Ubuntu: An African Jurisprudence

Ubuntu: An African Jurisprudence

T W BENNETT

assisted by

AR MUNRO and P J JACOBS

JUTA

First Published 2018

© Juta and Company (Pty) Ltd
First Floor,
Sunclare Building,
21 Dreyer Street,
Claremont 7708

This work is based on the research supported in part by the
National Research Foundation of South Africa

ISBN: 978 1 48512 6 713

Typeset in 11/12 Times New Roman
Typeset by Helanna Typesetting

PREFACE

This book was seven years in the making, and writing it has been a challenging task, especially in view of the many claims that ubuntu is now dead in South Africa. I can confidentl say, however, that, as far as the law is concerned, it is very much alive, and its prospects for continuing to thrive seem excellent. I therefore persevered with this project.

The general purpose of the book is to examine how and why the courts have been using ubuntu; to reflec views from the ever burgeoning academic literature on the subject and, above all, to proclaim the importance of this new addition to South African jurisprudence. The ground had, of course, already been tilled. Judges, notably those in the Constitutional Court, had clearly established ubuntu as a force to be reckoned with in the law, as had many scholars, notably, Drucilla Cornell who deserves a special mention in this preface. It was after listening to an inspiring talk by her that I — until then an ubuntu sceptic — came to realise its potential for transforming South African law.

Whatever is said about ubuntu, it is undeniably of great moral and, latterly, of legal value. Although borne of a pre-colonial society, when it was applicable to small social units — families, clans and neighbours — its basic precepts of caring, compassion and seeking social harmony give it an inherently inclusive scope. Ubuntu is therefore quite capable of embracing the much larger groups that make up the large, heterogeneous populations of modern day South Africa.

Indeed, at the start of the country's new democracy, ubuntu was chosen as a catchword for a new national ideology and as a guiding principle for the work of the Truth and Reconciliation Commission. The courts, however, took ubuntu much further. They used it to infuse all branches of the law with a new sense of right-doing in cases where application of the strict rules of law produced morally or ethically wrong decisions.

Ubuntu's similarity to equity then prompted me to embark on a somewhat lengthy chapter on this topic. When I began writing it, I was struck by ubuntu's close resemblance to the doctrine of equity in early English law, but closer examination revealed marked differences. Hence, the purpose of the chapter on equity changed, to argue that it, and the equitable principles of Roman-Dutch law, differed from ubuntu in both content and function. In addition, it became apparent that the courts would be ill-advised to allow ubuntu to follow the same path of development as equity in English law.

Two other chapters in the book — on imbizo and indaba — also require a word of explanation. They were included to give a sense of the traditional institutional settings for the realisation of ubuntu, and to show how these concepts can be deployed by courts and law-makers to implement, in the case of imbizo, the new constitutional requirement of participation in governance, and, in the case of indaba, to draw attention to the value of an African form of consensual decision-making as opposed to majority voting.

After a long and careful study of ubuntu, I ended up more convinced than ever that ubuntu offers something extraordinarily valuable to South Africa and, in fact, the wider world. Its emphasis on concern for others and on responsibility for the welfare of a community acts as a timely antidote to both the typically rationalist, disinterested system of justice in Western law and the sense of anomie so prevalent in Western societies. In the words of Drucilla Cornell,

'uBuntu requires us to come out of ourselves so as to realise the ethical quality of humanness. We are required to take that firs ethical action without waiting for the other person to reciprocate. uBuntu then is not a contractual ethic. It is up to me. And, in a certain profound sense, humanity is at stake in my ethical action. Thus, if I relate to

v

another person in a manner that lives up to uBuntu, then there is at least an ethical relationship that exists between us.' (Inaugural lecture, University of Cape Town, 2008)

TWB
January 2018

ACKNOWLEDGEMENTS

My thanks go to Barry Dean, James Patrick and Alan Rycroft, for their helpful suggestions and advice on writing this book, not to mention their help with the more mundane tasks of reading and checking drafts of the text. Especial thanks are, of course, due to my assistant authors, Reg Munro and Jacques Jacobs. Without their contributions this book could not have been written.

CONTENTS

TABLE OF CASES

ix

TABLE OF STATUTES

JOURNAL ABBREVIATIONS

Acad Manage Exec	Academy of Management Executive
Acad Manag J	Academy of Management Journal
Afr J Legal Stud	African Journal of Legal Studies
African J on Conflic Resolution	African Journal on Conflic Resolution
AHRLJ	African Human Rights Law Journal
AJCR	African Journal on Conflic Resolution
AJIL	American Journal of International Law
Am Anthropol	American Anthropologist
Am J Comp L	American Journal of Comparative Law
Am Polit Sci Rev	American Political Science Review
Anthro SA	Anthropology Southern Africa
ARSP	Archiv für Rechts- und Sozialphilosophie
ADRJ	Australasian Dispute Resolution Journal
British J of Criminology	British Journal of Criminology
British J of Psychology	British Journal of Psychology
Brown J of World Affairs	Brown Journal of World Affairs
Buff Hum Rts L Rev	Buffalo Human Rights Law Review
Can J Afr Stud	Canadian Journal of African Studies
CCR	Constitutional Court Review
CILSA	Comparative & International Law Journal of Southern Africa
Colum L Rev	Columbia Law Review
Comp Stud Soc Hist	Comparative Studies in Society & History
Crit Arts	Critical Arts
Crit Inquiry	Critical Inquiry
Crit Sociol	Critical Sociology
EJCL	Electronic Journal of Comparative Law
Harv L Rev	Harvard Law Review
Heidelberg J Int L	Heidelberg Journal of International Law
Hum Rights Rev	Human Rights Review
ICLQ	International Comparative Law Quarterly
ILJ	Industrial Law Journal
Int J Hum Resour Man	International Journal of Human Resource Management
Int J of African Renaissance Studies	International Journal of African Renaissance Studies
Int Rev of Administrative Sciences	International Review of Administrative Sciences
Int'l J Const L	International Journal of Constitutional Law
J Black Stud	Journal of Black Studies

J Hum Ecol	Journal of Human Ecology
J Human Rights	Journal of Human Rights
JL Prop & Soc'y	Journal of Law, Property & Society
J Law & Soc	Journal of Law & Society
J Legal Educ	Journal of Legal Education
J Legal Pluralism & Unofficial L	Journal of Legal Pluralism & Unofficial Law
J Lit Res	Journal of Literacy Research
J Manage Psychol	Journal of Managerial Psychology
J Modern African Studies	Journal of Modern African Studies
J Moral Educ	Journal of Moral Education
J of Chinese Philosophy	Journal of Chinese Philosophy
J of Media Ethics	Journal of Media Ethics
J of Planning Education & Research	Journal of Planning Education & Research
J Philosophy, Science & Law	Journal of Philosophy, Science & Law
J Polit Philos	Journal of Political Philosophy
J Public Admin	Journal of Public Administration
JHRE	Journal of Human Rights & the Environment
JICL	Journal of International & Comparative Law
JJS	Journal for Juridical Science
J Estate Planning L	Journal for Estate Planning Law
JPCL	Journal of Pidgin & Creole Languages
JSAS	Journal of Southern African Studies
Juridical Rev	Juridical Review
Law Contemp Probl	Law & Contemporary Problems
Law & Soc Rev	Law & Society Review
LDD	Law, Democracy & Development
Ling & Edu	Linguistics & Education
Loyola LA L Rev	Loyola of Los Angeles Law Review
LQR	Law Quarterly Review
MJECL	Maastricht Journal of European & Comparative Law
MLR	Modern Law Review
New York Rev of Law & Social Change	New York Review of Law & Social Change
New Zealand LR	New Zealand Law Review
Notre Dame L Rev	Notre Dame Law Review
PELJ	Potchefstroom Electronic Law Journal
Philos Afr	Philosophia Africana
Quinnipiac L Rev	Quinnipiac Law Review
Real Prop Prob & Tr J	Real Property, Probate & Trust Journal
Rev Afr Polit Econ	Review of African Political Economy
SA Crime Quarterly	South African Crime Quarterly

SA Criminal LJ	South African Journal of Criminal Justice
SA J of Higher Education	South African Journal of Higher Education
SA J Philosophy	South African Journal of Philosophy
SA Mercantile LJ	South African Mercantile Law Journal
SA Tydskr Etnol	Suid Afrikaanse Tydskrif vir Etnologie
SABJT	South African Baptist Journal of Theology
SAJ of Education	South African Journal of Education
SAJHR	South African Journal on Human Rights
SALJ	South African Law Journal
SAPL	South African Journal of Public Law
Soc Identities	Social Identities
Stell LR	Stellenbosch Law Review
Tex L Rev	Texas Law Review
Third World Legal Stud	Third World Legal Studies
THRHR	Tydskrif vir die Hedendaagse Romeins-Hollandse Reg
TSAR	Tydskrif vir die Suid Afrikaanse Reg/Journal of South African Law
Tul Eur & Civ LF	Tulane European & Civil Law Forum
Tul L Rev	Tulane Law Review
Universal Hum Rights	Universal Human Rights
UTLJ	University of Toronto Law Journal
UW Ontario L Rev	University of Western Ontario Law Review
Virginia J Int L	Virginia Journal of International Law

Chapter 1

INTRODUCTION

[Ubuntu is] 'an activist ethic of virtue in which what it means to be a human being is ethically performed, on a day-to-day basis, in a context in which how we are supposed to live together is constantly evoked and at the same time called into question.'[1]

1 INTRODUCTION

This book examines a remarkable process, which started nearly thirty years ago and is still underway, whereby three features typical of African customary law and governance were incorporated into the mainstream of South African law. These features are ubuntu, imbizo and indaba. The fact that the three terms were accepted without translation into English and Afrikaans, the principal languages of the legal system, sent a clear signal that new concepts were needed to express ideas lacking in the existing legal and linguistic environments.

Ubuntu is a prescriptive value or a quality of character denoting the humane treatment of others. Imbizo is a social institution, the gathering of a group of people to deliberate and decide on issues of common concern. Indaba is the actual process of decision-making within a group.[2] Ideally, these three elements work in conjunction with one another to build better human relationships.

Notwithstanding its demographic makeup, South Africa has always looked to Europe for its laws and legal institutions. Little regard was paid to its African heritage. Since the introduction of a new, fully democratic Constitution, however, ubuntu, imbizo and indaba have been used to interpret and enrich South African law, making it more relevant to the needs and history of the great majority of the country's population. The trio of terms have, in other words, begun to infuse the legal system with a long overdue sense of cultural legitimacy.

In addition to this function, these terms were put to the service of a much larger project, that of constitutional transformation. South Africa's new Constitution called for a long-term programme of radical social change but to be achieved through peaceful processes guided by the law.[3] The violent, authoritarian rule of apartheid had left a society demoralised by widespread poverty and injustice. This legacy now had to be repaired to create a new society based on justice, equality, dialogue and redistribution of resources. Ubuntu, imbizo and indaba were ideally suited to the purpose.

Of the three terms to be examined in this book, ubuntu will be the main focus of inquiry. Not only is it the most complex concept, but it has also had the most

---

[1] Cornell *Law and Revolution in South Africa: ubuntu, dignity, and the struggle for constitutional transformation* 40.

[2] Matters of definitio are explored in Chapters 3 and 4.

[3] Klare 'Legal culture and transformative constitutionalism' (1998) 14 *SAJHR* 150. See further the Conclusion Chapter 5.

pervasive impact on the law. The influenc of imbizo and indaba has been more limited in that they are applicable only in situations of group decision-making.

The process of integrating these terms into the legal system began with the word 'ubuntu'. It firs appeared in an epilogue to the Interim Constitution,[4] which was described as a 'historic bridge' to span 'the past of a deeply divided society characterised by strife, conflict untold suffering and injustice, and a future founded on the recognition of human rights, democracy and peaceful co-existence . . .'.[5] Although ubuntu was subsequently invoked in many judgments, as were imbizo and indaba, no comprehensive study has been undertaken to detail the functions of these terms, the circumstances in which they were used and their capacity to transform the South African legal order. The book therefore seeks to establish the current meanings, functions and implications of the three terms.

Linguistics and comparative law supplied a general framework of analysis, for they give valuable insights into how items that have been transferred from one language or legal system to another can be assimilated or rejected. On the basis of functionalist theory, the two disciplines assume that the items concerned may prove to be irrelevant or disruptive to the needs of their host systems, or be capable of performing useful and necessary functions. As will become apparent, the adoption of ubuntu, imbizo and indaba into South Africa's legal system has been a remarkable success.

To have a full appreciation of why this has been the case, earlier state policies on the country's indigenous systems of customary law must be explained. Since colonial conquest, Western laws and legal thinking have dominated South African law. The system is generally described as hybrid or 'mixed'.[6] The firs component was provided by the Netherlands, which introduced Roman-Dutch law to the Cape of Good Hope in the mid-seventeenth century. The second component arrived in 1806, when the Cape was ceded to Britain,[7] which then introduced new laws of its own. Through two centuries of statutory intervention and judicial law-making, these two components were gradually combined to produce an integrated system that it is now taken to be the 'common law' of South Africa.[8]

The legal regimes in operation prior to colonial occupation are a noticeable omission from this account of South African legal history.[9] Throughout the colonial period, the indigenous customary laws of the region were considered the

---

[4] Entitled 'National Unity and Reconciliation' in Act 200 of 1993.

[5] Cited by Chaskalson P in the firs decision of the newly established Constitutional Court: *S v Makwanyane and another* 1995 (2) SA 391 (CC) para 7.

[6] See Reid 'The idea of mixed legal systems' (2003) 78 *Tul L Rev* 8ff.

[7] See below p 18.

[8] In South Africa, the term 'common law' is ambiguous. It often refers to English as opposed to Roman-Dutch law, but in this book it will usually refer to all law that is not indigenous customary law. See Fagan 'Roman-Dutch law in its South African historical context' in Zimmerman & Visser *Southern Cross: civil law and common law in South Africa* 62.

[9] In South Africa, the terms 'indigenous' and 'customary' law are usually used interchangeably. 'Indigenous' was used by the courts and in statutes prior to 1994, for example, in s 1(1) of the Law of Evidence Amendment Act 45 of 1988. 'Customary' was the term used in the fina Constitution of the Republic of South Africa 108 of 1996, and has since been preferred in subsequent legislation and court cases.

product of an inferior civilisation, and were either actively suppressed[10] or given only limited recognition for purposes of civil litigation amongst Africans.[11] The subordinate status of customary laws was marked in various ways, notably by a so-called 'repugnancy' proviso,[12] which stipulated that they were not to be applied unless they conformed to British principles of public policy and natural justice.[13]

In fact, colonial jurisprudence consigned all such systems of indigenous law to the lesser status of mere habit or custom.[14] In consequence, none of the courts, other than those dedicated to African litigation, which were the courts of native commissioners and traditional rulers, could treat indigenous law as law. Instead, courts dispensing the common law treated customary rules as facts, to be proved in each case in which they arose.[15] It was only in 1988 that all courts in South Africa were given the power to apply customary law as law.[16]

British legal policy on customary law reflecte its curious relationship with the African colonies, one that has been described as an unhappy blend of tyranny and paternalism.[17] Admittedly, certain European travellers and explorers admired qualities that had been lost in their own past: the nobility of warrior nations, such as the Ashanti, Herero and Zulu, or the primordial innocence of cattle-keepers, such as the KhoeKhoe, Maasai and Nuer.[18] But, by and large, when colonists encountered Africa, they chose to see only the primitive and the backward.[19] Even so, the colonial powers had to accept the fact that, with minimal resources and personnel at their disposal, they were in no position to force their subjects to obey European laws. Hence, the courts were permitted to apply customary law in

---

[10] As in the case of lobolo and customary marriages: Simons 'The status of customary unions'1961 *Acta Juridica* 17-19.

[11] Which, in South Africa, was formerly regulated by the (now repealed) Black Administration Act 38 of 1927.

[12] Contained in s 11(1) of the Black Administration Act, which was repealed and replaced by s 1(1) of the Law of Evidence Amendment Act 45 of 1988.

[13] The effect of this proviso was symbolic rather than actual, because it was in practice very seldom invoked: Peart 'Section 11(1) of the Black Administration Act No 38 of 1927: the application of the repugnancy clause' 1982 *Acta Juridica* 105-110.

[14] Hartland *Primitive Law* 15.

[15] According to the rule for taking account of common-law custom: *Van Breda and others v Jacobs and others* 1921 AD 330. See *Ex parte Minister of Native Affairs: In re Yako v Beyi* 1948 (1) SA 388 (A) at 394-395; *Mosii v Motseoakhumo* 1954 (3) SA 919 (A) at 930. Cf *Shilubana and others v Nwamitwa* 2009 (2) SA 66 (CC) paras 54 and 56.

[16] The apartheid system began to be dismantled when the court system was integrated in terms of the Special Courts for Blacks Abolition Act 34 of 1986. Two years later, s 1 of the Law of Evidence Amendment Act 45 of 1988 removed any mention of race from the terms for recognising customary law, which was, as a result, made potentially applicable to any person and by any court in the country.

[17] Mamdani *Citizen and Subject: contemporary Africa and the legacy of late colonialism* 23.

[18] See, for example, Le Vaillant, *Voyages de M. le Vaillant dans l'Intérieur de l'Afrique par le Cap de Bonne-Espérance dans les années 1780-85* 132.

[19] See Kuper *Invention of Primitive Society: transformations of an illusion* 2-3 and Mogoeng CJ's dictum in *City of Tshwane Metropolitan Municipality v Afriforum and another* 2016 (6) SA 279 (CC) para 2.

domestic disputes between Africans, provided that it did not conflic with European values.[20]

After 1948, when a Nationalist government came to power in South Africa, the same, ostensibly tolerant view of indigenous law was maintained, but it became a strategic device to further the policy of apartheid. Customary law served to emphasise the differences distinguishing whites from blacks, and thus the need to reinforce racial segregation.[21] Accordingly, in line with its 'homelands' policy, the government entrenched traditional structures of government,[22] and gave homeland leaders full rein to implement customary laws as they saw fit [23]

On the eve of South Africa's new constitutional dispensation, the legal system comprised two distinct legal orders. On the one hand, there was the 'common-law' blend of Roman-Dutch and English law, and, on the other, a subordinate system of indigenous customary laws. The two orders operated almost entirely independently of one another. Most private-law aspects of the common law were not applicable to members of the population deemed 'black' (inevitably a contentious term in South Africa's highly racialised society).[24] This law was the preserve of the higher courts, namely, the Supreme Court and the magistrates' courts. Customary law applied only to 'blacks' or 'Africans', who constituted the great majority of the population. This law was the preserve of the courts of traditional rulers[25] or, occasionally, when specially pleaded, the higher courts.[26]

South Africa's firs truly democratic Constitution promised a complete break with the past. Because Africans were to be given the franchise on terms of equality with all other members of the citizen body, any discrimination based on race had to be eliminated. The time was therefore ripe for giving African customary law equal recognition on a par with the common law. Some degree of integration of the two legal orders might have been achieved — and was mooted in the academic literature[27] — but the issue was never further explored. Even more radical

---

[20] A notable casualty in this regard was the customary form of marriage: because it was potentially polygynous it fell foul of the Western dogma of monogamy: Bennett *A Sourcebook of African Customary Law for Southern Africa* 170ff. Full recognition was granted only with the Recognition of Customary Marriages Act 120 of 1998.

[21] Oomen 'Group rights in post-apartheid South Africa: the case of the traditional leaders' (1999) 31 *J Legal Pluralism* 93; Chanock 'Law, state and culture: thinking about customary law after apartheid' 1991 *Acta Juridica* 55.

[22] Black Authorities Act 68 of 1951.

[23] Hence, under the Transkei Marriage Act 21 of 1978, for example, polygyny was deemed acceptable even in the case of civil marriages.

[24] Bennett *Application of Customary Law in Southern Africa* (1985) 67-69.

[25] Woolman & Swanepoel 'Constitutional history' in Woolman & Bishop *Constitutional Law of South Africa* 2-8 to 2-23.

[26] Section 1(1) of the Law of Evidence Amendment Act 45 of 1988.

[27] Prinsloo 'Pluralism or unificatio in family law in South Africa' (1990) 23 *CILSA* 334; Bekker 'Interaction between constitutional reform and family law' 1991 *Acta Juridica* 15; Prinsloo 'Unifikasi van inheemse regstelsels' (1990) 4 *TSAR* 615; South African Law Reform Commission *Harmonisation of the Common Law and Indigenous Law — Report on Customary Marriages* (1999) Project 90; South African Law Commission, *Marriages and Customary Unions of Black Persons* (1985) Project 51 para 11.2.

proposals were made to 'africanise' the law,[28] but these, too, were not taken seriously, and were soon quietly abandoned.

Due largely to the lobbying of traditional leaders, customary law nevertheless gained special mention in the fina 1996 Constitution.[29] Section 211(3) provided that: 'The courts must apply customary law when that law is applicable, subject to the Constitution and any legislation that specificall deals with customary law.'[30] Further weight was given to the position of customary law by provisions in the Bill of Rights protecting the right to culture.[31]

The new Constitution might have done much to improve the formal status of customary law, but South Africa continues to operate with what is still, in essence, a dual legal system.[32] Even so, the courts[33] — and even the legislature[34] — began assimilating ubuntu, imbizo and indaba into the general law of the law of the land, although without reference to grander designs of integration or africanisation. Given previous attitudes to customary law, the ready reception of these terms and all they stood for has, in many ways, been an extraordinary event.

While there has always been a traffic of ideas between the common law and customary law, it has never been from the latter to the former.[35] The flo , however, has now been reversed. South Africa's new Constitution, a product

---

[28] See, for example, Nhlapo 'Cultural diversity, human rights and the family in contemporary Africa: lessons from the South African constitutional debate' (1995) 9 *Int J of Law, Policy & the Family* 219. See the more recent proposal, however, by Hutchison 'Decolonising South African contract law: an argument for synthesis' in Siliquini-Cinelli & Hutchison (eds) *The Constitutional Dimension of Contract Law: a comparative perspective* 151ff.

[29] Customary law was considered only late in the process of drafting the Interim Constitution, when, as a result of bargains struck with the National Party and the ANC, traditional rulers were promised that their existing position would be maintained in the future legal order. See Albertyn 'Women and the transition to democracy in South Africa' 1994 *Acta Juridica* 57-60.

[30] The firs proviso requires compliance with the Bill of Rights, and has occasioned significan litigation, as for example, in *Alexkor Ltd v The Richtersveld Community* 2004 (5) SA 460 (CC); *Gumede v President of the Republic of South Africa* 2009 (3) SA 152 (CC); *MM v MN and another* 2013 (4) SA 415 (CC); *Shilubana v Nwamitwa* 2009 (2) SA 66 (CC); *Bhe and others v Magistrate, Khayelitsha, and others (Commission for Gender Equality as Amicus Curiae); Shibi v Sithole and others; South African Human Rights Commission and another v President of the Republic of South Africa and another* 2005 (1) SA 580 (CC).

[31] Thus, s 30 provides that '[e]veryone has the right to use the language and to participate in the cultural life of their choice', although 'subject to the Bill of Rights'. Section 31(1) continued to provide that: 'Persons belonging to a cultural, religious or linguistic community may not be denied the right, with other members of that community — (a) to enjoy their culture, practise their religion and use their language; and (b) to form, join and maintain cultural, religious and linguistic associations and other organs of civil society.'

[32] In fact, a *plural* legal system, because, alongside indigenous customary laws, religious systems of law, notably, Islamic and Hindu laws, have also benefite from the rights to culture and religion: *Daniels v Campbell NO and others* 2004 (5) SA 331 (CC); *Singh v Ramparsad* (KZN564/2002) [2007] ZAKZHC paras 17-18. See, generally, Mofokeng *Legal Pluralism in South Africa: aspects of African customary, Muslim and Hindu family law*.

[33] Notably in *S v Makwanyane and another* 1995 (2) SA 391 (CC) paras 130, 223-227, 237, 243-245, 260, 307-313.

[34] As in the Child Justice Act 75 of 2008.

[35] Van Niekerk 'Reflection on the interplay of African customary law and state law in South Africa' (2012) 5 *SUBB Jurisprudentia* 5ff describes how this process has resulted in two forms of

typical of Western legal thinking, was taken to provide all the values necessary for a modern democratic state.[36]

Ubuntu, imbizo and indaba have introduced an African way of thinking. This entails a shift from the traditional Western concern with the rights of an individual,[37] to a concern with the individual as a member of a community of fellow human beings, all of whom deserve equal respect.[38]

Sceptics have claimed that this African ethos is now no more than an empty ideal, one that has ceased to be observed in our competitive, individualistic age, and even the courts have alluded to this situation.[39] It is no doubt true that many people do not realise traditional values in their lives, but ubuntu is an ideal that transcends everyday behaviour. It is now the basis of a compelling discourse, one which has attracted an expanding jurisprudence and a burgeoning academic literature.[40]

Indeed, many contend that ubuntu is essential for the transformation of South Africa's legal culture if the system is to be legitimated in African minds. But the appeal of ubuntu extends further than one particular section of society. It is an inclusive value calling on all of us to show consideration and respect for everyone within our reach. It is, accordingly, an 'ideal overarching vehicle for expressing shared values', one well suited to the development of a genuinely plural legal culture.[41] As Sachs J observed:[42]

---

customary law: one an 'official' law applied in the higher courts, and the other a 'living law', which is actually lived by the people. See below 166.

[36] Davis 'Constitutional borrowing: the influenc of legal culture and local history in the reconstitution of comparative influence the South African experience' (2003) 1 *Int'l J Const L* 185-188; Kende *Constitutional Rights in Two Worlds: South Africa and the United States* 31; Du Plessis 'Learned Staatsrecht from the heartland of the Rechtsstaat' (2005) 1 *PELJ* 13.

[37] With the notable exceptions made for socio-economic rights: Liebenberg *Socio-economic Rights: adjudication under a transformative constitution* 59-63; Liebenberg 'South Africa's evolving jurisprudence on socio-economic rights: an effective tool in challenging poverty' (2002) 6 *LDD* 164. See for example: *Government of the Republic of South Africa and others v Grootboom and others* 2001 (1) SA 46 (CC); *Port Elizabeth Municipality v Various Occupiers* 2005 (1) SA 217 (CC); *Minister of Health and others v Treatment Action Campaign and others* (No 2) 2002 (5) SA 721 (CC).

[38] See below pp 35–46.

[39] See *Johannesburg Housing Corporation (Pty) Ltd v Unlawful Occupiers of the Newtown Urban Village* [2013] 1 All SA 192 (GSJ) para 117, where, with reference to the hijacking of land by a third party who collected rentals from the occupants, the judge commented ironically: 'I am aware of the fact that there is no shortage of cash in Soweto. Ubuntu, working in tandem with capitalism, has gone a long way in this part of the world.' See, too, Mogoeng J in *The Citizen 1978 (Pty) Ltd and others v McBride (Johnstone and others, Amici Curiae)* 2011 (4) SA 191 (CC) para 216: 'The law, order, generosity, peace and common decency that previously characterised many communities in South Africa were attributed to an unwavering commitment to the philosophy of *ubuntu*. . . . [but] sadly, a new culture has taken root and continues to cancerously eat at *botho*.'

[40] For a broad overview of how ubuntu has developed as a special legal discourse in South Africa, see especially the contributions made by Drucilla Cornell under the auspices of the Ubuntu Project: http://theubuntuproject.org/ [Accessed 28 August 2015]. See further below p 27 fn 34.

[41] Keep & Midgley 'The emerging role of ubuntu-botho in developing a consensual South African legal culture' in Bruinsma & Nelken (eds) *Recht der Werkelijkheid* 48.

[42] *Port Elizabeth Municipality v Various Occupiers* 2005 (1) SA 217 (CC) para 37.

'The spirit of ubuntu, part of the deep cultural heritage of the majority of the population, suffuses the whole constitutional order. . . . It is a unifying motif of the Bill of Rights, which is nothing if not a structured, institutionalised and operational declaration in our evolving new society of the need for human interdependence, respect and concern.'

Chapter 2

LANGUAGE AND COMPARATIVE LAW

1 METHODOLOGY: TWO FRAMEWORKS FOR ANALYSIS

The three concepts ubuntu, imbizo and indaba, all of which were quite alien to the mainstream of South Africa's common law, have been assimilated into the system with remarkable ease. This phenomenon can, of course, be explained by South Africa's constitutional change and the improved status of customary law. Another explanation, however, lies in the hybrid nature of the common law. Lawyers in this country are used to working with different legal regimes, whether Roman-Dutch and English, or, to a lesser extent, customary and common law. Hence, they are, by force of circumstance, accustomed to dealing with different legal concepts, cultures and languages. The disciplines of comparative law and linguistics therefore present themselves as two useful frameworks for analysing the manner and effect of incorporating ubuntu, imbizo and indaba into the legal system's common law.

To explain the workings of their subjects of inquiry, linguistics and comparative law rely heavily on structural-functionalist theory.[1] In other words, they work with an assumption that the language or the law in question is a more or less coherent system in which all the parts contribute to its efficient operation as a unit.[2] It follows that the introduction of an alien element raises the possibility of its

---

[1] In this regard, linguistics drew on the structuralist theory of Saussure's *Cours de linguistique générale* (published 1916) which distinguished between *langue* (language) and *parole* (speech). Speech is individual and intentional, each speech act relying on and departing from the abstract structures of language. Saussure concentrated on language because it is systematic, and therefore facilitates a scientifi method for investigation. See Harris *Language, Saussure and Wittgenstein* ix.

[2] Regarding law as a system, see Hart *The Concept of Law* 82. The problems with this assumption in functionalism are explored below pp 16–17. See further: Ohlendorf 'Against coherence in statutory interpretation' (2014) 90 *Notre Dame L Rev* 735-782; Dagan 'The Realist conception of law' (2007) 57 *UTLJ* 624.

maladjustment to the system or even its complete rejection. These are issues that are central to determining the prospects for the future of ubuntu, imbizo and indaba.

The South African legal system operates primarily in English, and primarily according to laws of a Western European tradition, despite the fact that people speak many different languages and live according to a plurality of different laws.[3] Given these circumstances, ubuntu and its associated terms can be described, for linguistic purposes, as loan words in their new English environment, and, for legal purposes, as transplants in the common law.[4]

Ubuntu, which for the sake of convenience will be taken as the focus of this chapter, declares itself a word of distinctively African origin, and one of the significan features of its entry into the common usage of South African English has been the absence of an accompanying translation. Although English speakers may have known — more or less — what ubuntu meant, the fact that the word was not translated sent a clear signal: it was a newcomer to the language, and as such, has been co-opted to fulfi a specifi semantic, and indeed social, need. The ready reception of ubuntu into English therefore suggested that English speakers required a word derived from an indigenous African language to perform functions that their own language could not.

From a linguistic standpoint, therefore, a loan word can be examined with a view to determining its acceptance into the adoptive language, and in addition, its capacity for establishing a new discourse. An analogy can then be drawn between the effect of introducing ubuntu to mainstream legal discourse and the effect of transplanting a new concept to South African law, an inquiry that has the potential to teach us much about the current, and even future, use of both the word and the legal concept.

Likewise, from the standpoint of comparative law, if ubuntu is treated as a legal transplant, we have a useful way of thinking about how the transfer of a law/concept from one legal system to another can affect the laws (and social order) in the recipient system. To illustrate this type of analysis, a comparison will be made with the adoption of the trust from English into Roman-Dutch law and ubuntu from indigenous customary law to the common law.

2 LANGUAGE AND LINGUISTICS

'A new word is a solution to a problem. Often the need is obvious, but sometimes it is unseen or barely felt, and then it is only in findin something to plug the gap that we actually realize the gap was there in the firs place.'[5]

'[A]dditions to a language may signal a new political movement, a recent discovery or a sweeping revision of attitudes.'[6]

---

[3] As provided by ss 6, 30 and 31 of the Constitution of the Republic of South Africa 108 of 1996.

[4] A term coined in the 1970s by Watson *Legal Transplants: an approach to comparative law* (1974) 27.

[5] Hitchings *The Secret Life of Words* 5.

[6] Hitchings op cit 6.

(a) The emergence of ubuntu in public discourse

Ubuntu is a word occurring in the everyday vocabulary of most, if not all, South Africans. Although it derives from the Nguni family of languages, ie, isiXhosa, isiZulu, siSwati[7] and siNdebele, it has equivalents in seSotho and sePedi (*botho*), XiTsonga (*bunhu*) and TshiVenda (*vhuthu*).[8] Variants of ubuntu are also found in other African languages, for example, *unhu* (Shona), *utu* (Swahili) and *umundu* (Kikuyu).[9]

Use of this word signifie a core cultural concept for the linguistic communities from which it originated. Like any word, ubuntu is embedded in a network of culturally specifi meanings, and it was obviously because of the resonance of these meanings that ubuntu was incorporated into South Africa's general public discourse.[10] The process of incorporation became most noticeable during the early 1990s, which was a time when the country was undergoing fundamental political and legal changes.

Ubuntu is of course alien to English,[11] which is the most widely used language in South Africa's public discourse,[12] and a lingua franca for most of the population.[13] Even so, ubuntu was readily embraced in thought, word, and sometimes even deed by politicians, advertising agencies, religious leaders, businesses and law-makers to mark some significan type of change. While sceptics have claimed that referring to ubuntu did no more than pay lip service to traditional African values,[14] there can be no doubt that, for most people, it implied some degree of commitment to a new way of thinking about law, government, management, services and general attitudes.

The business sector, in particular, was quick to appropriate ubuntu as an advertising strategy and a basis for reformulating decision-making procedures in order to engender a better understanding of the market. Hence, to grapple with

---

[7] For siSwati *buntfu*: Taljaard, Khumalo & Bosch *Handbook of Siswati* 22.

[8] For these various terms, see Broodryk *Ubuntu: life lessons from Africa* 17; Gade 'What is *ubuntu*? Different interpretations among South Africans of African descent' (2012) 31 *S Afr J Philosophy* 488-593.

[9] See Kamwangamalu 'Ubuntu in South Africa: a sociolinguistic perspective to a pan African concept' (1999) 13 *Crit Arts* 25ff.

[10] See below pp 26ff.

[11] For Afrikaans see Odendaal & Gouws (eds) *HAT Verklarende Woordeboek van die Afrikaanse Taal* 1383: 'Lewensingesteldheid van medemenslikheid, hulpvaardigheid en barmhartigheid. For example "ons streef daarna om daagliks al die waardes van ubuntu uit te leef".'

[12] Although it is a second language for the great majority of the population. According to Statistics South Africa *Census 2011*, only 4,892,623 (9.6%) of the population use English as a firs language: *Census in brief* available at http://www.statssa.gov.za/census/census_2011/census_products/Census_ 2011_Census_in_brief.pdf [Accessed 28 August 2015] 23–25.

[13] Harms 'Law and language in a multilingual society' (2012) 15 *PELJ* 25-26 and 29; Motsaathebe 'Language, Afrikology and the tremor of the political moment: English as a main language of discourse in Africa' (2010) 9 *Indilinga* 97.

[14] English 'Ubuntu: the quest for an indigenous jurisprudence' (1996) 12 *SAJHR* 641. See too Wilson *The Politics of Truth and Reconciliation in South Africa: legitimizing the post-apartheid state* 13, who, after tracing the popularisation of ubuntu by organs of state, concludes that it was 'the Africanist wrapping used to sell a reconciliatory version of human rights talk to black South Africans'.

issues of equality and transformation, management principles had to undergo a paradigm shift,[15] one that has been described as a change in style from 'dictatorship to relationship' or from 'manager to mentor'.[16]

Ubuntu started its journey into the legal system somewhat later, as a minor term in an epilogue to the Interim Constitution of 1993,[17] but, soon thereafter, the courts began to invoke the word in a wide variety of different situations, so that ubuntu now constitutes a substantial new discourse.[18] This process entailed uprooting ubuntu from its original languages and cultures and deploying it in new contexts, with consequent shifts in form and meaning.

(b) Loan words

From a linguistic point of view, when a word like ubuntu appears in a new and quite different language, it is termed a 'loan' word.[19] This epithet indicates that a word, relevant to discourse in one language, has come to be regarded as highly significan to a similar, but not same, discourse in another language. Its presence in the receiving language may then be flagge by the use of the original term as a 'loan' word, rather than a calque (translation).[20]

The appearance of a loan word signifie semantic change. The word is an intruder in its new environment, lacking any semantic connections with its new host.[21] What is more, its connections with developments in its language of origin have been severed, leaving the loan word marooned and therefore open to new interpretations.[22] At the same time as the loan word starts to absorb new meanings, so, too, do the meanings of words with which it is now associated.[23]

The reasons for 'borrowing' or appropriating loan words are many, but two reasons are usually paramount: to denote an idea or phenomenon that was not previously expressed or to denote something that already had many different forms of expression. Those sceptical about the value of ubuntu would say that it falls into the second category. They claim that, as a catch-all term, it signifie concepts already existing in many other languages and legal systems, or that it is

---

[15] Mbigi 'Ubuntu' (1995) November *Enterprise* 57.

[16] Sachs 'Changing the law, changing the mind' in Lessem & Nussbaum (eds) *Sawubona Africa: embracing four worlds in South African management* 155. Cf the critical remarks by Kamwanga-malu (n9) 32.

[17] Chapter 16 of the Interim Constitution Act 200 of 1993. See further below p 27.

[18] Especially in the academic literature, as for example, that produced by Johan Broodryk, founder of the Ubuntu School of Philosophy at the University of Pretoria ttp://www.ubunturesearch.co.za/ [Accessed 2 November 2017] and by Drucilla Cornell under the auspices of the Ubuntu Project (publications cited below p 27 fn 24: http://www.up.ac.za/en/jurisprudence/article/17597/ubuntu-project [Accessed 2 November 2017].

[19] 'Loan' is of course not a really suitable term, because the word will not be returned to source.

[20] A calque or translation implies that the meaning is borrowed rather than the lexical item itself. The term loan word is itself a calque of the German *Lehnwort*, while *calque* is a loan word from French.

[21] Deroy *L'Emprunt linguistique* 215.

[22] Ball 'The vocabulary of English' in Bolton & Crystal (eds) *The English Language* 182-183.

[23] Hitchings (n5) 12.

so generalised that its meaning overlaps with terms in the new language.[24] What seems more probable, however, is that ubuntu signifie a culturally specifi concept that cannot be compressed into a single English word.[25]

(c) The shift from oral to written form

A key issue to be considered when exploring the incorporation of ubuntu into mainstream South African law is the fact that it is entering a written discourse. As a result, ubuntu now regularly appears in written texts, and, when a word deriving from an oral tradition is transcribed into this form, it undergoes inevitable, although often imperceptible, changes in function and meaning.

In a predominantly oral discourse, the meanings of words are porous and malleable,[26] with the result that meanings are likely to overlap and contradict one another.[27] It follows that the words are difficult to differentiate from one another, and are in consequence, less amenable to classificatio according to similarities and differences of meaning. More precise distinctions between words become possible only when the words are defined a process in which writing plays a critical role.[28]

The transcription of a language to writing allows the speakers/writers to become more objective about its use, and thereby to engage in reflectio on and analysis of words and their meanings.[29] Once this process is underway, definitio can begin, and with it, classification Words may then be arranged into sets, and ultimately integrated into a coherent system.[30]

The processes of definition classificatio and systematisation are, in their turn, preconditions for, and the effects of, specialisation in language and thought. Specialised forms of language and thinking thus contribute to the emergence of a professional class of people trained to work with the subject matter of the language in question. Accordingly, we fin that, for legal regimes derived from an oral tradition, there is no group of people devoted solely to the application, interpretation or making of rules.[31] When laws are written down, however, a professional discipline becomes necessary to interpret and apply them.[32] Law then ripens into an esoteric subject that is moved beyond the reach of ordinary people.

---

[24] See below p 37.

[25] See the problem of definitio below pp 29ff.

[26] Although in verbal communication, the specifi meaning of words can nonetheless be fixe by use of gesture, intonation, expression and various references to the context of a speech act. See Ong *Orality and Literacy: the technologizing of the word* 11.

[27] See Hamnett *Chieftainship and Legitimacy* 9-10 regarding the customary laws of Lesotho. It should not be inferred that customary law is *disorganised*, but rather that its logical coherence is not a prime value, as is the case with Western legal systems.

[28] Goodrich *Reading the Law: a critical introduction to legal method and techniques* 21; Goody *The Interface Between the Written and the Oral* 6.

[29] Danet & Bogoch 'From oral ceremony to written document: the transitional language of Anglo-Saxon wills' (1992) 12 *Lang & Communication* 95; Harris 'How does writing restructure thought?' (1989) 9 *Lang & Communication* 102.

[30] Ong (n26) 9.

[31] Friedman *Law and Society: an introduction* 21.

[32] Goodrich (n28) 21.

All the processes described above have been shaping the use and current meanings of ubuntu in South African law. Once introduced to a written form of law, starting with the Interim Constitution, and continuing with the judgments of the courts and an accompanying academic literature, the originally flui meanings of ubuntu started to become more define and fixe in relation to other legal terms. In this way, the word has gradually been brought into line with the requirements of the overall legal system.

(d) Discourse and register

Once words in an oral tradition are transcribed into writing, and once they become the subject of a professional legal system, with its attendant science of jurisprudence, they begin to emerge as a specifi discourse and a secondary register in a language. Hence, yet another linguistic consideration when studying ubuntu is the formation of a particular legal discourse about the word and the change in the register of the language involved in that discourse.

A discourse develops from the basis of certain key terms, which then enjoy a privileged position in relation to other terms.[33] Over time, the meanings of the various competing terms are modifie to accommodate the key terms. As a discourse becomes accepted, the meanings of the other terms in the system stabilise, which requires the exclusion of certain competing or redundant meanings.[34] These then fall into a reservoir of surplus meanings.[35]

Because ubuntu is now a key term in South African law, and is generating an expanding case law, it has created a specialised discourse, which brings it into competition with the Western legal discourse.[36] This, the dominant discourse in South African law, has been constructed on such terms as 'justice' and 'equality'. Now a rival African discourse is being constructed on the basis of ubuntu.

The process of creating the new ubuntu discourse has been accompanied by a change of register, namely, a shift to a distinct species of language usage. In socio-linguistics, the term 'register' is used to denote the selection of particular words and linguistic structures[37] according to the requirements of specifi social situations.[38] 'Register' therefore implies reference to the factors determining the

---

[33] What Laclau & Mouffe *Hegemony and Socialist Strategy* 112 call 'nodal points'.

[34] Laclau & Mouffe op cit 110 term words which still have multiple meanings 'elements' or 'floatin signifiers' Laclau *New Reflections on the Revolution of our Time* 28. A discourse seeks to establish a 'closure', or a temporary stop to the fluctuation in the meanings of signs. Cornell 'Socialism or radical democratic politics?: on Laclau and Mouffe' in Cornell *Law and Revolution in South Africa: ubuntu, dignity, and the struggle for constitutional transformation* 42.

[35] Which Laclau & Mouffe (n33) term a 'fiel of discursivity' 111.

[36] Fairclough *Analysing Discourse — textual research for social research* 24 and 227 calls this an 'order of discourse' or 'interdiscursivity', which denotes a limited range of discourses in competition for the same terrain.

[37] Halliday *Language as Social Semiotic: the social interpretation of language and meaning* 111. Halliday's 'systemic functional linguistics' approaches the study of language 'from a social semiotic perspective': Halliday & Hasan *Language, context, and text: aspects of language in a social-semiotic perspective* 3.

[38] With regard to law see Danet 'Language in the legal process' (1979/80) 14 *Law & Soc Rev* 465ff and Goody (n28) 263ff.

form of the language to be used. These include the subject-matter of a speech/text, its function, the event at which it is given, the nature of the chosen language (spoken, written, extempore or prepared) and the roles played by the participants.[39]

Legal English is a typical secondary or formal register of discourse, one that is so different from ordinary language in grammar, form and vocabulary that it has been referred to as a 'sublanguage',[40] with the implication that it needs to be taught to first-languag speakers as if it were a second language.[41] This type of discourse can therefore be distinguished from a 'primary' discourse, which is acquired by children during the process of socialisation, and continues to serve them throughout their lives.[42]

Ubuntu exists as a core term — and concept — in the primary and secondary discourses of African languages. As part of a secondary legal discourse, however, it must now comply with the constraints of its new setting. Legal language relies heavily on authority and precedent; it is marked by long, complex sentence structures and contains many special words and phrases unique to law.[43] While the purpose of this register is to reduce ambiguity so as to ensure legal certainty and predictability,[44] the effect is to render the language beyond the comprehension of non-professionals.[45]

When viewed in terms of discourse and register, it is evident that ubuntu has been undergoing the following process. From an established base as a core term and concept in the primary and secondary discourses of millions of South Africans, use of the *term* ubuntu has spread through informal interaction between those for whom it is a core concept and those for whom it is not (yet). In these interactions, when we use a word 'we wake into resonance . . . its entire previous history',[46] but we would obviously not all have the same understanding of the *concept*. Over time, and in the course of many interactions, the meanings of a term are then refined

Hence, at its present point on this path of development, ubuntu is now a term in a specialist, secondary register of discourse. It has been — and still is — subject to two powerful influences one is a concerted effort to fi its meaning and the other is to determine its connection with the existing terms of the dominant discourse.

---

[39] Eggins *An Introduction to Systemic Functional Linguistics* 42.

[40] Wydick *Plain English for Lawyers: teacher's manual* 10.

[41] Ramsfiel *Culture to Culture: a guide to US legal writing* 145. Even within legal discourse there are different genres, including academic writing, court judgments, statutes and contracts. See generally V K Bhatia *Analyzing Genre: language in professional settings*.

[42] See Gee *Social Linguistics and Literacies: ideology in discourses* 1-2; Gee 'Critical issues: reading and the new literacy studies: reframing the national academy of sciences report on reading' (1999) 31 *J Lit Res* 355ff.

[43] See Danet (n38) 465ff and Goody (n28) 263ff.

[44] Danet (n38) 474ff; Goodrich 'Law and language: an historical and cultural introduction' (1984) 11 *J Law & Soc* 188.

[45] Giving language a significan power of social control: Williams cited in Benson 'The end of legalese: the game is over' (1984–1985) 13 *New York Rev of Law & Social Change* 530; Boyd White *Heracles Bow — essays on the rhetoric and poetics of law* 63.

[46] Steiner *After Babel: aspects of language and translation* 24.

3 COMPARATIVE LAW AND LEGAL TRANSPLANTS

When we turn to comparative law, our focus shifts from words and their meanings to different laws and legal institutions. A topic of particular interest in this discipline is the legal transplant, a term that denotes the transfer of laws, principles or doctrines from one legal environment to another, generally in order to effect an improvement in the recipient's socio-legal order. Comparative law directs our attention to the effectiveness of the transplant and to the conceptual adjustments needed to ensure its assimilation to its new environment.

Views among comparative lawyers on the ease — and indeed the value — of transplanting laws used to be sharply divided. The debate was framed, on the one hand, by Alan Watson's view that the transfer of rules from one legal system to another is easy to accomplish,[47] and Pierre Legrand's view, on the other, that it runs the risk of rendering the rules 'a meaningless form of words'.[48] Although it seems that Legrand went too far,[49] he did establish the need for a deep understanding of cultural and linguistic contexts before attempting a legal transplant. And, subsequently, more moderate voices have conceded that, although transplanted laws obviously do not have the same meanings as laws in the receiving systems, the degree of their accommodation (or 'fit' will depend on many variables,[50] notably the differences between the cultures, languages[51] and structures of the receiving legal systems.[52]

Those engaged in the process of transplanting legal concepts, however, have ways of minimising, or even avoiding, such challenges, one of which is to use a calque[53] or to qualify the concept to be transferred to make it more accessible to lawyers in the receiving legal system.[54] Otherwise, if a concept proves too difficult to translate, the original term can be used, which is the case with ubuntu.

As it happens, attempts have been made to translate ubuntu — the two obvious candidates were 'humanity'[55] and 'humaneness'[56] — and, as direct translations of an abstract noun, these English terms are unobjectionable. Even so, they convey a

---

[47] See Watson A *Legal Transplants and European Private Law* (2000) 4 *EJCL* available at http://www.ejcl.org/44/art44-2.html?iframe=true&width=100%&height=100% [Accessed 28 August 2015].

[48] Legrand 'The impossibility of "legal transplants"' (1997) 4 *MJECL* 120. See too Legrand 'What are "legal transplants"?' in Nelken & Fest (eds) *Adapting Legal Cultures* 63.

[49] Graziadei 'Comparative law as the study of transplants and receptions' in Reimann & Zimmermann (eds) *The Oxford Handbook of Comparative Law* 468-469. In fact, Legrand's disagreement with Watson has been generally disposed of as a misunderstanding: transplanted laws obviously do not have the same meaning in the receiving systems, since the degree of 'fit will depend on various similarities in the cultural context. See Du Plessis 'Comparative law and the study of mixed legal systems' in Reimann & Zimmermann op cit 488.

[50] Du Plessis op cit 488. See, too, Graziadei op cit 468-469.

[51] Galdia *Legal Linguistics* 226.

[52] De Groot 'Het vertalen van juridische teksten' in Balkema & De Groot (eds) *Recht en Vertalen* 18-19.

[53] Heikki *Comparative Legal Linguistics* 119.

[54] Galdia (n51) 229.

[55] Tutu *No Future without Forgiveness* 35.

[56] The Afrikaans translation is *menswaardigheid*: *S v Makwanyane and another* 1995 (3) SA 391 (CC) paras 307 and 308.

dull, neutral sense of the word that is far less appealing than the meanings carried by ubuntu's manifold connotations.[57] It is hardly surprising, then, that courts and law-makers have abandoned translations in favour of the original term.

In fact, as we have seen, the use of a loan word is a useful way of signalling the arrival of a brand new concept, and in addition, reducing the likelihood of confusion with similar concepts in the receiving law.[58] Loan words, however, have the disadvantage of a reduced 'informativity' in the new environment;[59] they are also subject to different interpretations,[60] not to mention the misunderstandings that may arise between 'legal communicators' from different backgrounds.[61] All these problems have, to some extent, been realised in the case of ubuntu.

Aside from what has been said above, the functionalist theory used in comparative law to explain the success — or effectiveness — of a legal transplant can offer only limited assistance in predicting whether ubuntu will be fully assimilated into mainstream South African law with any positive social effects.[62] The principal reason is because the functionalist test is usually applied at a high level of abstraction without engaging in any empirical research.[63]

Functionalism is in itself, however, a problematic theory. It cannot explain the frequent persistence of dysfunctional institutions in a legal system or those that appear to have no apparent use.[64] Nor is it helpful in dealing with functional equivalence, namely, the successful performance of the same function by different rules or institutions.[65] In such situations, the rules or institutions appear to be of

---

[57] See below p 29.

[58] Mattila 'European integration and legal communication' in Petersen et al (eds) *Paradoxes of European Legal Integration* 268.

[59] Galdia (n51) 237.

[60] Watson (n4) 11.

[61] Kock 'Legal aspects of language policy for European communities: language risks, equal opportunities and legislating a language' in Coulmas (ed) *A Language Policy for the European Community: prospects and quandaries* 147.

[62] Mattila (n58) 270. Lawyers are all too willing to side-step the difficult problem of determining 'success'. Those bent on reform are usually unaware or uninformed of the full social contexts, or indeed the limits of law-making. An even more egregious neglect on the part of legal reformers is their failure to pay sufficient attention to matters of political will and the long-term problems of enforcement and maintenance. Hence, the law reformer's claim that a legal transplant will achieve 'better law' could be said to be chimerical, which explains why 'so many comparative studies list similarities and differences and then run out of criteria to determine which law is better': Michaels 'The functional method in comparative law' in Reimann & Zimmermann (n49) 375.

[63] Instead, empirical research is left to the social sciences and legal pluralism, a discipline that is concerned with the interaction of individuals living according to different 'semi-autonomous social fields' Moore *Law as Process* 56. For an overview of legal pluralism see: Von Benda-Beckmann 'Who's afraid of legal pluralism?'(2002) 34 *J Legal Pluralism & Unofficial L* 44-45.

[64] A classic example was the practice of suttee, which was explored by Geertz 'Ritual and social change: a Javanese example' (1957) 59 *Am Anthropol* 32. In this regard, note should be taken of the critique of old style functionalism by Merton *Social Theory and Social Structure* 81 who said that it failed to distinguish latent and patent functions or take account of the degree of social integration in a society.

[65] If a criterion were to be found to measure the effectiveness of a transplant, it would be either in the costs of importing a new law or its (dys)functionality relative to the social problems it was

equal value, and so cannot provide criteria for assessing efficacy. Yet another problem with functionalism is its assumption that law is a coherent system, whereas a legal system could — somewhat cynically — be described as 'a collage of legal artefacts'[66] that gives no guarantee that it can meet all social needs.[67]

These problems pose considerable obstacles to the possibility of proving or disproving the success of a legal transplant. Comparative lawyers nevertheless continue to use the functionalist test, and continue to avoid empirical research by referring to legal — not social — factors. They will therefore ask whether courts and law-makers consistently applied a transplant over a period of time. Explicit marks of the failure of a transplant can, moreover, be found if the courts declare that it lacked sufficient precedent or authority,[68] or failed to form congruent relationships with other legal concepts.[69] In other words, the elusive idea of the 'success' of a transplant can be measured by its *doctrinal* assimilation into the receiving legal system.

Following this line of thinking, and in keeping with the metaphor of a 'transplant', Kahn-Freund compares two situations: the transplant of a kidney and the changing of a carburettor in a car.[70] The former suggests an organic process, with the implied risk of conee rejection; the latter implies a mechanical process, with no risk of rejection. Although lawyers tend to think only in terms of the mechanical process,[71] Kahn-Freund argued that the organic and mechanical images should be better conceived of as poles at the ends of a continuum. The legal transplant lies somewhere in the middle. In other words, it *might* be assimilated. If so, what are the chances of successful implementation at the legal and social levels? Kahn-Freund proposed the following criteria for predicting the outcome:

- whether the new law involves reform of a comprehensive or selective nature;
- whether the new law concerns widely accepted norms (such as laws about trade and transport. which are fairly internationalised) or whether the law is specifi to a particular society (such as laws governing family relationships);

---

supposed to solve, an assessment that makes comprehensive evaluation almost impossibly complex. Michaels (n62) 374-376, 380.

[66] See Graziadei in Reimann & Zimmermann (n49) 471, according to whom further study of legal transplants was needed to challenge 'the philosophical emphasis on the law's overall intellectual coherence, rationality and responsiveness to society's needs'.

[67] Which leads to scepticism about validity of the popular 'mirror theory' (a term probably introduced by Friedman *A History of American Law* 12 and 959) which contends that law and legal policy reflec the environment in which they developed. The theory was attacked by Watson *Society and Legal Change* 106-111; Watson 'Legal transplants and law reform' (1976) 92 *LQR* 79-84; Ewald 'Comparative jurisprudence II: the logic of legal transplants' (1995) 43 *Am J Comp L* 492. Cf Cotterrell 'Is there a logic of legal transplants?' in Nelken & Fest (n48) 71ff.

[68] See below on the *exceptio doli* p 115.

[69] As in the case of the trust. See below pp 18ff.

[70] Kahn-Freund 'On uses and misuses of comparative law' (1974) 37 *MLR* 1. See further in this regard Teubner 'Legal irritants: good faith in British law or how unifying law ends up in new divergences' (1998) 61 *MLR* 11.

[71] Prompted by the requirements of predictability, certainty and coherence in Western legal systems.

•   whether organised groups, such as political, environmental or cultural
     lobbies, are available to make and maintain legal institutions.

These tests will be applied in the following section to examine the importation
of the trust from English into Roman-Dutch law. The study can then be compared
with the situation of ubuntu in South African law to determine the likelihood of its
permanent assimilation into the legal system.

4 A LEGAL TRANSPLANT IN SOUTH AFRICA: THE TRUST

Although South Africa's common law is derived from two different legal
traditions,[72] they were never completely blended into a single system. The law
governing private relationships was — and in most cases still is — Roman-
Dutch.[73] The colonial government imported English laws to fil what it saw as
gaps in Roman-Dutch law,[74] or to displace existing law considered unsuitable.[75]
Thus, statutory intervention remedied deficiencie in such areas as companies,[76]
wills,[77] freedom of testation[78] and intellectual property.[79] As a result, the original
and imported laws could usually be distinguished, and the judiciary was left with
the task of accommodating the importations within a Roman-Dutch legal
framework.

An outstanding example of the challenges experienced in this regard was the
English-law trust[80] which was introduced to the Cape in 1815.[81] The origins of the
trust lie in an Anglo-Norman phrase *cestui que trust,* which formed the basis for
an English doctrine that was gradually developed in order to overcome problems
caused by the intricacies of medieval feudal law.[82] With many adjustments over
the centuries, English courts and law-makers fashioned the trust concept to give
effect to its most distinctive feature, a divided form of ownership, whereby legal
ownership of trust assets vested in a trustee, giving that person control of the

---

[72] See above p 2.

[73] As established by the treaty of cession between Britain and the Netherlands. See Hahlo 'The
trust in South African law' (1961) 78 *SALJ* 195.

[74] Or areas in which Roman-Dutch law was not as well developed. On the idea of legal gaps, see
below p 104 fn 24.

[75] See generally Beinart 'The English legal contribution in South Africa: the interaction of civil
and common law' 1981 *Acta Juridica* 7ff.

[76] Joint-Stock Companies Limited Liability Act of 1861. See Hosten et al (eds) *Introduction to
South African Law and Legal Theory* 880.

[77] In 1845, the underhand will was introduced to the Cape.

[78] In 1874, the Roman-Dutch legitimate portion, a major restriction on freedom of testation, was
abolished: Hahlo & Kahn *The South African Legal System and its Background* 578 and Beinart (n75)
18.

[79] The Patents, Designs, Trade Marks and Copyright Act 9 of 1916, which repealed prior
legislation in the four provinces, was taken directly from its British counterpart.

[80] De Waal 'In search of a model for the introduction of the trust into a civilian context' (2001) 12
Stell LR 82.

[81] Cameron, De Waal & Wunsh *Honore's South African Law of Trusts* 2; De Waal op cit 76.

[82] For a general background see: Scott 'The nature of the rights of the "cestui que trust"' (1917)
Colum L Rev 269ff; Coertze *Die Trust in die Romeins-Hollandse Reg* 28; De Waal 'Core elements of
the trust: aspects of the English, Scottish and South African trusts compared' (2000) 117 *SALJ*
552-554.

assets to administer them for special person(s) or for a general section of the public for charitable purposes. The latter individual(s) or group acquired a beneficia interest.[83]

Throughout the nineteenth century, courts in South Africa proved to be willing to enforce the trusts created by wills and other juridical acts, but they were slow to address the problem of how to bring this concept into line with similar Roman-Dutch institutions, not to mention the laws required to enforce trusts, especially those pertaining to the protection of property and ownership. It was only in the early twentieth century that an opportunity arose in the then Appellate Division of the Supreme Court to give an authoritative pronouncement on the matter.

Estate Kemp v McDonald's Trustee[84] involved a trust that had been created by a will drawn up in England. The court began by noting that, although the terms 'trust' and 'trustee' were freely used in South Africa, the English doctrine was not part of the basic law of the land. But, because the use of trusts was so widely spread in South Africa, the court concluded that the practice would be impossible to eradicate. Hence, as a matter of legal policy, it held that a testamentary disposition expressed in the form of a trust should be accepted and enforced.[85]

In searching for a suitable Roman-Dutch law niche into which to place this institution, the court decided on the Roman-law *fideicommissum*.[86] When conceived of in these terms, the trustee was deemed to be a fiduciar with legal ownership of the trust assets,[87] while equitable (or beneficial ownership vested in the beneficiar .[88] The duties of the trustee were mainly administrative: to manage trust property on behalf of the beneficiar .[89] The beneficiar had only a personal right of recourse against the trustee. In this way, the court sought to solve the conundrum of a divided ownership.

To complicate matters, South African legal practitioners found a second equivalent for the trust, this time in Dutch law, the *bewind*.[90] Practitioners used this institution, rather than the *fideicommissum*, mainly to accommodate the requirements of Afrikaans speakers. Hence, for purposes of registration and for providing security by the trustee/administrator, both the *bewind* and the trust were

---

[83] Cameron, De Waal & Wunsh (n81) 1

[84] 1915 AD 491 at 502.

[85] Supra 499.

[86] Supra 491. See too *CIR v Estate Crewe* 1943 AD 656. Other Roman and Roman-Dutch principles governed the standard of care required of trustees, namely, the *bonus et diligens paterfamilias* (*Sackville West v Nourse* 1925 AD 516 at 519-520) and the trust beneficiary s remedy against the trustee for breach of trust, the *actio legis Aquiliae* (*Yorkshire Insurance Co Ltd v Barclays Bank (Dominion, Colonial & Overseas)* 928 WLD 199 at 206-207).

[87] As well as liabilities. See *Braun v Blann and Botha NNO and another* 1984 (2) SA 850 (A) 859; *Commissioner for Inland Revenue v MacNeillie's Estate* 1961 (3) SA 833 (A) at 840.

[88] *Kemp's* case supra 502.

[89] *Braun's* case supra 850.

[90] *Bafokeng Tribe v Impala Platinum and others Ltd* 1999 (3) SA 517 (BH) at 542. See in general Du Toit 'Reflection on the bewind trust in light of the Dutch testamentary bewind' (2011) *TSAR* 540-546.

treated alike. Unlike a *fideicommissum*, however, the beneficiar of a *bewind* owned the property and the fiduciar administered it.[91]

As it happened, the *fideicommissum* devised by *Kemp's* case came under increasing criticism, from both academics[92] and the courts.[93] Accordingly, seventy years after the decision in *Kemp*, the Appellate Division again intervened to reconsider the problem of how to accommodate the trust in Roman-Dutch law. In *Braun v Blann and Botha NNO and another*,[94] it was held that the judgment in *Kemp* had been wrong to identify trusts with *fideicommissa*.[95] The court began by observing that the trust had not been officially received into South African law.[96] It stressed the differences between the two institutions, each of which had its own set of legal rules,[97] and noted that *fideicommissa* and trusts were the products of quite different legal traditions, the former Roman law and the latter Germanic law.[98]

The court then sought to discover whether trusts and *fideicommissa* could be deemed equivalents in view of their respective implications. For instance, could the role of a fiduciar under a *fideicommissum* be equated with that of a trustee? Did a fiduciary s legal ownership include administrative powers over the estate on a par with those of a trustee? *Kemp's* case[99] had held that, if the *fideicommissum* were *purum*, Roman law allowed such interpretations, but the court in *Braun*[100] found that this decision was wrong: the *fideicommissum purum* had been misinterpreted, and suitable Roman-law authority was lacking.[101] The court also adverted to the possibility, under a *bewind*, to appoint an administrator (*bewindhebber* or *bewindvoerder*) to manage fideicommissar property, but, in this case, legal ownership did not vest in the administrator. The result was that neither the *fideicommissum* nor the *bewind* could provide a suitable conceptual framework to house both legal and equitable ownership.[102]

Braun's case identifie the structure of ownership as the main difference between the trust and the *fideicommissum*. The trust's dual structure permitted concurrent ownership, whereas a fideicommissary s ownership began when the

---

[91] Honoré, in his authoritative work on the subject of trusts, *The South African Law of Trusts* (firs published in 1966) 9, 64, treated the *bewind* as a species of trust, which he termed 'bewind-trust', as opposed to the English-law trust, which he termed an 'ownership-trust'. Joubert ''n Kritiese opvatting van Honoré se beskouings oor die trustreg' (1969) 31 *THRHR* 124-146 criticised this contention for confusing two different institutions, which Joubert argued should rather be kept separate.

[92] See, for example, Keeton *Law of Trusts* 14; Scott *The Law of Trusts* para 1.9; Ryan *The Reception of the Trust in the Civil Law* 225-226 (as cited in *Braun v Blann and Botha NNO and another* 1984 (2) SA 850 (A) at 865).

[93] *Greenberg and others v Estate Greenberg* 1955 (3) SA 361 (A) at 368; *Crookes NO and another v Watson and others* 1956 (1) SA 277 (A) at 297.

[94] 1984 (2) SA 850 (A).

[95] Supra at 866. See De Waal (n82) 570 and Coertze (n82) 54, as cited in *Braun's* case 859.

[96] De Waal (n82) 556.

[97] Scott (n92) para 1.9, as cited in *Braun's case* 859.

[98] *Braun's* case supra 859.

[99] 1915 AD 491 at 502.

[100] 1984 (2) SA 850 (A).

[101] Supra 864.

[102] Ibid.

fiduciary s ownership ended, ie, with the cessation of the *fideicommissum*.[103] It followed that, in the case of a trust, a beneficiar did not have a right against a *bona fide* buyer who had received interests in trust property alienated *bona fide* by the trustee. With *fideicommissa*, on the other hand, the fideicommissar had a claim to the property once it had vested.[104] Hence, unlike a trustee, a fiduciar could not burden or alienate the property.[105] For these reasons the court in *Braun* found that critical implications of the trust ownership structure were unsuited to *fideicommissa*.[106] It therefore held the trust must be considered a *sui generis* institution in South African law, one that was still developing.[107]

In spite of the confused state of the law following *Braun's* decision, legal practitioners continued to make use of both trusts and *bewind*-trusts, and eventually legislative intervention became necessary. In 1988, a Trust Property Control Act[108] was passed creating a *sui generis* institution to harmonise the trust and *bewind,* and to regulate most aspects of control over trust property. As a result, the trust in South Africa is now seen as a single institution that differs from the English version and shows its Roman-Dutch influenc by maintaining a unitary concept of ownership, and allowing ownership to vest in the trustee or the beneficiar .[109]

The handling of the trust in South Africa provides a good example of the introduction of a foreign institution that could not be accommodated in the receiving system without generating problems caused by conflict with the rules of existing institutions. Is the case of ubuntu comparable? On a superficia level, the trust and ubuntu may seem similar in that they both concern single terms, but this is a flims basis for comparison. They differ in many respects.

The firs clue to their differences is apparent in language and purpose. Trust is a well-established word in both the primary and secondary discourses of English. The legal institution denoted by this term was introduced to South African law not in order to benefi from a particula cultural connotation but rather to meet a very specifi socio-legal need. Ubuntu, on the other hand, is an Nguni word with a distinct cultural provenance that has been co-opted into secondary register English to signify a general change in approach to a wide range of legal problems.

The second difference appears from the history of the two terms. The origins of ubuntu lie in an oral and unspecialised legal tradition. It therefore retains a

---

[103] Supra 865. In other words, a *fideicommissum* created a 'succession of interests, not the concurrent interests of the trustee and beneficiary' Ryan (n92) 225-226, as cited in *Braun's case* 865. See Coertze (n82) 156.

[104] Lee *Introduction to Roman-Dutch Law* 5ed 374.

[105] *Abdul Hameed Sitti Kadijc v De Saram* 1946 AC 208 (PC) (Ceylon) at 216; Lee op cit 374-375. In essence, therefore, trusts separated control of the property from the benefits while *fideicommissa* allowed for successive entitlements: Ryan (n92) 225-226.

[106] In *Braun v Blann and Botha (NNO) and another* 1984 (2) SA 850 (A) at 860, the court dismissed an argument that the concept of trust could be developed to include the *fideicommissum*. See further *In Estate Watkins-Pitchford and others v Commissioner for Inland Revenue* 1955 (2) SA 437 (A) at 460; *Greenberg and others v Estate Greenberg* 1955 (3) SA 361 (A) at 368.

[107] Supra 859.

[108] 57 of 1988.

[109] Cameron, De Waal & Wunsh (n81) 5-7.

relatively porous, malleable meaning. The trust in its various guises, however, had a long history in literate legal cultures. Its meaning was therefore well defined

A third difference now becomes evident. Ubuntu is a single, general concept, as yet not fully defined and it is still in the process of establishing a new legal discourse. The trust, on the other hand, was a foundational concept of English law which headed a well-developed infrastructure of rules, and had evolved to meet certain social and legal needs. These infrastructural entailments made it difficult to accommodate in Roman-Dutch law, for the division between legal and equitable forms of ownership did not match up to the Roman-Dutch conception of unitary ownership, which vested all rights and powers in a single owner (or joint owners).[110]

Hence, as far as the future of ubuntu is concerned, several lessons can be drawn from a comparison with trusts. The most obvious is that, when the courts were presented with a particular social need, and found that a foreign legal concept was at hand to meet that need, they gave effect to the concept. Only later did they turn to address the doctrinal problem of assimilating the concept into the local conceptual framework. In the case of the trust, assimilation proved impossible,[111] although it continued to perform a function that Roman-Dutch institutions could not.[112] Thus, the trust eventually had to be established as a new *sui generis* institution.

None of these technical problems stands in the way of assimilating ubuntu into South African law. As a single, general concept it is applicable in a variety of situations with consequences that are still being determined. And, as will appear in chapter 4, it has, so far, not provided a basis for any particular rights or duties that might bring it into a direct conflic with those in the existing law. Instead, ubuntu works primarily as a principle of interpretation to modify the effect of applying rights in specifi factual situations. In this regard, it forms a convenient association with similar, existing concepts, such as dignity, good faith and public policy, thereby facilitating the introduction of a range of distinctively African values in the application of these concepts to particular facts.

5 CONCLUSION: PRELIMINARY OBSERVATIONS
Linguistics and the comparative law theory on legal transplants provide both an interesting and a useful method for analysing the progress of ubuntu in South

---

[110] Ibid.

[111] It is significant in this regard, that *Braun's* case was decided during the apartheid era by a court still pursuing a 'purist' approach to South African law, ie, was hostile to English-law transplants. Zimmermann ' "Double cross": comparing Scots and South African law' in Zimmermann, Visser & Reid (eds) *Mixed Legal Systems in Comparative Perspective: property and obligations in Scotland and South Africa* 31; De Waal & Paisley 'Trusts' in Zimmermann, Visser & Reid op cit 823.

[112] Hahlo (n73) 196 and 197, however, submitted that the essential nature of the trust as compared with 'the shape it happened to assume in the law of England' was *illustrated* by the *fideicommissum*. Cf Olivier *Trust Law and Practice* 8, who says, in no uncertain terms, that: 'Although it may be tempting to equate the trust idea with the *fideicommissum* of Roman law, such a comparison is no more than an intellectual exercise. The origin and development of the trust in English law has no connection with Roman law and efforts to try to establish a link between the two institutions are futile.' Olivier's opinion appears to be supported by Joubert JA's judgment in *Braun v Blann and Botha NNO and another* 1984 (2) SA 850 (A) 858-866.

African law. In fact, the rapid and extensive spread of ubuntu into a system of law so solidly grounded on Western legal traditions presents itself as a perfect case study of loan words and legal transplants: seldom has it been possible to track the development of such occurrences with any degree of accuracy.

The linguistic perspective draws attention to the fact that ubuntu is a loan word, ie, one that has been retained in its original vernacular form. The word thereby signals its strong African cultural associations and announces the arrival of a new concept in mainstream South African law — for which there is no exact equivalent. By becoming a key legal term, ubuntu establishes its position of authority in relation to similar terms in the receiving law, and lays the foundation for a new legal discourse. This process is occurring in terms of a secondary register of English, which demands a high degree of precision in language use. As a result, ubuntu is being constantly define in relation to the meaning of other, related terms so as to institute a coherent system of meanings.

Comparative law turns the focus of inquiry to legal transplants, and the need for a full understanding of the socio-legal contexts of both the giving and receiving systems to determine whether a transplant can be successfully assimilated into its new environment. South African lawyers are used to legal transplants, since they have a long history of taking from common- and civil-law jurisdictions to fil what are perceived to be gaps or deficiencie in the local law. In this regard, however, Mogoeng J's observations in *The Citizen 1978 (Pty) Ltd and others v Mcbride (Johnstone and others, Amici Curiae)*,[113] sounded a caution: we should be slow to take from comparable jurisdictions 'which do not necessarily share the same history and experience with us'.

Even so, ubuntu is very much part of South Africa's history and experience. Moreover, if we are to judge the courts' handling of ubuntu against Kahn-Freund's criteria for determining the success of legal transplants, and if we compare the history of ubuntu in South African law with that of the trust, the prospects for ubuntu seem excellent. Its application does not involve the complexities entailed by the adoption of a cumbersome infrastructure of foreign legal rules (as with the trust), and ubuntu has the support of a significan body of political and social sentiment in favour of its continued use.

What is more, as will become apparent in Chapter 4, ubuntu provides a convenient answer to issues for which South African law offers no immediate solution. It has helped to introduce a system of restorative justice to South Africa, thus contributing to the reconciliation of a divided people during the transition from apartheid to a new constitutional dispensation; it has provided a new standard for interpreting and applying existing rules and principles and, perhaps most important, it has functioned as a new, transcendent metanorm to supply equitable solutions for hard cases.

---

[113] 2011 (4) SA 191 (CC) para 243.

Chapter 3

UBUNTU: THE CONCEPT AND ITS VALUE

1   UBUNTU AS A NATIONAL VALUE

'[U]buntu expresses the ethos of an instinctive capacity for and enjoyment of love towards our fellow men and women; the joy and the fulfilmen involved in recognising their innate humanity; the reciprocity this generates in interaction within the collective community; the richness of the creative emotions which it engenders and the moral energies which it releases both in the givers and the society which they serve and are served by.'[1]

Ubuntu is a term signifying a particular type of ethical value in traditional African cultures.[2] It is a word in everyday use in the indigenous languages of South

---

[1] *S v Makwanyane and another* 1995 (3) SA 391 (CC) para 263 per Mohamed J.

[2] Mokgoro 'Ubuntu and the law in South Africa' (1998) 4 *Buff Hum Rts L Rev* 17-18. On the moral nature of ubuntu, see Mnyaka & Motlhabi 'The African concept of *Ubuntu/Botho* and its socio-moral significance (2005) 3 *Black Theology* 215ff.

Africa,[3] but, since the advent of the country's new constitutional democracy, it is now fully established in both English and Afrikaans,[4] and has come to play a significan role as a national value in unifying the country's diverse and divided society.

In this regard, ubuntu is functioning in much the same way as iconic words chosen in other postcolonial African states to evoke new national ideologies.[5] Looking to past African traditions, the leaders of these states coined terms that could operate as normative goals to assert the dignity and independence of nations demoralised by colonial rule.[6] *Ujamaa* was the term used by Nyerere in Tanzania,[7] *uhuru* by Kenyatta in Kenya,[8] *Consciencism* by Nkrumah in Ghana,[9] *Zambian humanism* by Kaunda in Zambia[10] and *négritude* by Senghor in Senegal.[11] When South Africa finall gained democratic government, the same need was felt to knit together a society suffering a legacy of segregation and apartheid.[12] Ubuntu then formed part of the initiative which Thabo Mbeki called the 'African Renaissance'.[13]

The firs written appearance of ubuntu dates back to an 1846 translation of the Bible into isiXhosa.[14] At that time, the principal meaning of the word was a

---

[3] See above p 10.

[4] Silva *A Dictionary of South African English on Historical Principles* 749 attributes the firs reference to 'ubuntu' in English to Callaway *Fellowship of Veld* (1926) 25: 'the qualities that go to make up ubuntu, the qualities that make an umntu (person), are largely social.'

[5] For an overview see: Ruch & Anyanwu *African Philosophy: an introduction to the main philosophical trends in contemporary Africa*; Sebidi 'Toward a definitio of *ubuntu* as African humanism' in Khabela & Mzoneli (eds) *Perspectives on Ubuntu* 62ff.

[6] Gade 'The historical development of the written discourses on *Ubuntu*' (2011) 30 *SA J Philosophy* 304 described it as a 'narrative of return'. See too Praeg *African Philosophy and the Quest for Autonomy: a philosophical investigation* 41 and 89ff.

[7] Stråth '*Ujamaa*: the evasive translation of an elusive concept' in Fleisch & Stephens (eds) *Doing Conceptual History in Africa* 204.

[8] Kenyatta *Facing Mount Kenya: the tribal life of the Gikuyu*.

[9] Nkrumah *Consciencism* 70.

[10] Ranganathan & Kaunda *The Political Philosophy of President Kenneth D Kaunda of Zambia*.

[11] Senghor *On African Socialism*.

[12] See the epilogue to the Interim Constitution Act 200 of 1993, below p 27.

[13] Mulemfo *Thabo Mbeki and the African Renaissance: the emergence of a new African leadership*; 'I am an African — Thabo Mbeki's speech at the adoption of The Republic of South Africa Constitution Bill', Cape Town, 8 May 1996, available at http://www.anc.org.za/content/i-am-african-thabo-mbekis-speech-adoption-republic-south-africa-constitution-bill [accessed 29 March 2017].

[14] This firs complete edition of the New Testament was translated from both English and German by Dugmore et al *Itestamente Entsha Yenkosi Yetu Kayesu Kristu, Gokwamaxosa* (1842-1846). Six references to ubuntu can be found in the books of Mark 12:14, Romans 6.6-7, 1 Peter 3.18 and Jude 1:7-8. Ubuntu was chosen to translate the general idea of the carnal as opposed to the spiritual. It appears more specificall in the texts as sexual desire and sins of the flesh See, for example, Jude 1: '7. . . . just as Sodom and Gomorrah and the surrounding cities, which likewise indulged in sexual immorality and pursued unnatural desire, serve as an example by undergoing a punishment of eternal fire. 8. Yet in like manner these people also, relying on their dreams, defile the flesh, reject authority, and blaspheme the glorious ones.' '7. . . . ekela **ubuntu** bumbi, zimi- siweke ukuban-gumzekeliso, zibuva ubuhlungu bomlilo o- bungunapakade. 8 Kanjalo ababapupi aba- ncolileyo bayancolisa **ubuntu**, bayadeka ubukosi bayateta okukohlakeleyo gamatshawe.'

special human quality.[15] An additional meaning — that of an abstract virtue or ethic — emerged only later at a time when ubuntu was being used to achieve political purposes.[16]

Ubuntu in the latter sense began to appear in a national discourse during the 1920s, when the Zulu cultural movement, Inkatha, made it a catch-word of a programme designed to restore Zulu identity.[17] The term was then taken to stand for the virtues of an African[18] or, more specificall , a Zulu culture.[19] Although Inkatha's activities flagge during the 1930s, the organisation was revived forty years later under the leadership of Dr Mangosuthu Buthelezi.[20] He was largely responsible for launching the Inkatha National Cultural Liberation Movement,[21] a national body aimed at liberating all black South Africans from apartheid rule.

While Inkatha had initially supported the African National Congress during the party's years of exile, it changed its focus in the 1970s to become a bastion of rural traditionalists. In 1981, the organisation formally converted itself into a political party, the Inkatha Freedom Party (IFP), with Buthelezi as its president. The value of African thought and philosophy, in which ubuntu-botho was a key concept, continued to be central to the IFP's manifesto.[22] Thus the Party, and by association, ubuntu, came to be seen as a system of patriarchal values closely linked to Zulu ethnicity.[23]

1980 saw the publication of the firs book devoted exclusively to the study of

---

[15] According to Gade (n6) 308, the biblical and other texts are ambiguous as to whether ubuntu inhered only in individuals, in all members of the human race or whether it implied only humanity or a complex set of qualities.

[16] Cf Gade (n6) 306, 309-310 and 319, who claims that this meaning appears in about 1980. He concedes, however, that his periodisation of the meanings of ubuntu was provisional only.

[17] See Bhengu *Ubuntu: the essence of democracy* 10. King Solomon kaDinuzulu founded the Inkatha organisation in 1922-23 with a view to resisting the radicalism of the trades union movement and British/Afrikaner domination. In its early years, Inkatha was controlled by converts to Christianity, who were Zulu nationalists in favour of re-establishing the Zulu monarchy: Mahoney *The Other Zulus: the spread of Zulu ethnicity in colonial South Africa* 219-220.

[18] In this regard Ngcobo 'The Bantu peoples' in Calpin (ed) *South African Way of Life: values and ideals of a multi-racial society* 56 said: 'To the Bantu the Europeans, probably because of their materialistic outlook, lack the essential quality of human beings, which is best conveyed by the Zulu word "Ubuntu".'

[19] See generally on Inkatha, Maré & Hamilton *An Appetite for Power: Buthelezi's Inkatha and South Africa* ch 4.

[20] Harries 'Imagery, symbolism and tradition in a South African Bantustan: Mangosuthu Buthelezi, Inkatha, and Zulu history' (1993) 32 *History & Theory* 113.

[21] This organisation emerged at the same time as the Black Consciousness Movement to fil a vacuum in black politics, which arose because of the banning of the ANC and PAC: Maré & Hamilton (n19) 142-143.

[22] See Bhengu (n17) 10. Thus, the IFP's 2009 National Manifesto declared that: 'The IFP exists as a political party to serve the people of South Africa, and to do so in the spirit of *ubuntu/botho*. . . . We recognise *ubuntu/botho* as the foundation of all human interaction.' available at http://archive.ifp.org. za/2009/2009NATIONALMANIFESTO-FULL.pdf [Accessed 29 September 2015] 7.

[23] See below p 42.

ubuntu. This was the work of two Zimbabwean brothers,[24] who set out to promote ubuntu as a political and ideological goal for the newly independent state of Zimbabwe. Rather than pursue the Western ideologies of Marxism or capitalism, they called for an indigenous ubuntu (in Shona *unhu*) which they translated as 'humanism'. While their proposal had no lasting influenc on the future political development of Zimbabwe,[25] it had an immediate resonance with earlier, comparable ideas elsewhere in Africa.[26]

In the early 1990s, ubuntu was to serve a similar political and ideological purpose for South Africa, where a new democratic constitution was in the process of being negotiated. Indigenous African values became a critical factor in planning strategies for creating a sense of national unity.[27] Given these momentous events, ubuntu made what could only be described as a diffident entry into the country's legal system. For still undisclosed reasons,[28] it was included in an epilogue — entitled 'National Unity and Reconciliation' — to South Africa's Interim Constitution of 1993.[29]

'The adoption of this Constitution lays the secure foundation for the people of South Africa to transcend the divisions and strife of the past, which generated gross violations of human rights, the transgression of humanitarian principles in violent conflict and a legacy of hatred, fear, guilt and revenge. These can now be addressed on the basis that there is a need for understanding but not for vengeance, a need for reparation but not for retaliation, a need for *ubuntu* but not for victimisation.'[30]

After these clauses, a further provision followed, which was designed to advance 'reconciliation and reconstruction' through the granting of amnesty for offences 'associated with political objectives and committed in the course of the conflict of the past'.[31] In pursuit of these goals, ubuntu then appeared again in 1995, in the preamble to the Promotion of National Unity and Reconciliation Act[32] which established a Truth and Reconciliation Commission. Ubuntu proved to be the principle guiding the Commission through its painful process of hearing the accounts of victims of apartheid and granting amnesties to the offenders.[33]

In the same year that the TRC was founded, Augustine Shutte launched the 'Common Good Project'.[34] This Project coincided with the publication of a new

---

[24] Samkange & Samkange *Hunhuism or Ubuntuism: a Zimbabwe indigenous political philosophy*.

[25] Gade (n6) 309-310.

[26] See above p 25 and Gade (n6) 304.

[27] See above p 25.

[28] Gade (n6) 312.

[29] 200 of 1993.

[30] See further: *S v Makwanyane and another* 1995 (3) SA 391 (CC) paras 220-228; *Dikoko v Mokhatla* 2006 (6) SA 235 (CC) para 113.

[31] Epilogue to the Interim Constitution.

[32] 34 of 1995.

[33] See the Truth and Reconciliation Commission of South Africa *Report* 125-127.

[34] See Gade (n6) 321-322. See, too, the later 'Ubuntu Project' launched by Drucilla Cornell in 2003 under the auspices of the Stellenbosch Institute for Advanced Study: http://theubuntuproject.org/ [Accessed 28 August 2015]. As a result of the Project various conferences were convened resulting in the following publications: Cornell 'Is there a difference that makes a difference between uBuntu and dignity?' (2010) 25 *SAPL* 382ff; Cornell & Panfili *Symbolic Forms for a New Humanity: cultural*

edition of Shutte's book, *Philosophy for Africa*, a work which presented ubuntu as 'something of great value we can offer to the rest of the world'.[35] Shutte is said to be responsible for the association of ubuntu with a general saying in African languages: *umuntu ngumuntu ngabantu* [isiXhosa: a person is a person through people].[36] In other words, the constitutional transformation of South Africa would require a sense of community and caring for fellow human beings. The time when this connection was made was of course significant for it was a period when preparations were underway for voting in a new democratic government.[37]

In the following passage, Mabogo More brings together the different aspects and functions of ubuntu then prevalent in the country.

> 'In one sense *ubuntu* is a philosophical concept forming the basis of relationships, especially ethical behaviour. In another sense, it is a traditional politico-ideological concept referring to socio-political action. As a moral or ethical concept, it is a point of view according to which moral practices are founded exclusively on consideration and enhancement of human well-being; a preoccupation with "human". It enjoins that what is morally good is what brings dignity, respect, contentment, and prosperity to others, self and the community at large. *uBuntu* is a demand for respect for persons no matter what their circumstances may be.'[38]

Ubuntu was to have an impact beyond South Africa's borders. As the leitmotif of the country's remarkable constitutional revolution, it soon attracted the attention of those seeking to transform social relations in their own states.[39] Hence, ubuntu is now being investigated in various parts of the world for new ideas about ethical behaviour in order to revive the waning legitimacy of the established Western discourses of democracy and human rights.[40]

---

and racial reconfigurations of critical theory; Cornell (ed) *Law and Revolution in South Africa: uBuntu, dignity, and the struggle for Constitutional Transformation*; Cornell 'uBuntu and subaltern legality' in Praeg & Magadla (eds) *uBuntu: curating the archive* 167-176; Cornell 'A call for a nuanced constitutional jurisprudence: ubuntu, dignity, and reconciliation' (2004) 19 *SAPL* 666; Cornell & Van Marle 'Exploring ubuntu: tentative reflections (2005) 5 *AHRLJ* 195; Cornell 'Ubuntu, pluralism and the responsibility of legal academics in the New South Africa' (2009) 20 *Law & Critique* 43-58; Cornell 'The significanc of the living customary law for an understanding of law: does custom allow for a woman to be Hosi?' (2009) 2 *CCR* 395.

[35] Shutte *A Philosophy for* Africa v.

[36] Gade (n6) 314.

[37] See Shutte (n35) vi.

[38] More 'South Africa under and after apartheid' in Wiredu (ed) *A Companion to African Philosophy* 149 and 156-157.

[39] See, for example, Gade 'What is *Ubuntu*? Different interpretations among South Africans of African descent' (2012) 31 *SA J Philosophy* 500.

[40] For example, Boaventura de Sousa Santos's ALICE project (a motto standing for 'alternatives are not lacking in the world. What is indeed missing is an alternative thinking of alternatives'). Available at http://alice.ces.uc.pt/en [Accessed 29 March 2017].

2 LEGAL DEFINITIONS: THE PROBLEM AND SOME PRELIMINARY ANSWERS

Everyone would agree that ubuntu is 'like life and love ... a difficult word or concept to define'[41] Indeed, even before its adoption into legal discourse, ubuntu was, in the famous words of Credo Mutwa, 'veiled in a heavy *kaross* of mystery'.[42] Like any abstraction, however, the meaning of ubuntu is necessarily vague. Its very ambiguity 'speaks to the idea that it is law without a center'.[43]

Nevertheless, much of the work of law is to fi the meanings of key terms,[44] and, since ubuntu has entered a legal discourse, the word has been no exception to the rule. In fact, as was evident in the previous chapter,[45] the transition of ubuntu from spoken to written form, together with its shift to a secondary, legal register, means that the word will inevitably be subject to definition[46]

(a) The problem of definition

In general terms, definitio implies an attempt to link a word to a precise referent, and to stabilise its meaning by fixin the boundaries of its semantic fiel by excluding overlapping field of meaning. A complication in this process is the fact that words have two forms (or orders) of signification denotation and connotation.[47]

Denotation is popularly taken to be the 'literal', 'obvious' or 'universal' meaning of a word. Once this meaning has been learned and accepted, it can function as the basis for conscious, analytical inquiry in professional disciplines, such as the law.[48] Connotation, on the other hand, refers to shades of meaning that are associative, expressive, attitudinal and evaluative.[49] As such, connotations derive from a word's socio-cultural or personal connections, which are polysemic,[50] and hence less amenable than denotations to having their meanings defined[51]

Establishing a precise and permanent denotation for ubuntu is obviously a herculean task. At the outset, it must be appreciated that its meaning is inherently vague, because it is a noun with an abstract, generalised referent. What is more,

---

[41] Bohler-Muller 'The story of an African value: focus: ten years after' (2005) 20 *SAPL* 266. See further Himonga, Taylor & Pope 'Reflection on judicial views of ubuntu' (2013) 16 *PELJ* 376ff.

[42] Credo-Mutwa *Indaba, My Children* 555-556. See, too, Mokgoro (n2) 15.

[43] Ramose 'An African perspective on justice and race' (2001) 3 *Polylog: Forum for Intercultural Philosophy* available at https://them.polylog.org/3/frm-en.htm#f4 para 6 [Accessed 29 March 2017].

[44] See above p 12.

[45] See above pp 12ff.

[46] Mnyongani 'De-linking ubuntu: towards a unique South African jurisprudence' (2010) 31 *Obiter* 135. Cf Ramose 'Uburtu: affirming a right and seeking remedies' in Praeg & Magadla (n34) 134.

[47] Trask *Language and Linguistics: the key concepts* 51 and 67.

[48] Silverman *The Subject of Semiotics* 31.

[49] Connotation often indicates that a denotative meaning is being made to stand for the user's values. Fiske & Hartley *Reading Television* 33, 84 (following Roland Barthes) regard connotations as manifest signs of ideology, so that the way in which they fi together to form a coherent pattern is evidence of an underlying, invisible, organising principle, ie, an ideology.

[50] O'Sullivan et al (eds) *Key Concepts in Communication and Cultural Studies* 231.

[51] Barthes *Elements of Semiology* 89-91.

any meaning of ubuntu in its original, oral context is bound to be elusive, and of course, because ubuntu is a loan word, it occupies a position in its host language rendering its meaning even more malleable.[52]

Finally, and most importantly, the speakers and writers who appropriate a word like ubuntu add or subtract nuances of meaning to serve their own particular purposes.[53] It follows that the meaning of ubuntu, as currently used, has been moulded to meet various political, ideological and other agendas, each of which has entailed certain semantic shifts.[54] Adoption into a legal discourse is a prime example of this process, and lawyers, as the agents active in constructing the meanings of ubuntu, are well placed to manipulate meaning, because their goal is to maintain a self-referential[55] and authoritative code of rules. Hence, when ubuntu fell into the domain of law, the very flexibilit of its meaning made it an immediate target for definition

Nevertheless, although the law rarely tolerates technical terms with open-ended meanings, certain words are deliberately allowed to remain ambiguous so as to permit judges discretion in applying them to diverse factual situations. Words such as 'wrongful'[56] and 'reasonable'[57] are typical examples. Ubuntu falls into this category. While judges and academics have fille many pages with debate about definition its meaning in law will persist in remaining fluid

A search for definitio all too often results in recourse to a dictionary.[58] This quick fi solution, however, has serious shortcomings. For a start, if ubuntu is to be used in English, the dominant language in South African law, it has to be translated. It must then be appreciated that, in any natural language, words have to be define in terms of other words, with the result that a search for meaning ultimately becomes a circular process. Furthermore, not all dictionary definition take full account of connotations and the contexts of usage. Yet, in the case of the ubuntu, these matters are all important, since the word has powerful cultural connotations.[59] Lastly, when applied to a word like ubuntu, the dictionary type of definitio works on an assumption that the word refers to some core concept that

---

[52] See above p 11.

[53] Cornell & Van Marle (n34) 207.

[54] Cornell (n34 2010) 397; Himonga, Taylor & Pope (n41) 394; Richardson 'Reflection on reconciliation and ubuntu' in Nicolson (ed) *Persons in Community: African ethics in a global culture* 80.

[55] In this regard, see Teubner *Autopoietic Law: a new approach to law and society* 221; Luhmann 'Autopoiesis of social systems' in Geyer & Van der Zouwen (eds) *Sociocybernetic Paradoxes: observation, control and evolution of self-steering systems* 172ff.

[56] Cockrell ' "Can you paradigm?" — another perspective on the public law/private law divide' 1993 *Acta Juridica* 243.

[57] Alexy 'Reasonableness of law' in Bongiovanni, Sartor & Valentini (eds) *Reasonableness and Law* 7.

[58] Which will usually give common usage denotations: Bolinger 'The atomization of meaning' (1965) 41 *Language* 555ff. Lexical definition are descriptive, since they do no more than report an actual usage by speakers of a language, and (possibly) the changes following from usage. They are seldom prescriptive, ie, suggesting a 'correct' version of a term, regardless of changed meaning.

[59] Which the courts have been deploying in their judgments: Mokgoro 'Ubuntu, the Constitution and the rights of non-citizens' (2010) 21 *Stell LR* 224.

synthesises an actual way of being.[60] The meaning is then fixe and essentialised which has the effect of precluding additional meanings constructed by past and present users.

It is therefore suggested that, to the extent that definitio is an inevitable process in law, the task is best tackled through the 'sense' of the word, ie, its current usage and relationship to other words in a given linguistic system, rather than the referential, dictionary approach.[61] Thus, the meaning of ubuntu may be more profitabl explored through the ways in which it is used in legal writings and its connections with other legal terms.[62] Modern semantic theory certainly prefers the sense approach, contending that the referent (particularly social and abstract referents) is constantly being reconstructed through acts of communication.[63] If it is conceded, as it must be, that we have no direct access to meaning outside language, then it is to the actual use of ubuntu in current legal discourse that we must look.

Finally, it is important to be aware of the fact that a term such as ubuntu, which is providing a foundation for a system of thought, is likely to have several different uses and functions. In consequence, it will never be susceptible to being reduced to a single meaning.[64] For many reasons, then, we must not be too quick to settle on one meaning for ubuntu.[65] To do so would impose boundaries on the scope of the term and restrict its semantic range, an approach that would be ill-advised at this time in South Africa, when the country is undergoing a wide-ranging socio-legal transformation,[66] a process in which ubuntu is playing a small but significan role.

(b) Basic meanings of ubuntu: being human and the right way of being human

Notwithstanding the above caveat, we still need some rule-of-thumb understanding of the present meaning of ubuntu before we can start an inquiry into its

---

[60] Ramose *African Philosophy through Ubuntu* 92. Cf Mokgoro (n2) 15, who says that the Western use of abstractions 'defie the very essence of the African world-view', which describes ideas through real contexts.

[61] Every word is a sign implying its physical manifestation in sound or writing, the fact that it stands for something other than itself and the fact that it is recognised by people other than the speaker/writer. A referential approach to meaning thus implies that a word signifie an object or concept external to the user. By contrast, a 'sense' approach indicates that meaning is to be found in the relationship of a word to others in a linguistic system. See O'Sullivan et al (n50) 262 and 284.

[62] Which in the case of South African law includes terms such as *boni mores*, equity, dignity or equality.

[63] Bruner *Acts of Meaning* 69 and 158; Bruner 'The narrative construction of reality' (1991) *Crit Inquiry* 17; Hasan 'The disempowerment game: Bourdieu and language in literacy' (1998) 10 *Ling & Edu* 59.

[64] In fact, the concept of ubuntu forms the basis for sub-sets of meaning, and, accordingly must be broad enough to encompass them. Praeg 'An answer to the question: what is [ubuntu]?' (2008) 27 *SA J Philosophy* 368. The terms currently associated with ubuntu are numerous. See the list given in *Afriforum and another v Malema and another* 2011 (6) SA 240 (EqC) para 19.

[65] Hence Cornell & Van Marle (n34) 205 argue that the generality of ubuntu is its strength. See further below p 109 on the problems that arose with the development of equity in English law.

[66] Langa 'Transformative constitutionalism' (2006) 17 *Stell LR* 354.

function as a metanorm in the law. To this end, a right way of living or attitude to life will probably serve as a broadly accepted meaning.[67] We can then think of ubuntu as a virtuous form of behaviour, whether as an individual's personal attribute or as a more general ethical duty to care for a community of fellow human beings.[68]

Within this general understanding, two core meanings can be identified [69] The firs is the experience of being a person, an *umuntu*. Ubuntu can be likened to a 'life force' or 'breath' [isiZulu, isiXhosa: *moyo*; seSotho: *moya*],[70] a meaning that includes self-understanding and self-identity. From this basis, the second meaning of ubuntu arises, one signifying a set of qualities and norms concerning the way a person behaves — and ought to behave — as a human, towards other humans. Basic qualities encompass the connotations: 'caring, compassion, unity, tolerance, respect, closeness, generosity, genuineness, empathy, consultation, compromise, and hospitality'.[71] The list could be extended further to include the notions of fullness of human life, truthfulness, self-respect and integrity.[72]

These understandings of ubuntu are reflecte in the conceptions of personhood elsewhere in Africa. Wiredu's work on Akan culture, for instance, shows that a person has two aspects. One is ontological, ie, the experience of being human, and the other is the set of normative qualities expected of a human. Built into this expectation is a presupposition that, when individuals are conscious of and have due respect for their responsibilities, they have a will free to realise this ethical code. They are therefore people not only by the fact of birth, but also by evolving through events and experiences that induce ethical action.[73]

Being *umuntu*, then, is a value, because it is underpinned by aspirational standards which can be described as *ubuntu*.[74] It follows that a person can be described as such if he or she has *ubuntu* or embodies its virtues and ethical norms.[75] It also follows that the realisation of this normative code has many implications for membership of a community of fellow human beings and their general welfare.

---

[67] Ramose (n60) 43.

[68] Metz & Gaie 'The African ethic of *ubuntu/botho*: implications for research on morality' (2010) 39 *J Moral Educ* 284.

[69] Gade (n39) 487.

[70] Forster *Self Validating Consciousness in Strong Artificial Intelligence: an African theological contribution* (2006) unpublished Doctoral thesis, UNISA 62. Cf Ramose (n60) 61 for the various meanings of *moya*. Metz 'Developing African political philosophy: moral theoretic strategies' (2012) 14 *Philos Afr* 66-67 discusses this conception under the rubric of 'vitality', 'a valuable spiritual or invisible energy that inheres in everything'.

[71] Masina 'Xhosa practices of *ubuntu* for South Africa' in Zartman (ed) *Traditional Cures for Modern Conflicts: African conflict 'medicine'* 170. See, too, the list noted by Gade (n6) 307-308.

[72] Forster (n70) 60.

[73] Wiredu *Cultural Universals and Particulars: an African perspective* 127 and 130-133.

[74] Gade (n6) 314.

[75] Forster (n70) 60 and Forster 'Identity in relationship: the ethics of ubuntu as an answer to the impasse of individual consciousness' in Du Toit (ed) *The Impact of Knowledge Systems on Human Development in Africa* 266.

(c) Further basic meaning of ubuntu: humanity through community

Ubuntu signifie the affirmation of an individual's humanity by accepting that others are equally human, and by being willing to share the world with them.[76] Shutte, for example, says that '[o]ur deepest moral obligation is to become more fully human. And this means entering more and more deeply into community with others. So, although the goal of our lives is personal fulfilment selfishnes is excluded.'[77]

Hence, although ubuntu means humanity, it is not humanity as a quality of character inhering in only some individuals, but as the vital force we share and participate in through 'the interplay which takes place when people come into contact or live together'.[78] For that reason, ubuntu implies a 'collective personhood',[79] which invokes images of 'group support, acceptance, co-operation, care, sharing and solidarity'.[80]

From this foundation arises a strong sense of interconnectedness in a community of fellow beings.[81] When used in relation to ubuntu, the idea of community is captured in the isiXhosa adage mentioned earlier: *umuntu ngumuntu ngabantu* (or in seSotho *motho ke motho ka batho*).[82] Usually translated as 'I am because we are', *umuntu ngumuntu ngabantu* could also be rendered as 'a person becomes a person through other people',[83] which expresses a better sense of *inter*dependence.[84] This adage is not peculiar to Africa. A much quoted English equivalent is a line from John Donne: 'No man is an island, entire of itself; every man is a piece of the continent, a part of the main.'[85]

The feeling of community can be expressed in many ways. In a very profound sense, for example, it appears in sayings found throughout Africa that 'it takes a

[76] Which then includes caring, respect and other virtuous acts: Bhengu (n17) 5. Msila 'African leadership models in education: leading institutions through ubuntu' (2014) 18 *Anthropologist* 1109: 'Ubuntu is the innate policy used to run the village. As members are born or join the village they are socialised to the principles of this policy. This keeps the fabric of the society intact and members learn about unity.'

[77] Shutte *Ubuntu: an ethic for a new South Africa* 30. Hence, those who lack ubuntu, ie, behave in an antisocial manner, may be dubbed 'animals': Bhengu (n17) 27.

[78] Setiloane *African Theology: an introduction* 14.

[79] Masina (n71) 170.

[80] Mbigi 'Ubuntu' (1995) November *Enterprise* 57; Metz & Gaie (n68) 276.

[81] See *S v Makwanyane and another* 1995 (3) SA 391 (CC) para 224.

[82] Quoted often in the cases, for example: *Makwanyane* supra para 308; *MEC for Education, KwaZulu-Natal, and others v Pillay* 2008 (1) SA 474 (CC) para 53; *South African Police Service v Solidarity obo Barnard* 2014 (6) SA 123 (CC) para 174; *Bhe and others v Magistrate, Khayelitsha, and others (Commission for Gender Equality as Amicus Curiae); Shibi v Sithole and others; South African Human Rights Commission and another v President of the Republic of South Africa and another* 2005 (1) SA 580 (CC) para 163.

[83] Forster (n70) 60.

[84] See Bhengu (n17) 2; Mbigi & Maree 'Introduction' in Mbigi & Maree (eds) *Ubuntu: the spirit of African transformation management* 2.

[85] *From Devotions upon Emergent Occasions* xxvii, cited in *MEC for Education, KwaZulu-Natal, and others v Pillay* 2008 (1) SA 474 (CC) para 53; *Port Elizabeth Municipality v Various Occupiers* 2005 (1) SA 217 (CC) para 37; *Union of Refugee Women and others v Director: Private Security Industry Regulatory Authority and others* 2007 (4) SA 395 (CC) para 145; *South African Police Service v Solidarity obo Barnard* 2014 (6) SA 123 (CC) para 174.

whole village to raise a child'.[86] In other words, a child is held to be the common concern of everyone in the group, and all members are expected to ensure that the child is cared for and fully integrated into the group.[87]

When talking of community, however, a note of caution is necessary. Community is a contentious term bearing several meanings,[88] and the word has been appropriated by many interest groups to serve their own ends. Nevertheless, as an analytical term of social science, community is used to signify a closely knit social unit, typically based on relationships of kin, whereby members share common interests and values.[89] The community should not therefore be conceived of as a simple association of individuals, whose interests happen to coincide for a particular purpose. It is a collection of people who are united by powerful interpersonal bonds, whether biological or social.[90]

Considered in this way, the individual should be thought of in terms of social ties rather than personal traits.[91] Ramose, for instance, talks of African communities as dynamic associations of individuals.[92] Each has a special commitment to others and a distinct sense of a shared life, whereby promotion of the group works to benefi the individual (and vice versa).[93] A community thereby generates 'a public discursive space which members construct through action-in-concert'.[94] An individual's life is, accordingly, a history of transactions with the group.

---

[86] An Igbo Yoruba proverb, expressed in other forms elsewhere, such as 'your child is mine [and] my child is yours': Van Wyk 'Performativity in higher education transformation in South Africa' (2005) 19 *SA J of Higher Education* 15.

[87] Van Wyk 'Higher education transformation in the Western Cape: on the transformative potential of ubuntu and communalism' in Waghid et al (eds) *African(a) Philosophy of Education: reconstructions and deconstructions* 108.

[88] Boonzaier & Sharp 'Introduction: constructing social reality' in Boonzaier & Sharp (eds) *South African Keywords* 3.

[89] *Gemeinschaft* as opposed to *Geselleschaft*: Tönnies *Community and Society* 37; Almgren 'Community' in Borgatta & Borgatta (eds) *Encyclopedia of Sociology* vol 1 244-249.

[90] Gyekye *An Essay on African Philosophical Thought: the Akan conceptual scheme* 155-158 define African communalism as a kinship-oriented social order, which is informed by an ethic of reciprocity, and in which the individual is raised with a strong sense of solidarity with the group. See, too, Khoza *Let Africa Lead: African transformational leadership for 21st century business* 266, who describes communalism as 'a concept that views humanity in terms of collective existence and intersubjectivity, serving as the basis for supportiveness, cooperation, collaboration and solidarity'.

[91] Mabovula 'The erosion of African communal values: a reappraisal of the African ubuntu philosophy' (2011) 3 *Inkanyiso* 38ff.

[92] Cited by Mabovula op cit 38. See Ramose 'The philosophy of ubuntu and ubuntu in philosophy' in Coetzee & Roux (eds) *The African Philosophy Reader: a text with readings* 274.

[93] See too Metz 'Just the beginning for ubuntu: reply to Matolino and Kwindingwi' (2014) 33 *SA J Philosophy* 71; Metz 'Ethics in Africa and in Aristotle: some points of contrast' (2012) 13 *Phronimon* 104; Metz 'African values and human rights as two sides of the same coin: a reply to Oyowe' (2014) 14 *AHRLJ* 311.

[94] See in Coetzee 'Morality in African thought' in Coetzee & Roux (n92) 322.

As a result, ubuntu stands both for the individual and the group joined in a vibrant and interactive process of *becoming*.[95] It is best seen, not as the end but as the process of day-to-day involvement with other people, and the consequent enlargement of the self and the consciousness of others. People who live in a community come together whenever problems of mutual concern arise. They can then share ideas and seek solutions, which are generally solutions designed to promote peace and living together in a respectful harmony.[96] Responding to the needs and wants of others is not merely descriptive of community relationships, but is also a moral or ethical duty.[97]

The extent to which the individual retains his or her identity in a community is one of the most troubled issues regarding ubuntu, because it is on this point that Western and African philosophies diverge. The former takes a largely subjectivist approach to the definitio of a person, which can be summed up in the Cartesian maxim, 'I think therefore I am',[98] or put in another way, 'I am known, therefore we are'.[99] Here the emphasis is on the autonomy of the individual.[100] According to this way of thinking, individuals are the basic given. They lie at the centre of things; society is an intellectual construct.[101] Each person is thus a distinct and independent unit, linked to the others as a bearer of rights and duties; groups are social abstractions, and in consequence, not deserving of the same respect or attention.

African philosophy, on the other hand, takes a relational approach to the idea of individual identity: 'I participate therefore I am.'[102] In Shutte's words, 'the human self is not something that firs exists on its own and then enters into relationship .... [instead] these relationships are what it is'.[103] From this perspective, ubuntu may be described as a living sense of human relationships.[104] Hence, 'an individual human person cannot develop and achieve the fullness of his potentials

---

[95] Much of the text that follows in this section can be attributed to James Patrick whose work has made an invaluable contribution to the understanding of ubuntu. See Bennett & Patrick 'Ubuntu: the ethics of traditional religion' in Bennett (ed) *Traditional African Religions in South African Law* 226ff.

[96] Metz & Gaie (n68) 276.

[97] Ramose 'The ethics of ubuntu' in Coetzee & Roux (n92) 329.

[98] Forster (n70) 260.

[99] Bujo *Foundations of an African Ethic: beyond the universal claims of Western morality* 4. Following Bujo, Metz (n70) 68 acknowledges that community 'is a reliable epistemic means by which *to know how* to behave' and thereby to promote the life-force itself.

[100] As Forster (n75) 254 points out, however, this is an inadequate theory, particularly in light of the technical and scientifi advances of modern society.

[101] Ramose 'The ontology of invisible beings' in (1989) 2 *Boleswa Occasional Papers* 16: 'Individualism is part of the legacy of fragmentation in science and society and, as such, it detracts from the wholeness which is characteristic of African traditional thought.'

[102] Forster (n75) 268.

[103] Shutte (n77) 23.

[104] Ubuntu also gives expression to what the Indian nationalist turned spiritual philosopher, Sri Aurobindo Ghose *The Ideal of Human Unity* 298 described as 'a living sense of human oneness and practice of human oneness in thought, feeling and life'.

without the concrete act of relating to other individual persons'.[105] As Ramose says, the community ascribes ontological primacy to the group,[106] through which individuals can come to know themselves and their surrounding world.[107]

This view of ubuntu helps us to appreciate that we are not dealing with a mere intellectual construct. Ubuntu arises from the actual experience of life, and so it acts as a corrective to such abstractions as 'humanity' or 'the individual'. Individuals are neither to be lumped together in a mass nor separated into discrete units, but rather to be located in a web of living relationships. This does not mean that individual interests are to be sacrifice in favour of the group; just as others within the group deserve our respect and care, so does the individual giving respect and care.

It follows that ubuntu poses a radical challenge to the deeply entrenched Western model of the detached ego. The individual is always one-in-society: 'There is no truly human existence without community and that community is not an extra that gets added on but is of the very essence.'[108] When seen in these terms, ubuntu offers a counterbalance to the dehumanised and atomised individual that has been the product of the modern Western world.[109]

3 OBJECTIONS TO UBUNTU

The arrival of ubuntu in South African law has not been greeted with universal approval. Several scholars have expressed doubt as to whether it can make any useful contribution to the existing system, and it is worth examining their claims in some detail if only to refute them, because it is through the process of refutation that a deeper understanding of the positive qualities of ubuntu can be revealed.

The objections to ubuntu may be grouped into fiv categories: it is too general and vague to be of any legal use; it serves only the interests of an insider group

---

[105] Gyekye *Person and Community: Ghanaian philosophical studies* reprinted as 'Person and community in African thought' in Coetzee & Roux (n92) 353, cited in *MEC for Education, KwaZulu-Natal, and others v Pillay* 2008 (1) SA 474 (CC) para 53. Thus Gyekye builds an African system of ethics on the performance of deeds that promote the general good of the human weal 'without treating individuals disrespectfully'. See Metz (n70) 63-64; Gyekye 'African ethics' in Zalta (ed) *Stanford Encyclopaedia of Philosophy* (available at http://plato.stanford.edu/entries/african-ethics/ [accessed at 30 September 2015].

[106] De Tejada 'The future of Bantu law' (1979) 11 *ARSP* 304 as cited in Ramose (n43): '*Ubu* and *ntu* are mutually founding in the sense that they are two aspects of being as a oneness and an indivisible whole-ness. *Ubu* as the generalized understanding of being may be said to be distinctly ontological; *ntu* as the nodal point at which being assumes concrete form or a mode of being in the process of continual unfoldment may be said to be distinctly epistemological. Accordingly, *ubuntu* is the fundamental ontological and epistemological category in the African thought of the Bantu-speaking people.'

[107] Ramose (n60) 56; Gyekye (n90) 155; Gyekye 'Person and community in African thought' in Kimmerle (ed) *I, We, and Body* 53-54.

[108] Macquarrie *In Search of Humanity: a theological and philosophical approach* 88.

[109] The philosophy of ubuntu is therefore aligned with post-modern thinking in that it: 'goes beyond the mere rational into other dimensions of knowing and experiencing . . . . The postmodern scientifi approach rehumanizes — it has a marked influenc on what is human . . . . The importance of the non-rational and trans-rational is again receiving a place in the experience of human beings.' See Oosthuizen 'The place of traditional religion in contemporary South Africa' in Olupona (ed) *African Spirituality: forms, meanings and expressions* 39.

and promotes a majoritarian tyranny; because it is derived from a traditional society, it cannot contribute to the solution of contemporary problems; it is open to manipulation to serve political and ideological ends; it is redundant to the requirements of South African law.[110]

(a) Too general and vague

A major criticism brought against ubuntu is that it is too general and hence too vague.[111] As a result it can be so loaded with meanings that it either 'means all things to all men'[112] or 'collapses under the weight of the expectations' heaped upon it.[113] These objections, however, can be immediately refuted. As a foundational legal norm,[114] the meaning of ubuntu is necessarily broad and generalised — and so it should remain if it is to perform its function as a metanorm contributing to the transformation of South African law.[115]

The same generality and vagueness have led to the further criticism that ubuntu does not easily fi into a normative hierarchy as either a rule or principle.[116] This criticism is indeed true. As a signifie of the right way of living,[117] ubuntu is closer to a value.[118] An ambiguous quality such as this, however, should be no reason for

---

[110] Himonga, Taylor & Pope (n41) 384ff; Mokgoro & Woolman 'Where dignity ends and uBuntu begins: an amplificatio of, as well as an identificatio of a tension in, Drucilla Cornell's thoughts' (2010) 25 *SAPL* 403-404.

[111] Klug *Constituting Democracy: law, globalism and South Africa's political reconstruction* 164; English 'Ubuntu: the quest for an indigenous jurisprudence' (1996) 12 *SAJHR* 641; Van der Walt *Law and Sacrifice: towards a post-apartheid theory of law* 109-115. Richardson in Nicolson (n54) 78.

[112] English op cit 646. Another problem with the ambiguity of ubuntu is that it encompasses contradictory principles, but this is to be expected of any broad normative concept: Himonga, Taylor & Pope (n41) 385.

[113] Kroeze 'Doing things with values II: the case of ubuntu' (2002) 13 *Stell LR* 260-261. Kroeze argues that the Constitutional Court's definition of ubuntu in *Makwanyane* resulted in words with no 'self-evident meaning', leaving ubuntu 'over-loaded with empty concepts'.

[114] See above p 13 and Metz 'Toward an African moral theory' (2007) 15 *J Polit Philos* 321ff, who claimed that African philosophy had failed to construct such a foundational norm. Cf Ramose 'But Hans Kelsen was not born in Africa: a reply to Thaddeus Metz' (2007) 26 *SA J Philosophy* 347ff, who argues that Metz's thesis was based on Hans Kelsen's conception of a *Grundnorm* which is alien to African thinking.

[115] Cornell & Muvangua 'Introduction: the re-cognition of *uBuntu*' in Cornell & Muvangua (eds) *Ubuntu and the Law: African ideals and postapartheid jurisprudence* 18. See, too, Mokgoro & Woolman (n110) 403: 'the presence of "uBuntu" as a guiding norm in the interpretation of our basic law is essential, in the minds of ordinary people, for the legitimation of our legal system.'

[116] Mboti 'May the real ubuntu please stand up?' (2015) 30 *J of Media Ethics* 143. See, too, Keevy 'Ubuntu versus the core values of the South African Constitution' (2009) 34 *JJS* 34-35, who, in addition, argues that ubuntu cannot be considered a 'philosophy' in the Western conception of the term.

[117] In this sense, ubuntu is akin to the Hindu notion of *dharma,* which can be translated as 'righteous duty, law, morality or religion': Menski *Hindu Law: beyond tradition and modernity* 98. See, too, the similarity to Confucianism: Bell & Metz 'Confucianism and ubuntu: reflection on a dialogue between Chinese and African traditions' (2011) 38 *J of Chinese Philosophy* 81.

[118] Ramose (n60) 40.

excluding ubuntu from the legal system, since its role as a metanorm means that, while it is superordinate to both rules and principles, it informs their meaning.[119]

(b) Promotes the interests of insiders and majorities

The next objection to ubuntu goes to matters of substance rather than form. Because ubuntu is concerned with the spirit of community, it favours insiders as opposed to outsiders and the majority as opposed to the individual or minority.[120] The answer to both these objections has already been given above. In the firs place, the outsider, the visitor, the lone traveller, the one who is not a member of the family or nation should never fall outside the generous embrace of ubuntu.[121] Although exclusion may happen in practice, such incidents cannot be regarded as conforming to the spirit of ubuntu.

The response to the second claim — majoritarianism — can also be found in what has been said about the position of the individual in the community. While the community provides the basis for ubuntu's value system, the well-being of the individual is not necessarily suppressed; rather it is realised in and through the community.[122] In keeping with this line of reasoning, Metz construes the good of the community in a utilitarian sense, namely, promotion of the group works to benefi the individual (and vice versa).[123] He therefore contends that the communal ethic integral to the idea of ubuntu should be understood to involve both identity and solidarity.[124] Identity means that people think of themselves as members of a group, and 'take pride or feel shame in the group's activities', as well as a sense of duty to 'engage in joint projects, co-ordinating their behaviour to realise shared ends'.[125] Solidarity means that people not only empathise with the group, but also assist one another to their mutual benefit Although Metz notes

---

[119] Metz (n93 2014) 309; Van Niekerk 'A common law for Southern Africa: Roman law or indigenous African law?' (1998) 31 *CILSA* 166-167.

[120] Marx '*Ubu* and *Ubuntu*: on the dialectics of apartheid and nation building' (2002) 29 *Politikon* 53; Kroeze (n113) 261; Van Binsbergen 'Ubuntu and the globalisation of Southern African thought and society' (2001) 15 *Quest* 78; Metz '*Ubuntu* as a moral theory and human rights in South Africa' (2011) 11 *AHRLJ* 533; Cornell (n34 2004) 671; Louw 'Ubuntu and the challenges of multi-culturalism in South Africa' (2001) 15 *Quest* 19; Magadla & Chitando 'The self become god: *ubuntu* and the "scandal of manhood"' in Praeg & Magadla (n34) 188. Cf *Prince v President, Cape Law Society, and others* 2002 (2) SA 794 (CC) para 157 and Botha 'Human dignity in comparative perspective' (2009) 20 *Stell LR* 205, who quotes from *Prince's* case the need to resist the 'hydraulic insistence on conformity'.

[121] See the quote from Mandela below p 48.

[122] See above p 33ff, and, in addition, Himonga, Taylor & Pope (n41) 419ff, who argue that the apparent conflic between Western liberalism and ubuntu communitarianism is too simplistic.

[123] Metz (n93 2014) 311; Metz (n93 'Just the beginning for ubuntu') 71; Metz (n93 2012) 104.

[124] Metz 'African conceptions of human dignity: vitality and community as the ground of human rights' (2012) 13 *Hum Rights Rev* 32; Metz 'African moral theory and public governance: nepotism, preferential hiring and other partiality' in Murove (ed) *African Ethics: an anthology for comparative and applied ethics* 341; Metz '(n93 'Reply to Matolino and Kwindingwi' 2014) 69; Metz & Gaie (n68) 276.

[125] Metz (n120) 538.

that the two principles are conceptually discrete, the African ethic requires both to be realised in order to achieve ubuntu.[126]

(c) Unsuited to modern conditions

Ubuntu derives of course from a traditional African culture, and is therefore associated with the predominantly small-scale societies of pre-colonial Africa. These were typifie by the cohesiveness and spirit of sharing typical of the relationships amongst kinfolk. With such a background, ubuntu sceptics have argued that its system of values is neither practised nor workable in the heterogeneous, urban environments of today's South Africa. The response to this contention has two parts.

The firs concerns the claim that ubuntu is no longer realised in people's everyday behaviour.[127] Given the difficulty of findin empirical proof of people's attitudes to such profound moral questions, this claim cannot be accepted on face value. In fact, two snapshot inquiries using different methods in two very different subject groups produced widely divergent results.

The one study was conducted amongst school children from different kinds of community between 2004 and 2008. It revealed that the children had scant regard for the ubuntu ideal: they showed very little respect for their principals in schools, their parents, teachers, elders or friends. Many failed to meet their commitments at school, and they displayed both a violent behaviour and a selfis philosophy.[128] The other study was conducted amongst Bafokeng villagers. It showed that their prevailing sentiments were much closer to the values of ubuntu. While the villagers were well aware of their rights under the South African Constitution, their ideology conformed more closely with 'communal best interests rather than that of individual preferences' and 'the ideal of village consensus'.[129]

All things considered, it would seem that there can be no definit answer to the claim that ubuntu has lost its relevance for most, or even some, South Africans. The diversity of our multicultural society with its fast changing traditions presents too many variables to reach a reliable conclusion. Hence, instead of attempting empirical inquiries to determine current attitudes to ubuntu, the matter could be better approached by understanding the dynamics of culture.

The complex concept of culture refers to the means whereby a consciousness of separate identities is forged when two or more groups have a history of close relations.[130] Such an awareness of cultural difference implies, in turn, that the

---

[126] Metz (n120) 538. See, too, Metz (n70) 68-69; Metz (n124 2012) 27; Metz 'An African theory of dignity and a relational conception of poverty' in De Gruchy (ed) *The Humanist Imperative in South Africa* 236.

[127] See above p 6.

[128] Mabovula (n91) 38ff.

[129] Cook 'Chiefs, kings, corporatization, and democracy: a South African case study' (2005) 12 *Brown J World Aff* 135.

[130] See Roosens *Creating Ethnicity: the process of ethnogenesis* 12-13. Cf Chanock ' "Culture" and human rights: orientalising, occidentalising and authenticity' in Mamdani (ed) *Beyond Rights Talk and Culture Talk: comparative essays on the politics of rights and culture* 21, who contends that

people concerned had gained a certain distance from their past. Hence the paradox: those who claim respect for their culture are in the process of losing it.[131]

It is not surprising, then, that thinking about ubuntu as a cultural ideal in the present day may be pervaded by an awareness of a fading — and usually essentialised — past. Such a situation, however, is not sufficient to discredit the value of the concept, especially if it is consistently applied by an institution, such as the law. Here it has in fact taken on a new life, empowered by those committed to creating a new national ideology. Nor should we think that ubuntu has been so totally discredited that it is incapable of being revived. After all, societies worldwide are constantly reviving traditional rituals, customs and values to serve new purposes.[132]

The second part of the answer concerns the workability of values formulated in one type of society in a radically different one. Modern day South Africa, for instance, poses issues unheard of — or not talked about — in pre-colonial times.[133] Bujo identifie acceptance of homosexuality as one such issue. In Africa, men and women were considered bipolar in nature, and the most basic unit of the community was seen as the husband and wife, with the eventual addition of children.[134] The modern idea of equality for all,[135] regardless of sexual orientation,[136] and the consequent recognition of same sex relationships,[137] is alien to the idea of humanity in traditional Africa.

Bujo, however, believes that problems of this nature may be solved by the likelihood that communities will gradually and inevitably accept shifts in values and behaviour, and he points to the major changes in norms surrounding all sexual acts in recent years. He gives as an example the dictates of hospitality requiring a man to offer his guest a wife for the night,[138] a practice that would now strike modern South Africans as completely unacceptable. Bujo contends that, for this reason, we should focus not on the immediate practice but on a higher value,[139]

---

conflic *internal* to the group concerned, rather than conflic with outsiders, leads to the essentialising of cultures.

[131] Roosens op cit 9 and 47. See also Eriksen *Ethnicity and Nationalism: anthropological perspectives* 71.

[132] See Hobswam 'Introduction: inventing traditions' in Hobswam & Ranger (eds) *The Invention of Tradition* 1-2.

[133] In this regard, urbanisation is said to be responsible for the decay of the sense of ubuntu: Smit, Deacon & Shutte *Ubuntu in a Christian Perspective* 32.

[134] Bujo (n99) 6-7.

[135] Section 9(4) of the Constitution of the Republic of South Africa 108 of 1996.

[136] *National Coalition for Gay and Lesbian Equality and another v Minister of Justice and others* 1999 (1) SA 6 (CC); *National Coalition for Gay and Lesbian Equality and others v Minister of Home Affairs and others* 2000 (2) SA 1 (CC); *Du Toit and another v Minister of Welfare and Population Development and others* 2003 (2) SA 198 (CC); *Satchwell v President of the Republic of South Africa and another* 2003 (4) SA 266 (CC).

[137] Civil Union Act 17 of 2006; *Minister of Home Affairs and another v Fourie and another (Doctors for life International and others, Amici Curiae); Lesbian and Gay Equality Project and others v Minister of Home Affairs and others* 2006 (1) SA 524 (CC).

[138] Bujo (n99) 37.

[139] Metz (n93 'African values and human rights') 309 and 312-313.

which, in this case, is the principle of being hospitable. In this way, a community can modify their ideas of what is acceptable and what is meant by ubuntu.

Another contemporary issue is the need to conserve the environment. In this respect, however, ubuntu is already well equipped to handle the problem.[140] As a spiritual worldview, it perceives the universe 'as a graded system of life-force, emanating from the source of all force, God, and then going from the strongest — the ancestors,[141] who have died, and the heads of clans and families — to the weakest — animals and material objects'.[142] Humans are at the centre, open both to nature and to the spiritual forces immanent in nature. As such, they have a responsibility of stewardship over their environment,[143] a principle that has a contemporary ring to it, because it resonates with the rediscovered Western sense of the web of life.[144]

To answer then the contention that ubuntu has no role to play in the modern world, Bhengu's summing up of the concept is especially germane. He says that ubuntu's greatest value lies in its precept that ignorance is the only limitation of life. One's neighbour should be viewed as a wealth of knowledge.[145] We should therefore accept our neighbours as the reverse of ourselves, and learn from them. In so doing, we can accept the differences and at the same time celebrate the similarities.

(d) Manipulable to achieve political and ideological ends

This claim has much truth to it — and is to be expected. Any abstract concept is subject to manipulation to suit the needs of certain persons or groups at particular times. In the case of ubuntu, many South Africans will have memories of its ideological use during the apartheid years — and even before — when it was deployed to privilege 'dangerous hierarchies [and] corrupt tribal authorities'.[146] In this regard, the Inkatha Freedom Party under the leadership of Mangosuthu

---

[140] Le Grange 'Ubuntu/Botho as ecophilosophy and ecosophy' (2015) 49 *J Hum Ecol* 307.

[141] Metz 'Recent work in African ethics' (2010) 39 *J Moral Educ* 383. Mkhize 'African traditions and the social, economic and moral dimensions of fatherhood' in Richter & Morrell (eds) *Baba: Men and Fatherhood in South Africa* 183ff, says that ubuntu is characterised by 'connectedness to and on-going fellowship with the ancestors'. Ramose 'The death of democracy and the resurrection of timocracy' (2010) 39 *J Moral Educ* 300: 'The concept of community in the African philosophy of Ubuntu/Botho (humanness) is comprised of three tiers, namely, the living, the living-dead ('ancestors') and the yet to be born.'

[142] Shutte (n77) 22.

[143] Bavikatte & Bennett 'Community stewardship: the foundation of biocultural rights' (2015) 6 *JHRE* 18.

[144] See, for example, Capra *The Web of Life: a new scientific understanding of living systems*. See further Drengson & Inoue (eds) *The Deep Ecology Movement: an introductory anthology*; Sessions *Deep Ecology for the Twenty-first Century*; Baird Callicott *In Defense of the Land Ethic: essays in environmental philosophy* 174: 'since nature is the self fully extended and diffused, and the self, complementarily, is nature concentrated and focused . . . nature is intrinsically valuable to the extent that the self is intrinsically valuable.'

[145] Bhengu (n17) 3.

[146] Cornell (n34 2010) 395. See further: Keevy (n116) 41; Nkondo '*Ubuntu* as a public policy in South Africa' (2007) 2 *Int J of African Renaissance Studies* 92; Metz (n120) 533.

Buthelezi was a particular culprit,[147] and women were particular victims.[148] The emphasis on community had the effect of entrenching a patriarchal African tradition, which bestowed full authority and power on senior males, with all the potential for abuse that it entailed.[149]

The proper response to the charge of manipulation, however, is to consider the specifi application of the concept rather than its inherent quality. In other words, the problem lies with the ends sought to be achieved rather than the values embodied in the conceptual means. We could in similar vein, for instance, criticise the concept of equality, one of foundations of Western law. When gender and racial discrimination were firs prohibited in Western systems of law, law-makers could claim a triumph for equal treatment, although equality was taken to mean no more than formal non-discrimination. Application of this principle paid only lip service to improving the actual living and working conditions of women and blacks. Much critical scholarship was necessary to correct this problem,[150] and, under South Africa's Bill of Rights, substantive equality is now required.[151]

Hence, it must be borne in mind that, regardless of how ubuntu might have been applied by certain people or groups, the concept still stands for values that are positive, not negative. Moreover, the current application of ubuntu is in a formative stage. We are not bound by its earlier applications and interpretations. New meanings are being fashioned by courts and scholars, and these highlight the values needed to achieve the transformation of South African society.[152] To this end, the courts have made full use of the many connotations of ubuntu, such as civility, respect, dignity, harmony and compassion, when interpreting the concept in keeping with the Bill of Rights.[153]

---

[147] See above p 26. Mdluli '*Ubuntu-botho*: Inkatha's peoples' education'(1987) 5 *Transformation* 67 regarding the manipulation of ubuntu in school syllabuses for political ends. Golan 'Inkatha and its use of the Zulu past' (1991) 18 *History in Africa* 121 and 124: 'The contradictions in Inkatha ideology and the organization's patriarchal tendencies are reflecte in studies and speeches about the Zulu past as well as in the *Ubuntu/Botho* texts. The primary use of the Zulu past is to establish continuity from Shaka's days to the present and to present Inkatha and its leader as the legitimate heirs of the Zulu kings.' Mapadimeng '*Ubuntu/botho*, the workplace and "two economies": part two: policy and political choices' (2007) 37 *Africanus* 263-264.

[148] Hassim 'Family, motherhood and Zulu nationalism: the politics of the Inkatha Women's Brigade' (1993) 43 *Feminist Review* 6 shows how ubuntu principles were distorted in order to promote apartheid politics, and argues that Buthelezi's conception of the ideal Zulu woman was deployed to reinforce the subordinate position of women. See too Roberts 'South Africa: a patchwork quilt of patriarchy' (2010) 3 *Skills at Work: Theory & Practice J* 64.

[149] Matolino & Kwindingwi 'The end of *ubuntu*' (2013) 32 *SA J Philosophy* 202; Mbaya 'Social capital and the imperatives of the concept and life of *ubuntu* in the South African context' (2010) 104 *Scriptura* 374. See, too, Cornell & Van Marle (n34) 196.

[150] For an overview, see Albertyn & Goldblatt 'Equality' in Woolman & Bishop (eds) *Constitutional Law of South Africa* ch 35.

[151] Which at the same time works to ensure the fulfilmen of socio-economic rights. See Preamble to the Promotion of Equality and Prevention of Unfair Discrimination Act 4 of 2000; *Minister of Finance and another v Van Heerden* 2004 (6) SA 121 (CC) para 31.

[152] Cf Davis & Klare 'Transformative constitutionalism and the common and customary law' (2010) 26 *SAJHR* 403ff. See, too, Ramose (n141) 300.

[153] See the following judgments: *Dikoko v Mokhatla* 2006 (6) SA 235 (CC) paras 68-69; *Afriforum and another v Malema and another* 2011 (6) SA 240 (EqC) para 18; *S v Makwanyane and another*

(e) Not a legal concept

Given that the origins of ubuntu lie in an ancient religion and a normative order that is preserved in an oral tradition,[154] the question could well be asked whether it is capable of functioning as a true legal concept, at least as one understood by a Western legal system. Ubuntu sceptics have identifie the following doubts: ubuntu is not susceptible to the rationalism expected in Western legal thinking; violation of ubuntu does not entail a secular sanction; the obligations implicit in ubuntu do not resolve themselves into clear rights and duties; and observance of ubuntu does not require performance of a specifi duty.

(i) *Intrinsically religious*

It is undeniable that ubuntu has a powerful spiritual dimension.[155] While the maxim 'I am a person through people' may to the Western mind have no apparent spiritual significance ubuntu suggests something more: humane behaviour towards others results in individuals not only becoming more fully developed as persons, but also becoming eligible to join their ancestral spirits.[156] In other words, those who uphold the values of ubuntu during their lives will, in death, achieve a unity with those departed, and thereby become worthy of veneration.[157]

In traditional — and even contemporary[158] — African thinking the ancestors play an omniscient role in everyday life.[159] Like living humans, they exercise a

---

1995 (3) SA 391 (CC) paras 225, 250, 263 and 308; *Port Elizabeth Municipality v Various Occupiers* 2005 (1) SA 217 (CC) para 37. *Masetlha v President of the Republic of South Africa and another* 2008 (1) SA 566 (CC) para 238; *Union of Refugee Women and others v Director: Private Security Industry Regulatory Authority and others* 2007 (4) SA 395 (CC) para 145; *Hoffmann v South African Airways* 2001 (1) SA 1 (CC) para 38; *Bhe and others v Magistrate, Khayelitsha, and others (Commission for Gender Equality as Amicus Curiae); Shibi v Sithole and others; South African Human Rights Commission and another v President of the Republic of South Africa and another* 2005 (1) SA 580 (CC) paras 45 and 163. Mokgoro & Woolman (n110) 406.

[154] See above p 12 for the characteristics of oral legal systems.

[155] Broodryk *Ubuntu: life lessons from Africa* 139; Turaki *Tribal Gods of Africa: ethnicity, racism, tribalism, and the Gospel of Christ* 54; Bhengu *Ubuntu: the global philosophy for humankind* 90 and 101, for instance, says that the moral and spiritual dimensions of ubuntu are emphasised rather than the legal. Cf Oladipo 'Religion in African culture: some conceptual issues' in Wiredu (ed) *A Companion to African Philosophy* 360, who argues that ubuntu is humanistic rather than spiritual, and thus the ideal 'spiritual' qualities are no more than what is expected of a person of good character. His argument rests on the contention that the spiritual aspect results from the imposition of Christian beliefs. See, too, Imbo 'Okot p'Bitek's critique of Western scholarship on African religion' in Wiredu op cit 364ff, who calls John Mbiti Africa's chief 'intellectual smuggler', ie, the surreptitious importer of Western concepts (at 370).

[156] Bujo (n99) 5, too, distinguishes between mere communitarian ethics and ubuntu. He also notes that African thought is not limited to the tangible environment, since the community encompasses those who came before, those still to come and those currently in existence (see above p 41).

[157] Louw 'Ubuntu: an African assessment of the religious other' (1998) paper delivered at Twentieth World Congress of Philosophy. Available at https://www.bu.edu/wcp/Papers/Afri/AfriLouw.htm [Accessed on 28 March 2017].

[158] Masondo 'The practice of African traditional religion in contemporary South Africa' in Bennett (n95) 19ff.

[159] See, for example, Hunter *Reaction to Conquest: effects of contact with Europeans on the Pondo of South Africa* 232.

strong force (as do certain animals and even inanimate objects).[160] All living people and all things, together with the ancestors, are linked together in an enduring relationship, the unifying force of which is *ntu*.[161] This unity of being is evident in the fact that the African conception of a person knows of no strict separation between the corporeal and the spiritual. If 'the physical and metaphysical are aspects of reality', the transition from the living to the spirit becomes as natural as life itself.[162] Death, therefore, is not the end of existence, but rather a change of status: there can be no hiatus between living humans and their spiritual forebears.[163]

The ancestral spirits are the supreme guardians of the social order.[164] During their mortal incarnation, their good deeds, as captured in the term ubuntu, set the standards of good conduct,[165] and they are always on hand to sanction bad behaviour.[166] A person should therefore be in communion not only with those in his or her mortal community but also with the ancestors. Ubuntu implies the realisation of this communion in three respects: an increase of being, a unity of life and participation.

First, the increase of being: Shutte says that, '[t]o the extent that I identify with this common humanity I develop my own humanity, my own identity, and I enter into the hearts and minds of others.'[167] Humanity in this sense is something 'unlimited and all-inclusive and can be shared in by all without being divided or diminished'.[168] Diminution would result from such acts as violence, wickedness or sorcery (the latter constituting both a social and a spiritual injury).[169]

Second, the unity of life implies that, whenever individuals choose to assert the life force (*ntu*), their acts are 'favourable to the blossoming of life, capable of conserving and protecting life, of making it flowe and increasing the vital potential of the community'. These worthy acts may be contrasted with evil deeds, which are prejudicial to the life and interests, whether moral or material, of the individual and the community. 'In this *muntu* ideal, it is in relation to life and afterlife, that every human act is judged.'[170]

---

[160] Shutte (n77) 22.

[161] Bhengu (n17) 2. The notion of *moyo*, also translated as 'life' or 'breath', can also be used in this context. See above p 32.

[162] Onwuanibe 'The human person and immortality in Ibo (African) metaphysics' in Wright (ed) *African Philosophy: an introduction* 184, cited by Ramose (n60) 81. As Mbiti *Introduction to African Religion* 93 remarks, 'personhood is, therefore, acquired and not merely established by virtue of the fact of being human'.

[163] Hunter (n159) at 232. See, too, Zahan 'Some reflection on African spirituality' in Olupona (n109) 10.

[164] Ebo 'Indigenous law and justice: some major concepts and practices' in Woodman & Obilade (eds) *African Law and Legal Theory* 39.

[165] Opoku *West African Religion* 39, cited by Kalu 'Ancestral spirituality and society in Africa' in Olupona (n109) 55.

[166] See Mbon 'African traditional socio-religious ethics and national development: the Nigerian case' in Olupona *African Traditional Religions in Contemporary Society* 102.

[167] Shutte (n77) at 23.

[168] Shutte (n77) ibid.

[169] Mulago 'Traditional African religion and Christianity in Africa' in Olupona (n166) 123.

[170] Mulago in Olupona (n166) 123.

Third, acts of participation physically manifest the union of the individual with the community and with the ancestral spirits, links which are both horizontal and vertical.[171] 'The life of the individual is understood as participated life. The members of the tribe, clan, the family know that they live not by a life of their own but by that of the community. . . . [A]bove all they know that their life is a participation in that of ancestors.'[172] Welfare of the individual is therefore a function and a consequence of the welfare of the community.

These senses of being, unity and participation, keys to the understanding of ubuntu, feed into custom and tradition, and, in this way, supply the ethical content of the traditional African social and belief system. To this end, Ramose posits a triad of the 'three interrelated dimensions' of the living, the living dead and the yet to be born as 'an unbroken chain and infinit chain of relationships which are characteristically of a one-ness and wholeness at the same time'.[173]

In view of the profound spiritual dimension of ubuntu, can the concept be accommodated in a modern, secular legal system? The answer is that it can — regular reference to it by courts and law-makers is clear evidence that it does — although no mention may have been made of its spiritual origins. We need only to look to the common law to fin comparable rules originating in Christian belief. The oath taking required of witnesses, for instance, harks back directly to a spiritual sanction, and other rules, such as the celebration of marriages before duly ordained ministers of religion, derive from biblical precepts.[174]

(ii) *Lack of a secular sanction*

Even though rules stemming from religious belief may be recognised and applied in a secular environment, Western legal systems now require a secular sanction for non-compliance.[175] Compensation and punishment are typical examples. Such forms of sanction, however, seem to be opposed to the fundamental character of ubuntu, which is about 'caring, compassion, unity, tolerance . . . empathy . . . compromise'.[176] In fact, sanctions appear superfluou to ubuntu. Because its principles are so deeply ingrained in people from birth,[177] ubuntu is a way of life,

---

[171] Mulago in Olupona (n166) 120.

[172] Mulago in Olupona (n166) 120.

[173] Ramose (n60) 50–51 and 94 as cited in Keevy 'The Constitutional Court and ubuntu's "inseparable trinity"' (2009) 24 *JJS* 23-24.

[174] Hahlo & Khan *The South African Legal System and its Background* 447-448.

[175] Metz & Gaie (n68) 278.

[176] Masina (n71) 170.

[177] Masina (n71) ibid. As Mogoeng CJ said, in *The Citizen 1978 (Pty) Ltd and others v McBride (Johnstone and others, Amici Curiae)* 2011 (4) SA 191 (CC) para 217: 'A forgiving and generous spirit, the readiness to embrace and apply restorative justice, as well as a courteous interaction with others, were instilled even in the young ones in the ordinary course of daily discourse. The unforgiving, the arrogant and the unduly abusive were described by the Batswana, and presumably other African communities, as those who are bereft of *botho*.'

and therefore functions both as an aid to resolving conflict and as a prophylactic against conflict [178]

As it happens, the South African courts have not sought to apply their usual enforcement mechanisms against those who failed to display ubuntu. For instance, plaintiffs suing for defamation were granted an apology, not damages[179] and land owners demanding the eviction of unlawful occupiers were required to wait until the defendants were provided with appropriate housing.[180] Similarly, those exercising public powers were not punished but rather were ordered to modify their demands by exercising compassion, humanity, civility or respect for the dignity of others.[181]

Another line of cases has used the non-retributive nature of ubuntu as a basis for establishing the principle of restorative justice in South Africa.[182] In this regard, ubuntu was a critical factor in the workings of the Truth and Reconciliation Commission (TRC),[183] which had the difficult task of guiding a strife torn nation towards peace and harmony.[184] Even though the law prescribed punishment, or at least compensation, for wrongs committed in the apartheid era, the goal of the TRC was reconciliation, which entailed forgiveness.[185] Hence, provided that the perpetrators of offences confessed their wrongdoing, they could be forgiven and granted amnesty.[186]

---

[178] If conflict arise, they can be resolved more effectively, because the community is more responsive to the idea of co-operating with extended family members, elders and the community in order to fin a satisfactory solution. See restorative justice below p 79.

[179] See *Dikoko v Mokhatla* 2006 (6) SA 235 (CC).

[180] See *City of Johannesburg v Rand Properties (Pty) Ltd and others* 2007 (1) SA 78 (W).

[181] See *Koyabe and others v Minister for Home Affairs and others (Lawyers for Human Rights as Amicus Curiae)* 2010 (4) SA 327 (CC).

[182] As in the call put out in the epilogue to the Interim Constitution 1993: [The legacy of hatred, fear, guilt and revenge] '. . . can now be addressed on the basis that there is a need for understanding but not for vengeance, a need for reparation but not for retaliation, a need for ubuntu but not for victimisation.'

[183] Which was established by ch 2 of the Promotion of National Unity and Reconciliation Act 34 of 1995. See Ramose (n43).

[184] According to the TRC of South Africa *Report* ch 4 at 48, the Commission 'was conceived as part of the bridge-building process designed to help lead South Africa away from a deeply divided past to a future founded on the recognition of human rights and democracy'. Ubuntu was expressly mentioned in the preamble to the Promotion of National Unity and Reconciliation Act 34 of 1995. The official report on the TRC proceedings describes what ubuntu meant and how it substantiated restorative justice: TRC op cit 125-127. The Commission justifie this approach by heavy reliance upon the judgments of Langa and Mokgoro JJ in *S v Makwanyane and another* 1995 (3) SA 391 (CC): TRC op cit 127. See further Gade 'Restorative justice and the South African Truth and Reconciliation process' (2013) 32 *SA J Philosophy* 10-35; Metz & Gaie (n68) 278.

[185] Ubuntu has also played a valuable role in realising transitional justice in other parts of Africa. See, for instance, Mekonnen 'Indigenous legal tradition as a supplement to African transitional justice initiatives' (2010) 10 *AJCR* 101ff with reference to Eritrea; Hapanyengwi-Chemhuru 'Reconciliation, conciliation, integration and national healing: possibilities and challenges in Zimbabwe' (2013) 13 *AJCR* 95.

[186] Sections 20-22 of the Promotion of National Unity and Reconciliation Act 34 of 1995. As it happened, amnesty did much to secure South Africa's peaceful transition to a fully inclusive democracy: TRC (n184) 112, cited by *Albutt v Centre for the Study of Violence and Reconciliation, and others* 2010 (3) SA 293 (CC) para 58.

In *Azanian Peoples Organisation (AZAPO) and others v President of the Republic of South Africa and others*,[187] the validity of these amnesties was contested in the Constitutional Court, but the challenge failed. Thereafter, certain judges — mainly in the Constitutional Court — began to use the term ubuntu as an indigenous basis for their decisions,[188] and these judgments attracted a positive academic commentary. This body of case law and articles thus became responsible for creating what can now be considered an established policy of restorative justice in the criminal justice system.[189]

(iii) *Implies no specific duties*

Associated with the absence of secular sanctions for the infringement of ubuntu is the apparent absence of a duty with a corresponding right. In this regard, however, ubuntu is not the only concept in customary law that find no appropriate expression in the common law.[190] Indeed, rather than thinking about ubuntu in terms of a right/duty dyad, which corresponds to the individualism typical of Western legal systems, it is preferable to conceive of it in terms of *relationships*.[191] These suggest more diffuse *responsibilities* to a wider community.[192]

In order to explain the problem of translating African ideas of proper normative behaviour into Western law, it is necessary to understand the different views in African and Western thinking about the individual as opposed to the group. In Africa, the family is the focus of social concern,[193] and loyalty to this unit is a prime value.[194] In consequence, personal interests tend to be conflate with the

---

[187] 1996 (4) SA 671 (CC) para 4.

[188] Notably in *S v Makwanyane and another* 1995 (3) SA 391 (CC) para 308; *Bhe and others v Magistrate, Khayelitsha, and others (Commission for Gender Equality as Amicus Curiae); Shibi v Sithole and others; South African Human Rights Commission and another v President of the Republic of South Africa and another* 2005 (1) SA 580 (CC); *Port Elizabeth Municipality v Various Occupiers* 2005 (1) SA 217 (CC); *Barkhuizen v Napier* 2007 (5) SA 323 (CC) and *Dikoko v Mokhatla* 2006 (6) SA 235 (CC) paras 68-70 and 112-121.

[189] See below pp 79ff.

[190] In this regard see Merry *Human Rights and Gender Violence: translating international law into local justice* who explores in detail the problems of translating transnational human rights into local vernaculars.

[191] See the interesting argument by Englund 'Human rights and village headmen in Malawi: translation beyond vernacularisation' in J Ekert et al (eds) *Law against the State: ethnographic forays into law's transformation* (2012) CUP 70ff.

[192] See, for example, Langa J in *Bhe and others v Magistrate, Khayelitsha, and others (Commission for Gender Equality as Amicus Curiae); Shibi v Sithole and others; South African Human Rights Commission and another v President of the Republic of South Africa and another* 2005 (1) SA 580 (CC) paras 162-163. See further Metz (n141) 383 citing Bujo 'Springboards for modern African constitutions and development in African cultural traditions' in Murove (ed) *African Ethics: an anthology of comparative and applied ethics* 115.

[193] Metz & Gaie (n68) 279.

[194] By contrast, in Western thinking, each person is an isolated entity, protected by rights opposable against the group: Donnelly 'Human rights and human dignity: an analytical critique of non-western conceptions of human rights' (1982) 76 *Am Polit Sci Rev* 311. Hence, as Kiwanuka 'The meaning of "people" in the African Charter on Human and Peoples' Rights' (1988) 82 *AJIL* 82 says, the human rights lawyer sees 'individuals as locked in a constant struggle against society for the redemption of their rights'.

common weal,[195] and responsibilities become more important than individual rights.[196] Such thinking is apparent in the African Charter on Human and People's Rights (1982), which, unlike other bills of rights,[197] rejects the conception of a person 'who is utterly free and utterly irresponsible and opposed to society'.[198]

As members of a group, people are expected to be responsible for one another, but even this idea should not be thought of as imposing legally enforceable rights and duties.[199] Such a way of thinking is not part of ubuntu. At the heart of this concept — and it is a case of 'the heart' — lies the sense that each person's need or call for help should elicit a natural response.[200] The sense of responsibility thus activated, however, is not conceived to be only between individuals but also between individuals and society: 'Each one of us is responsible for making up our togetherness.'[201]

In yet another sense, ubuntu does not recognise the simple correlation between a right and a duty. It requires the individual to do more than the expected minimum in fulfillin his or her responsibilities. We are, in other words, expected to 'go the extra mile'. As Mandela himself put it: 'A traveller through a country would stop at a village and he didn't have to ask for food or for water. Once he stops, the people give him food, entertain him.'[202] Ubuntu is thus *creative* of 'generosity and unselfishness even to the point of self-sacrifice'[203]

---

[195] Mojekwu 'International human rights: the African perspective' in Nelson & Green (eds) *International Human Rights: contemporary issues* 86-87. Emphasis on the group is not seen as threatening, however, because the group provides the individual with support and sustenance: Mutua 'The Banjul Charter and the African cultural fingerprint an evaluation of the language of duties' (1995) 35 *Virginia J Int L* 360.

[196] Donnelly (n194) 306 and M'Baye *'Human Rights* in Africa' in Vasak (ed) *The International Dimensions of Human Rights* 588-589. Thus Langa J in *S v Makwanyane and another* 1995 (3) SA 391 (CC) para 224 remarks that '[m]ore importantly, [ubuntu] regulates the exercise of rights by the emphasis it lays on sharing and co-responsibility and the mutual enjoyment of rights by all.'

[197] Cf Article 29 of the Universal Declaration of Human Rights (1948), which introduced the idea of including duties in a human rights document.

[198] President Senghor's 1979 address to a meeting of experts engaged in preparing the draft African Charter (cited in Mutua (n195) 368). Chapter 2 of the Charter is devoted to the duties owed by the individual to the family, the community and the nation at large. Hannum 'The Butare colloquium on human rights and economic development in Francophone Africa: a summary and analysis' (1979) 1 *Universal Hum Rights* 69, however, says that, while 'traditional society offered a balance between individual and collective rights that perhaps tilted toward the latter . . . it is essential to maintain a balance rather than merely expand one set of rights at the expense of the other.'

[199] Fletcher *Moral Responsibility* 234 cites Hart, who 'always insisted that responsibility means blameworthiness' and is a matter of 'imputability and culpability — a matter of assessing guilt, related to vincibility and invincibility in a "forum of conscience" where response to law . . . is required of the agent'.

[200] Fletcher loc cit.

[201] Cornell & Van Marle (n34) 206.

[202] Nelson Mandela, speaking in an interview incorporated in a promotional video for the Ubuntu Linux distribution. Available at http://www.youtube.com/watch?v=ODQ4WiDsEBQ. [Accessed on 7 May 2016].

[203] Shutte (n77) 53. Bhengu (n17) 8 identifie a spirit of ubuntu in the Islamic religious act of *beital mal* which involves the giving of money into a community pool which serves to succour widows and their children.

As will be shown later, the courts in South Africa have not attempted to transform ubuntu into the formula of rights and duties.[204] (The one apparent exception was a majority judgment by the Constitutional Court in *Tshwane City v Afriforum and another*,[205] where ubuntu was spoken of in terms of a right.)[206] In general, the courts have used ubuntu as a metanorm to prescribe the manner in which existing rights and duties are to be exercised, ie, by demonstrating a sense of compassion and understanding, not only for the other party involved in a dispute but also for the wider community.[207] In this manner the generosity and tolerance that mark the character of ubuntu have been deployed to soften the blunt impact of the law.

(iv) *Not susceptible to rationalist thinking*

Following what has been said above, it is evident that application of ubuntu does not comfortably fi in with the typically rationalist approach of Western law. Indeed, an ubuntu approach to life has close similarities to the normative ideal of love in the Graeco-Christian sense of *agape*. Like ubuntu, love is an emotive term: it induces feelings of content; it ingenuously disarms any opposition and effectively forestalls any critical reflection Love, it is commonly believed, is enough in itself.[208] It is the highest ideal of the Christian faith, and is therefore central to Christian ethics.

If ubuntu functions in much the same way as the Christian idea of love/*agape*,[209] it is both an end and a means, and, with respect to the means, it is useful to consider ubuntu in terms of situation ethics.[210] According to a situationist approach, the evaluation of an act must take into account its context, not only the relevant ethical standards. Once treated as an interactive ethic, the manner in which ubuntu is to be applied will depend on the circumstances, with the result that it cannot be captured by any hard and fast rules.[211] It then follows that to the

---

[204] See below pp 93-94.

[205] 2016 (6) SA 279 (CC) para 11.

[206] A powerful dissenting judgment, however, questioned the possibility of findin a corresponding duty: paras 135-139.

[207] See above pp 34-36.

[208] Love, however, is a 'swampy' word, a 'semantic confusion': Fletcher *Situation Ethics* 15. As Archbishop Desmond Tutu *No Future without Forgiveness* 31 said: 'A person with Ubuntu is open and available to others, affirming of others, does not feel threatened that others are able and good, for he or she has a proper self-assurance that comes from knowing that he or she belongs in a greater whole and is diminished when others are humiliated or diminished, when others are tortured or oppressed.' See, too, Metz & Gaie (n68) 276.

[209] Such an interpretation of ubuntu has penetrated the law: *S v Makwanyane and another* 1995 (3) SA 391 (CC) para 263; *The Citizen 1978 (Pty) Ltd and others v McBride (Johnstone and others, Amici Curiae)* 2011 (4) SA 191 (CC) para 216: '*Ubuntu* gives expression to, among others, a biblical injunction that one should do unto others as he or she would have them do unto him or her.' See Bennett & Munro 'Ubuntu, incaba and Baptist congregationalism' (2012) 21 *SABJT* 27.

[210] A movement that exerted a significan influenc on the broader fiel of Christian ethics during the 1960s and 70s: Fletcher (n208) 15 and 33.

[211] Keevy (n173) 64.

extent that ubuntu is not adaptable to legislation, it will resist 'the dictate of Western logic and Western rites of argumentation'.[212]

Ubuntu is not, however, antinomian, as in the existentialist ethics of Jean-Paul Sartre and Simone de Beauvoir, for whom there could be no 'connective tissue between one situation or moment of experience and another . . . no fabric or web of life, hence no basis for generalizing moral principles'.[213] Ubuntu represents another way of thinking. Because it is situationist, its application in practice will vary with the context. The one constant, sole standard, is ubuntu itself. As self-realisation, it has parallels in the *summum bonum* of Aristotelian ethics,[214] or 'the greatest happiness of the greatest number' of utilitarianism.[215]

If this is the case, two questions arise. The firs is whether ubuntu is purely emotional, a matter of feelings, as opposed to the Western concept of law, which is volitional, a matter of will and determination. This question, however, appears to be a false opposition. Ubuntu is not simply about sentiment, but rather *sensitive* to the situation. Its purpose is to satisfy the neighbour's need, not one's own. It is a disposition of the will, and its ethical content is attitudinal not emotional. Just as law is 'conative, volitional, decision-oriented, purposive, dispositive',[216] so is ubuntu. Thus, ubuntu and law are not different, one a matter of feeling and the other a matter of willing: they work in the same way.

Secondly, should ubuntu be regarded as personal and interpersonal, and law as impersonal and objective? The answer, again, must be in the negative. Ubuntu is not limited to people with whom we have direct personal relationships. Because it embraces more people than we know, it too may operate impersonally and disinterestedly, although it never reduces people to abstractions. It regulates behaviour and provides a standard of judgment, against which failures and infractions may be gauged. Ubuntu is a pervasive, all-controlling norm, to which the workings of the law can give force and substance.

In summary, the relationship between ubuntu and law should not be treated as one of opposites, but can rather be described as 'co-inherence'.[217] This term signifie the indwelling of elements that exist in a symbiotic relationship with one another, each as an innate component of the other.[218] The way in which such a relationship works is currently manifesting itself in the South African legal system in two ways.

One is by directing the claimants of rights and powers to comply with virtuous standards of behaviour. These standards are sensitive to the overall socio-legal

---

[212] Koka *Sage Philosophy: the significance of ubuntu philosophy in post-colonial Africa* cited in Bhengu (n155) 46. Indeed, feeling and intuition, rather than rationality, underlie traditional African thought: Irele 'Francophone African philosophy' in Coetzee & Roux (n92) 137.

[213] Fletcher (n208) 25; Ramose (n60) 62.

[214] Metz (n93 2012) 104; Metz & Gaie (n68) 275.

[215] And the *agape* of Christian ethics: Fletcher (n199) ch 4.

[216] Fletcher (n199) 49.

[217] This term was coined by Charles Williams to denote a concept central to his theology. See, for example, Williams *The Figure of Beatrice: a study of Dante* 92.

[218] See Malan 'The suitability and unsuitability of ubuntu in constitutional law — inter-communal relations versus public office-bearing' (2014) 47 *De Jure* 239.

context of the particular case and to the circumstances of the parties involved.[219] The other is by acting as a norm with a highly generalised scope of meaning, making it sufficiently flexibl and all-encompassing so that it can be invoked to address an indefinit variety of social needs as occasions arise. Such metanorms serve as superordinate standards,[220] providing criteria against which decision-makers can judge both norms of a lower order and the actions of individuals.[221] Examples of other metanorms similar to ubuntu are justice, equity and reasonableness.[222]

(f) Redundancy

> 'We should only borrow what we do not have. Our firs port of call should be the interpretation and development of our Constitution and our law in general based on our unique history, experience and conditions. . . .'[223]

A fina objection to ubuntu is that it is surplus to the requirements of our legal system.[224] South African law is said to be well equipped with the rules and principles needed to do whatever work ubuntu can do.[225]

When considering the merits of this objection, it must immediately be conceded that precepts on the right way of living exist in all cultures,[226] and the notion of an ethical or moral code cutting across cultures has ancient origins. The Graeco-Roman ideas of justice and equity,[227] for instance, were absorbed into the political

---

[219] See below pp 98-99

[220] Metz (n93 2014) 309.

[221] Motha 'Rationality, the rule of law, and the sovereign return' (2011) 4 *CCR* 132.

[222] For the concept of reasonableness. see Lord Atkin's famous dictum in *Donoghue v Stevenson* [1932] AC 562 at 580: 'The liability for negligence . . . is no doubt based upon a general public sentiment of moral wrongdoing for which the offender must pay. But acts or omissions which any moral code would censure cannot in a practical world be treated so as to give a right to every person injured by them to demand relief. In this way rules of law arise which limit the range of complainants and the extent of their remedy. *The rule that you are to love your neighbour* becomes in law, you must not injure your neighbour; and the lawyer's question, Who is my neighbour? receives a restricted reply. You must take reasonable care to avoid acts or omissions which you can reasonably foresee would be likely to injure your neighbour.'

[223] Mogoeng J in *The Citizen 1978 (Pty) Ltd and others v McBride (Johnstone and others, Amici Curiae)* 2011 (4) SA 191 (CC) para 243.

[224] Kroeze (n113) 260-61, for instance, argues that, if ubuntu is simply a particular manifestation of a universal phenomenon, it is redundant. Metz 'Ubuntu: curating the archive' (2014) 43 *Philosophical Papers* 448. See further Cornell & Van Marle (n34) 196; Matolino 'A response to Metz's reply on the end of ubuntu' (2014) 34 *SA J Philosophy* 214ff; Matolino & Kwindingwi (n149) 203. Himonga, Taylor & Pope (n41) 390 note the link between the arguments of redundancy and the ambiguity of ubuntu. Hence, it is only when the meaning and content of the term have been clarified that its potential redundancy can be assessed.

[225] Van Binsbergen (n120) 62 went so far as to say that ubuntu is simply an 'academic construct, called forth by the same forces of oppression, economic exploitation, and cultural alienation that have shaped Southern African society over the past two centuries'. Cf the counterargument by Bewaji & Ramose 'The Bewaji, van Binsbergen and Ramose debate on ubuntu' (2003) 22 *SA J Philosophy* 380.

[226] Broodryk 'Is ubuntuism unique?' in Malherbe (ed) *Decolonizing the Mind: proceedings of the second colloquium on African philosophy* 32.

[227] See below pp 104ff on justice and equity.

creed of the eighteenth century Enlightenment in Europe and North America. They were then taken up by the international human rights movement, to become an established feature of international law and most systems of national law.[228] If ubuntu shares this 'world spirit', then the most it can add to our law would be to accentuate that spirit and remind us of its importance as an African contribution.[229]

The assumption that there are such timeless universals, however, is contested by cultural relativists.[230] In this respect, ubuntu apologists argue that, although the concept may have parallels in Western philosophy, it is nevertheless distinctively African,[231] and therefore offers something different and unique.[232] Indeed, as we have seen above, essential features of Western thinking, such as rationality and rights and duties,[233] have no particular resonance with ubuntu.

What is more, a major difference between African and Western thinking is the former's concern with the community rather than the individual.[234] It might then be argued that African philosophy is comparable with Marxist theory,[235] in terms of which individual interests are subordinate to the greater good of society.[236] Such an understanding, however, would be wrong. According to ubuntu, all humans are equal and of concern to the community:[237] humanity is of the essence, not simply the individual in relation to the group.[238]

With this idea in mind, it would probably be better to understand ubuntu as a way of living that contributes positively to the welfare of *both* the individual and the community. This proposition leads directly to a consideration of dignity, the most serious candidate for the argument of redundancy.

---

[228] Falk 'Cultural foundations for the international protection of human rights' in An-Na'im (ed) *Human Rights in a Cross Cultural Perspective: a quest for consensus* 45; Morsink *The Universal Declaration of Human Rights: origins, drafting, and intent* 282.

[229] Prinsloo 'The ubuntu style of participatory management' in Malherbe (n226) 120.

[230] Mokgoro & Woolman (n110) 405. Hence, in 1947, the American Anthropological Association warned that the Universal Declaration of Human Rights (1948) would simply encode the ethnocentric values of Europe and America: The Executive Board, American Anthropological Association 'Statement on Human Rights' (1947) 49 *Am Anthropologist* 539ff.

[231] Cf Broodryk (n155) 16, who argues that, although ubuntu and Western concepts may have similarities, the former is deeper and more intense. See, further, Mazrui *Africanity redefined: collected essays of A A Mazrui* vol 1 as cited in Mbigi & Maree (n84) ix.

[232] Broodryk in Malherbe (n226) 31, for instance, argues that the qualities in a person suggested by ubuntu, although recognised in other cultures, are incomparable and extraordinary.

[233] Keep & Midgley 'The emerging role of ubuntu-botho in developing a consensual South African legal culture' in Bruinsma & Nelken (eds) *Recht der Werkelijkheid* 33.

[234] See Mangena 'Towards a *hunhu/ubuntu* dialogical moral theory' (2012) 13 *Phronimon* 1ff; Mnyongani (n46) 142. Ubuntu thereby provides a more plausible basis for social contract theory: Zandberg *The Philosophy of Ubuntu and the Origins of Democracy* 102-106.

[235] Metz (n93 'African values and human rights') 318, citing Karl Marx 'On James Mill' (1843) in McLellan (ed) *Karl Marx: selected writings* 126.

[236] Oyowe 'Strange bedfellows: rethinking ubuntu and human rights in South Africa' (2013) 13 *AHJRL* 108-109.

[237] Metz (n93 'African values and human rights') 314-315 and 317.

[238] Shutte (n77) 52.

(i) *Dignity*

> 'Perhaps a Twainian twist is in order: ∟Buntu and dignity do not map directly on to one another, but they do rhyme.'[239]

Dignity is the cynosure of South Africa's new constitutional order.[240] Specifi provision is made for it as a fundamental value of the Republic,[241] and, in addition, as a right specifie in the Bill of Rights.[242] Hence, when construed as both a value and a right, dignity operates as a guiding principle and an enforceable right against another. Ubuntu, on the other hand, does not (at present) provide the sole basis for rights and duties.[243] It functions mainly as a principle or value that can be called upon to temper the application of strict rules of law.[244] At firs glance then, dignity would seem to be able to do the work of ubuntu, because it is the more versatile concept.

The cardinal importance of dignity for our law has often been repeated by the Constitutional Court.[245] As a foundational concept, it forms the basis for a discourse that has generated its own sub-set of rules.[246] It follows that human dignity is not only a 'justiciable and enforceable right that must be respected and protected', and thus a *means* for achieving the human rights order, but also one of its ultimate *goals*.[247] Dignity therefore serves to protect individual freedoms and to secure the right to equality;[248] it informs the interpretation of all the other rights,[249] and any limitation of a constitutional right is permissible only if it leaves intact, *inter alia*, dignity.[250]

It so happens that ubuntu has often been equated with dignity by both scholars and courts. According to Cornell, the two concepts are banners of high ethical endeavour,[251] and according to Vervliet, '*ubuntu* is rooted in a search towards African dignity'.[252] The Constitutional Court, in particular, has done much to

---

[239] Cf Mokgoro & Woolman (n110) 407.

[240] Chaskalson 'Third Bram Fischer Lecture — human dignity as a foundational value of our Constitutional order' (2000) 16 *SAJHR* 196.

[241] Section 1(a).

[242] Section 10: 'Everyone has inherent dignity and the right to have their dignity respected and protected.'

[243] See below pp 93-94.

[244] See below p 61.

[245] For example, *National Coalition for Gay and Lesbian Equality and another v Minister of Justice and others* 1999 (1) SA 6 (CC) para 28 held that: '[a]t its least, it is clear that the constitutional protection of dignity requires us to acknowledge the value and worth of all individuals as members of our society.' See, too, *August and another v Electoral Commission and others* 1999 (3) SA 1 (CC) para 17.

[246] See above p 13.

[247] Currie & De Waal *The Bill of Rights Handbook* 253.

[248] Currie & De Waal op cit 250.

[249] Currie & De Waal op cit 251.

[250] *Christian Education South Africa v Minister of Education* 2000 (4) SA 757 (CC) para 15. Cornell 'Dignity violated: rethinking AZAPO through ubuntu' in Cornell (ed) *Law and Revolution in South Africa: uBuntu, dignity, and the struggle for constitutional transformation* 54.

[251] Cornell (n34 2010) 389.

[252] Vervliet *The Human Person: African Ubuntu and the dialogue of civilisations* 20. See, too, Ackermann *Human Dignity: lodestar for equality in South Africa* 78; Nhlapo 'Cultural diversity,

cement the relationship between the two, as in its firs case, *S v Makwanyane and another*,[253] where Langa J held that:

'An outstanding feature of *ubuntu* in a community sense is the value it puts on life and human dignity. The dominant theme of the culture is that the life of another person is at least as valuable as one's own. Respect for the dignity of every person is integral to this concept.'[254]

In the circumstances, we might be forgiven for questioning the relevance of ubuntu when we already have a right to dignity.

(ii) *Definition of dignity*

To examine the similarity of dignity and ubuntu the meaning of dignity must firs be understood. Unfortunately, however, the definitio of dignity is as elusive as that of ubuntu. Although the concept has a long history in Western European philosophy, few attempts have been made to establish an exact meaning,[255] which should not be surprising, because metanorms must remain indeterminate if they are to perform their function as criteria for adjudicating a wide variety of norms and factual situations.

Nevertheless, in general terms, dignity has been taken to express the idea that individual human beings have an innate right to be respected and valued.[256] On the basis of this understanding, dignity provided a key concept in the Enlightenment endeavour to justify the inherent and inalienable nature of human rights. Although some have contended that human rights must be observed for purely utilitarian reasons — for instance, to improve the lot of society as a whole — this is not the predominant view of human rights theorists. Metz, for example, says that 'to observe human rights is to treat an individual as having a dignity, roughly, as exhibiting a superlative non-instrumental value'.[257]

Kant, in particular, was influentia in presenting dignity as the underpinning of Western philosophical discourse. He contended that certain things could not, and should not, be discussed in terms of their value, because value is inevitably relative, and thus dependent on a particular person's judgment. According to this reasoning, whatever is not relative is beyond value, and is therefore an end in itself, but only if it has a moral dimension, ie, posed a choice between right and

---

human rights and the family in contemporary Africa: lessons from the South African constitutional debate' in Lowe & Douglas (eds) *Families Across Frontiers* 249-250.

[253] 1995 (3) SA 391 (CC) para 225.

[254] See further: Mokgoro & Woolman (n110) 400-407; Cornell 'Where dignity ends and uBuntu begins' in Cornell (n250) 171 fn8; Cornell (n34 2004) 66; Metz (n120) 532.

[255] International conventions, for instance, did not venture a definition McDougal, Lasswell & Chen *Human Rights and World Public Order: the basic policies of an international law of human dignity* 376.

[256] Woolman 'Dignity' in Woolman & Bishop (eds) *Constitutional Law of South Africa* vol 3 36-17; Davis 'Human dignity: lodestar for equality in South Africa, Laurie Ackermann' (2013) 130 *SALJ* 882.

[257] Metz (n120) 542.

wrong. Hence, '[m]orality, and humanity as capable of it, is that which alone has dignity'.[258]

Such thinking pervades most modern human rights discourse, and work on dignity in South African law has drawn freely from Kantian philosophy.[259] Dignity is therefore interpreted to signify whatever gives human beings their intrinsic worth,[260] or to signify a fundamental norm that all individuals must be recognised 'as ends-in-themselves capable of self-governance'.[261] It follows that all humans are entitled to equal respect[262] and self-governance,[263] with the implication of a collective responsibility[264] to maintain the material conditions necessary for realising these rights.[265]

---

[258] Kant *Fundamental Principles of the Metaphysics of Morals* 64.

[259] See *South African Police Service v Solidarity obo Barnard* 2014 (6) SA 123 (CC) para 172. Woolman (n256) ch 36; Woolman 'Humility, Michelman's method and the Constitutional Court: rereading the *First Certification* judgment and reaffirming a distinction between law and politics' (2013) 24 *Stell LR* 281ff; Ackermann 'The legal nature of the South African Constitutional revolution' (2004) 4 *New Zealand LR* 650.

[260] *S v Makwanyane and another* 1995 (3) SA 391 (CC) para 329; *Dawood and another v Minister of Home Affairs and others; Saalabi and another v Minister of Home Affairs and others; Thomas and another v Minister of Home Affairs and others* 2000 (3) SA 936 (CC) para 35; *S v Jordan and others (Sex Workers Education and Advocacy Task Force and others as Amici Curiae)* 2002 (6) SA 642 (CC) para 74; *MEC for Education, KwaZulu-Natal, and others v Pillay* 2008 (1) SA 474 (CC) para 64; *Nyathi v MEC for Department of Health, Gauteng and another* 2008 (5) SA 94 (CC) para 45. See Ackermann 'Equality in the South African Constitution: the role of dignity' (2000) 60 *Heidelberg J Int L* 540-542; Botha (n120) 197 and 204.

[261] Woolman (n256) 36-6.

[262] *S v Makwanyane and another* 1995 (3) SA 391 (CC) paras 223-225; *President of the Republic of South Africa and another v Hugo* 1997 (4) SA 1 (CC) para 41; *Harksen v Lane NO and others* 1998 (1) SA 300 (CC) paras 46, 50, 51, 53, 91, 92; *MEC for Education, KwaZulu-Natal, and others v Pillay* 2008 (1) SA 474 (CC) para 65; *Minister of Home Affairs and another v Fourie and another (Doctors for life International and others, Amici Curiae); Lesbian and Gay Equality Project and others v Minister of Home Affairs and others* 2006 (1) SA 524 (CC) para 50; *South African Police Service v Solidarity obo Barnard* 2014 (6) SA 123 (CC) para 174.

[263] *Ferreira v Levin NO and others; Vryenhoek and others v Powell NO and others* 1996 (1) SA 984 (CC) para 4; *Masiya v Director of Public Prosecutions, Pretoria and another (Centre for Applied Legal Studies and another, Amici Curiae)* 2007 (5) SA 30 (CC) para 84. Jordaan 'Autonomy as an element of human dignity in South African case law' (2009) 9 *J Philosophy, Science & Law* available at http://jpsl.org/archives/autonomy-element-human-dignity-south-african-case-law/ [Accessed 31 October 2017].

[264] *Khosa and others v Minister of Social Development and others, Mahlaule and others v Minister of Social Development and others* 2004 (6) SA 505 (CC) para 74.

[265] See generally Woolman (n256) 36-6-36-19. *Ferreira v Levin NO and others; Vryenhoek and others v Powell NO and others* 1996 (1) SA 984 (CC) para 49. Cf *S v Jordan and others (Sex Workers Education and Advocacy Task Force and others as Amici Curiae)* 2002 (6) SA 642 (CC) para 74. See also Botha (n120) 211ff. For the relationship between dignity and other values, such as freedom, equality and democracy, see: *Government of the Republic of South Africa and others v Grootboom and others* 2001 (1) SA 46 (CC) paras 23, 44, 83; *Khosa's* case supra paras 40-41; *Jaftha v Schoeman and others; Van Rooyen v Stoltz and others* 2005 (2) SA 140 (CC) para 21; *Minister of Home Affairs and others v Watchenuka and another* 2004 (4) SA 326 (SCA) para 32; *Somali Association of South Africa and others v Limpopo Department of Economic Development, Environment and Tourism and others* 2015 (1) SA 151 (SCA) paras 22, 43. See further Liebenberg 'The value of human dignity in interpreting socio-economic rights' (2005) 21 *SAJHR* 15.

(iii) *Similarities to ubuntu*

The similarity between ubuntu and dignity was firs commented on in *S v Makwanyane and another*,[266] where the Court noted that they both demanded respect for the worth of each human being.[267] It has therefore been established that, in so far as ubuntu advocates respect for others, it clearly embraces dignity.[268]

Cornell notes a further connection between ubuntu and Kantian philosophy in a common concern with freedom and morality, obligation and necessity.[269] The conjunction of these principles would imply that, when expressing our freedom, we lay down laws to govern ourselves, and create obligations for others through moral precepts. 'Moral personality', according to Kant, allows us dignity and humanity.[270] It is by means of our capacity for practical reason and our potential to be guided by the dictates of the moral law that humanity itself becomes a moral ideal.[271] Thus, our very humanity can be seen to set an ethical ideal. In this regard, ubuntu and Kantian philosophy would converge.[272]

Wiredu would support such thinking, but from a theological perspective: the derivation of human value from God.[273] The source therefore creates an entitlement to respect for all beings, which is the basis of human dignity.[274] Closely related to the entitlement to respect is every person's right 'as recipient of a destiny, to pursue that unique destiny assigned to him by God'.[275] As a result, '[o]ne is enjoined, yes, commanded as it were, to actually become a human being'.[276] This right to self-fulfilmen shows, in its turn, an association with the 'western understanding of human dignity', especially Kantian philosophy.[277]

---

[266] 1995 (3) SA 391 (CC) paras 307-313. As Mokgoro J para 308 says: 'While it [ubuntu] envelops the key values of group solidarity, compassion, respect, human dignity, conformity to basic norms and collective unity, in its fundamental sense it denotes humanity and morality.'

[267] A point followed in a later judgment: *Hoffmann v South African Airways* 2001 (1) SA 1 (CC) para 38. In this case the court endorsed Langa and Mokgoro JJ's description of ubuntu in *Makwanyane's* case. For Ackermann (n252) 115, human dignity vests in individual morality, responsibility and accountability, which underlie the concept of freedom, and in this respect the concept of ubuntu should be taken into account.

[268] Oyowe (n236) 310; Pieterse ' "Traditional" African jurisprudence' in Roederer & Moellendorf (eds) *Jurisprudence* 444.

[269] Cornell (n34 2010) 397. Ackermann (n252) 81 and 114 makes the same argument.

[270] Kant *Religion within the Boundaries of Mere Reason* 552.

[271] Cornell (n34 2010) 397. Although Metz (n286) 370-371, too, shows that Kant claimed 'all persons share a rational mind', Metz rejects universalism because societies are different.

[272] Ackermann (n252) 78.

[273] Wiredu (n73) 157-158; Ackermann (n252) 77.

[274] Ackermann (n252) 77-78.

[275] Wiredu 'The Akan perspective on human rights' in An-Na'im & Deng (eds) *Human Rights in Africa: cross-cultural perspectives* 244-245; Ackermann (n252) 77.

[276] Ramose 'The philosophy of ubuntu and ubuntu in philosophy' in Coetzee & Roux (n92) 272.

[277] Cornell & Van Marle 'Ubuntu feminism: tentative reflections (2015) 36 *Verbum et Ecclesia* 5-6; Ackermann (n252) 78. Dzobo 'Values in a changing society: man, ancestors and God' in Wiredu & Gyekye (eds) *Person and Community: Ghanaian philosophical studies* 229: 'A person, therefore, is good not because he is good for something, but primarily because he has a creative humanity and so is a creator of the good.'

(iv) *Differences from ubuntu*

From the above it would appear that there is a significant degree of overlap between ubuntu and dignity. Of the three major authors putting the counterargument, Metz is the most definite.[278] The views of Ackermann and Cornell are not as categorical.[279]

In stressing his Kantian approach, Ackermann does not reject 'associational aspects of a human being',[280] and, adverting to various provisions in the Constitution, he finds support for the view that dignity does not treat an individual as an isolated or unencumbered being.[281] The *Second Certification* case,[282] for instance, observed that dignity was protected by means of 'associational individual rights',[283] which *in casu* were the rights of cultural, religious and linguistic communities contained in s 31 of the Constitution.[284] Nevertheless, while accepting that human beings realise themselves through others, Ackermann argues that this condition does not constitute 'total humanity' or 'total human dignity'.[285] And he sees danger in communitarian views because of their potential to undermine individual responsibility by giving too much weight to the group, thereby facilitating totalitarianism.[286]

Cornell shares certain common ground with Ackermann, for she too accepts that 'it is only through the engagement and support of others that a person is able to realise a true individuality'.[287] She rejects, however, a purely communitarian

---

[278] Metz (n120) 542-543 rejects a conception of dignity founded in 'life force', the soul or other such metaphysical notion, in favour of a conception consonant with a more secular, multicultural society. Individuals may, accordingly, develop their human qualities by 'communing with those who have a dignity in virtue of their capacity for communing', ie, 'the inherent capacity to exhibit identity and solidarity with others' (op cit 544). See too Metz (n93 2014) 309-310 and 318.

[279] See too Nhlapo (n252) 251.

[280] Ackermann (n252) 79.

[281] Ackermann (n252) 109-110.

[282] *Ex parte Chairperson of the National Assembly: In re Certification of the Amended Text of the Constitution of the RSA, 1996* 1997 (2) SA 97 (CC) paras 22-27. In further support, Ackermann draws on O'Regan J's judgment in *Khumalo and others v Holomisa* 2002 (5) SA 401 (CC) para 27.

[283] Namely, 'those rights which cannot be fully or properly exercised by individuals otherwise than in association with others of like disposition' (para 24).

[284] Langa CJ expanded on this notion in *MEC for Education, KwaZulu-Natal, and others v Pillay* 2008 (1) SA 474 (CC) para 53, where he stated that human identity is an inseparable part of human dignity and self-worth. Dignity thus allows a person to belong to a community and participate in its culture.

[285] Ackermann (n252) 79.

[286] Ackermann (n252) 79. Ramose 'Ecology through ubuntu' in Murove (n192) 309 agrees on this point, arguing that a morality which places prime value on ubuntu and social harmony is a product of 'absolutism and dogmatism'. Cf Metz 'Ubuntu as a moral theory: reply to four critics' (2007) 26 *SA J Philosophy* 374-375.

[287] As quoted by Ackermann (n252) 80 from an unpublished memorandum of 2011. See too Cornell (n34 2010) 393 and Oyowe (n236) 108, who claims that 'grounding dignity in a yet-to-be-realised capacity for community represents the individual as existing in principle outside the network of relationships that constitutes community.' See also *MEC for Education, KwaZulu-Natal, and others v Pillay* 2008 (1) SA 474 (CC) paras 53-54, 64; *Minister of Home Affairs and another v Fourie and another (Doctors for Life International and others, Amici Curiae); Lesbian and Gay Equality Project and others v Minister of Home Affairs and others* 2006 (1) SA 524 (CC) para 78.

view of ubuntu as a 'profound misunderstanding',[288] and contends that ubuntu differs from Kantian philosophy, because, as the source of dignity, it is not an ethical concern, but a direct product of the '[e]mbeddedness as part of the human community'. Kant, on the other hand, imagined dignity as *a priori* rooted in moral individuals living subject to a social contract with others to live in harmony. Dignity therefore implied a human being as an *a priori* self-legislating being.[289]

Metz takes a somewhat different standpoint. He argues that ubuntu stands for a uniquely African ethical theory drawn from African intuitions.[290] Thus, for Metz, dignity represents individualistic values while ubuntu stands for communitarian values,[291] thereby expressing a moral claim that human beings are entirely constituted and dependent on each other.[292]

In support of this argument, Metz distinguishes values that are shared in Western and African cultures and those that are distinctively African. The latter include the following: decisions should be based on consensus rather than a majority vote; reconciliation should be the central aim of justice;[293] wealth should be created on a co-operative (as opposed to competitive) basis, and should be distributed on the basis of need (not individual rights).[294] These normative propositions can be derived from ubuntu, because they are essential to the individual's life, well-being and right to self-realisation.[295] Ubuntu is therefore embedded in a social bond with others, outside of the individual, and responsibilities arise from the web of relationships definin individuals. Thus ubuntu grows out of its instrumentality; it does not have an *a priori* existence.[296]

Whichever line of argument is pursued regarding the differences between ubuntu and dignity, it is difficult to avoid the fact that the two concepts are the products of their own distinctive African and Western histories. They therefore bring with them a train of different associations. No doubt their functions do, to some extent, coincide, but certain differences persist. The dignity discourse remains centred on the individual, whether as a bearer of a right or freedom, or flowin simply from the fact of human life itself. Ubuntu, on the other hand, sees

---

[288] Cornell ibid.

[289] Cornell (n34 2004) 668 says that 'for Kant, the notion of law and the founding principle of legality can only be a hypothetical experiment in the imagination, in which self-legislating human beings contracted to their own restraint on the basis of mutual accordance of each other's dignity as free persons, limited only by the internal restrictions of dignity as an ideal.'

[290] Metz (n286) 379. This seems to bear more than a passing relationship to the 'imagination' of Kantian philosophy.

[291] Metz 'Human dignity, capital punishment, and an African moral theory: towards a new philosophy of human rights' (2010) 9 *J Human Rights* 84. Woolman (n256) 36-16 makes a similar argument with relation to Kant that 'does not amount to the subordination of the inherent worth and dignity of the individual to notions of "collective" dignity, but rests instead upon the identificatio of the dignity of the individual with a Kantian "realm of ends" in which everyone's dignity is recognised'. See too Botha (n120) 210.

[292] Metz (n291) 84.

[293] The latter two matters are explored below pp 151-153 and p 150.

[294] See further Gyekye 'Person and community in African thought' in Wiredu & Gyekye (n277) 113-121.

[295] Metz (n114) 333.

[296] Metz (n114) 337.

the individual as rooted in a community, and has thereby introduced a new discourse that emphasises the community and a sense of responsibility towards all members of that community. Finally, it must be noted that ubuntu has even influence interpretation of the right to dignity itself by drawing attention to a need to create harmony between groups or individuals.[297]

4 CONCLUSION

Ubuntu is a core ethical and religious concept of traditional African society. As such, it is necessarily general and indeterminate in meaning. Now, however, it has been adopted by the courts, and, in line with the general demand of Western law for precision and clarity in legal terms, definitio of ubuntu has been a major preoccupation of courts and writers. It is nonetheless argued here that we should not be too quick to establish a fixe meaning for the term. Because it has to be applied in many different situations to achieve different goals, a high degree of flexibilit is necessary.[298]

Most of the doubts about introducing ubuntu into modern South African law can be readily disposed of. It is a workable legal concept that is neither too vague nor ambiguous to perform the functions it is put to by the courts. It does not necessarily favour only insider or majoritarian interests, nor is it too rooted in a bygone age to suit the needs of modern society. It is, admittedly, being used to achieve political and ideological ends, but, in the hands of the courts, these ends are set by South Africa's new constitutional order.

The charge that ubuntu is superfluou to the needs of South African law, and thus, as a legal transp ant, is i danger of rejection,[299] is a more difficult issue to contest. The answer, however, lies in the existence of an ever expanding number of judgments in which it has been applied without demur. The courts are readily invoking ubuntu, thereby implying that it has a necessary role to play in our legal system. In the prophetic words of Langa J, ubuntu is now regularly called into play to regulate 'the exercise of rights by the emphasis it lays on sharing and co-responsibility and the mutual enjoyment of rights by all'.[300]

In fact, ubuntu has many features that recommend it to a South African society in the process of transformation:

'the African-ness of its name; that it is not tied to Western origins; that it is not associated with a particular religious dogma or philosophy; and, above all, that ubuntu is inclusive, aspirational and also accessible, all of these seem to make it an ideal worth striving for in post-apartheid South Africa.'[301]

The next chapter will examine the circumstances in which the courts have been applying ubuntu in order to discover more precisely the function it is fulfillin in our law.

---

[297] Pieterse (n268) 461
[298] Himonga, Taylor & Pope (n4) 388 regard the lack of specificit as an advantage.
[299] See above pp 16-18.
[300] *S v Makwanyane and another* 1995 (3) SA 391 (CC) para 224.
[301] Himonga, Taylor & Pope (n41) 391.

Chapter 4

APPLICATION OF UBUNTU

1 INTRODUCTION: UBUNTU AS A METANORM

> [Ubuntu is] 'the embodiment of a set of values and moral principles which informed the peaceful co-existence of the African people in this country'.[1]

Since ubuntu's entry into the South African legal system as a single word in an epilogue to the Interim Constitution of 1993,[2] it has appeared in at least 39 reported cases.[3] This is, perhaps, a modest number of decisions, but account should be taken of the fact that the highest courts of the land were responsible for the great majority of these references, which have in turn generated a vigorous

---

[1] *S v Makwanyane and another* 1995 (3) SA 391 (CC) para 217.

[2] 'The adoption of this Constitution lays the secure foundation for the people of South Africa to transcend the divisions and strife of the past, which generated gross violations of human rights, the transgression of humanitarian principles in violent conflict and a legacy of hatred, fear, guilt and revenge. These can now be addressed on the basis that there is a need for understanding but not for vengeance, a need for reparation but not for retaliation, a need for *ubuntu* but not for victimisation. . . .'

[3] Ubuntu has been given serious attention in 19 Constitutional Court cases and 2 Supreme Court of Appeal cases.

academic literature.[4] Hence, although some might claim that the practice of ubuntu is dead,[5] it is clear that the concept is still very much alive in the law.[6]

In the previous chapter, it was established that ubuntu is quite capable of working as a legal norm, and we can now proceed to consider how it has been used by the courts. This chapter therefore explores the courts' judgments in order to discover ubuntu's functions, the meanings attributed to it and the weight of authority it carries for the development of a legal discourse. An inquiry of this nature requires an account of the legal and factual contexts in which the concept has been applied, because, as was pointed out earlier, if we are to establish both the current meanings and functions of ubuntu, an understanding of context is critical.[7] Furthermore, the outcomes in specifi cases and their subsequent precedent value depend on particular factual scenarios and the legal principles that have influence the way in which ubuntu has been interpreted.

The following survey of the cases shows that ubuntu has been invoked in a wide variety of contexts, and has permeated all branches of South African law. In constitutional and administrative law, for instance, it has been employed to mediate conflict between rights, refin and interpret rights and temper discretionary powers. In the criminal justice system, it has contributed to the determination of standards for arrest, sentencing and parole, and has provided an indigenous basis for the idea of restorative justice. In the fiel of private law, it has reinforced the duty of support in family law, modifie the rights of property owners and, in contract, has given added meanings to the principles of fairness, justice, good faith and public policy.

In all these situations, the general function of ubuntu has remained constant: to act as a new and independent metanorm in South Africa's legal system. Norms of this nature are of a higher order in that they do not apply directly to the facts of cases, which is the work of lower order rules.[8] The role of higher order norms is to regulate the application of lower order rules to bring about more equitable results. In this sense, ubuntu works in a way similar to equity in both the civilian legal systems and the early English doctrine of equity.[9]

It will become evident therefore that the courts have been using ubuntu to modify the effect of strict application of the law. In so doing, they have set new goals and standards of behaviour in line with African values and the spirit of the Constitution.

---

[4] See above for example p 6 fn 40 and p 11 fn 18.

[5] Matolino & Kwindingwi 'The end of ubuntu' (2013) 32 *SA J Philosophy* 204; Eliastam 'Exploring ubuntu discourse in South Africa: loss, liminality and hope' (2015) 36 *Verbum et Ecclesia* 5.

[6] Including Namibian law. See the case of *BV Investment Six Hundred and Nine CC v Kamati* (I 1074/2013) [2016] NAHCMD 216 para 41, where a witness was commended for having the character of ubuntu.

[7] See above pp 30-31.

[8] Typical second order norms are the rules for interpreting statutes and the choice of law rules provided by private international law to determine which of two or more legal systems is applicable to facts connected to a foreign jurisdiction.

[9] See below pp 106ff.

2 THE COURTS' USE OF UBUNTU

The cases considered below are loosely classifie according to the functions assigned to ubuntu by the courts.[10] The presentation of each case includes a brief summary of the facts, together with the applicable rules and any key terms used in association with ubuntu. By this means, we can gauge how ubuntu entered the legal system, what meanings were ascribed to it and the roles it has played all of which help to show the path of its future development. Accordingly, when reading the cases, four points need to be borne in mind: the precedent value of the judgments; the legal context in which ubuntu appeared, namely, the rules and principles with which it was associated and the meanings attributed to ubuntu.

(a) Mediating conflicting laws

When performing this function, ubuntu has determined which of two conflictin rules (or rights) should be applied in particular situations. It was used, in other words, to weigh the merits of applying one or other rule, which is akin to the balancing process that becomes necessary when conflict arise between constitutional rights. Four examples are given here.[11]

The firs is *Bophuthatswana Broadcasting Corporation v Ramosa and others.*[12] In this instance, a dispute had arisen during negotiations between the applicant (the BBC) and the respondents (employees of the applicant and members of a trade union). The respondents had protested in a group at the entrance to the BBC, sometimes resorting to violent behaviour towards the Corporation's staff. The BBC therefore sought an urgent interdict to prevent the respondents from disrupting their working day. Khumalo J was called on to deal with an argument raised by the respondents that their rights to protest and demonstrate under s 17 of the Constitution were not subject to the rights of others. In the course of his judgment, Khumalo equated ubuntu with the 'golden mean', a classic concept denoting moderation in behaviour in order to reconcile conflictin interests. He noted that, as a keystone of many different moral systems,[13] the golden mean

---

[10] Cf Himonga, Taylor & Pope 'Reflection on judicial views of ubuntu' (2013) 16 *PELJ* 373, who take a different approach by categorising the cases chronologically in order to identify 'two major epochs in the development of ubuntu, marked by the constitutional decisions in *Makwanyane . . .* and *PE Municipality . . .* respectively'. They contend that the former established 'the central avenue of development for ubuntu' and 'the latter marked the start of the thematic development of the concept in the direction of restorative justice' (421).

[11] Other cases falling into this category are considered below: *The Citizen 1978 (Pty) Ltd and others v McBride (Johnstone and others, Amici Curiae)* 2011 (4) SA 191 (CC) (both concerned with freedom of expression); *City of Johannesburg Metropolitan Municipality v Blue Moonlight Properties 39 (Pty) Ltd and Another* 2012 (2) SA 104 (CC) and *Resnick v Government of the Republic of South Africa and another* 2014 (2) SA 337 (WCC) (concerned with the right to evict unlawful occupiers of property).

[12] [1997] JOL 283 (B).

[13] Khumalo J referred in this regard to the moral systems of Confucius and Christianity (in which he included Justinian's *Corpus Juris Civilis*). He cited the following axioms: Confucius, you should 'do not do unto others what you would not want others to do unto you'; St Matthew, 'all things whatsoever ye would that men should do to you, do ye even so to them: for this is the law and the

requires reciprocity in so far as 'to be human is a communal enterprise', and he found that this idea was inherent in ubuntu. The judge accordingly held that the respondents' planned method for exercising their constitutional right to protest could not be considered appropriate because it unduly violated the rights of others (presumably freedom of movement under s 21(1) of the Constitution).

In *Crossley and others v National Commissioner of South African Police Service and others,*[14] the two rights to be weighed against each other were dignity and access to the courts as guaranteed by ss 10 and 34 of the Constitution respectively. The applicants stood accused of the murder of a farm employee (whom they had allegedly severely assaulted and thrown to a pride of lions on a game farm). They sought an interdict to stay the deceased's funeral so that they would examine his remains with a view to obtaining forensic evidence which they could then present at their criminal trial. As it happened, the application was dismissed because its urgency was not established. Nevertheless, part of Patel J's reasoning concerned the applicants' failure to inform the deceased's family of their application (to which the family should have been joined as respondents). In this regard, the judge raised *obiter* the constitutional right of the deceased and his relatives to dignity, as opposed to the applicants' right to a fair trial. And, as an additional reason for refusing the application, ubuntu was associated with the maxim *umuntu ngumuntu ngabantu.* Patel held that '*ubuntu* embraces humaneness, group solidarity, compassion, respect, human dignity, conformity to basic norms and collective unity, humanity, morality and conciliations'.[15]

In *Manyatshe v M&G Media Ltd and others,*[16] the respondents had sent the appellant a questionnaire asking him to comment on allegations that he had been involved in the irregular award of a contract while serving as the CEO of the South African Post Office. The appellant refused to comply, arguing that publication would not only cause him great prejudice, but also that the notion of ubuntu recognised 'a person's status as a human being, entitled to unconditional respect, dignity, value and acceptance from the members of the community, that such a person may be part of'.[17] The Supreme Court of Appeal held that the law of defamation required a balance to be struck between the constitutional rights of freedom of expression (s 16) and dignity and privacy (ss 10 and 14). It found that the appellant's public profil could 'add weight to both sides of the scale' and that 'considerable recognition should be given to the values embodied in the notion of ubuntu, under the rubric of dignity'.[18] Whether sufficient weight had been given to

---

prophets'; Justinian, *Digest* 1.1.10 'the precepts of the law are these: to live honestly, to hurt no other, to give everyone his due'.

[14] [2004] 3 All SA 436 (T).

[15] Paragraph 18.

[16] [2009] JOL 24238 (SCA).

[17] Paragraph 21 citing here Jajbhay J in *Tshabalala-Msimang and another v Makhanya and others* 2008 (6) SA 102 (W) para 2.

[18] Paragraph 22.

these factors, however, was held to be a matter of fact. The factors were therefore deemed irrelevant to the appeal which dealt only with matters of law.[19]

Finally, there is the unusual case of *S v Mandela*,[20] the only instance in which ubuntu was invoked in the context of criminal liability, where it appeared in connection with a defence of necessity.[21] This case involved an accused who had been charged with several offences, including murder. He entered a plea of not guilty, invoking the defence of necessity. The court held that this defence required a delicate balance between two rights to life: that of the person who was safeguarding his or her own life at the expense of another's life.[22] As a result, a plea of necessity could be upheld only when the threat of death was unavoidable except by a heroic act exceeding the capacity of an ordinary person. On the evidence, the court found that there had been 'no immediacy of life threatening compulsion'. It held that to lower the threshold of this defence would be to lower regard for life and to undermine 'the very fabric of the attempt to build a constitutional community, where each and every person is deserving of equal concern and respect and in which community grows, sourced in the principle of *ubuntu*'.[23]

A few points need to be considered in these four cases. The firs is a feature that will become apparent in all but two cases concerning ubuntu: it was not asserted as a principal reason for judgments, but rather by way of *obiter dicta*, ranging in weight from *Bophuthatswana Broadcasting*, where it was a significan factor, to *Mandela*, where it was clearly incidental. Secondly, although ubuntu was not a decisive element in the fina judgments, it helped to tip the balance of arguments in favour of one rather than the other. Thirdly, ubuntu was interpreted in different ways: in *Bophuthatswana Broadcasting*, it was likened to a golden mean, or a general standard of moderation requiring reciprocal action in human behaviour; in *Crossley* and *Manyatshe*, it was seen in terms of a right to dignity (in the former case, demanding a humane approach to those mourning the loss of a deceased relative) and in *Mandela* it was taken to mean equal concern and respect.

(b) Interpreting terms of contracts and statutes

In the following four cases, ubuntu's role as a higher norm determining the application of lower norms involved the interpretation of clauses in contracts and statutes. To decide what meaning to attach to the terms in question, the courts

---

[19] Moreover, the article had already been published which made the interdict meaningless. This case may be compared with *Tshabalala-Msimang and another v Makhanya and others* 2008 (6) SA 102 (W), where the firs applicant (who was South Africa's Minister of Health) and the second applicant (Medi-Clinic Ltd) sought an order against the respondents seeking *inter alia* an interdict restraining the respondents from publishing or commenting on her medical records or any other private information concerning her medical condition. Jajbhay J held that publication of certain information about Tshabalala-Msimang's health condition should be permitted. He considered that, notwithstanding the value of dignity and privacy, publication of the Minister's medical condition was of considerable public importance. Although the judgment began (para 2) with a vivid description of ubuntu, linking it to dignity and respect, the concept played no significan role in the case.

[20] *S v Mandela* [2001] JOL 7754 (C).

[21] Define in Burchell *Principles of Criminal Law* 164ff.

[22] *S v Mandela* [2001] JOL 7754 (C) at 21.

[23] Supra at 23.

drew on the established common-law principles of interpretation — good faith and public policy — to which they added the Bill of Rights and the ethical qualities of ubuntu, ie, concern for the community, compassion and social justice.

The first case, chronologically speaking, was *Port Elizabeth Municipality v Various Occupiers*.[24] In this matter, the Municipality had sought, in terms of the Prevention of Illegal Eviction from and Unlawful Occupation of Land Act (PIE),[25] to evict some 68 unlawful occupiers from its land. As an organ of state, the City's power to do so depended upon conditions specifie in the Act, namely, whether the eviction was 'just and equitable' and also whether it was in 'the public interest'.[26] The Constitutional Court refused to grant the eviction order. Its decision rested on a delicate balancing of 'conventional rights of ownership against the new, equally relevant right not to be arbitrarily deprived of a home',[27] as well as the interpretation of the terms 'just and equitable' in the PIE.[28] With regard to the latter, Sachs J commented in a *dictum* (quoted frequently in subsequent cases) that the PIE

> 'expressly requires the court to infuse elements of grace and compassion into the formal structures of the law. It is called upon to balance competing interests in a principled way and to promote the constitutional vision of a caring society based on good neighbourliness and shared concern. The Constitution and PIE confir that we are not islands unto ourselves. The spirit of *ubuntu*, part of the deep cultural heritage of the majority of the population, suffuses the whole constitutional order.'[29]

The City's application was therefore denied on the ground that it was not just and equitable. In support of this decision, the Court alluded to: the long period of time that the occupiers had lived on the land; the absence of any evidence to show that either the Municipality or the owners needed to evict the occupiers in order to put the land to productive use; the Municipality's failure to listen to the occupiers' problems, and the serious effect the eviction would have on a small group of homeless and needy people.[30]

Barkhuizen v Napier[31] dealt with the interpretation of a clause in a contract. This was a time-limitation clause, the enforcement of which would have entailed a restriction on the claimant's access to the courts, a right enshrined in s 34 of the Constitution. The Court held that clauses such as the one before it were generally considered to be contrary to public policy — because they barred individual rights to legal redress for injuries suffered — unless they had been freely consented to. The principle of public policy was informed by considerations of fairness, justice,

---

[24] 2005 (1) SA 217 (CC).

[25] 19 of 1998.

[26] Section 6(2) of PIE. 'Public interest' is define to include 'the health and safety of those occupying the land and the public in general'.

[27] Paragraph 23. See too s 26(1) of the Constitution: 'Everyone has the right to have access to adequate housing.'

[28] Section 6(3).

[29] Paragraph 37 [footnotes omitted]. Cited also in *Thubelisha Homes and others v Various Occupants and others* [2008] JOL 21559 (C) para 51. See, too, *Transnet Limited v Tebeka and others* [2013] JOL 30987 (SCA).

[30] Paragraph 59.

[31] 2007 (5) SA 323 (CC) para 51.

equity and reasonableness — and in addition, ubuntu. Once the objective terms of the contract were found to be consistent with public policy (a 90-day period was held to be neither unfair nor inadequate), a second inquiry then became necessary to determine whether the terms were contrary to public policy in the light of the relative circumstances of the contracting parties, especially their respective bargaining powers.[32] As it turned out, the appeals to public policy and ubuntu in this case failed on the facts, since the Court found no evidence to show a significan inequality of bargaining power or to show that the contract had not been freely negotiated.[33] Moreover, the applicant gave no reasons to explain why he did not comply with the time clause or why he had waited for two years before instituting action against the respondent.[34]

In *Dula Investments (Pty) Ltd v Woolworths (Pty) Limited,*[35] the applicant, a franchise holder of three of the respondent's stores, sought to extend its franchise beyond the agreed period by means of an extension clause. Although it was accepted that the applicant had given timeous notice of an intention to extend the agreement in terms of that clause, it had breached a sub-clause in which it undertook 'not [to] have committed any breach of any of the provisions of this agreement at any time during the initial period'. The applicant claimed, partly on the basis of ubuntu, that the respondent, Woolworths, was obliged to act in good faith, such that it would be unfair for the respondent to rely on a breach of the conditions of the contract as a reason for refusing to extend the franchise. The applicant's argument failed. The Court held that: 'concepts of "good faith" and *ubuntu* constitute a two-way street and are not unilateral obligations owed by one party to the other.'[36] Instead, the Court emphasised business efficacy in a commercial sense. The fact that Woolworths might have overlooked minor breaches of the franchise agreement during its subsistence would not have prevented the company from relying on the extension clause if it did not wish to continue doing business with the applicant after the termination date.[37]

---

[32] Paragraphs 57–59.

[33] Paragraph 66. Due to the absence of stated facts, it was impossible for the Court to decide whether the enforcement of the clause against the applicant would be unfair and contrary to public policy (paras 84–86).

[34] *Advtech Resourcing (Pty) Ltd t/a Communicate Personnel Group v Kuhn and another* 2008 (2) SA 375 (C) para 14 involved a restraint of trade clause in an employment contract. Such clauses are permissible under common law unless they are contrary to public policy, which *in casu* required weighing *pacta sunt servanda* against dignity and the freedom to work (protected by s 22 of the Constitution). The attempt to achieve an equitable outcome to the dispute succeeded, in that the restraint clause was declared unenforceable, but ubuntu played only a minor role in the judgment, where it was spoken of as an equivalent of good faith and community interests. See, too, *Burmbuild (Pty) Ltd v Ndzama* [2013] 2 All SA 399 (ECG) which also concerned the enforceability of a clause in restraint of trade in light of s 22 of the Constitution. While reference was made to the need to develop the law by means of ubuntu, the concept was not directly applied.

[35] [2013] JOL 30323 (KZD).

[36] Paragraph 48.

[37] Paragraph 48.

NM v Presiding Officer of Children's Court, Krugersdorp, and others[38] dealt with the entitlement of a caregiver who bore a duty to support a child to be appointed the child's foster parent. Paradoxically, such an appointment was contrary to the plain wording of the Children's Act.[39] According to a literal interpretation of the provision in question, only the children living with caregivers, who had no common-law duty of support towards those children, could become foster parents — a curious outcome, and one that would result in the creation of different categories of dependent children. It was held that such an interpretation constituted unjustifie discrimination, which would be contrary to the Bill of Rights and thus not in keeping with the spirit of ubuntu or with the best interests of children.[40]

In these cases, the precedent value of ubuntu was again weak, because the principle was raised only *obiter*. Nonetheless, the assertion of ubuntu provided a justification on the facts, for securing more equitable outcomes than application of strict rules of law (notably in *Port Elizabeth Municipality*). Another development, noticeable in the previous section, but gaining further traction here, is ubuntu's association with existing concepts in South African law: just and equitable (*Port Elizabeth Municipality*), public policy (*Barkhuizen*), good faith (*Dula Investments*) and equal treatment and best interests of the child (*NM*). In one case, this association in turn provided the basis for infusing the existing terms with new meanings: grace and compassion (*Port Elizabeth Municipality*).

(c) Developing the common and customary law according to the Bill of Rights

Section 39(2) of the Constitution requires the courts 'when developing the common law or customary law' to 'promote the spirit, purport and objects of the Bill of Rights'. An early landmark decision, which confronted a problem that had been long awaiting a solution, dealt with the conflic between the constitutional requirement of gender equality and the customary-law rule of patrilineal succession. In *Bhe and others v Magistrate, Khayelitsha, and others*,[41] the solution decided upon by a majority judgment of the Constitutional Court was an interim measure: to replace customary law with the Intestate Succession Act[42] until Parliament enacted suitable legislation to reform customary law.[43]

---

[38] 2013 (4) SA 379 (GSJ).

[39] Section 156(1)(e) of Act 38 of 2005.

[40] Which are protected under s 28(2) of the Bill of Rights (para 24). It should be noted in addition that, under s 39(2) of the Constitution, courts are obliged to interpret any legislation in a way that will 'promote the spirit, purport and objects of the Bill of Rights'.

[41] The full citation is *Bae and others v Magistrate, Khayelitsha, and others (Commission for Gender Equality as Amicus Curiae); Shibi v Sithole and others; South African Human Rights Commission and another v President of the Republic of South Africa and another* 2005 (1) SA 580 (CC).

[42] 81 of 1987.

[43] Reform of Customary Law of Succession and Regulation of Related Matters Act 11 of 2009.

In a separate dissenting judgment, however, Ngcobo J argued that, rather than resort to the Intestate Succession Act to ensure compliance with the Constitution, the customary system of succession could be developed to achieve the same ends.[44] He noted that the existing customary laws should be understood in terms of their inherent capacity to adjust to social needs and context, whereby the emphasis fell, not on rights, but on a network of duties and responsibilities amongst family members ensuring that everyone had access to the basic necessities of life.[45] The Judge then identifie ubuntu, as captured in the maxim *umuntu ngumuntu ngabantu*, as a prevailing value of this type of social order.[46] Subsequent academic commentary on this case applauded Ngcobo's judgment not only for coming closer to realising constitutional standards (notably the best interests of the child), but also equal recognition for customary law on a par with the common law.[47]

Everfresh Market Virginia (Pty) Ltd v Shoprite Checkers (Pty) Ltd[48] dealt with a quite different matter, a grey area in South African contract law: whether parties have a duty to negotiate a new contract in terms of a renewal clause in the old contract. On the termination of a lease between Everfresh (the lessee of premises in a shopping centre) and Shoprite Checkers (the lessor), a renewal clause in the contract came into operation. It provided that Everfresh had the right to renew the lease for a further specifie period on the same terms as those contained in the lease agreement, except for the rental which would have to be agreed upon by the two parties. Everfresh was prepared to renew the lease at a new rental, but Shoprite Checkers contended that the clause was not legally binding.

When the High Court found in favour of Shoprite Checkers, and Everfresh's application for leave to appeal to the Supreme Court of Appeal was refused, the matter was taken to the Constitutional Court. Here, Everfresh advanced a new argument: that the common law of contract should be developed so as to require parties who undertake to negotiate to do so reasonably and in good faith. The Court held that it was too late in the proceedings to deal with this argument, but

---

[44] Paragraph 139. Another landmark decision referring to the development of customary law was *Mayelane v Ngwenyama and another* 2013 (4) SA 415 (CC) which dealt with the validity of a polygamous marriage, in particular whether a husband was obliged to secure his firs wife's consent before contracting a second or subsequent marriage. Because it was uncertain whether 'living' XiTsonga law had this rule, the Constitutional Court held that customary law ought to be developed to bring it into line with the requirement of gender equality in the Bill of Rights (paras 71ff).

[45] Paragraphs 162-163.

[46] Citing *S v Makwanyane and another* 1995 (3) SA 391 (CC) para 163 per Langa DCJ: 'it is a culture which "regulates the exercise of rights by the emphasis it lays on sharing and co-responsibility and the mutual enjoyment of rights".' Because Ngcobo J considered the interim measure proposed in the majority judgment inappropriate, he held (para 240) that the parties should be allowed to decide for themselves whether succession should be governed by customary law. If disputes arose as to when it was applicable, they could be referred to a magistrate's court, which must then have regard to what would be fair, just and equitable, especially regarding the interests of minor children and other dependants of the deceased.

[47] See Mnisi Weeks 'Customary succession and the development of customary law: the Bhe legacy: part III: reflection on themes in Justice Langa's judgments' 2015 *Acta Juridica* 252-254; Lehnert 'The role of the courts in the conflic between African customary law and human rights' (2005) 21 *SAJHR* 270.

[48] 2012 (1) SA 256 (CC).

both the majority and minority judgments accepted, in principle, that the law of contract should be developed in terms of s 39(2) of the Constitution.[49] Speaking for the majority, Moseneke DCJ held that two principles could tilt the argument in favour of Everfresh: good faith (underlying the law of contract) and ubuntu (implying humaneness, social justice and fairness) which both contribute to South Africa's constitutional order.[50] For the minority, Yacoob J observed that a contract between two business entities (of equal power) might not entail an assertion of ubuntu, but it had to be remembered that contracts were often undertaken between 'poor, vulnerable people on one hand and powerful, well-resourced companies on the other. The idea that people or entities can undertake to negotiate and then not do so because this attitude becomes convenient for some or other commercial reason, certainly implicates *ubuntu.*'[51] In other words, the call for ubuntu suggested that those in weak bargaining positions should not be sacrifice to the interests of the more powerful for the sake of business convenience.[52]

In neither of these cases was ubuntu critical to the fina judgment. In *Bhe's* case, it was used simply to demonstrate an aspect of customary law that was compatible with the Constitution, thereby implying that customary law could be developed rather than overridden by the common law in order to comply with the Bill of Rights. In *Everfresh*, reference to ubuntu was *obiter*, and was linked to good faith, the long established interpretive principle in contract law. In this context, ubuntu was construed to mean humaneness, fairness and social justice, and as such, was used as a reason in the minority judgment to correct inequalities of bargaining power.

(d) Modifying the exercise of rights and powers

(i) *Criminal justice*
The following set of cases to typify this function of ubuntu fall within the realm of the criminal justice process, primarily the powers of sentencing and parole.[53] The firs was *S v Makwanyane and another.*[54]

---

[49] As per Yacoob J for the minority (para 34) and Moseneke DCJ for the majority (para 48). See below p 162.

[50] Paragraphs 71-72.

[51] Paragraph 24. The *Everfresh dictum* in favour of good faith and ubuntu was approved in another lease agreement, but one subject to administrative law and hence the Promotion of Administrative Justice Act 3 of 2000: *Mkululi Lumumba Kubukeli t/a Four Seasons Fashions v King Sabata Dalindyebo Municipality and others* [2013] JOL 30220 (ECM) para 23.

[52] Cf *Dula Investments (Pty) Ltd v Woolworths (Pty) Limited* [2013] JOL 30323 (KZD) above p 66. *Everfresh* was referred to with approval, albeit *obiter*, in *Makate v Vodacom (Pty) Ltd* 2016 (4) SA 121 (CC) para 100, a case concerned with payment of compensation for Vodacom's appropriation of the applicant's idea to develop a lucrative new product. The applicant argued that Vodacom was obliged to negotiate in good faith, claiming that the common law should be developed in order to infuse it with the constitutional values of ubuntu and good faith. In an *obiter dictum*, the Constitutional Court accepted this argument (para 100), and ordered Vodacom to commence negotiations with the applicant. In *Maharaj v Gold Circle (Pty) Ltd* [2016] JOL 35727 (KZD) para 61, on the other hand, a case concerning allegations of racial discrimination arising from the respondent's refusal to extend facilities for equestrian racing and transformation benefit to appellant, the *Everfresh* argument was not applied on the ground that it had been given *obiter*.

[53] One case, *Bertie Van Zyl (Pty) Ltd and another v Minister for Safety and Security and others* 2010 (2) SA 181 (CC), concerned the power of arrest which a SAPS official had used to harass

The issue in this instance was the constitutionality of a court's power to impose the death penalty in terms of the Criminal Procedure Act.[55] Exercise of this power was reserved to the superior courts in cases of conviction for, *inter alia*, murder. The Constitutional Court was called upon to weigh a death sentence against an accused's fundamental rights to life, dignity and freedom from cruel or unusual punishment.[56] In accordance with the epilogue to the Interim Constitution, the Court held that retribution ought not to be given undue weight when balancing the fundamental rights against the power to impose capital punishment. The extensive judgments in *Makwanyane* gave ubuntu its firs and fullest judicial exposition. Indeed, six of the eleven Constitutional Court judges highlighted ubuntu as a reason for favouring abolition of the death penalty.[57] Chaskalson J, who delivered the main judgment, held that: 'to be consistent with the value of "ubuntu" South Africa should be a society that 'wishes to prevent crime . . . not to kill criminals simply to get even with them'.[58] And, in his separate judgment, Langa J found that the epilogue in the Interim Constitution on National Unity and Reconciliation implied 'a change in mental attitude from vengeance to an appreciation of the need for understanding, from retaliation to reparation and from victimisation to "ubuntu" '.[59] One of the principal features of ubuntu 'was the value that it put on life and human dignity . . . the life of another person was at least as valuable as one's own'.[60] Instead of the death penalty, therefore, the Court ruled in favour of imprisonment.

In *Makwanyane's* case, ubuntu was used to strengthen an argument that the courts' general power to impose the death penalty should be permanently removed from the law. The following cases differed, in that ubuntu was used as a reason for tempering the exercise of powers of sentencing and parole in terms of the facts of each case. In other words, no change to the law was required.

S v Matiwane[61] serves as an example of three cases concerned with granting more lenient sentences.[62] The accused had been arrested for a petty theft. He had pleaded guilty, and in view of 17 previous convictions, a magistrate's court had

---

members of the applicant company. It was held that the SAPS conduct was 'reminiscent of the abuse of power and police harassment . . . which were rife in our past', and that public service policing had to pay due regard to the values of ubuntu (para 77).

[54] 1995 (3) SA 391 (CC).

[55] Section 277(1) of Act 51 of 1977.

[56] Sections 9, 10 and 11(2), respectively, of the Interim Constitution.

[57] In the judgments of Judges Chaskalson, Langa, Madala, Mohammed, Mokgoro and Sachs.

[58] Paragraph 131, citing Brennan J in *Furman v Georgia* [1972] USSC 170 at 305. Note the call by Judges Madala, Mokgoro and Sachs to explore traditional African jurisprudence to determine the issue (paras 259, 304 and 374ff, respectively).

[59] Paragraph 223. Kriegler J (para 203) held that, although the protections given by the Constitution were applicable to everyone, especially those who were poor, weak and vulnerable, they were also applicable to those who might not appear to need special protection, 'even the worst and most vicious criminals'.

[60] Paragraph 225. See too Mokgoro J para 309. In *Makwanyane's* case, the Court began the search for a suitable definitio of ubuntu (paras 224, 263, 307 and 312).

[61] [2016] JOL 35378 (WCC).

[62] In a similar case, *S v Koikoi* (CC 37/05) [2005] ZANWHC 23 (17 March 2005), the court found that a 19 year old convicted of rape showed none of the 'the element of remorse or ubuntu factor', and that his sincerity was 'in short supply'. Nonetheless, the accused's personal circumstances

sentenced him to three years, imprisonment. He was, however, 32 years old, unemployed, with child dependants, and he suffered from serious injury requiring medical attention. The High Court found the sentence unfairly severe, and held that the court *a quo* should have been more aware of the accused's socio-economic background and should have applied the principle of ubuntu. The accused was accordingly cautioned and discharged.

When we turn to consider parole, we fin that ubuntu was a major influenc in two judgments. *Du Plooy v Minister of Correctional Services*[63] is an example. Parole had initially been refused although the prisoner was terminally ill. The High Court, however, found this decision to be irrational and in contravention of the Correctional Services Act,[64] as well as several provisions of the Constitution. The applicant was declared to be a person

> 'in need of humanness, empathy and compassion. These are values inherently embodied in *ubuntu*. When these values are weighed against the applicant's continued imprison-ment, then, in my view his continued incarceration violates his human dignity and security, and the very punishment itself becomes cruel, inhuman and degrading.'[65]

In summarising the impact of these cases on the law, it is evident that ubuntu did not affect the main issues,[66] although it played a significan role in *Matiwane* and *Du Plooy*. *Makwanyane* is exceptional in that ubuntu was arguably one of the principal grounds for effecting a major change to the law, and was at the same time established as a core, constitutional value on a par with life and dignity. Not surprisingly, given the context in *Makwanyane*, ubuntu was associated with the rights to life, dignity and freedom from cruel or unusual punishment.

When the circumstances of parolees or convicted persons were concerned, however, ubuntu was associated not with rights, but rather with such virtues as empathy, humanity and compassion (*Du Plooy*), and these qualities were taken as reasons for tempering the exercise of public powers. In all these cases, the factual circumstances of the particular individual were of key importance. Only in *Makwanyane* was an entire class of people involved. In this regard, Langa J spoke of constitutional protections being applicable to every person, especially 'the weak, the poor and the vulnerable', but he went on to include others who might not appear to require special protection, such as those who 'placed themselves on the wrong side of the law'.[67]

---

tipped the scales in favour of leniency (para 7). *S v Sibiya* 2010 (1) SACR 284 (GNP) involved reference to restorative justice, and it is considered below pp 79ff.

[63] [2004] 3 All SA 613 (T).

[64] 111 of 1998.

[65] Paragraph 29. Similarly, in *Derby-Lewis v Minister of Justice and Correctional Services and others* 2015 (2) SACR 412 (GP), the court approved a parole application, referring to s 12(1)(e) of the Constitution which provides that: 'Everyone has the right to freedom and security of the person, which includes the right not to be treated or punished in a cruel, inhuman or degrading way.' Considering that the applicant was terminally ill, the court held that the provisions of a statute should be construed in such a manner that 'upholds basic tenets of our law' as entrenched in the Constitution. One such principle was ubuntu 'which recognises the inherent dignity in every human being and enjoins people of South Africa to treat one another in a humane manner' (paras 54 and 55).

[66] And was incidental to the fina judgments in *Bertie Van Zyl* and *Mandela* supra.

[67] *S v Makwanyane and another* 1995 (3) SA 391 (CC) para 230.

(ii) *Property*

In the general fiel of private law, we fin that most of the cases dealt with property and the restrictions imposed on the rights and powers of property owners. Ubuntu was deployed in this context mainly in order to serve the ends of social justice. Colonialism and apartheid had left whites with overwhelming control of South Africa's resources, a situation facilitated in part by the exclusive, individualistic notion of property inherited from Roman-Dutch law.[68] The result was a grossly disproportionate distribution of land in favour of whites, and a concomitant problem of homelessness for blacks.[69]

Section 25, the property clause in the Constitution is, in consequence, one of the longest and most complex section in the Bill of Rights, because it sets out not only to guarantee security of tenure,[70] but also to restore land to those dispossessed by racially discriminatory laws[71] and to promote just and equitable land reform.[72] Additional provisions are made in s 26 to give citizens 'adequate housing' and to prevent arbitrary evictions of unlawful occupiers.[73] To give effect to these provisions, Parliament passed the Prevention of Illegal Eviction from and Unlawful Occupation of Land Act (PIE),[74] in terms of which eviction orders may be issued only if they are 'just and equitable to do so, after considering all the relevant circumstances'.[75]

The firs case in the category of property to deal explicitly with ubuntu was *City of Johannesburg v Rand Properties (Pty) Limited and others.*[76] Here the City had applied to have poverty-stricken occupiers evicted from properties deemed unfi for human occupation. Application for the eviction order was not brought under the PIE, however, but in terms of an inner city renewal programme,[77] as a result of which the action was governed by administrative law. Although the eviction order was upheld, the court interdicted the City from evacuating the respondents until it had developed 'a pragmatic, constructive and coherent programme' to deal with the respondents' predicament.[78] This programme was to include findin the occupiers temporary accommodation, but not as mere shack dwellers in an

---

[68] Van der Walt 'Dancing with codes — protecting, developing and deconstructing property rights in a constitutional state' (2001) 118 *SALJ* 290.

[69] Van der Merwe 'Land tenure in South Africa: a brief history and some reform proposals' (1989) 4 *TSAR* 679-680.

[70] Section 25(1): 'No one may be deprived of property except in terms of law of general application, and no law may permit arbitrary deprivation of property.' See too s 25(6).

[71] Section 25(7).

[72] Section 25(8).

[73] Section 26.

[74] 19 of 1998. See also Pienaar *Land Reform* 659ff and, in this regard, the comments on the *mandament van spolie* in *Tswelopele Non-Profit Organisation and others v City of Tshwane Metropolitan Municipality* 2007 (6) SA 511 (SCA) paras 20ff.

[75] '[I]ncluding the rights and needs of the elderly, children, disabled persons and households headed by women' (s 4(6)). The leading authority on evictions is *Port Elizabeth Municipality v Various Occupiers* 2005 (1) SA 217 (CC), which was considered above p 65.

[76] 2007 (1) SA 78 (W).

[77] Governed by the National Building Regulations and Building Standards Act 103 of 1977.

[78] Paragraph 67.

informal settlement.[79] A solution such as the latter would 'fl[y in the face of the concept that a "person is a person through persons" (*ubuntu*)'. The court held that experience had shown that placing evictees in informal settlements was 'fundamentally skewed'; as occupiers of shacks, they 'not only lost their possessions through flood and fir but also their lives'.[80]

Similar issues were at stake in another case, *Resnick v Government of the Republic of South Africa and another.*[81] When determining whether the South African Police Service should be granted an eviction order against a widow who had been in long-term occupation of its land, the 'just and equitable' requirements of s 4 of the PIE arose. The court held that important guides in the inquiry were the 'spirit of ubuntu [which] promotes a normative notion of humanity, of human beings who recognise the "other", of values of solidarity, compassion and respect for human dignity'. As it happened, the appellant was a divorcee who had occupied the dwelling with her two children on a minimal income; she grew her own vegetables in order to stretch the little money she received as maintenance from her former spouse; she suffered from stress and ill health. The court granted the eviction order, but, in line with the 'just and equitable' requirements, ruled that the appellant be given some significan period of time to fin alternative accommodation.[82]

Aside from the eviction cases, ubuntu has played a prominent role in two matters concerned with developing property rights to include an owner's responsibilities towards the broader community.[83] To this end, the Constitutional Court made a strong statement in favour of ubuntu and community interests in *Shoprite Checkers (Pty) Ltd v MEC for Economic Development, Eastern Cape and others.*[84] This case was concerned with the harm that would be done to a corporate enterprise (Shoprite Checkers) whose licence to sell wine (a matter of intellectual property) was threatened by a provincial government's change to regulations controlling sale of liquor.[85] It was argued that the effect of the enactment was to deprive Shoprite Checkers of its property, a right protected by

---

[79] Note that the City successfully appealed against this judgment, with the result that the occupiers were evicted: *City of Johannesburg v Rand Properties (Pty) Ltd* 2007 (6) SA 417 (SCA).

[80] Paragraph 64. *City of Johannesburg Metropolitan Municipality v Blue Moonlight Properties 39 (Pty) Ltd and another* 2012 (2) SA 104 (CC) concerned a private landowner's application for an eviction order under the PIE. Here the occupiers' right to secure housing was again a prominent issue. After noting the connections between justice, equity and ubuntu, the court went on to state that those who acquire land for commercial purposes, and are aware that it has been occupied for a lengthy period of time, should not expect to put an eviction order into immediate operation, but nor should they be expected 'to provide free housing for the homeless' for an indefinit period of time. 'An owner's right to use and enjoy property at common law can be limited in the process of the justice and equity enquiry mandated by PIE' (para 40). Note that s 26(3) of the Constitution provides that: 'No one may be evicted from their home, or have their home demolished, without an order of court made after considering all the relevant circumstances.'

[81] 2014 (2) SA 337 (WCC).

[82] Which aligned justice and equity with the requirements of 'grace, compassion and a commitment to ubuntu in these circumstances' (para 344).

[83] Van der Walt (n68) 290.

[84] 2015 (6) SA 125 (CC).

[85] Eastern Cape Liquor Act 10 of 2003.

s 25(1) of the Constitution. One of the questions in issue was whether a liquor licence constituted property. In answering this question in the affirmative, a majority judgment of the Constitutional Court observed *obiter* that rights protected by the Constitution were not simply those envisaged in the traditional idea of private ownership, and that the individual's rights were not absolute, but rather were subject to social considerations.[86] Emphasising communality and interdependence, the Court then repeated the well-known saying 'that we are not islands unto ourselves', which was mirrored in the adage *umuntu ngumuntu ngabantu*.[87] It followed that, when making use of their property, owners should take into account the public good.[88]

A subsequent judgment echoing the same sentiments, but this time in connection with land, was given in *Savage and others v Sisters of the Holy Cross, Cape Province and others*.[89] The applicants (and their forebears) were tenants living gratuitously in six cottages on land owned by the Catholic Church. When, through economic necessity, the Church decided to sell the land, the applicants sought to interdict the transfer, arguing, *inter alia*, that alienation was precluded by the communitarian ethic of ubuntu.[90] Although the judgment ultimately went in favour of the Church on the basis of its need to address its financia woes, the court agreed that property rights could not be understood without regard to ubuntu,[91] and that they ought to 'evolve structurally in our law so that institutional change can follow'.[92] In addition, the court held that ubuntu could be used to repair the fractured relationship between the parties, because it could serve as a means through which the Church could appreciate the damaging effect of its actions.[93]

In these cases, ubuntu featured by way of forceful *dicta* aimed either at circumscribing owners' rights to evict unlawful occupants or at developing the

---

[86] Davis & Klare 'Transformative constitutionalism and the common and customary law' (2010) 26 *SAJHR* 485. See also *Port Elizabeth Municipality v Various Occupiers* 2005 (1) SA 217 (CC) para 16; *Jaftha v Schoeman and others; Van Rooyen v Stoltz and others* 2005 (2) SA 140 (CC) para 57.

[87] See above p 33.

[88] Paragraph 47. See, too, Ncube 'Calibrating copyright for creators and consumers: promoting distributive justice and ubuntu' in Giblin & Weatherall (eds) *What if We could Reimagine Copyright?* 253ff who argues that the public interest underlying existing copyright laws should be reimagined in order to promote the creation of literature (especially for children) in the neglected languages of disadvantaged communities by applying the principles of distributive justice inherent in ubuntu.

[89] 2015 (6) SA 1 (WCC).

[90] Paragraph 36. The communitarian spirit of ubuntu was also argued in *Langebaan Ratepayers' and Residents' Association v Dormell Properties 391 (Pty) Ltd and others* 2013 (1) SA 37 (WCC). This case concerned a public servitude of right of way based on immemorial use. In the argument for the existence of the servitude, counsel contended closure of the road would subject the public to a much longer walk in order to gain access to the beaches, which would run counter to ubuntu (para 36). The court did not address this issue, but determined a reasonable apprehension of harm to the public, and therefore interdicted the landowner from closing the road.

[91] Paragraph 36, citing here *Everfresh Market Virginia (Pty) Ltd v Shoprite Checkers (Pty) Ltd* 2012 (1) SA 256 (CC).

[92] Paragraph 39. It is noteworthy that the court did not refer here to 'developing' the law in terms of s 39(2) of the Constitution.

[93] Paragraph 36.

concept of ownership with due consideration for the owners' responsibilities to a wider community (*Shoprite Checkers* and *Savage*). As for the legal context, ie, the terms and principles with which ubuntu was associated, reference was made to the constitutional right of property, or where eviction was involved, the 'just and equitable' requirement stipulated in PIE, as well as the constitutional right to secure housing (*Resnick*). Ubuntu was expressed in terms of, humanity, interconnectedness, solidarity and respect for human dignity (*Resnick*),[94] and, more fulsomely, as 'the capacity to express compassion, justice, reciprocity, dignity, harmony and humanity in the interests of building, maintaining and strengthening the community' (*Rand Properties*). Another theme emerging in the cases was the interconnectedness of an individual property owner's legal and social responsibilities to care for others (*Shoprite Checkers* and *Rand Properties*).[95]

(iii) *Freedom of expression*

Section 16 of the Bill of Rights guarantees freedom of expression, including specificall freedom of the press.[96] In *The Citizen 1978 (Pty, Ltd and others v McBride (Johnstone and others, Amici Curiae)*,[97] *The Citizen* newspaper had described Robert McBride, the firs respondent, as a 'murderer' on the ground that he, as an ANC operative, had been convicted of murder following a car bomb attack on a Durban bar and restaurant in 1986. McBride sued for defamation, claiming that he had been reprieved and given amnesty by the TRC under the Promotion of National Unity and Reconciliation Act.[98] Two issues arose: the effect of the Act to expunge convictions for politically motivated offences, so that they were deemed never to have been committed, and *The Citizen's* defence of fair comment.[99]

The court addressed the firs issue by stating that the Act affected only the legal, not the linguistic consequences of conviction. In other words, it did not make it untrue that McBride had committed the act alleged, and public discussion of it as 'murder' was therefore permissible. With regard to this line of argument, and in a separate minority judgment, Ngcobo CJ (Khampepe J concurring) alluded to ubuntu as a foundation of the reconciliation and nation building process in post-apartheid South Africa.[100] These goals had been achieved through disclosing the truth of what had happened so that a lesson could be learnt from the 'past so as to prevent gross human rights violations from ever occurring in the future'.[101] In

---

[94] Paragraphs 63 and 343, respectively.

[95] *Shoprite Checkers (Pty) Ltd v MEC for Economic Development, Eastern Cape and others* 2015 (6) SA 125 (CC) para 63; *Resnick v Government of the Republic of South Africa and another* 2014 (2) SA 337 (WCC) para 343.

[96] Section 16(1)(a). Another case involving freedom of expression, *Manyatshe v M&G Media Ltd and others* [2009] JOL 24238 (SCA), was dealt with above p 63.

[97] 2011 (4) SA 191 (CC).

[98] 34 of 1995.

[99] For which the requirements were that the statements concerned were comment or opinion; were 'fair', ie, not malicious and were true and related to a matter of public interest (para 80).

[100] Paragraphs 167-168. As outlined in the epilogue to the Interim Constitution and *Azanian Peoples Organisation (AZAPO) and others v President of the Republic of South Africa and others* 1996 (4) SA 671 (CC).

[101] Paragraph 169.

order to achieve this aim, freedom of expression was essential.[102] The Citizen's defence of fair comment was therefore upheld, allowing reference to past deeds notwithstanding the granting of amnesty. In a dissenting judgment, however, Mogoeng J ruled in favour of the respondent, invoking ubuntu to support McBride's right to dignity. Mogoeng spoke of South Africa's 'shameful history of institutionalized human rights violations' and its unique 'commitment to make a decisive break with this past as well as our pursuit of the noble objectives of national unity and reconciliation'.[103] He accordingly held that this history should inform the interpretation and exercise of constitutional rights, and that the law of defamation could not be applied without considering the Truth and Reconciliation process and ubuntu.[104]

The court, in *Afriforum and another v Malema and another*,[105] considered freedom of expression in the different context of hate speech. The action in this instance was directed at Julius Malema, leader of the Economic Freedom Fighters, for singing the anti-apartheid song *'Dubula ibhunu'* (shoot the Boers/farmers). Afriforum brought its claim to restrain hate speech under the Promotion of Equality and Prevention of Unfair Discrimination Act.[106] In his judgment in favour of Afriforum, Lamont J held that the right to freedom of expression had to be limited partly in order to foster the spirit of ubuntu in South Africa.[107] One of the principal reasons for this decision was ubuntu, and Lamont sought to give a full definitio of the concept. He therefore listed various qualities of ubuntu, such as the value it places on life, dignity, compassion, humaneness, civility, mutual tolerance and respect for the humanity of others. In addition, he paid particular attention to ubuntu's potential for achieving restorative justice and what it entailed, primarily a shift from confrontation to mediation and conciliation.[108]

Ubuntu appeared in *The Citizen* in the form of strong dicta, and arguably as a *ratio decidendi* in *Afriforum*. It was associated with the right to dignity, as well as reconciliation, nation building and restorative justice; indeed the latter three goals served to focus the overall direction of argument in both the cases. Ubuntu was invoked, however, for quite different reasons: in *The Citizen* it appeared as a justificatio for upholding freedom of speech and fair comment (cf Mogoeng J's dissenting judgment); in *Afriforum* it limited freedom of speech in order to encourage national reconciliation.

(e) Promoting national unity and reconciliation

As we have seen, ubuntu began its journey into South African law from its starting point in the epilogue to the Interim Constitution entitled 'National Unity and Reconciliation'.[109] In view of the country's violent history and the deep divisions

---

[102] Paragraph 170.
[103] Paragraph 241.
[104] Paragraph 243. On the TRC, see above pp 27 and 46.
[105] 2011 (6) SA 240 (EqC).
[106] 4 of 2000.
[107] Paragraph 108.
[108] Paragraph 18. See further below p 79.
[109] See above p 27.

in its society, the epilogue declared that: 'The pursuit of national unity, the well-being of all South African citizens and peace require reconciliation between the people of South Africa and the reconstruction of society.'[110] These goals featured in a number of cases thereafter,[111] three of which referred to ubuntu.

The firs two cases involved the right to freedom of expression and dignity. In *The Citizen 1978 (Pty) Ltd and others v McBride (Johnstone and others, Amici Curiae)*,[112] a minority judgment held that McBride's amnesty granted by the Truth and Reconciliation Commission (TRC) had had the effect of expunging his conviction for an offence committed during apartheid. Their reasoning was guided by the need for ubuntu, which was a foundation for reconciliation and nation building.[113] Mogoeng J, however, used ubuntu for another purpose: to protect McBride's dignity and prevent the newspaper from vilifying him, on the ground that such action ran counter to the 'generosity, peace and common decency' of an ubuntu culture.[114]

McBride's case can be compared with *Afriforum and another v Malema and another*,[115] which was concerned with an action to restrain the leader of the Economic Freedom Fighters from singing an anti-apartheid song inciting the death of white Afrikaans-speaking South Africans on the ground that it constituted hate speech. Lamont J reasoned that, in terms of the political agreements and laws establishing the new democratic South Africa, 'the enemy had become the friend, the brother. Members of society were enjoined to embrace all citizens as their brothers. It must never be forgotten that in the spirit of ubuntu this new approach to each other had to be fostered.'[116] The court accordingly interdicted the respondents from singing the song because it violated the principles of ubuntu and national unity.[117]

The third case under the rubric of national reconciliation involved the right to culture, which is protected by s 31 of the Constitution. In *City of Tshwane Metropolitan Municipality v Afriforum and another*,[118] the Tshwane City Council appealed against an urgent interim interdict brought by Afriforum to halt the City's removal of colonial and apartheid-era street names in the Pretoria area. Although the main issues before the Constitutional Court were the conditions for granting interim interdicts and whether the Council had engaged in proper

---

[110] Cf Van der Walt (n68) 259ff who criticises Mureinik's depiction of the interim Constitution as a 'bridge' facilitating the transition 'from a culture of authority to a culture of justification' See Mureinik 'A bridge to where? Introducing the interim Bill of Rights' (1994) 10 *SAJHR* 31-32.

[111] Although counsel sometimes argued these goals, the courts did not engage with them, as, for instance, in *Du Toit v Minister for Safety and Security and another* 2009 (1) SA 176 (SCA) para 14. On other occasions, the courts engaged fully, as in *Azanian Peoples Organisation (AZAPO) and others v President of the Republic of South Africa and others* 1996 (4) SA 671 (CC) para 3; *Du Toit v Minister for Safety and Security and another* 2009 (6) SA 128 (CC); *Albutt v Centre for the Study of Violence and Reconciliation and others* 2010 (3) SA 293 (CC) para 54.

[112] 2011 (4) SA 191 (CC). See above p 75.

[113] Paragraphs 167-168.

[114] Paragraph 215.

[115] 2011 (6) SA 240 (EqC).

[116] Paragraph 108.

[117] Ibid.

[118] 2016 (6) SA 279 (CC).

consultation, part of the judgment dealt with ubuntu and Afriforum's contention that, if the interdict were not upheld, its right to culture would be violated.

The bench was divided: a majority (nine judges) supported the City Council, and a minority (two judges) supported Afriforum. Mogoeng CJ delivered the majority judgment. He prefaced his ruling with an account of the injustices that would be perpetrated by retaining the colonial and apartheid-era names of cities, towns, streets and institutions of South Africa.[119] To accede to Afriforum's objection to the renaming of streets would be to withhold the honour due to the African people and their history, and to fl in the face of the 'all-inclusive constitutional project, geared at achieving national unity and reconciliation'.[120] Underlying this opening statement was an implicit need to realise the spirit of ubuntu in order to overcome 'racial intolerance, racial marginalisation and insensitivity'.[121] The Chief Justice then went even further, however, to say that '[a]ll peace- and reconciliation-loving South Africans whose world-view is inspired by our constitutional vision *must* embrace the African philosophy of "ubuntu" ' (italics added).[122]

When Mogoeng CJ turned to decide whether or not to uphold the interdict in favour of Afriforum, he observed that the Forum's argument required evidence showing that the removal of existing street names would violate its right to culture, thereby causing emotional hurt and irreparable harm, ie, a gradual loss of place or sense of belonging.[123] The Chief Justice held that to rely on such an argument was both divisive and selfish [124] In this regard, he weighed the factors both for and against the claims made by the City Council and Afriforum: the interests of a previously disadvantaged majority as opposed to those of a white minority;[125] the national obligation to afford a sense of belonging to all those living in South Africa; the removal of any potential 'to open up wounds and divisions of the past'; the need to remedy the injustices of the past by honouring all South Africans regardless of their colour; and the degree of harm inflicte on Afriforum by the change of a mere 25 street names.[126] The preponderance of factors clearly came down in favour of the City Council.

A dissenting judgment was delivered by Cameron and Froneman JJ. They contested the idea that the Constitution imposed *an obligation* on people to observe ubuntu, although they agreed that it 'would be beneficia if all South Africans approached matters with appreciation and respect for others'.[127] In

---

[119] Paragraphs 2ff.

[120] Paragraph 6.

[121] Paragraph 11.

[122] Ibid. This obligation was repeated (para 14) in somewhat different terms: 'Through the Preamble and the entire Constitution we imposed on ourselves the duty to transform. Recognition of the injustices of the past is neither a slogan nor an empty or meaningless assertion of recognition. It heralds an obligation to actively participate not in the perpetuation, but in the eradication of the injustices of the past.'

[123] Paragraph 57.

[124] Paragraph 58.

[125] Paragraph 64.

[126] Paragraph 65.

[127] Paragraph 137.

support of this argument, they posed a question: what would be the legal consequence of failing to embrace ubuntu? They said that answer could not be a loss of constitutional protections for existing rights.[128] The two judges then posed a further rhetorical question, one that is central to the role of ubuntu in the law: should ubuntu not work to the benefi of all South Africans, rather than a particular group? In other words,

> '[s]hould members of Afriforum not be given the same kind of space when renaming streets they hold dear is at issue? Would the transformation of our society under the Constitution be endangered if they were given that space? For our part, we very much doubt it. It may merely suggest the growing power of our democracy.'[129]

Unfortunately, Cameron and Froneman did not propose a solution for accommodating all interests. The only feasible answer to that problem would seem to lie in an indaba-like process,[130] or the techniques advocated for attaining restorative justice.[131] Both of these methods would involve face-to-face encounters by all interested parties, a sympathetic listening to the views of others and (hopefully) a consensual resolution.[132]

In the three cases considered here, the concept of ubuntu played a significan role in the fina judgments. The *City of Tshwane* case came closest to using it as a full *ratio decidendi*; in *Afriforum* ubuntu was the principal, although not exclusive reason for the decision, and in *The Citizen*, it was a key aspect of the policy of national reconciliation (in both the majority and minority judgments). Ubuntu was fully define in *Afriforum*, and, as with the other two cases, was conceived in general terms of reconciliation. In addition, it was described as embodying the qualities of generosity, peace and common decency (*McBride*). Application of ubuntu was associated with the right to dignity (in all three cases), with freedom of expression (*The Citizen* and *Afriforum*) and with culture (*City of Tshwane*).

(f) Complementing the policy of restorative justice

Closely connected to reconciliation is restorative justice. Although this general policy initiative was derived from Anglo-American jurisdictions, it was found to have a close connection with one of the central tenets of ubuntu, namely, seeking a harmonious resolution to conflict [133] Ubuntu therefore provided a justificatio for introducing restorative justice to South Africa,[134] where it has been invoked to

---

[128] Hence it was argued (para 139) 'that even if Afriforum members had the kind of right they claimed — a sense of historic belonging and space — their loss of that sense can never qualify as irreparable harm. But this denial of that kind of possibly irreparable harm is not extended in our law to other infringements of rights whose loss cannot be quantifie in material terms.'

[129] Paragraph 161.

[130] See below Chapter 7.

[131] See below pp 79ff.

[132] Cf *City of Tshwane* supra para 21, where it appeared that consultations had been held with only 0 out of 76 city wards.

[133] See Rautenbach 'Legal reform of traditional courts in South Africa: exploring the links between ubuntu, restorative justice and therapeutic jurisprudence' (2015) 2 *JICL* 275ff.

[134] Perhaps the most famous South African example of a search for reconciliation was the work of the Truth and Reconciliation Commission (TRC). In order to achieve a settlement between apartheid

determine sentencing policy for crimes and, in other contexts, to achieve reconciliation and rehabilitation.[135] This section considers more specificall the use of restorative justice to divert cases from the regular criminal process by seeking to reconcile victims and offenders, and to substitute an award of monetary compensation with an apology in defamation suits.[136]

The traditional Western approach to crime concentrates on retribution for wrongdoing.[137] The procedure to determine guilt or innocence then places the state and offender in opposition to one another in an adversarial hearing. When it comes to sentencing, the state, as the notionally aggrieved party, may pursue one or a combination of goals, the main ones being punishment, deterrence and rehabilitation. In the case of civil suits, where the proceedings are also adversarial, the court is obliged to enforce the winner's rights regardless of the effect on the parties' future relationship.[138] By contrast, a restorative justice approach to both criminal and civil offences sets out to repair the harm caused by an offence rather than to impose a punishment. Hence, although offenders are still held responsible for their deeds, all the parties affected, including (potentially) members of the community, are given an opportunity to voice their interests at the hearing. The aim is to fin 'a resolution that affords healing, reparation and reintegration, and prevents future harm'.[139]

Restorative justice in its current form originated in America during the 1970s, which was a time when legal activists were campaigning to correct the many deficiencie in the Western model of criminal justice.[140] It entered South African

---

offenders and their victims, the Commission relied on forgiveness by the former and remorse and full disclosure of the truth by the latter in order to achieve reconciliation. See further Truth and Reconciliation Commission *Report* vol 1 (1999) 125ff available at http://www.justice.gov.za/Trc/report/finalreport/ olume%201.pdf [Accessed 11 April 2017]; Van Antwerpen 'Reconciliation as heterodoxy' in Llewellyn & Philpott (eds) *Restorative Justice, Reconciliation, and Peacebuilding* 91. See, too, Gade 'Restorative justice and the South African Truth and Reconciliation process' (2013) 32 *SA J Philosophy* 10ff; Metz & Gaie 'The African ethic of *ubuntu/botho*: implications for research on morality' (2010) 39 *J Moral Educ* 278.

[135] See, for instance, *Van Vuren v Minister of Correctional Services and others* 2012 (1) SACR 103 (CC) para 51; *Barnard v Minister of Justice, Constitutional Development and Correctional Services and another* 2016 (1) SACR 179 (GP) para 67.

[136] Himonga, Taylor & Pope (n10) 371ff, on the other hand, argue that one of the main functions of ubuntu has been to introduce restorative justice more generally into conflic situations, such as eviction, which 'might be ameliorated or even resolved through mediation, apology, dialogue and other restorative measures' in order to achieve reconciliation (408).

[137] This is, of course, an overgeneralisation, since, in many areas, Western legal systems also encourage compromise solutions to disputes, such as out-of-court settlements or mediation or arbitration (although usually in labour and matrimonial cases). See Van Velsen 'Procedural informality, reconciliation, and false comparisons' in Gluckman (ed) *Ideas and Procedures in African Customary Law* 137ff.

[138] Elias *Nature of African Customary Law* 268.

[139] A useful thumbnail sketch of restorative justice can be found in *S v Maluleke* 2008 (1) SACR 49 (T) para 28 (quoting Tshehla 'The restorative justice bug bites the South African criminal justice system' (2004) 17 *SA Criminal LJ* 7).

[140] Notably, overcrowded prisons and high rates of recidivism.

case law in 2000.[141] Some eight years later, the court in *S v Maluleke*[142] identifie restorative justice with the customary-law approach to dispute resolution,[143] which was taken to be an authoritative basis for applying restorative principles in South African law.[144] From there it was but a short step to linking restorative justice with ubuntu.[145]

The courts, however, did not make this connection until the decision in *Dikoko v Mokhatla*,[146] a case where the applicant had been sued for a defamatory statement made by the respondent. One of the applicant's issues concerned the quantum of compensatory damages, which the High Court had assessed to be at R110, 000. The Constitutional Court changed this ruling by ordering instead an apology, arguing in favour of this quite different form of reparation to address a need for reconciliation and social harmony.

Authority for introducing these principles into the law of defamation was found, in part, in indigenous customary law, where the main objective of the legal process was to restore social relationships when they were disrupted by the

---

[141] As an *obiter dictum* in *S v Baloyi (Minister of Justice and another intervening)* 2000 (2) SA 425 (CC) paras 17-18.

[142] 2008 (1) SACR 49 (T). See, too, *S v Shilubane* 2008 (1) SACR 295 (T).

[143] Skelton has produced many valuable works on this topic: Skelton 'Tapping indigenous knowledge: traditional conflic resolution, restorative justice and the denunciation of crime in South Africa' 2007 *Acta Juridica* 228ff; Skelton 'International trends in the re-emergence of traditional systems' in Petty & Brown (eds) *Justice for Children: challenges for policy and practice in Sub-Saharan Africa* 99ff; Skelton 'Restorative justice as a framework for juvenile justice reform: a South African perspective' (2002) 42 *British J of Criminology* 496ff; Skelton & Frank 'Conferencing in South Africa: returning to our future' in Morris & Maxwell (eds) *Restorative Justice of Juveniles: conferencing, mediation and circles* 103ff. See, too, Kgosimore 'Restorative justice as an alternative way of dealing with crime' (2002) 15 *Acta Criminologica* 69ff; Tshehla (n139) 1ff.

[144] The court found (para 39) that such countries as New Zealand and Canada had also drawn on the restorative principles of their indigenous cultures to improve local criminal justice systems. For a discussion of restorative justice and customary law, see Bekker & Van der Merwe 'Indigenous legal systems and sentencing: *S v Maluleke* 2008 (1) SACR 49 (T)' (2009) 42 *De Jure* 239ff.

[145] See further Cornell & Muvangua 'Introduction: the re-cognition of *ubuntu*' in Cornell & Muvangua (eds) *Ubuntu and the Law: African ideals and postapartheid jurisprudence* 14-15. *Maluleke's* case received the weighty support of the Constitutional Court in *M v S (Centre for Child Law Amicus Curiae)* 2007 (12) BCLR 1312 (CC), where Sachs J held (para 62) that the offender's prison time should be suspended, but with the addition of a correctional supervision order. In coming to this conclusion, the Judge commended the fact that restorative justice places crime control in the hands of the community rather than organs of state, pointing out that, if the offender were kept out of prison, she would have a better chance of social rehabilitation, and would not suffer the negative effects of prison life, loss of a job and probable damage to family networks. Himonga, Taylor & Pope (n10) 396 note that, in *Port Elizabein Municipality v Various Occupiers* 2005 (1) SA 217 (CC), while Sachs J did not refer explicitly to 'restorative justice', he advocated mediation, dialogue, compromise and reintegration into the community, thereby arguably reflectin this notion, together of course with ubuntu. This argument is supported by Sachs J's judgment in *Dikoko's* case infra para 114.

[146] 2006 (6) SA 235 (CC). In the criminal justice system, ubuntu was later linked to restorative justice via a *dictum* in *S v Sibiya* 2010 (1) SACR 284 (GNP) paras 13 and 14, where the court noted that short terms of imprisonment were likely to do young, first-tim offenders more harm than good. As a more effective punishment, the court opted instead for a suspended sentence, or a sentence based on ubuntu, which would involve a restorative form of justice, namely, reconciling the victim and offender.

violation of community norms.[147] The Court held that the same objective should be part of the common law, because monetary damages did no more than 'enlarge the hole in the defendant's pocket, something more likely to increase acrimony, push the parties apart and even cause the defendant financia ruin'.[148] In addition, the Court considered that a remedy based on the values of ubuntu would go further to restore human dignity than a monetary award in which 'the size of the victory is measured by the quantum ordered and the parties are further estranged rather than brought together by the legal process'.[149]

Another source of authority for ordering an apology was found in the Roman-Dutch remedy of an *amende honorable*.[150] In this regard, the Court held that, regardless whether the remedy was still part of the South African legal system, the law of defamation should be developed with a view to promoting ubuntu and accentuating restorative justice.[151]

> 'The goal should be to knit together shattered relationships in the community and encourage across-the-board respect for the basic norms of human and social interdependence. It is an area where courts should be proactive, encouraging apology and mutual understanding wherever possible.'[152]

The Court held that, when developing the law concerning reparations for defamation, the remedies should be reconceived 'so as to focus more on the human and less on the patrimonial dimensions of the problem'.[153] It followed that the principal goal should be to repair relationships, not punish offending behaviour.[154]

---

[147] Paragraph 68.

[148] Ibid.

[149] Ibid. The Court continued: 'The primary purpose of a compensatory measure, after all, is to restore the dignity of a plaintiff who has suffered the damage and not to punish a defendant. . . . It could indeed give better appreciation and sensitise a defendant as to the hurtful impact of his or her unlawful actions, similar to the emerging idea of restorative justice in our sentencing laws.'

[150] For the psychological benefit underlying apology, see Sachs J para 119.

[151] See Sachs J para 116: 'Although *ubuntu-botho* and the *amende honorable* are expressed in different languages intrinsic to separate legal cultures, they share the same underlying philosophy and goal. Both are directed towards promoting face-to-face encounter between the parties, so as to facilitate resolution in public of their differences and the restoration of harmony in the community. In both legal cultures the centre-piece of the process is to create conditions to facilitate the achievement, if at all possible, of an apology honestly offered, and generously accepted.'

[152] Paragraph 69. Mokgoro J held further that the focus on monetary compensation distracts from basic principles of the law on defamation: that the reparation does not, in essence, represent a proprietary loss, but rather an injury to honour, dignity and reputation, and that the courts should endeavour to restore a respectful relationship between the parties, a point that recognises the need for ubuntu. Note that, in cases of hate speech, the Equality Court may also order that an apology be made in addition to, or instead of, other remedies: s 21(2)(j) Promotion of Equality and Prevention of Unfair Discrimination Act 4 of 2000.

[153] Paragraph 112 per Sachs J. Although it has been held in principle that punitive damages should have no place in the South African law of delict, the large amounts of damages that can be sought in actions for defamation may intimidate defendants and prevent them from exercising their right to freedom of expression (*National Media Ltd and others v Bogoshi* 1998 (4) SA 1196 (SCA)). See Mukheibir 'Ubuntu and the amende honourable — a marriage between African values and medieval canon law' (2007) 28 *Obiter* 583ff.

[154] The judgment in *Dikoko* was subsequently referred to in *The Citizen 1978 (Pty) Ltd and others v McBride (Johnstone and others, Amici Curiae)* 2011 (4) SA 191 (CC) para 130. See above p 77 and

In the criminal justice field the link between ubuntu and restorative justice was further cemented by the decisions in *Afriforum v Malema*[155] and *Van Vuren v Minister of Correctional Services and others*.[156] In the latter, which was a case concerned with the granting of a parole, the Constitutional Court held that the applicant, who was serving a sentence of life imprisonment, should be considered for placement under community correction. Delivering the majority judgment, Nkabinde J remarked (*obiter*) on the connection between restorative justice and ubuntu in South African jurisprudence. She held that both principles aimed at rehabilitating offenders so that they could be 'repossessed of the fuller scope of [their] rights', thereby acknowledging their dignity.[157]

The most comprehensive and systematic implementation of ubuntu and restorative justice, however, has not been in the case law but in legislation concerning juvenile offenders. The two principles are major features of the Child Justice Act,[158] section 2(b) of which declares that the objects of the Act are to promote the spirit of ubuntu in the child justice system through, *inter alia*, 'supporting reconciliation by means of a restorative justice response'.[159]

In the cases considered above, ubuntu appeared both as *obiter dicta* (*Van Vuren*) and as major reasons for the judgments (*Afriforum* and *Dikoko*). Ubuntu was naturally associated with restorative justice and reconciliation, and indeed, its

---

see, too, *Le Roux and others v Dey* 2011 (3) SA 274 (CC). In *The Citizen*, the newspaper had described Robert McBride as a 'murderer', but the possibility of the newspaper tendering an apology in line with restorative justice was dismissed, in part because there was no personal relationship to repair and in part because the parties did not agree on the acceptability of an apology, which the Court held was one of the key conditions for reconciliation (paras 132-135). Thus Descheemaeker 'Old and new learning in the law of amende honorable' (2015) 132 *SALJ* 937 argues that ubuntu and restorative justice are not a proper consideration for the law of delict: 'the very fact one party is bringing another to court is proof that they have been unable to "get over" their dispute apart from the law'. Moreover, the courts are powerless to force a genuine reconciliation; the best they can do is 'exhort the wrongdoer to apologise to the wronged party before sending them both away'.

[155] 2011 (6) SA 240 (EqC) para 18. See further above p 76.

[156] 2012 (1) SACR 103 (CC).

[157] Paragraph 51. Nkabinde J also noted, however, that 'these interests must be balanced against those of the community, which include the right to be protected against crime'. This *dictum* was cited with approval in *Barnard v Minister of Justice, Constitutional Development and Correctional Services and another* 2016 (1) SACR 179 (GP) para 66.

[158] 75 of 2008. See Van der Merwe 'A new role for crime victims? An evaluation of restorative justice procedures in the Child Justice Act 2008' (2013) 46 *De Jure* 1022ff for a commentary on the Act.

[159] Section 51(g). Restorative justice is now regularly employed for sentencing in criminal cases, and it is officially promoted by the Department of Justice. See the booklet issued by the Department of Justice: *Restorative Justice: a road to healing* available at http://www.justice.gov.za/rj/2011rj-booklet-a5-eng.pdf. Reconciliation and restorative justice also featured in Clause 2(a) of a proposed Traditional Courts Bill (B-15 2008), where much was made of the need to 'affirm the values of the traditional justice system, and to align the goals of restorative justice and reconciliation with the Constitution'. This Bill was withdrawn, however, on 2 June 2011 and a new Bill (B1-2017) is under consideration by the National Assembly. See the explanatory summary of the Bill in *GG* 40487 N 872 of 9 December 2016 available at http://pmg-assets.s3-website-eu-west-1.amazonaws.com/b_1_-_2017_traditional_courts.pdf [Accessed 13 April 2017]. In addition, the South African Law Commission proposed a restorative justice approach for the community tribunals it had recommended establishing in urban townships: *Project 94: Alternative Dispute Resolution* (1996) Issue Paper 8 paras 3.45-3.46.

main function was to give the policy of restorative justice an indigenous cultural legitimacy by relating it to customary-law methods of dispute resolution. The courts held that, by this means, the plaintiff's dignity could be restored in defamation actions without resort to financia compensation, and criminal offenders could be kept out of the prison system, thereby improving the likelihood of maintaining their dignity and being rehabilitated back into society.

(g) Requiring fairer and more efficient service procedures

Cases in this category were generally related to administrative and executive action. As a background to the application of ubuntu in this respect, it is necessary to be aware of the reforms undertaken by government to ameliorate not only the law but also the policies regulating a public service that had been schooled under the apartheid regime. The general aim of the reforms can be summed up as a commitment to treat all people in the country with equal dignity and respect.

In the past, the government was often able to escape liability for poor decision-making and service delivery (especially the services provided to persons deemed 'black') because of deficiencie in South African administrative law.[160] A foundation for the general reform of administrative law was laid by the 1996 Constitution, s 33 of which guaranteed just administrative action.[161] Four years later, the Promotion of Administrative Justice Act (PAJA)[162] was passed. This enactment was designed to ensure administrative action that was 'lawful, reasonable and procedurally fair'.[163]

A case that fell squarely within the purview of the PAJA was *Union of Refugee Women and others v Director: Private Security Industry Regulatory Authority and others.*[164] In this instance, the Authority had refused to permit refugees from African countries to take up employment in the security industry in terms of the Private Security Industry Regulation Act,[165] a provision of which required those applying for registration to be either 'a citizen of or ha[ve] permanent resident status in South Africa'.[166] The Constitutional Court held that, although individuals without citizenship or permanent resident status were barred from registration in the security industry, an exemption clause in the Act allowed the Minister to exercise a wide discretion if 'good cause' was shown.[167] The majority judgment found that the Authority's conduct fell short of the standards of procedurally fair

---

[160] See, for example, Corder 'Crowbars and cobwebs: executive autocracy and the law in South Africa' (1989) 5 *SAJHR* 1ff; Corder 'Establishing legitimacy for the administration of justice in South Africa' (1995) 6 *Stell LR* 202-207.

[161] See *Masetlha v President of the Republic of South Africa and another* 2008 (1) SA 566 (CC) para 238: 'The Constitution ... therefore presupposes that public power will be exercised in a manner that is not arbitrary and not unduly disrespectful of the dignity of those adversely affected by the exercise.'

[162] 3 of 2000.

[163] Preamble of the PAJA.

[164] 2007 (4) SA 395 (CC) para 1. See Mokgoro 'Ubuntu, the Constitution and the rights of non-citizens' (2010) 21 *Stell LR* 227.

[165] 56 of 2001.

[166] Section 23(1).

[167] Section 1(2).

administrative action demanded by the PAJA.[168] In a separate judgment, however, Sachs J went further to hold that the Authority's blanket refusal amounted to unfair discrimination.[169] It should of its own accord have informed the applicants of the possibility of an exemption, but it had failed to do so. In his reference to ubuntu, Sachs spoke of '[t]he culture of providing hospitality to bereft strangers seeking a fresh and secure life for themselves'.[170] While these words had been used in relation to homeless South Africans, the Judge considered that they should be a reminder that we are not islands unto ourselves,[171] and, on the basis of this metaphor, proceeded to apply the principle to the state's dealings with foreigners.[172]

In *Masetlha v President of the Republic of South Africa and another,*[173] the State President had dismissed the head of the National Intelligence Agency (NIA). His action was not governed by the Labour Relations Act,[174] since the Constitution gave the President sole power to appoint and implicitly to dismiss the head of the NIA,[175] nor was the dismissal an administrative action reviewable under the PAJA.[176] It therefore appeared that, as an executive function,[177] the action was not susceptible to review.[178] According to the majority judgment, however, this apparent lacuna in the law[179] could be fille by referring to the principles of ordinary contract law.[180] But Ngcobo, Madala and Sachs JJ relied on the broader principle of fairness,[181] which Sachs J elaborated upon in the following terms:

---

[168] Paragraph 79.

[169] Paragraph 147.

[170] Citing, in this respect, Hammond-Tooke *The Roots of Black South Africa* 99, who said that, in traditional society, 'the hospitality universally enjoined towards strangers, [is] captured in the Xhosa proverb: *Unyawo alunompumlo* ("the foot has no nose"). Strangers, being isolated from their kin, and thus defenceless, were particularly under the protection of the chief and were accorded special privileges.'

[171] Paragraph 37: 'Today the concept of human interdependence and burden-sharing in relation to catastrophe is associated with the spirit of *ubuntu-botho.*' Here Sachs J cited *Port Elizabeth Municipality v Various Occupiers* 2005 (1) SA 217 (CC) para 37.

[172] Paragraph 150.

[173] 2008 (1) SA 566 (CC).

[174] 66 of 1995.

[175] Under s 209(2) of the Constitution.

[176] 3 of 2000.

[177] Under s 85(2)(e) of the Constitution.

[178] Paragraph 76.

[179] While the Constitution and the PAJA brought significant improvements to administrative law, certain loopholes remained, notably those that involved matters falling outside the definitio of 'administrative action': Kohn 'Our curious administrative law love triangle: the complex interplay between the PAJA, the Constitution and the common law' (2013) 28 *SAPL* 22-23. In *Fedsure Life Assurance and others v Greater Johannesburg Metropolitan Council and others* 1999 (1) SA 374 (CC) para 58, however, the Constitutional Court held that *any* exercise of public power, including executive power, was subject to a general principle of legality.

[180] Paragraphs 87ff.

[181] Paragraph 189.

'In this regard fair dealing and civility cannot be separated. Civility in a constitutional
sense involves more than just courtesy or good manners. It is one of the binding elements
of a constitutional democracy. It presupposes tolerance for those with whom one
disagrees and respect for the dignity of those with whom one is in dispute. Civility,
closely linked to ubuntu-botho, is deeply rooted in traditional culture, and has been
widely supported as a precondition for the good functioning of contemporary democratic
societies.'[182]

In 1997, even before adoption of the PAJA, the new ANC government had
announced a fundamental change to its policy on public service in a White Paper
on *Transforming Public Service Delivery*.[183] This initiative was described as
Batho Pele (People First), in other words, a commitment to produce 'a
transformed South African public service [that] will be judged by one criterion
above all: its effectiveness in delivering services which meet the basic needs of all
South African citizens. Public services are not a privilege in a civilised and
democratic society: they are a legitimate expectation.'[184] Henceforth all citizens
were to be treated as 'customers' because, although citizens using public services
had little or no choice over their service providers or the services on offer, they
still deserved the highest standard of treatment normally accorded customers in
the private sphere.[185]

In *Koyabe and others v Minister for Home Affairs and others (Lawyers for
Human Rights as Amicus Curiae)*,[186] the Constitutional Court discerned a direct
link between the *Batho Pele* policy and ubuntu. The firs and second applicants
were Kenyan citizens who had been denied visas, admission to South Africa and
residence permits. In their application for a review of the decision, they were met
by the claim that they had not exhausted internal remedies before instituting legal
proceedings. Mokgoro J, delivering the Court's judgment, found that, '[i]n the
context of a contemporary democratic public service like ours, where the
principles of batho pele, coupled with the values of ubuntu enjoin the public
service to treat people with respect and dignity', the procedural requirement of
exhausting internal remedies could not be treated as absolute, nor should it be
used by administrators to frustrate the efforts of aggrieved persons or shield the
administration from judicial inquiry.[187]

---

[182] Paragraph 238.

[183] *GG* 18340 GN 1459, 1 October 1997.

[184] Paragraph 1.1.1.

[185] Paragraphs 1.2ff. 'To treat citizens as "customers" implies: listening to their views and taking
account of them in making decisions about what services should be provided; treating them with
consideration and respect; making sure that the promised level and quality of service is always of the
highest standard; and responding swiftly and sympathetically when standards of service fall below
the promised standard' (para 1.2.3).

[186] 2010 (4) SA 327 (CC). See Mokgoro (n164) 227.

[187] Paragraph 62. Another decision linking the *Batho Pele* policy with ubuntu was *Joseph and
others v City of Johannesburg and others* 2010 (4) SA 55 (CC), this time with regard to a local
authority's disconnection of electricity supply to the occupants of a block of flat owned by a private
individual. Although there was no direct contractual relationship between the City and the
consumers, the Court held that, as customers, they were entitled to electricity as a basic human right,
and could therefore claim an administrative-law remedy (under s 3(1) of the PAJA) to demand
procedural fairness if the City wished to terminate services. When delivering the Court's judgment,

In these the cases, ubuntu was used in *obiter dicta* to supplement the just and fair administrative action prescribed in both the Constitution and the PAJA, and to support the government's *Batho Pele* policy (*Koyabe*). It was accordingly associated with words such as fairness (*Masethla*), non-discrimination (*Union of Refugee Women*), dignity, respect and civility. By eschewing procedural technicality (*Union of Refugee Women* and *Koyabe*) and by protecting the more vulnerable members of society (refugees, employees and tenants), ubuntu thereby contributed to more equitable outcomes.

(h) Ensuring equality

In view of South Africa's long history of racial discrimination, the Constitution declared equality to be not only a cardinal value[188] but also a justiciable right.[189] Along with dignity, equality can therefore be considered a cynosure of South Africa's constitutional order.

Hoffmann v South African Airways[190] was the first case in which ubuntu was invoked in support of the right to equality. The appellant in this matter had been refused employment as a cabin attendant by South African Airways on the ground of his HIV positive status. He argued that he had been unfairly discriminated against contrary to the equality provisions in s 9 of the Bill of Rights. On an appeal to the Constitutional Court, it was held that discrimination against persons living with HIV harmed one of most vulnerable groups in society, since they were subject to intense prejudice. SAA's refusal to engage him could therefore be viewed both as an infringement of the right to equality and as an assault upon dignity. Ngcobo J held that '[p]eople who are living with HIV must be treated with compassion and understanding. We must show ubuntu towards them.'[191]

The next case concerning ubuntu and equality was *National Lotteries Board v South African Education and Environment Project*.[192] In this instance, the Supreme Court of Appeal reviewed the National Lotteries Board's rejection of applications by two registered charities for financial grants from the Lottery's Trust Fund on the ground that they did not comply with the requisite guidelines. Although not included in the guidelines, one reason for the Lotteries' declining the second respondent's application was the difference between the racial composition of the board and the community it intended to assist. Cachalia JA found the Board's overall approach to the applications formulaic. With specific reference to its reason for declining the second respondent's application, he held that the Board had replicated the apartheid era welfare policy of racial discrimination, and that '[t]o repeat that error would be so inimical to the founding values of our

---

Skweyiya J observed in a footnote (para 46 fn 39) that *Batho Pele* gave 'practical expression to the constitutional value of *ubuntu*', meaning that the government was required 'to act in a manner that is responsive, respectful and fair when fulfilling its constitutional and statutory obligations'.

[188] Subsections 1(a) and (b) respectively.

[189] Section 9.

[190] 2001 (1) SA 1 (CC).

[191] Paragraph 38. The Court went on to say that: 'They must not be condemned to "economic death" by the denial of equal opportunity in employment. This is particularly true in our country, where the incidence of HIV infection is said to be disturbingly high.'

[192] 2012 (4) SA 504 (SCA)

Constitution — non-racialism, equality and human dignity (as it relates to ubuntu) — that it is an unimaginable basis for public policy'.[193]

The fina case, *South African Police Service v Solidarity obo Barnard*,[194] involved equal access to promotion. The respondent claimed she had been unfairly discriminated against by reason of an affirmative action policy in the police service. Her claim did not succeed. For purposes of securing socio-economic rights, the Court read the rights of dignity and equality together, reasoning that the Constitution provides the foundation for a society that must take seriously its responsibilities to promote equality and respect for all. To this end, it contains specifi provisions aimed at ensuring an affirmative and substantive equality:[195] '[t]hese measures can enhance the dignity of individuals, even those who may be adversely affected by them'.[196] Dignity must therefore be read in two ways: first the manner in which individuals interact with others in society, whether members of advantaged or disadvantaged groups; secondly, fulfilmen of a duty to embrace 'every other individual in a manner that extends beyond the interests of our more parochial selves'.[197]

The aspect of this case pertinent to ubuntu can be found in the concurring minority judgment of Van der Westhuizen J. When analysing the concept of equality, he asked whether Ms Barnard 'was treated as a mere means to reach an end, on the basis of her race only'.[198] Although readily accepting that each person should be treated as an end in herself, and that the concept of dignity entails the individual's sense of self-esteem and entitlement to develop fully her talents,[199] the Judge found that Ms Barnard was 'also a member of a society deeply scarred by past and present inequality'. Accordingly, he held that: [a]n atomistic approach to individuals, self-worth and identity is not appropriate. This court has recognised that we are not islands unto ourselves. The individual, as the bearer of the right to dignity, should not be understood as an isolated and unencumbered being.'[200] Van der Westhuizen J therefore found in favour of the SAPS, since the collectivist attributes of dignity mean 'that we are "social beings whose humanity is expressed through . . . relationships with others"' [a principle finding resonance in the South African idea of *Ubuntu*, which foregrounds 'interdependence of the members of a community'.[201]

---

[193] Paragraph 17. See, too, above pp 66-67 *NM v Presiding Officer of Children's Court, Krugersdorp, and others* 2013 (4) SA 379 (GSJ), which dealt with s 156(1)(e) of the Children's Act 38 of 2005. The court held that a literal interpretation of this provision would produce the curious result of creating different categories of dependent children, which would constitute unjustifie discrimination, and would not be in keeping with the spirit of ubuntu (para 24).

[194] 2014 (6) SA 123 (CC).

[195] Section 9(2).

[196] Paragraph 175 per Van der Westhuizen J.

[197] Ibid.

[198] Paragraph 171.

[199] Paragraph 173.

[200] Paragraph 172: 'Because the right to human dignity affirms the intrinsic worth of every person, it is foundational to several other rights in the Bill of Rights. The right to and value of dignity therefore also inform constitutional interpretation and adjudication at multiple levels.'

[201] Paragraph 174.

In these four cases, ubuntu was referred to only by way of *obiter dicta* and had no marked outcome of any of the judgments. While it was mentioned by the courts mainly in order to secure the right to equality, it was also related to dignity (construed in a collectivist sense in the *SAPS* case) and public policy (*National Lotteries Board*). Ubuntu was interpreted to mean compassion, understanding (*Hoffmann*) and interdependence (*SAPS*).

(i) Promoting cultural diversity

Prior to its new Constitution, only Western culture and religions enjoyed the benefit of state support in South Africa (although limited recognition was given to African customary law).[202] The Constitution, however, brought about a far-reaching change by requiring equal respect and protection for the cultures and religions of all individuals and groups.[203]

In terms of this new dispensation, *Ryland v Edros*[204] began the (still unfinished process of securing legal recognition for marriages celebrated under Islamic law. Since colonial times, the potentially polygamous nature of these, and other such religious marriages, had been denied full legal effect on the grounds that they were contrary to South African public policy and *boni mores*.[205] Farlam J declared that a fresh approach was required. On the basis of the spirit of communality and interdependence in ubuntu,[206] he held that the plural nature of South African society, together with the new principles of equality and tolerance of diversity, meant that no one group was entitled to impose its values upon another. It followed that a marriage contract could be deemed offensive to public policy or *boni mores* only if it violated the values of 'all right-thinking people in the community' at large and not simply one section.[207]

Kievits Kroon Country Estate (Pty) Ltd v Mmoledi and others[208] dealt with a similar issue but in a different context: the need to understand and tolerate a particular individual's cultural/religious beliefs. Mrs Mmoledi had been dismissed for staying away from work in order to attend a traditional healer's course. The Commission for Conciliation, Mediation and Arbitration[209] found her dismissal unfair, noting that she was deeply afraid of suffering serious misfortune if she did not respond to the call of her ancestors. This decision was upheld on appeal. The Labour Appeal Court held that: 'Accommodating one another is nothing else but "*botho*" or "*ubuntu*" which is part of our heritage as a society.'[210]

In these two cases, ubuntu again appeared by way of *obiter dicta*. In both cases, it was associated with the constitutional freedom of religion and right to culture,

---

[202] Bennett *Customary Law in South Africa* 188ff.
[203] Section 9(3) as read with s 15 (freedom of religion), and ss 30 and 31 (right to culture).
[204] 1997 (2) SA 690 (C) at 708.
[205] *Ismail v Ismail* 1983 (1) SA 1006 (A).
[206] As featured in the epilogue to the Interim Constitution and *S v Makwanyane and another* 1995 (3) SA 391 (CC) para 224.
[207] Page 707.
[208] (2012) 33 ILJ 2812 (LAC) para 26.
[209] Established under the Labour Relations Act 66 of 1995.
[210] Paragraph 26.

which required tolerance and understanding if the practices and beliefs of others were to be accommodated in a pluralist society.[211]

(j) Setting new norms of conduct

In the following fiv cases, the courts drew on the concept of ubuntu to set certain standards of acceptable behaviour for normative regimes that do not fall within the strict purview of the law. In the firs two cases, ubuntu was linked to morality and the common-law concept of *boni mores*,[212] and in the three thereafter, the broad fiel of ethics.

In *Fosi v Road Accident Fund and another*,[213] a parent claimed damages for loss of the support of a deceased child. Although the action could have been based on the common law, Dlodlo J noted that he was required by the Constitution to apply customary law 'when that law is applicable'.[214] He accordingly held that a child's failure to maintain his or her parents is, according to customary law, not only *contra bonos mores* but also morally reprehensible. Such a child 'would be ostracised and be looked down upon as a person who has no *ubuntu*'.[215]

JT v Road Accident Fund[216] was another case involving a dependant's action for loss of support. In this instance, although the child had been adopted by her grandmother, her natural father had continued to provide her with maintenance. When the father died the grandmother sued the RAF on the child's behalf for loss of his support. The RAF claimed that the deceased father's legal obligation of support was extinguished when the adoption took place. The court, however, held that, when the father decided to maintain his child, he undertook a continuing duty of support. This ruling was supported by reasoning that a duty of support between *de facto* family members was an area in which the law reflecte the moral views of society, and that the common law should be developed to include this norm.[217] In this respect, the court cited with approval Dlodlo's judgment in *Fosi's* case, where ubuntu was linked to the duty to support.[218]

---

[211] *Kukard and others v Molapo Technology (Pty) Ltd* [2006] 4 BLLR 334 (LC) was another case concerned with tolerance and understanding, but not falling within the category of cultural or religious diversity. It dealt with a group of employees wanting to celebrate a national holiday of especial significanc to South Africans, 'a historic event in the history of the land'. The Labour Court held (para 41) that 'the values of dignity, freedom and ubuntu' required employers to respect their employees' desire.

[212] As in *Ryland v Edros* 1997 (2) SA 690 (C) at 708.

[213] 2008 (3) SA 560 (C).

[214] Section 211(3).

[215] Paragraph 17.

[216] 2015 (1) SA 609 (GJ).

[217] Paragraphs 29-31. A case similarly concerned with a moral rather than a legal issue was *Badenhorst v Badenhorst* 2005 (2) SA 253 (C) para 24. Here a married couple's claim to the husband's parents' farm was found to be an abuse of parental generosity. The court spoke of the wife's claim as 'an irresistible temptation of greed', and added that 'her attitude in this regard undermined *ubuntu*, that godly value with which all human beings are ordained' (para 24).

[218] Paragraph 17. See too the judge's reference (para 26) to a *dictum* by Grogan AJ in *Jacobs v RAF* 2010 (3) SA 263 (SE)): 'a culturally imbedded notion of "family", constituted as being a network of relationships of reciprocal nurture and support, informs the common law's appetite to embrace, as worthy of protection, the assumption of duties of support and the reciprocal right to claim support,

The following trio of cases involved the ethical duties of a judge, an attorney and an arbitrator. *Pharmaceutical Society of South Africa and others v Tshabalala-Msimang and another NNO; New Clicks South Africa (Pty) Ltd v Minister of Health and another*[219] concerned, *inter alia*, a lower court's undue delay in giving judgment on an application for leave to appeal. In the Supreme Court of Appeal, Harms JA referred to the principle 'justice delayed is justice denied', holding that the spirit of ubuntu should apply to both the relationship between courts and between organs of state and citizens, and that courts have an ethical duty to ensure speedy judgment.[220]

Law Society, Northern Provinces v Mogami and others,[221] related to an action against the respondent, an attorney, which called for his suspension or removal from the roll for various acts of misconduct and unprofessional behaviour. The Supreme Court of Appeal ordered his suspension from practice and a reprimand. It observed that, while the respondent may not have infringed any written rule of ethics, his ethical duties extended to observation of the basic principles of ubuntu.[222]

In *National Union of Metalworkers of SA and another v Wainwright NO and others*,[223] the Labour Court was called on to review an arbitration award, in which it was clear that the arbitrator had not only failed in his duties as an arbitrator but had also ignored the overriding principles of fairness and social justice, attributes required of all arbitrators. The court held that social justice was based on treating all people equally with dignity and respect, which in the South African context could be summed up as ubuntu.[224]

The references to ubuntu in these cases constituted *obiter dicta*, and could not be considered sufficiently significan to have influence the law, since they fell outside the ambit of legal norms. Nonetheless, the normative regimes in question — public policy, *boni mores* and morality (*Fosi* and *JT*), ethics and basic fairness (*National Union of Metalworkers*) — are frequently invoked by the courts to help interpret legal duties (the duty of support in *Fosi* and *JT*) or to fil gaps where no strict rule of law is applicable (*Pharmaceutical Society of South Africa, Law Society* and *National Union of Metalworkers*).

---

by persons who are in relationships akin to that of a family. This norm is not parochial but rather is likely to be universal, it certainly is consonant both with norms derived from the Roman-Dutch tradition . . . and, no less, from norms derived from African tradition, not least of all as exemplifie by the spirit of *Ubuntu*. . . .'

[219] 2005 (3) SA 238 (SCA) para 39.

[220] Paragraph 39.

[221] 2010 (1) SA 186 (SCA).

[222] Paragraph 22.

[223] (2015) 36 ILJ 2097 (LC).

[224] Paragraphs 41-43. Cf *Tlale NO and another v Momentum Group Limited and others* [2016] JOL 35531 (FB), where an attorney argued that it would be wrong and contrary to the ethics of ubuntu to attach a debtor's movable goods in excess of 'necessary furniture and household utensils'. He also alluded to the relative inequalities of the parties: a large corporation and a poor widow. This argument did not succeed, and it was noted that a creditor also has rights.

3 CONCLUSION: ANALYSIS OF THE CASES

This chapter surveyed, in broad outline, the South African courts' use of ubuntu, paying particular attention to the legal/factual contexts in which it was invoked and the purposes to which it was put. From these readings, we can now return to the aim of this inquiry: to discover the functions of ubuntu, the meanings attributed to it and its weight in the legal system.

The appearance of ubuntu in the 1993 Interim Constitution[225] gave it no sure basis as a legal term, for the unusual context — an epilogue, an apparent afterthought — seemed to imply that it was merely an aspirational ideal. The maiden decision of the Constitutional Court, *S v Makwanyane and another,*[226] did not help to counter this inference. Despite the Judges' frequent references to ubuntu, no attempt was made to clarify its position in the law.

It was only later, in the Constitutional Court decision on *Azanian Peoples Organisation (AZAPO) and others v President of the Republic of South Africa and others,*[227] that ubuntu was acknowledged as a legal principle (and then only indirectly). In terms of the epilogue to the Interim Constitution, Parliament had been obliged to put in place legislation to regulate the granting of amnesties to apartheid offenders.[228] It accordingly promulgated a Promotion of National Unity and Reconciliation Act,[229] under which a Truth and Reconciliation Commission (TRC) was created, which in turn established a special Committee to hear amnesty applications.[230] The applicants in the *AZAPO* case sought a declaration that grants of amnesty by the Committee were unconstitutional on the ground, *inter alia*, that they denied the applicants a constitutional right of access to the courts to have their grievances against apartheid offenders heard.[231] The Court, however, held that the epilogue itself[232] permitted violation of the right, and that this instrument had full legal effect on a par with other provisions of the Constitution.[233] Hence, as part of the epilogue, ubuntu achieved a legal status.[234]

What then is the nature of this status? Have the courts' many references to ubuntu constituted sufficient authority to give any of the decisions the obligatory force of binding precedents? To begin with the second question: since the decisions in *Makwanyane* and *AZAPO*, ubuntu has been invoked in virtually all

---

[225] For the text of which see above p 60 fn 2.

[226] 1995 (3) SA 391 (CC).

[227] 1996 (4) SA 671 (CC).

[228] 'In order to advance such reconciliation and reconstruction, amnesty shall be granted in respect of acts, omissions and offences associated with political objectives and committed in the course of the conflict of the past. To this end, Parliament under this Constitution shall adopt a law ... providing for the mechanisms, criteria and procedures, including tribunals, if any, through which such amnesty shall be dealt with at any time after the law has been passed.'

[229] 34 of 1995.

[230] As define   in s 20(2) and (3) of the Act.

[231] Section 22.

[232] See p 60 fn 2 above.

[233] Referring here to s 232(4) of the Constitution which provided that the epilogue was not to 'have a lesser status than any other provision of this Constitution'.

[234] Confirmin   what was said about ubuntu as a legal concept in the previous Chapter.

field of law,[235] but nearly always by way of *obiter dicta* in support of existing rules or principles. In none of the cases, with two possible exceptions,[236] did ubuntu provide the main reason for a judgment. Furthermore, although most of the judgments emanated from the highest courts in the land, they followed no consistent pattern of facts or legal circumstance to warrant the formation of a prevailing opinion indicating when ubuntu must be applied. In consequence, we have no binding precedent to determine when ubuntu is applicable. This matter still lies within the courts' discretion.

As to the firs question: it appears clear from the cases that ubuntu did not constitute a legal *rule*. Its very generality and ambiguity has made it resistant to any such designation.[237] Instead, the courts applied ubuntu in much the same way as they do with guiding principles (such as fairness and good faith)[238] or values (such as dignity).[239] This reading of the judgments, however, should not be taken to suggest that ubuntu lacks legal weight, nor does it allow an inference that ubuntu gives rise to enforceable rights and duties.[240]

---

[235] Notable exceptions are tax and company law. Ubuntu was, however, mentioned in the influentia King *Report on Corporate Governance in South Africa* III (2009). In one of the key aspects of the *Report*, ubuntu is referred to in connection with ethical leadership which is characterised as the 'values of responsibility, accountability, fairness and transparency . . . based on moral duties that fin expression in the concept of ubuntu' (para 8). Ubuntu was also mentioned in *South African Broadcasting Corporation Ltd and another v Mpofu* [2009] 4 All SA 169 (GSJ) paras 63-66 (a case concerning directors' duties), and has received extensive discussion in the context of black economic empowerment. See, for example, Schoeman 'The co-operative as an appropriate enterprise for black economic empowerment' (2006) 1 *J for Estate Planning Law* 23ff.

[236] *City of Tshwane Metropolitan Municipality v Afriforum and another* 2016 (6) SA 279 (CC) and *Afriforum and another v Malema and another* 2011 (6) SA 240 (EqC).

[237] See above pp 37-38.

[238] These distinctions correspond with those proposed by Dworkin *Taking Rights Seriously* 22ff. According to Dworkin, rules dictate a specifi result; principles (such as good faith) set out guides for behaviour without necessarily determining the result, and so may conflic with one another without affecting their validity. Policies establish goals to be attained, usually with reference to the prevailing socio-economic circumstances of a particular society. Dworkin also distinguishes rules, principles and policies on the basis of form: their level of particularity or generality and the corresponding degree of precision or vagueness. Cf Twining & Miers *How To Do Things with Rules* 132ff.

[239] Values are usually of a greater degree of generality and vagueness than rules or principles. They can be divided into two categories: whether their worth is intrinsic (such as promoting life, equality, care for others) or extrinsic (such as promoting a desirable result).

[240] See above pp 45ff regarding ubuntu and sanctions. The designation of a norm as a 'rule' involves its inclusion in a self-standing system that subjects human conduct to governance of a regime requiring such principles as predictability, consistency and non-retroactivity. See Fuller *The Morality of Law* 33-94. At present, use of ubuntu is neither predictable nor entirely consistent. Twining & Miers (n238) 132 and 139 point out that norms can be used in two ways in legal argument: normatively (ie prescriptively) to determine acts and behaviour, or as a justificatio for action or behaviour. The courts have used ubuntu mainly as a justification

The outstanding exception to this observation is the case of *City of Tshwane v Afriforum and another,*[241] where Mogoeng CJ said that ubuntu *must be observed* by all South Africans. Although forcefully pronounced, this statement should be read in light of the minority judgment of Froneman and Cameron JJ.[242] They posed the as yet unanswered question: what legal consequences would flo from failure to comply with a duty of ubuntu? Thus, notwithstanding Mogoeng's judgment, ubuntu is better regarded as a generalised legal norm, one lacking the specificit of a rule.

This being the case, what species of legal norm is ubuntu? Sometimes it is spoken of as a principle,[243] and sometimes as a policy or value.[244] The courts often use these words interchangeably. To some extent, context dictates the term to be used. For instance, when used in conjunction with good faith, ubuntu appears as a principle; when used together with justice it appears as a value[245] and, when talked about in the abstract, it is described more broadly as an ideal or as a philosophy.[246]

Given the lack of agreement about terminology, or indeed any special interest in the issue, we may well ask whether description as a principle, value or philosophy really matters. Doubtless, the precise use of terms helps to specify their function, but, as far as ubuntu is concerned, exact definitio is not essential. It is sufficient to think of the concept simply as a metanorm, one in an early stage of development with a flexibl (and hence indeterminate) form and meaning. This indeterminacy should not be seen as a fla in the concept: it is a necessary condition for norms that have to apply to a broad range of different situations. Parallels in the common law are good faith and equity, and, as it happens, the courts have ascribed a role to ubuntu much the same as that played by these two concepts.

---

[241] 2016 (6) SA 279 (CC).

[242] Paragraphs 79ff.

[243] Cases in which ubuntu could be interpreted in this way are: *Derby-Lewis v Minister of Justice and Correctional Services and others* 2015 (2) SACR 412 (GP); *Savage and others v Sisters of the Holy Cross, Cape Province and others* 2015 (6) SA 1 (WCC); *S v Matiwane* [2016] JOL 35378 (WCC); *S v Mandela* [2001] JOL 7754 (C); *S v Makwanyane and another* 1995 (3) SA 391 (CC) para 374; *Everfresh Market Virginia (Pty) Ltd v Shoprite Checkers (Pty) Ltd* 2012 (1) SA 256 (CC); *Law Society, Northern Provinces v Mogami and others* 2010 (1) SA 186 (SCA).

[244] Cases in which ubuntu could be interpreted as such are: *Makate v Vodacom (Pty) Ltd* 2016 (4) SA 121 (CC); *S v Makwanyane and another* 1995 (3) SA 391 (CC) paras 131 and 266; *Everfresh Market Virginia (Pty) Ltd v Shoprite Checkers (Pty) Ltd* 2012 (1) SA 256 (CC); *Joseph and others v City of Johannesburg and others* 2010 (4) SA 55 (CC); *Advtech Resourcing (Pty) Ltd t/a Communicate Personnel Group v Kuhn and another* 2008 (2) SA 375 (C); *Koyabe and others v Minister for Home Affairs and others (Lawyers for Human Rights as Amicus Curiae)* 2010 (4) SA 327 (CC).

[245] Writers who refer to ubuntu as a value include: Kroeze 'Doing things with values: the role of constitutional values in constitutional interpretation' (2001) 12 *Stell LR* 268; Van Niekerk '*Amende honorable* and *ubuntu*: an intersection of *ars boni et aequi* in African and Roman-Dutch jurisprudence?' (2013) 19 *Fundamina* 409; Tshoose 'The emerging role of the constitutional value of ubuntu for informal social security in South Africa' (2009) 3 *Afr J Legal Stud* 12. Cf Metz 'African values and human rights as two sides of the same coin: a reply to Oyowe' (2014) 14 *AHRLJ* 307.

[246] Cornell & Van Marle 'Exploring ubuntu: tentative reflections (2005) 5 *AHRLJ* 196; *Dikoko v Mokhatla* 2006 (6) SA 235 (CC) para 115.

We can turn now to consider the legal terms associated with ubuntu. These associations give useful clues about the way in which it has been accommodated in mainstream South African law, and, at the same time, they help to determine the general functions being performed by ubuntu. At least ten constitutional rights have been linked to ubuntu: equality,[247] privacy,[248] freedom of expression,[249] access to courts,[250] property,[251] housing,[252] work,[253] culture,[254] religion,[255] protest[256] and most often dignity.[257] Ubuntu has been linked to only one right in common- and customary-law: the support that can be claimed from kin and family.[258] Otherwise, it was associated with general principles of common

---

[247] *South African Police Service v Solidarity obo Barnard* 2014 (6) SA 123 (CC) para 175; *Hoffmann v South African Airways* 2001 (1) SA 1 (CC) para 38; *MM v MN and another* 2013 (4) SA 415 (CC) para 64.

[248] *The Citizen 1978 (Pty) Ltd and others v McBride (Johnstone and others, Amici Curiae)* 2011 (4) SA 191 (CC); *Tshabalala-Msimang and another v Makhanya and others* 2008 (6) SA 102 (W).

[249] *The Citizen* supra; *Tshabalala-Msimang* supra; *Afriforum and another v Malema and another* 2011 (6) SA 240 (EqC).

[250] *Crossley and others v National Commissioner of South African Police Service and others* [2004] 3 All SA 436 (T).

[251] *Langebaan Ratepayers' and Residents' Association v Dormell Properties 391 (Pty) Ltd and others* 2013 (1) SA 37 (WCC); *Savage and others v Sisters of the Holy Cross, Cape Province and others* 2015 (6) SA 1 (WCC).

[252] *City of Johannesburg v Rand Properties (Pty) Limited* 2007 (1) SA 78 (W); *City of Johannesburg Metropolitan Municipality v Blue Moonlight Properties 39 (Pty) Ltd and another* 2012 (2) SA 104 (CC).

[253] *City of Johannesburg* supra; *Advtech Resourcing (Pty) Ltd t/a Communicate Personnel Group v Kuhn and another* 2008 (2) SA 375 (C).

[254] *City of Tshwane Metropolitan Municipality v Afriforum and another* 2016 (6) SA 279 (CC) para 16.

[255] *Ryland v Edros* 1997 (2) SA 690 (C).

[256] *Bophuthatswana Broadcasting Corporation v Ramosa and others* [1997] JOL 283 (B).

[257] *Masetlha v President of the Republic of South Africa and another* 2008 (1) SA 566 (CC); *Koyabe and others v Minister for Home Affairs and others (Lawyers for Human Rights as Amicus Curiae)* 2010 (4) SA 327 (CC); *Bertie Van Zyl (Pty) Ltd and another v Minister for Safety and Security and others* 2010 (2) SA 181 (CC); *S v Makwanyane and another* 1995 (3) SA 391 (CC); *Van Vuren v Minister of Correctional Services and others* 2012 (1) SACR 103 (CC); *South African Police Service v Solidarity obo Barnard* 2014 (6) SA 123 (CC); *Dikoko v Mokhatla* 2006 (6) SA 235 (CC); *The Citizen 1978 (Pty) Ltd and others v Mcbride (Johnstone and others, Amici Curiae)* 2011 (4) SA 191 (CC); *Manyatshe v M&G Media Ltd & others* [2009] JOL 24238 (SCA); *Afriforum and another v Malema and another* 2011 (6) SA 240 (EqC); *Tshabalala-Msimang and another v Makhanya and others* 2008 (6) SA 102 (W); *MM v MN and another* 2013 (4) SA 415 (CC); *Advtech Resourcing (Pty) Ltd t/a Communicate Personnel Group v Kuhn and another* 2008 (2) SA 375 (C).

[258] *Fosi v Road Accident Fund and another* 2008 (3) SA 560 (C); *JT v Road Accident Fund* 2015 (1) SA 609 (GJ); *Bhe and others v Magistrate, Khayelitsha, and others (Commission for Gender Equality as Amicus Curiae); Shibi v Sithole and others; South African Human Rights Commission and another v President of the Republic of South Africa and another* 2005 (1) SA 580 (CC); *NM v Presiding Officer of Children's Court, Krugersdorp, and others* 2013 (4) SA 379 (GSJ); *MM v MN and another* 2013 (4) SA 415 (CC).

law, namely, reasonableness,[259] good faith,[260] fairness, justice and equity,[261] public policy (or public interest),[262] and of course *boni mores* and ethics.[263] What is more, ubuntu supported and was read together with a more recent arrival in South African law, restorative justice.[264]

Ubuntu's connection with these general concepts indicates one of its principal means of access to mainstream South African law: norms with a broad and indefinit scope of reference facilitate the deployment of new concepts into a legal system.[265] The indeterminacy of such terms as *boni mores*, good faith and public policy leaves them open to the exercise of judicial discretion to which courts must resort in the absence of a rule clearly applicable to the facts in issue. To preclude the appearance of subjectivity, they usually refer to social and moral factors extrinsic to positive law.[266] Ubuntu is one such factor.

Judicial discretion can, of course, be invoked in many different situations and in all branches of the law. Hence, whenever courts have to depart from the strict letter of the law, they can rely on existing general principles, such as equity or good faith. They can use these terms in tandem with ubuntu,[267] or, as ubuntu is now becoming better established as an independent principle in its own right, ubuntu alone.[268]

---

[259] *South African Police Service v Solidarity obo Barnard* 2014 (6) SA 123 (CC); *Pharmaceutical Society of South Africa and others v Tshabalala-Msimang and another NNO; New Clicks South Africa (Pty) Ltd v Minister of Health and another* 2005 (3) SA 238 (SCA); *Langebaan Ratepayers' and Residents' Association v Dormell Properties 391 (Pty) Ltd and others* 2013 (1) SA 37 (WCC); *Savage and others v Sisters of the Holy Cross, Cape Province and others* 2015 (6) SA 1 (WCC); *City of Johannesburg Metropolitan Municipality v Blue Moonlight Properties 39 (Pty) Ltd and another* 2012 (2) SA 104 (CC); *Barkhuizen v Napier* 2007 (5) SA 323 (CC).

[260] *Barkhuizen* supra; *Everfresh Market Virginia (Pty) Ltd v Shoprite Checkers (Pty) Ltd* 2012 (1) SA 256 (CC); *Dula Investments (Pty) Ltd v Woolworths (Pty) Limited* [2013] JOL 30323 (KZD); *Burmbuild (Pty) Ltd v Ndzama* [2013] 2 All SA 399 (ECG); *Advtech Resourcing (Pty) Ltd t/a Communicate Personnel Group v Kuhn and another* 2008 (2) SA 375 (C).

[261] *Masetlha v President of the Republic of South Africa and another* 2008 (1) SA 566 (CC); *Joseph and others v City of Johannesburg and others* 2010 (4) SA 55 (CC); *Port Elizabeth Municipality v Various Occupiers* 2005 (1) SA 217 (CC); *Everfresh* supra; *Resnick v Government of the Republic of South Africa and another* 2014 (2) SA 337 (WCC); *Barkhuizen* supra.

[262] *Burmbuild (Pty) Ltd v Ndzama* [2013] 2 All SA 399 (ECG); *Fosi v Road Accident Fund and another* 2008 (3) SA 560 (C); *Port Elizabeth Municipality* supra; *The Citizen 1978 (Pty) Ltd and others v McBride (Johnstone and others, Amici Curiae)* 2011 (4) SA 191 (CC); *Barkhuizen* supra; *Advtech Resourcing (Pty) Ltd t/a Communicate Personnel Group v Kuhn and another* 2008 (2) SA 375 (C); *Ryland v Edros* 1997 (2) SA 690 (C); *S v Makwanyane and another* 1995 (3) SA 391 (CC).

[263] *Law Society, Northern Provinces v Mogami and others* 2010 (1) SA 186 (SCA) para 22.

[264] *Dikoko v Mokhatla* 2006 (6) SA 235 (CC); *Afriforum and another v Malema and another* 2011 (6) SA 240 (EqC); *Van Vuren v Minister of Correctional Services and others* 2012 (1) SACR 103 (CC).

[265] See the discussion of legal transplants above pp 15ff, especially Graziadei 'Comparative law as the study of transplants and receptions' in Reimann & Zimmermann (eds) *The Oxford Handbook of Comparative Law* 468-469.

[266] See below p 105.

[267] As in Mogoeng J's judgment in *The Citizen 1978 (Pty) Ltd and others v McBride (Johnstone and others, Amici Curiae)* 2011 (4) SA 191 (CC).

[268] As in *City of Tshwane Metropolitan Municipality v Afriforum and another* 2016 (6) SA 279 (CC).

When we turn to consider the functions of ubuntu, it is evident that most were concerned with advancing the cause of constitutional transformation whether by promoting reconciliation, unity, equality and cultural diversity, or, more explicitly, by developing the law in line with the Bill of Rights.[269] In some cases, the effect of applying ubuntu was, paradoxically, to limit rights,[270] which strictly speaking should be regulated by s 36(1) of the Constitution.[271] Hence rights such as property[272] were limited to the extent that they had to be exercised so as to make allowance for the interests of others.

Aside from reinforcing South Africa's constitutional enterprise, ubuntu had a major political function, although one that was generally unacknowledged: to domesticate the Constitution by giving it a cultural legitimacy. This function operated in two ways. One was to read certain aspects of the Constitution, which is in essence the product of Western law, together with ubuntu to show that the Constitution includes indigenous African ideas. So, for example, the courts have frequently associated ubuntu with restorative justice,[273] reconciliation, unity and social harmony.[274] Another particular associate was dignity, because it is similar, although not identical, to ubuntu:[275] the similarity appears in the high level of

---

[269] In terms of s 39(2) of the Constitution. See *Advtech Resourcing (Pty) Ltd t/a Communicate Personnel Group v Kuhn and another* 2008 (2) SA 375 (C); *Dikoko v Mokhatla* 2006 (6) SA 235 (CC); *Burmbuild (Pty) Ltd v Ndzama* [2013] 2 All SA 399 (ECG); *Savage and others v Sisters of the Holy Cross, Cape Province and others* 2015 (6) SA 1 (WCC); *MM v MN and another* 2013 (4) SA 415 (CC); *Bhe and others v Magistrate, Khayelitsha, and others (Commission for Gender Equality as Amicus Curiae); Shibi v Sithole and others; South African Human Rights Commission and another v President of the Republic of South Africa and another* 2005 (1) SA 580 (CC); *Everfresh Market Virginia (Pty) Ltd v Shoprite Checkers (Pty) Ltd* 2012 (1) SA 256 (CC); *JT v Road Accident Fund* 2015 (1) SA 609 (GJ).

[270] As with freedom of expression in *Afriforum and another v Malema and another* 2011 (6) SA 240 (EqC).

[271] 'The rights in the Bill of Rights may be limited only in terms of law of general application to the extent that the limitation is reasonable and justifiabl in an open and democratic society based on human dignity, equality and freedom, taking into account all relevant factors, including — (a) the nature of the right; (b) the importance of the purpose of the limitation; (c) the nature and extent of the limitation; (d) the relation between the limitation and its purpose; and (e) less restrictive means to achieve the purpose.'

[272] For example, *Savage and others v Sisters of the Holy Cross, Cape Province and others* 2015 (6) SA 1 (WCC). See further on property, Van der Walt & Dhliwayo 'The notion of absolute and exclusive ownership: a doctrinal analysis' (2017) 134 *SALJ* 34ff.

[273] See especially *S v Makwanyane and another* 1995 (3) SA 391 (CC) paras 225, 308.

[274] Which are goals required by the epilogue to the Interim and the Preamble to the Final Constitutions. See, too, restorative justice in this regard: *Van Vuren v Minister of Correctional Services and others* 2012 (1) SACR 103 (CC); *South African Police Service v Solidarity obo Barnard* 2014 (6) SA 123 (CC); *S v Makwanyane and another* 1995 (3) SA 391 (CC); *Dikoko v Mokhatla* 2006 (6) SA 235 (CC); *Azanian Peoples Organisation (AZAPO) and others v President of the Republic of South Africa and others* 1996 (4) SA 671 (CC).

[275] See above pp 55ff. Moreover, the association of ubuntu and dignity as interpretive mechanisms find support in s 39(1) of the Constitution: 'When interpreting the Bill of Rights, a court, tribunal or forum . . . (a) must promote the values that underlie an open and democratic society based on human dignity . . . .'

abstraction of the two concepts as values;[276] the difference lies in dignity's status as a fundamental human right, one on which all others depend.[277]

The other way was to provide a filte for interpreting and fin tuning the rights so that they could be applied in a manner more sympathetic to an African world view and South Africa's own history. *Kievits Kroon Country Estate (Pty) Ltd v Mmoledi and others*[278] is a good example, in that ubuntu was deployed to interpret the right to fair labour practices to give effect to the cultural beliefs of an employee. Similarly, in *Hoffmann v South African Airways*,[279] the right to equal treatment was interpreted to allow account to be taken of the country's HIV/AIDS epidemic, and *Port Elizabeth Municipality v Various Occupiers*[280] is another case where the right to ownership in property was restricted in favour of the many South Africans bereft of land and housing.

The courts put ubuntu's domesticating function into operation by invoking the network of connotations it carried from its origins in an African system of ethics. These connotations thereby gave depth to ubuntu by elaborating its core meanings. They included 'respect' (which is generally paired with dignity),[281] 'humanity', 'grace', 'compassion',[282] 'civility',[283] 'tolerance' and 'understanding'.[284] One particular meaning of ubuntu, however, which was often remarked on in the judgments, was the precept that, when individuals exercise their rights, they have responsibilities towards a broader community — hence the repeated reference to the maxim *umuntu ngumuntu ngabantu*.

---

[276] Fletcher 'Human dignity as a constitutional value' (1984) 22 *UW Ontario L Rev* 174 and 178.

[277] See ss 1, 7(1) and 39 of the Consitution. See also *S v Makwanyane and another* 1995 (3) SA 391 (CC) paras 144 and 328; *National Coalition for Gay and Lesbian Equality v Minister of Justice* 1999 (1) SA 6 (CC) para 28. *South African Police Service v Solidarity obo Barnard* 2014 (6) SA 123 (CC) para 172: 'Because the right to human dignity affirms the intrinsic worth of every person, it is foundational to several other rights in the Bill of Rights. The right to and value of dignity therefore also inform constitutional interpretation and adjudication at multiple levels.'

[278] (2012) 33 ILJ 2812 (LAC) para 26.

[279] 2001 (1) SA 1 (CC).

[280] 2005 (1) SA 217 (CC).

[281] *Everfresh Market Virginia (Pty) Ltd v Shoprite Checkers (Pty) Ltd* 2012 (1) SA 256 (CC) paras 71-72; *The Citizen 1978 (Pty) Ltd and others v McBride (Johnstone and others, Amici Curiae)* 2011 (4) SA 191 (CC) para 215; *S v Makwanyane and another* 1995 (3) SA 391 (CC) para 308; *Masetlha v President of the Republic of South Africa and another* 2008 (1) SA 566 (CC) para 238; *Dikoko v Mokhatla* 2006 (6) SA 235 (CC) para 68.

[282] *Hoffmann v South African Airways* 2001 (1) SA 1 (CC); *Derby-Lewis v Minister of Justice and Correctional Services and others* 2015 (2) SACR 412 (GP); *Thubelisha Homes and others v Various Occupants and others* [2008] JOL 21559 (C) para 37 citing *Port Elizabeth Municipality v Various Occupiers* 2005 (1) SA 217 (CC).

[283] *Pharmaceutical Society of South Africa and others v Tshabalala-Msimang and another NNO; New Clicks South Africa (Pty) Ltd v Minister of Health and another* 2005 (3) SA 238 (SCA); *Masetlha v President of the Republic of South Africa and another* 2008 (1) SA 566 (CC).

[284] *Kievits Kroon Country Estate (Pty) Ltd v Mmoledi and others* (2012) 33 ILJ 2812 (LAC); *Ryland v Edros* 1997 (2) SA 690 (C); *Bhe and others v Magistrate, Khayelitsha, and others (Commission for Gender Equality as Amicus Curiae); Shibi v Sithole and others; South African Human Rights Commission and another v President of the Republic of South Africa and another* 2005 (1) SA 580 (CC); *City of Tshwane Metropolitan Municipality v Afriforum and another* 2016 (6) SA 279 (CC) para 11.

By referring to ubuntu's connotations, the courts obliged right-holders to conduct themselves with respect, grace, compassion, etc, in other words, to behave virtuously. Virtues are admirable character traits that are calculated to promote the common good.[285] The traits considered virtuous in a society obviously differ, depending on the needs and preoccupations of the time and the society in question.[286] The most important virtues associated with ubuntu are those denoting a distinctively African concern for the needs of others.

Two of the main targets of the courts' injunctions to behave in a virtuous manner were persons in the public service[287] and privileged members of society.[288] Hence, through reference to ubuntu, these groups were obliged to implement their rights and powers with compassion and understanding for the plight of others. Examples are the eviction of unlawful occupiers,[289] the dismissal of employees,[290] and the processing of applications for residence permits.[291] Given the indeterminate nature of ubuntu and the values it embraces, it would be going too far to configur these requirements as the imposition of precise legal duties. Virtues signify a mode of behaviour that is too general and ill-define to qualify as a duty of law in the accepted sense. Rather, as Kant would say, they are the handmaidens to the fulfilmen of our duties.[292]

One of the most significan results of applying ubuntu has been to benefi individuals who were vulnerable and marginalised in South African society, especially, consumers, workers and people classed as 'black'.[293] This outcome

---

[285] See Gade 'The historical development of the written discourses on *Ubuntu*' (2011) 30 *SA J Philosophy* 308-310.

[286] MacIntyre *After Virtue: a study in moral theory* 14 on the nature of virtues in different epochs and societies.

[287] See, for example, *Bertie Van Zyl (Pty) Ltd and another v Minister for Safety and Security and others* 2010 (2) SA 181 (CC) (police); *Pharmaceutical Society of South Africa and others v Tshabalala-Msimang and another NNO; New Clicks South Africa (Pty) Ltd v Minister of Health and another* 2005 (3) SA 238 (SCA) (courts), *Law Society, Northern Provinces v Mogami and others* 2010 (1) SA 186 (SCA) (attorneys); *Koyabe and others v Minister for Home Affairs and others (Lawyers for Human Rights as Amicus Curiae)* 2010 (4) SA 327 (CC) (Home Affairs) (public officials); *City of Johannesburg Metropolitan Municipality v Blue Moonlight Properties 39 (Pty) Ltd and another* 2012 (2) SA 104 (CC) (local authorities).

[288] *City of Tshwane Metropolitan Municipality v Afriforum and another* 2016 (6) SA 279 (CC) paras 2 and 11.

[289] *City of Johannesburg v Rand Properties (Pty) Limited* 2007 (1) SA 78 (W); *Resnick v Government of the Republic of South Africa and another* 2014 (2) SA 337 (WCC).

[290] *Masetlha v President of the Republic of South Africa and another* 2008 (1) SA 566 (CC).

[291] *Koyabe and others v Minister for Home Affairs and others (Lawyers for Human Rights as Amicus Curiae)* 2010 (4) SA 327 (CC).

[292] Kant *Groundwork of the Metaphysics of Morals* (1785) (trans Abbot, ed & rev Dennis) 101. See, in this regard, the dissenting judgment in *City of Tshwane Metropolitan Municipality v Afriforum and another* 2016 (6) SA 279 (CC) para 137.

[293] For consumer protection, *Joseph and others v City of Johannesburg and others* 2010 (4) SA 55 (CC); for immigration and administrative law, *Koyabe and others v Minister for Home Affairs and others (Lawyers for Human Rights as Amicus Curiae)* 2010 (4) SA 327 (CC); for evictions, *Port Elizabeth Municipality v Various Occupiers* 2005 (1) SA 217 (CC); *City of Johannesburg v Rand Properties (Pty) Limited* 2007 (1) SA 78 (W); *Resnick v Government of the Republic of South Africa and another* 2014 (2) SA 337 (WCC; *City of Johannesburg Metropolitan Municipality v Blue*

suggests that one of the principal objections to ubuntu — that it works only to the advantage of a privileged insider group[294] — is not in fact being realised in the case law. This effect appears clearly in Mogoeng CJ's judgment in *City of Tshwane v Afriforum and another.*[295] When weighing the interests of white and previously disadvantaged black South Africans, the Chief Justice said that:

> 'White South Africans must enjoy a sense of belonging. But unlike before, that cannot and should never again be allowed to override all other people's interests. South Africa no longer "belongs" to white people only. It belongs to all of us who live in it, united in our diversity. Any indirect or even inadvertent display of an attitude of racial intolerance, racial marginalisation and insensitivity, by white or black people, must be resoundingly rejected by all South Africans in line with the Preamble and our values, if our constitutional aspirations are to be realised.'[296]

If we were to look for common factors determining the circumstances in which ubuntu has been invoked in South African law, the most likely would be furthering constitutional transformation (which is discussed more fully in the Conclusion to this book) and solving hard cases, namely, those where application of the accepted rules of law appeared to work an injustice or a hardship. The latter factor suggests a compelling similarity between ubuntu and the conception of equity in the early stages of its development in English law, an issue to be dealt with in the next chapter.

Moonlight Properties 39 (Pty) Ltd and another 2012 (2) SA 104 (CC); for unfair contractual terms, *Everfresh Market Virginia (Pty) Ltd v Shoprite Checkers (Pty) Ltd* 2012 (1) SA 256 (CC); for protection of community interests from the exercise of individual rights, *Langebaan Ratepayers' and Residents' Association v Dormell Properties 391 (Pty) Ltd and others* 2013 (1) SA 37 (WCC); *Savage and others v Sisters of the Holy Cross, Cape Province and others* 2015 (6) SA 1 (WCC).

[294] See above p 38.
[295] 2016 (6) SA 279 (CC).
[296] Paragraph 11.

Chapter 5

UBUNTU: AN AFRICAN EQUITY?

1 INTRODUCTION: EQUITY, A LEGAL METANORM

As was apparent from the analysis of the cases in the previous chapter, the courts have been using ubuntu to modify the effect of rules of law when their application yielded morally or ethically unjust results. By performing this function, ubuntu took on the character of a metanorm, namely, a norm designed to regulate the operation of lower level rules or principles. Metanorms can be found in any legal system that distinguishes positive law from other normative regimes, such as custom, morality and ethics. The structuring begins when law moves from an oral to a literary form,[1] and ethnographic literature on this subject suggests that a typical metanorm, like equity, emerges only when power becomes vested in centralised organs of state,[2] and restraints begin to be imposed on the naked power of government.[3]

Ubuntu bears a close resemblance to the concept of equity during the early years of its development in English law. Although it is clear that ubuntu cannot be simply translated as equity — and in fact the South African courts have never done so — the overall function of the two concepts is remarkably similar. Differences appear in their content, the most obvious being equity's concern with

---

[1] See above p 12.
[2] Nader & Starr 'Is equity universal?' in Newman (ed) *Equity in the World's Legal Systems: a comparative study* 136.
[3] Cf Snyder 'Natural law and equity' in Newman op cit 42-43.

justice for the individual, whereas the concern of ubuntu is for the welfare of the community.[4]

In Europe, equity originated in Graeco-Roman philosophy,[5] and it became an important component of all Western legal systems. In English law, however, equity took on a life of its own, to generate not only a system of rules quite distinct from the common law but also to provide the basis for a separate branch of the courts. The firs objective of this chapter, therefore, is to examine the history of equity in order to determine its function as a metanorm in Western legal systems, and to compare that function with ubuntu. The second is an issue alluded to previously:[6] to ask whether the South African legal system actually needs a metanorm to do the work of equity or whether the system is already suitably equipped in this regard. The third objective is to outline the evolution of the English doctrine of equity to discover whether there are lessons to be learned for the development of ubuntu in South African law.

2   A NOTE ON TERMINOLOGY: EQUITY, JUSTICE, EQUALITY AND FAIRNESS

In the South African case law and the legal literature, frequent reference is made to three metanorms closely related to equity:[7] 'equality',[8] 'justice' and 'fairness' (the usual partner of justice).[9] All these terms signify highly abstract concepts, the etymology of which implies interrelated meanings.[10] Disentangling these meanings is a difficult task, first because the words tend to be define in terms of one another, and secondly, because they are often used in pairs (or 'doublets') suggesting synonymous meanings.

The firs problem is typically presented in dictionary definitions Justice, for instance, will be define as 'the quality of being equal or fair'.[11] Equity will likewise be define as 'doing justice' or 'conformity (of an action or thing) to moral right, or to reason, truth, or fact; rightfulness; fairness; correctness;

---

[4] See above p 33ff and 98-99.

[5] See generally Van Zyl 'The significanc of the concepts justice and equity in law and legal thought' (1988) 105 *SALJ* 272ff.

[6] In the discussion of loan words and the application of ubuntu by the courts. See above pp 11ff and Chapter 4.

[7] Onions, Friedrichsen & Burchfiel *The Oxford Dictionary of English Etymology* 321.

[8] Equality arrived in English in the fourteenth century, somewhat later than equity, via the Old French term *equalité* (modern French *égalité*), which was derived from *aequalitas* 'similarity, likeness'. From the 1520s onwards, equality was used in the context of civil rights and privileges.

[9] This word also entered English in the early fourteenth century via the Old French term *equité*, which was also derived from the Latin *aequitas*, but to mean 'conformity, symmetry, fairness'. See Van Zyl (n5) 272ff.

[10] The ambiguities can be traced to the etymological roots of the words in Latin. Law and justice share a Latin origin in the word *ius* (law or right) and *iustitia* (justice, fairness, equity). See Simpson *Cassell's New Latin-Engish, English-Latin Dictionary* 703. Equity and equality, on the other hand, originate, respectively, in two closely related words: *aequus* meaning even or level, or equal and just (noun *aequitas* meaning uniformity, evenness, impartiality, justice and equity) and *aequalis* also meaning level or equal (noun *aequalitatis* meaning evenness and equality). See Simpson loc cit.

[11] 'Justice' in Murray & Minor (eds) *Oxford English Dictionary* available at http://www.oed.com/view/Entry/102198?rskey=UgrlIc&result=1 [Accessed 25 February 2016].

validity'.[12] In their turn, both equity and justice are taken to imply equal treatment or equality,[13] which again in turn, is define as justice (or its near synonym fairness).[14]

The second problem, the pairing of words in legal English — termed legal doublets — can usually be ascribed to the traditions of the genre. The phrase 'just' and 'fair', for example, is a common feature of legalese.[15] In the early development of the legal discourse, two such words were often used instead of one to give greater cogency to a phrase.[16] The origin of one word would be Latin/French, and the origin of the other Anglo-Saxon.[17] Such pairings are of no great semantic consequence. Due to the dictates of professional tradition, they have been retained in modern legal language to do little more than signify a high register discourse.[18]

Because meaning plays such an important role in the analysis of ubuntu, however, especially when ubuntu is linked with equity and its cognate terms, meanings must be distinguished. The best way to do so is to refer to the contexts in which the words are used.[19] Accordingly, in order to differentiate justice, fairness, equity and equality (and their adjectival forms: just, fair, equitable and equal), the words need to be examined in terms of their associations.

To start with 'justice': this term is commonly used together with 'fair' to signify equal dealing for the individual,[20] and it has an obvious relationship with law, the legal system and courts, as implied in the phrases 'justice, law and order' and 'courts of justice'. Equality, on the other hand, carries the connotation of having the same status as a notionally privileged class of people. To achieve equality is to give all classes the same access to opportunities, resources or physical conditions as others, hence the rule that like people must be treated alike.[21]

---

[12] 'Equity' in Murray & Minor op cit http://www.oed.com/view/Entry/63838?redirectedFrom= equity [Accessed 25 February 2016].

[13] 'Equality' in Murray & Minor op cit http://www.oed.com/view/Entry/63702?redirectedFrom= equality [Accessed 25 February 2016].

[14] Murray & Minor op cit.

[15] Justice is of Latin/French origin, while fairness is of Germanic origin deriving from the Old English word *fæger* which meant beautiful, pleasing, and then, from the twelfth century, 'free from blemish' or 'favourable'. See Hoad (ed) *Concise Oxford Dictionary of English Etymology* 250.

[16] The same is true of liturgical discourse: David 'The sound of the Magic Flute in legal and religious registers of the Ramesside period: some common features of two "ritualistic languages"' in Hagedorn & Kratz (eds) *Law and Religion in the Eastern Mediterranean: from antiquity to early Islam* 13.

[17] Danet 'Language in the legal process' (1980) 14 *Law & Soc Rev* 469, 472-476; Bathia *Textbook on Legal Language and Legal Writing* 16.

[18] See above pp 13-14.

[19] See above p 31 regarding the definitio of ubuntu.

[20] The individualistic conception of justice derives from Plato's definition namely, that justice is the having and doing of what is one's own. A just man is a man in just the right place, doing his best and giving the precise equivalent of what he has received: Plato *Republic* 34.

[21] For an overview see Gosepath 'Equality' in Zalta (ed) *The Stanford Encyclopedia of Philosophy* (2011) available http://plato.stanford.edu/archives/spr2011/entries/equality/ [Accessed 25 Februray 2015]. In this regard, see Aristotle *Nicomachean Ethics* 10.3-5 (3.1131a–1131b). Since equality was elevated to the status of a fundamental human right, guaranteed in international and domestic legal instruments, its meaning has been progressively refined See, for example, Albertyn &

Equity differs from the above terms in the following way. While often used as a synonym for equality, justice and fairness, the word has another meaning, namely, the way in which these goals can be realised. This is done is by referring to the particular circumstances of individuals who stand to be seriously disadvantaged by application of the usual rules of law. An example might be an individual, who is a novice to complex commercial transactions, concluding a contract with a large corporation. The corporation normally drafts the contract in its own favour, and in a high register language unlikely to be understood by the average person. Although the standard rule in contract law is *pacta sunt servanda*, its application in these circumstances would be to the obvious disadvantage of the party entering such a contract for the firs time. In these circumstances, the courts may intervene to assist the weaker party by appealing to equity.

Used in this sense, equity may — paradoxically — supersede justice, when justice is taken to signify strict application of the established rules of law.[22] The key function of equity, therefore, is to correct moral dysfunctions in a legal system by providing a gateway to the factual contexts of specifi cases together with reference to a repertoire of metanorms, such as morality, ethics and good conscience.

3 HISTORY OF EQUITY IN WESTERN EUROPEAN LAW

All legal rules are, to a greater or lesser extent, generalised propositions. They are designed to regulate social problems that are perceived to be prevalent at a particular time, often ones that are lost in the past. Inevitably, however, factual situations later arise that fail to conform to the intended scenarios. Courts may then fin that the rules are either too vague or too narrowly conceived to provide an appropriate match for the facts of the cases before them,[23] or, occasionally, where there seems to be no rule relevant to the facts.[24] Adherence to the established set of rules is then likely to cause a sense of wrong.

Kentridge 'Introducing the right to equality in the Interim Constitution' (1994) 10 *SALJ* 149-178. Westen 'The empty idea of equality' (1982) 95 *Harv L Rev* 537ff shows that equality is in essence an 'empty' concept. He summarises his argument (542) as follows: '(1) the proposition "people who are alike should be treated alike" is tautological; (2) the entitlements people mistakenly attribute to the idea of equality all derive from external substantive rights; and (3) the idea of equality is logically indistinguishable from the standard formula of distributive justice — that is, that "every person should be given his due".'

[22] An interesting example can be found in St Germain's analysis of justice (the law) and equity. See below pp 107-108.

[23] Often termed a 'hard case' (see below p 105). This situation depends on the manner in which the antecedent law is conceived, ie, as a determinate system of rules or as an indeterminate repertoire of (often) contradictory rules. While traditional forms of positivism favour the former understanding, the Critical Legal Studies (CLS) movement favours the latter. See, for example, Kennedy 'Freedom and constraint in adjudication: a critical phenomenology' (1986) 36 *J Legal Educ* 562; Kennedy *A Critique of Adjudication [fin de Siècle]* 51; Tushnet 'Defending the indeterminacy thesis' (1996-1997) 16 *Quinnipiac L Rev* 341.

[24] Equity has also been said to fil gaps in the law (see equity *praeter legem* below p 110), but the idea that law can have 'gaps' is contentious. See Zahnd 'The application of universal laws to particular cases: a defense of equity in aristotelianism and Anglo-American law' (1996) 59 *Law Contemp Probl* 263ff esp 268ff. See further Shiner 'Aristotle's theory of equity' (1993) 27 *Loyola LAL Rev* 1247-1250, who discusses the debate between Hart *The Concept of Law* ch 7 and Dworkin

In Anglo-American jurisprudence, such a situation is typically described as a 'hard case',[25] calling for the exercise of judicial discretion to find a morally appropriate solution. Hard cases can be solved in one of two ways: by giving judges freedom to decide whatever they personally think is right or by referring to certain predetermined norms. Resort to a patently subjective discretion, however, conflict with the principle of judicial impartiality, and so judges normally base their decisions — or at least give the appearance of doing so — on normative criteria.[26]

Reference to norms deemed superior, and usually external,[27] to the established law is a matter that has preoccupied European jurisprudence since antiquity. As early as the sixth century BCE, Greek philosophers had identifie the need for these norms to solve morally incefensible situations.[28] Plato and Aristotle referred to them as *epieikeia* (equity), as opposed to *dikaiosyne* (justice), which involved application of the regular rules of law.[29] Some two centuries after Aristotle, Cicero

---

Taking Rights Seriously ch 2, in which the former contended that judicial discretion came into play when application of a legal rule was unclear. Dworkin interpreted Hart's contention to mean that judicial discretion could be invoked pre-eminently whenever gaps were perceived, a proposition that Dworkin considered ill-founded, since higher norms, ie, principles, were applicable. Moreover, according to Shiner, it would be a misreading of Aristotle's Greek texts to fin legal gaps in a system.

[25] A term usually used in the prediction that 'hard cases [will make] make bad law', an adage that can be traced back to the case of *Hodgens v Hodgens* [1937] 6 ER 257 (1694-1865) 275 (quoted in Shapiro *The Yale Book of Quotations* 614).

[26] Cf in this regard, the famous public lecture given by Holmes 'The path of law' (1897) 1 *Harv L Rev* 457-469 (republished in (1997-1998) *Harv L Rev* 991 at 997-998) describing how judges exercise their discretion, and how, in practice, they rely on the norms generated by social policy, history and morality.

[27] Dworkin (n24) 71 and 81ff, however, argued that the ethical principles forming equity should be considered to be part of, and not extraneous to, the law as conceived in positivist jurisprudence. In other words, in order to solve hard cases, law should be understood to contain more than mere rules, and judges should accordingly be guided by standards which are more general and abstract than rules, namely, policies concerning collective social goals, or principles concerning individual rights, such as liberty, equality, respect and dignity. In effect, Dworkin and the CLS movement highlight the 'background elements' of the legal system (Waldron's term), namely, 'the principles and policies that lie behind the rules and texts that positivists emphasize'. Waldron 'Did Dworkin ever answer the Crits?' in Hershovitz (ed) *Exploring Law's Empire: the jurisprudence of Ronald Dworkin* (repr 2012) 155. Nonetheless, according to the CLS, these elements are so contradictory that they cannot yield a clear result, and so cannot be of definit v use. See Waldron op cit 162. Cf Kellogg 'What precisely is a "hard" case? Waldron, Dworkin, Critical Legal studies, and judicial recourse to principle' (2013) *Discussion Paper for University of Edinburgh Legal Theory Research Group* http://ssrn.com/abstract=2220839 or http://dx.doi.org/10.2139/ssrn.2220839 [Accessed 14 January 2016] 20 who argues for a middle ground between these two approaches.

[28] Notably the work of Heraclitus of Ephesus (ca 536–470 BCE), who distinguished the laws of the *polis* from an ambiguous *logos* [word, principle, plan, formula]: Van Zyl *Justice and Equity in Greek and Roman Legal Thought* chs 2 and 4.

[29] In Plato's *Laws* 757 BCE, the adjective *epieikés* was define in terms of the decent as opposed to the bad man. Coupled with forgiveness, it denoted 'the perfection and exactness that belong to strict justice', so as to produce a division between *epieikeia* and *dike* or *themis* (namely justice), giving to the former the function of mitigating and adapting strict rules of law. In *Nicomachean Ethics* and *Rhetoric* (both c350 BCE), Aristotle define the notion of *epieikeia* in similar fashion by contrasting it with positive law, ie, the laws laid down by human lawmakers. For an overview, see Hamburger *Morals and Law: the growth of Aristotle's legal theory* 89ff.

continued to maintain the distinction between the rules of law and equity (which he subsumed under the idea of natural justice, the *ius naturale*).[30] These distinctions were later codifie in Justinian's *Digest* and *Institutes* (ca 533-536).[31]

The idea of the natural law was received into medieval ecclesiastical law.[32] In the firs definitiv compendium of canon laws, Gratian's *Decretum* (ca 1140),[33] the introductory definition provided that: 'The human race is ruled by two things, namely, natural law and customary usages.' The former was coupled with the time-honoured biblical precept requiring each person 'to do unto others what he wants done unto himself'.[34] These were the principles that informed the concept of equity in medieval Europe.

Thereafter, equity continued to permeate the civil-law jurisdictions of Europe, although without any define sphere of operation. Specifi effect was given to it by certain equitable remedies inherited from Roman Law. This was the form of equity in the Roman-Dutch law that eventually arrived in South Africa, and it will be explored further in section 5 below. In England, however, equity came to comprise a distinct, self-contained system of rules and remedies supported by a separate branch of the courts.[35]

Ubuntu, as an emergent of African metanorm, could now be developed to emulate one of two models: to remain a diffuse element in the law, similar to equity in Roman-Dutch law and the civil-law jurisdictions, or to become a separate doctrine of equity as happened in English law. An examination of these two possibilities helps to understand how ubuntu is currently being used by the courts, whether it is redundant to the requirements of South African law and, more importantly, to show the advantages and disadvantages of taking ubuntu down one path or the other.

4 EQUITY IN ENGLISH LAW

Prior to the Norman conquest, the laws of England consisted of a medley of Saxon customs, court rulings and occasional feudal statutes.[36] Although the Normans

---

[30] Cicero *De Partitione Oratoria* 37, 129-131. See commentary by Van Zyl *Justice and Equity in Cicero: a critical evaluation in contextual perspective* ch 4 and Van Zyl 'Cicero and Roman Law' (1991) 108 *SALJ* 496-502. Succeeding generations of Roman lawyers, for instance Gaius *Institutes* 1.1, drew yet a further distinction between the law observed by all people (*ius gentium*) and nature's law (*ius naturale*). The *ius gentium* differed from the *ius naturale* in that it was observed by humans only and was established by their customary usages.

[31] *Digest* 1.1.1.1.pr and *Institutes* 1.2.pr. and 1.2.11.

[32] Via the work of St Isidore of Seville (ca 600-625CE), who, in his *Etymologies* (5.4), combined the two traditions of the ancient world: that natural law was the law common to all nations which had been created at the instigation (*instinctus*) of nature, not as a result of human legislation.

[33] Quoting St Isodore *The Treatise on Laws (Decretum DD. 1-20) with the Ordinary Gloss (Studies in Medieval and Early Modern Canon Law, Volume 2)* (1582).

[34] *Matthew* 7.12.

[35] Hudson *Equity and Trusts* 4 define equity broadly to mean an element of private law that 'appears to imbue the courts with a general discretion to disapply statutory or common law rules whenever good conscience requires it'. See further Allen *Law in the Making* 423 and Kiralfy *Potter's Historical Introduction to English Law and its Institutions* 569.

[36] See Pollock & Maitland *The History of English Law before the Time of Edward I* Ch IV.

brought some sort of order to the system by introducing the doctrine of *stare decisis*,[37] the laws became ever more complex and formalistic as the volume of precedents grew.[38] In this early period, however, substantive law was not thought of as a set of predetermined general rules, but rather as divinely ordained justice. Less abstract, and much more relevant to everyday purposes, were the procedures for bringing disputes to courts of justice.[39]

The king was deemed to be the font and arbiter of justice. Any person could petition him to obtain redress for a wrong.[40] In such matters, the king's representative was the Lord Chancellor (the chief Minister in the royal Court),[41] and it was from the Chancellor's office that all 'writs' initiating legal actions were issued.[42] Actions could easily be lost because of procedural loopholes, fraud, bribery and political intervention.[43] In instances where the legal process did not work, the king — or more usually the Chancellor — could intervene by ordering the individuals involved to behave more ethically. When, in the mid-fourteenth century, the number of petitions to the Chancellor grew, a new system of courts was established: the Courts of Chancery.[44] Until they were eventually abolished in the 1870s, this specialised branch of the judiciary, one of the distinguishing features of English law, operated separately from courts of the common law.[45]

The principle by which the Chancellor and Courts of Chancery could implement corrections to the justice system was equity.[46] While the term 'equity' was derived from the Roman-law concept of *aequitas naturalis*,[47] and so had connections with equitable principles employed elsewhere in Europe, it evolved quite differently in England. By the early sixteenth century, it had come to provide the basis for a separate system of jurisprudence. St Germain, a barrister with 'extensive theological learning', was responsible for drawing a clear distinction

---

[37] Hudson (n35) 16-17.

[38] Kiralfy (n35) 569.

[39] In this regard, it should be noted that the development of the common law was in essence concerned with procedure, for it consisted primarily of rules designed to direct suits to the appropriate bodies for decisions according to justice. The task of lawyers was therefore 'to see that disputes were properly submitted to an appropriate deciding mechanism': Milsom *Historical Foundations of the Common Law* 83.

[40] Kiralfy (n35) 569; Hudson (n35) 9.

[41] During the fourteenth century, the Chancellor's powers expanded to hear matters on his own authority and to issue the necessary decrees: Pettit *Equity and the Law of Trusts* 2.

[42] Milsom (n39) 84 says that, at this stage, 'equity' did not exist as 'a nascent body of rules different from the common law. There was no common law, no body of substantive rules from which equity could be different. And the idea that the law could be unjust, if comprehensible at all, would have been abhorrent. Failures were mechanical.'

[43] Zweigert & Kötz *Introduction to Comparative Law* 4.

[44] Hudson (n35) 16-19.

[45] Fox 'The nature, history and courts of equity' in *McGhee* (ed) *Snell's Principles of Equity* 17. The Courts of Chancery thereafter became the Chancery Division of the High Court; the Queen's Bench Division heard matters pertaining to common law, although it too had the power to consider defences 'in equity': Zweigert & Kötz (n43) 207. If a conflic arose between common law and equity, the latter prevailed. See Pettit (n41) 7.

[46] Hudson (n35) 6 and 16.

[47] Buckland & Stein *A Text-Book of Roman Law: from Augustus to Justinian* 55 fn5. For the history of equity before its development in England see Allen (n35) 383ff.

between divine justice and the common law.[48] He identifie a positive human law conceived in terms of substantive rules, although, as a result of human agency, open to producing unjust results.[49] These results could be remedied by equity.

Application of equity allowed a defendant to seek an injunction[50] from the Lord Chancellor against a plaintiff who had relied on the positive law in support of his action, even though application of that law yielded an unjust result.[51] The injunction obliged the plaintiff to look to his conscience (which would be informed by a divine sense of right and wrong) and to abstain from further proceedings.[52] Equity therefore rectifie situations where parties had acted unconscionably, although abiding by the letter of the law.[53]

In this way, the doctrine of equity grew out of the nebulous idea of 'good conscience'. While Chancellors obviously had reference to the accepted moral standards of the time, which would have been informed by both canon and natural law, their decisions were nevertheless grounded on the simple notion of good conscience.[54] No other specifi source or reason for equity was acknowledged.[55]

Given such vagueness, it is not surprising that many cases were decided in terms of the Chancellor's personal sense of right and wrong, a practice that led to the criticism that:

> 'Equity is a roguish thing. For [common] law we have a measure . . . [but] equity is according to the conscience of him that is the Chancellor, and as that is larger or narrower, so is equity. Tis all one as if they should make the standard for measure . . . a Chancellor's foot.'[56]

Hence, to offset the vagaries in the application of equity, the Courts of Chancery followed their common-law counterparts by adopting a doctrine of precedent,[57] which had the effect of generating a more systematic body of rules.[58]

By now equity had come to be regarded as a jurisdictional supplement to the common law,[59] although a separate component of the English legal system with its

---

[48] Christopher St Germain *The Doctor and Student* (1518) 1 ch 17, http://lonang.com/library/reference/stgermain-doctor-and-student/ [Accessed 8 June 2017].

[49] Thus Milsom (n39) 89 says that: '[t]he true start of equity as well as the common law was the replacement of the divine test by a fallible human result', and that '[t]he achievement of St Germain was to reconcile this new concept of law with the medieval belief in divine justice.'

[50] Namely, a prohibitive writ issued by a court of equity, at the suit of a complainant, directed at the defendant in the action prohibiting him or her from doing some act.

[51] Allen (n35) 406-410; Hudson (n35) 406-407. Thus began the enduring debate about the need for laws that produced certainty and uniformity versus abstract justice: Milsom (n39) 94.

[52] St Germain (n48) *Dialogue* 1 ch 17.

[53] Worthington *Equity* 11. See, too, *Westdeutsche Landesbank Girozentrale v Islington LBC* [1996] AC 669.

[54] Or '[f]or the love of God and in the way of charity': Zweigert & Kötz (n43) 194. See, too, Kiralfy (n35) 570. Equity courts were called 'courts of conscience', and Chancellors were known as 'keepers of the King's conscience': Hudson (n35) 17 and 33, respectively.

[55] Which therefore contributed to the inherent vagueness of the doctrine, and its many different interpretations: Hudson (n35) 28.

[56] Selden *Table Talk: being the discourses of John Selden, Esq* 55-56; Hudson (n35) 17.

[57] Zweigert & Kötz (n43) 195.

[58] Especially after 1529 when the post of the Chancellor was secularised: Zweigert & Kötz ibid.

[59] Petit (n41) 2.

own technical rules and procedures.[60] Even so, equity, in its fully-fledge form, differed little from the common law; the primary point of distinction lay in the nature of the remedies it allowed. Courts applying common law were generally limited to ordering payment of monetary damages for failure to perform obligations or for loss of determinable property. Equitable remedies were more varied. They were effected by way of injunctions, ie, orders compelling particular parties to behave in a certain way.[61]

The doctrine of equity thus conceived had both strengths and weaknesses,[62] both of which can be attributed, largely, to the casuistic approach of English judges. Its strength lay in its flexibilit , aided by the courts' search for justice on an inductive, case-by-case basis.[63] This very flexibilit , however, led to uncertainty. Attempts were made to deduce certain common themes in equity jurisprudence,[64] but the manifold cases resisted any reduction to basic principles of natural law.[65] Although the doctrine of *stare decisis* brought some order to the cases,[66] the precedents became fixe into a set of binding rules, much like the common law.[67] Hence the irony that equity, too, could produce inequitable outcomes.[68]

According to Allen, the English courts used equity to perform two principal functions. One function, which has been termed equity *infra legem*, was to provide the criterion for 'a liberal and humane interpretation of the law in general . . . without actual antagonism to the law itself'. The other, termed equity *contra legem*, was to modify the law 'in exceptional cases not coming within the ambit of the general rule'. The former usage Allen calls 'equity in general' and the latter

---

[60] Petit ibid.

[61] Worthington (n53) 33. Examples would include orders to compensate or render specifi performance: Hudson (n35) 14.

[62] Worthington (n53) 17. Allen (n35) 425, for one, doubted whether the doctrine was of any benefi to English law.

[63] Zweigert & Kötz (n43) 196.

[64] Notably Francis's *Maxims of Equity* (1714-1739) cited in McFarlane 'The maxims of equity' in *McGhee* (n45) 87-103. The following are examples: 'Equity will not suffer a wrong to be without remedy.' 'Equity follows the law.' 'Where there is equal equity, the law shall prevail.' 'Where the equities are equal, the firs in time shall prevail.' 'Delay defeats equities.' 'He who seeks equity must do equity.' 'Equality is equity.' 'Equity looks to the intent rather that to the form.' 'Equity acts in personam.'

[65] The attempts to summarise equity into a set of simple principles produced propositions that were too vague to be useful: Smith 'Legal relief against the inadequacies of equity' (1933) 12 *Tex L Rev* 111; Klinck *Conscience Equity and the Court of Chancery in Early Modern England* 181-182.

[66] Hudson (n35) 33. 'Equity is not divined from philosophical foundations; rather, equity is found in the law reports, albeit derived on the basis of case law precedent and the principles [of equity]' Hudson (n35) 42.

[67] Kiralfy (n35) 569. Smith (n65) 11 observes that: '[E]quity, by this time, had been rounded out into a more or less closed system of rules and principles. The prerogative of grace had given place to *stare decisis*, and the Chancellor's foo, once suspected of being coterminous with the King's foot, had finall become an impersonal and an abstract and a standardized foot, and, whatever else might be said against it, the jibe at equity as ''loose and liberal, large and vague'' could no longer justly be applied.'

[68] Allen (n35) 425.

'particular equity'.[69] A third category could be added: the use of equity to fil ostensible gaps in the law, equity *praeter legem*.[70]

These terms of reference call attention to interesting similarities and differences between the functions of ubuntu and the English doctrine of equity. Like Allen's 'general' equity, ubuntu has been used for the purpose of interpreting rights and duties, and for correcting defects in the mechanics of the legal process,[71] such as undue expense, delays,[72] excessive technicality[73] and the absence of a suitable remedy.[74] Ubuntu has seldom, however, performed the 'particular' function of English equity, ie, to change the actual substance of specifi rules of law.[75] Rather, ubuntu has performed an additional teleological function aimed at attaining broader goals for the whole legal system, namely, transforming the law to meet the demands of the Constitution[76] and giving the Bill of Rights an African legitimacy.[77]

More generally, it is clear that, although ubuntu is generating a new discourse in South African law, it is not (yet) creating a specifi set of equitable rules. As a result, it is not being detached into a separate doctrine of equity — and is certainly never likely to found a separate judicial structure — with all the accompanying problems that arose in English law. Rather, ubuntu is still a pervasive element in our legal system, flexibl and amenable to application in a diverse range of situations.

---

[69] Allen (n35) 385.

[70] The Latin tags here refer to a classificatio derived from international law. Akehurst 'Equity and general principles of law' (1976) 25 *ICLQ* 801-802, however, notes that, in practice, the different categories may prove impossible to distinguish because their differences depend upon how a court chooses to solve a problem. It may decide that application of the letter of a particular rule of law is undesirable, because it runs contrary to the spirit of the law or that the law-maker intended an exception to the rules (equity *infra legem*). Alternatively, the court could assume that the rule does not fi the particular facts, causing a gap that should then be fille by referring to equity (equity *praeter legem*), or that the rule is simply unjust and should not therefore be applied (equity *contra legem*).

[71] Holdsworth *History of English Law* 279-288.

[72] For example, *Pharmaceutical Society of South Africa and others v Tshabalala-Msimang and another NNO; New Clicks South Africa (Pty) Ltd v Minister of Health and another* 2005 (3) SA 238 (SCA) para 39.

[73] For example, *Union of Refugee Women and others v Director: Private Security Industry Regulatory Authority and others* 2007 (4) SA 395 (CC) para 1; *Koyabe and others v Minister for Home Affairs and others (Lawyers for Human Rights as Amicus Curiae)* 2010 (4) SA 327 (CC).

[74] For a possible example, *Dikoko v Mokhatla* 2006 (6) SA 235 (CC).

[75] *Dikoko* supra and *S v Makwanyane and another* 1995 (3) SA 391 (CC) are potential exceptions. In English law, equity provided a basis for the creation of rules to govern trusts, for supplying a concept of deceit and giving protection against the imposition of penalties in agreements: Holdsworth (n71) 289-299.

[76] As in *Bhe and others v Magistrate, Khayelitsha, and others (Commission for Gender Equality as Amicus Curiae); Shibi v Sithole and others; South African Human Rights Commission and another v President of the Republic of South Africa and another* 2005 (1) SA 580 (CC) para 139; *Everfresh Market Virginia (Pty) Ltd v Shoprite Checkers (Pty) Ltd* 2012 (1) SA 256 (CC) paras 24 and 71-72.

[77] As in *Hoffmann v South African Airways* 2001 (1) SA 1 (CC).

5 EQUITY IN SOUTH AFRICAN LAW

Having established that the current usage of ubuntu in South Africa bears little resemblance to English equity, we can now ask whether it is more akin to equity in Roman-Dutch law and, if so, whether it is duplicating that form of equity. An answer to the latter question was alluded to earlier in the discussion on loan words: they fulfi a previously unacknowledged semantic function in the host language.[78] A more detailed, specificall legal answer, however, is now necessary, and a useful starting point for this inquiry is to revisit an argument that South African law had no need for the English doctrine of equity, because Roman-Dutch law was already amply equipped in this regard.

(a) The English doctrine of equity and Roman-Dutch law

South Africa, as a 'mixed' legal system combines elements of both the civil and common law.[79] When Britain acquired the Cape, it retained Roman-Dutch law as the basic law of the colony, although subject to any changes implemented by the new government.[80] The colonial administration then began to enact statutes modelled on English law to fil what it saw as 'gaps' in the local law.[81]

Wholesale acceptance of English transplants, however, was met with resistance, resulting in a *'bellum juridicum'* that grew in strength in the later part of the nineteenth century and reached its height in the firs part of the twentieth century. The warring parties were dubbed 'purists' and 'pollutionists' (or 'pragmatists').[82] While the latter could fin no harm in the courts looking to English methods and sources to develop South African law, the former claimed that it should remain true to its civilian tradition. Particular opposition was shown to the doctrine of equity.[83] According to the purists, such a doctrine would sully the purity of Roman-Dutch law:[84] not only did it offer a particular type of remedy, ie, not the usual award of damages, but it was also the product of a completely different legal system.

Here, the purists had a point. Equity was the product of a separate system of courts, which had a decidedly casuistic approach to the law, in marked contrast to

---

[78] See above pp 11-12.

[79] See above p 2.

[80] In accordance with the rule laid down in *Campbell v Hall* (1774) 1 Cowper 204 at 209.

[81] See generally Beinart 'The English legal contribution in South Africa: the interaction of civil and common law' 1981 *Acta Juridica* 7ff.

[82] Proculus *'Bellum juridicum*: two approaches to South African law' (1951) 68 *SALJ* 306; Proculus Redivivus 'South African law at the crossroads — or — what is our common law' (1965) 82 *SALJ* 17; Van Blerk 'The genesis of the modernist-purist debate: a historical bird's-eye view' (1984) 47 *THRHR* 257-258; Christie & Bradfiel *Christie's The Law of Contract in South Africa* 543.

[83] See *Mills & Sons v Trustees of Benjamin Bros* 1876 Buch 115 at 121; *Kent v Transvaalsche Bank* 1907 TS 765 at 774; *Bank of Lisbon v De Ornelas* 1988 (3) SA 580 (A) at 606; Hefer 'Billikheid in die kontraktereg volgens die Suid-Afrikaanse Regskommissie' (2000) 1 *TSAR* 144.

[84] See the cases of *Kent, Mills* and *Bank of Lisbon* supra, as well as the discussion of the latter by Van Blerk (n82) 268 and Van der Merwe, Lubbe & Van Huyssteen 'The *exceptio doli generalis*: *requiescat in pace — vivat aequitas*' (1989) 106 *SALJ* 238.

the deductive approach of the Roman-Dutch tradition.[85] Even more compelling was the argument that a specifi doctrine of equity was superfluou to the needs of Roman-Dutch law, which already had a battery of rules and remedies designed to ensure equitable solutions to unjust cases.[86] In this respect, the purists could point to the origins of equity in Roman law, from which Roman-Dutch law derived its infusion of equitable principles.[87] What is more, the Roman-Dutch remedies often resembled those available under the English doctrine of equity,[88] for they reflecte the same desire to seek fair and just solutions.[89]

The doctrine of English equity, then, was barred entry to South African law. Nonetheless, aspects of it came in through the back door, most of them by way of the rules of English commercial law, which were freely borrowed by South African courts. What is more, the very term 'equity', in its broader civilian sense, has a well established place in the country's legal discourse, being used both as an independent principle and in association with the Roman-Dutch remedies.

Nevertheless, the Roman-Dutch idea of equity was not fashioned into a single, overarching metanorm with a define sphere of operation. We may therefore ask whether this general idea of equity, together with the specifi equitable remedies it offers, is capable of functioning in the same way as an ubuntu metanorm, especially in light of South Africa's new Bill of Rights.

(b) Equitable concepts and remedies in Roman-Dutch and South African law

In South African law several institutions perform the function of equity: the *condictiones* (the remedies for unjust enrichment); the fiduciar duty (a legal relationship suffused with the principle of equity); and good faith and public

---

[85] Proculus (n82) 306; Van Blerk (n82) 258. Cf Van der Walt 'Horizontal application of fundamental rights and the threshold of the law in view of the *Carmichele* saga' (2003) 19 *SAJHR* 530-531.

[86] See the analysis by Neels 'Regsekerheid en die korrigerende werking van redelikheid en billikheid (deel 1)' (1998) 4 *TSAR* 702ff, who claims that the concepts of reasonableness and fairness in Roman-Dutch law perform three functions: providing a direct source of rules, a standard or goal to which the law must aspire and a reason for correcting existing rules or principles.

[87] Which meant that there was no need for a doctrine of equity separate from the ordinary law. See *Weinerlein v Goch Buildings Ltd* 1925 AD 282 at 295; *Le Roux v Dey* 2011 (3) SA 274 (CC) para 198; Hawthorne 'Public policy: the origin of a general clause in the South African law of contract' (2013) 19 *Fundamina* 301-302 and sources cited in fn13. See further regarding equity in the civil-law as opposed to common-law systems: Piers 'Good faith in English Law — could a rule become a principle' (2011) 26 *Tul European & Civil L Forum* 123ff.

[88] Burdick *The Principles of Roman Law and Their Relation to Modern Law* 4. See, for example, *Ferreira v Ferreira* 1915 EDL 9 at 15-16.

[89] The courts have therefore been unwilling to abandon these remedies in favour of equity, especially in the sphere of private law: Van der Walt (n85) 532; Christie & Bradfiel (n82) 543. See, for instance, *Estate Thomas v Kerr* (1903) 20 SC 354 at 366; *Umhlebi v Estate Umhlebi* (1905) 19 EDC 237 at 249; *Kent v Transvaalsche Bank* 1907 TS 765 at 774. Thus, in *Weinerlein v Goch Buildings Ltd* 1925 AD 282 at 295, Kotze JA declared that: 'Our common law, based to a great extent on the civil law, contains many an equitable principle, but equity, as distinct from and opposed to law, does not prevail with us. Equitable principles are only of force insofar as they have become authoritatively incorporated and recognised as rules of law.'

policy (two broad principles that readily respond to a call for equitable outcomes in particular cases).

(i) *Unjust enrichment and the* condictiones

Part of the Roman legacy to Roman-Dutch, and subsequently South African law, was the *condictiones,*[90] a set of equitable remedies for unjust enrichment.[91] These actions allowed the plaintiff to recover money or property that, for some unfair reason, had come into the possession of the defendant.

In Justinian's *Digest,*[92] the *condictiones* were particularised in the sense that they were offered only in specifi circumstances, which were determined by the reasons for liability. Accordingly, a *condictio* can be brought to restore property or money if: it was not owed or was given mistakenly (*indebiti*), given without cause (*sine causa*), given to achieve a purpose that had failed (*causa data causa non secuta*) or given for an immoral or illegal purpose (*ob turpem vel iniustam causam*).[93]

A plaintiff in South Africa can recover an unjust enrichment only by way of one of the *condictiones.*[94] They bear little relationship to a general equity doctrine, however, first because they apply only in very specifi situations — the enrichment of a party, which must be proved to be unjust — and, secondly, because the main remedy is compensation to the amount of the improper enrichment.[95]

(ii) *The fiduciary duty*

A broader concept in South African law, and one more closely related to the general idea of equity, both historically and doctrinally, is the fiduciar duty.[96] This duty is incurred whenever one person (the fiduciary acquires the power to act on behalf of another (the beneficiary) usually in order to manage that person's property.[97] In the typical case, the fiduciar has greater experience and knowledge of the affairs being handled than the beneficiar . A fiduciar relationship implies

---

[90] Glover 'Reflection on the *sine causa* requirement and the *condictiones* in South African law' (2009) 20 *Stell LR* 468ff esp 469-470

[91] For what follows in this paragraph, see Scott *Unjust Enrichment in South African Law: rethinking enrichment by transfer* 1-2; Du Plessis *The South African Law of Unjustified Enrichment* 64.

[92] Scott op cit 87; Du Plessis op cit 199; Visser *Unjustified Enrichment* 157.

[93] Du Plessis (n91) 199ff; Scott op cit 87-88; Sonnekus *Unjustified Enrichment in South African Law* 97ff; Visser (n92) 417. Unlike the specifi actions under Roman-Dutch law, English law offers a general equitable remedy for unjustifie enrichment, restitution, which, not surprisingly, has often been confounded with the remedies offered by equity. See Hudson (n35) 23.

[94] *Nortje en 'n ander v Pool NO* 1966 (3) SA 96 (A); *Kommissaris van Binnelandse Inkomste v Willers* 1994 (3) SA 283 (A); *McCarthy Retail Ltd v Shortdistance Carriers CC* 2001 (3) SA 482 (SCA). See Visser 'Unjustifie enrichment' in Zimmermann & Visser (eds) *Southern Cross: civil law and common law in South Africa* 533ff for the influenc of English law on this area of South African law.

[95] Lotz 'Enrichment' in Joubert (ed) *LAWSA* paras 208 and 243.

[96] The term derives from the Latin word *fiducia* (trust).

[97] *Land and Agricultural Development Bank of SA v Parker* 2005 (2) SA 77 (SCA) para 22.

the beneficiary s full trust in the fiduciar , who in turn owes the beneficiar duties of loyalty, good faith and honesty.[98]

A prime example of a fiduciar is a trustee,[99] although the duty may arise in a wide variety of other legal relationships,[100] such as guardian-ward, attorney-client, executor-heir, banker-client and company director-shareholder.[101] In all cases, the fiduciar is held to a standard of conduct[102] higher than that required of the ordinary person.[103] Two prophylactic rules are designed to maintain this standard: fiduciarie must avoid any conflic of interests with the beneficiaries [104] and must take no profi from their privileged position.[105] In addition, when managing the assets under their control, fiduciarie must act in the best interests of beneficia ries[106] and must treat a multiplicity of beneficiarie equally.[107]

In English law, the fiduciar duty was developed mainly through equity jurisprudence, more specificall with regard to trusts.[108] South African courts, however, held that our fiduciar duty derives from Roman and Roman Dutch law,[109] although they acknowledged that the concept is substantially the same as its English counterpart.[110] The courts therefore relied heavily on English (and to a

---

[98] Coetzee & Van Tonder 'The fiduciar relationship between a company and its directors' (2014) 35 *Obiter* 287.

[99] The concept of a trust (see above pp 18ff) is a prime example of the 'back door' reception of equity to South African law. Du Toit 'The fiduciar office of trustee and the protection of contingent trust beneficiaries (2007) 18 *Stell LR* 471ff. Note, however, that the office of trustee does not of itself imply the imposition of a fiduciar duty: *Hofer v Kevitt* 1996 (2) SA 402 (C); *Doyle v Board of Executors* 1999 (2) SA 805 (C) at 813.

[100] *Phillips v Fieldstone Africa (Pty) Ltd* [2004] 1 All SA 150 (SCA) para 27: 'There is no magic in the term "fiduciar duty". The existence of such a duty and its nature and extent are questions of fact to be adduced from a thorough consideration of the substance of the relationship and any relevant circumstances which affect the operation of that relationship.' Hence, *Volvo (Southern Africa) (Pty) Ltd v Yssel* [2009] 4 All SA 497 (SCA) para 16 held that: 'While certain relationships have come to be clearly recognised as encompassing fiduciar duties there is no closed list of such relationships.'

[101] *Robinson v Randfontein Estates Gold Mining Co Ltd* 1921 AD 168 at 177-178.

[102] Coetzee & Van Tonder (n98) 285 at 287.

[103] See s 9(1) of the Trust Property Control Act 57 of 1988.

[104] *Jowell v Bramwell-Jones* 2000 (3) SA 274 (SCA) para 16.

[105] See *Land and Agricultural Development Bank of SA v Parker* 2005 (2) SA 77 (SCA) para 22. The beneficiar may, of course, waive these rights, and often does so: Cameron, De Waal & Wunsh *Honore's South African Law of Trusts* 604.

[106] *Jowell v Bramwell-Jones* 1998 (1) SA 836 (W) at 89I and 894.

[107] *Lloyds Bank v Duker* (1987) WLR 1324 at 1330-1331.

[108] Conaglen 'Fiduciaries' in McGhee (n45) 138-140. Helfman 'Land ownership and the origins of fiduciar duty' (2006) 41 *Real Prop Prob & Tr J* 651ff shows how it developed from the feudal law governing real property.

[109] *Digest* 18.1.34.7; *Robinson v Randfontein Estates Gold Mining Co Ltd* 1921 AD 168 at 177-178; *Sackville West v Nourse* 1925 AD 516 at 533-534; *Fey and Whiteford v Serfontein* 1993 (2) SA 605 (A) at 612; *Phillips v Fieldstone Africa (Pty) Ltd* [2004] 1 All SA 150 (SCA) paras 30-31.

[110] *Transvaal Cold Storage Co Ltd v Palmer* 1904 TS 4 at 19-20; *African Claim & Land Co Ltd v W J Langermann* 1905 TS 494 at 504-505.

lesser extent American) judgments in developing the trust,[111] but only when those judgments had been authoritatively incorporated into South African law.[112]

Today, the most important fiduciar duties of the common law have been superseded by legislation, notably the Trust Property Control Act[113] and the Companies Act.[114]

Again, like the remedies for unjust enrichment, the fiduciar duty is too narrow in its scope to be compared with a general equitable doctrine or, indeed, ubuntu. The fiduciar duty gives rise to specifi rights and remedies, which ubuntu does not, and, again unlike ubuntu, it applies only to certain relationships.[115]

(iii) *Exceptio doli generalis*

The *exceptio doli generalis* used to play a general equitable role in the Roman-Dutch law of contract, but is now of historical interest only.[116] This remedy could be invoked by a defendant to defeat an action to enforce a contract by a plaintiff in unfair or unconscionable circumstances.[117] The exception originated in Roman law,[118] was subsequently developed in Roman-Dutch Law.[119] It then entered South African law as a basis for certain contractual remedies,[120] most of which had parallels in the English doctrine of equity.[121]

In 1988, notwithstanding frequent use of the *exceptio doli*, the former Appellate

---

[111] *Olifants Tin 'B' Syndicate v De Jager* 1912 TPD 305 (where reference was made to *Kimberley v Arms* 129 US Rep 512 and *Mitchell v Read* 61 NY 123); *Goldberg v Trimble & Bennett* 1905 TS 255 at 273 (where reference was made to *Kimberley* supra and *Latta v Kilbourn* 150 US Rep 524); *Transvaal Cold Storage* supra 20; *Jones v East Rand Extension Gold Mining Co Ltd* 1903 TH 325.

[112] *Weinerlein v Goch Buildings Ltd* 1925 AD 282 at 295. See, too, De Villiers CJ in *Mills & Sons v Trustees of Benjamin Bros* 1876 Buch 115 at 121: '[T]his Court is a Court of Equity as well as of Common Law, but it can administer equity only so far as it is consistent with the principles of the Roman-Dutch law.'

[113] Section 9 of Act 57 of 1988.

[114] Section 77 of Act 71 of 2008.

[115] Cf, however, the references to ubuntu in relation to directors' duties in the King *Report on Corporate Governance in South Africa* III (2009) above p 93 fn235.

[116] Neels 'Die aanvullende en beperkende werking van redelikheid en billikheid in die kontraktereg' (1999) 4 *TSAR* 688.

[117] *Weinerlein v Goch Buildings Ltd* 1925 AD 282 at 292-293. Resort to the *exceptio doli generalis* was considered necessary because of the absence of the 'law of equity': Hawthorne (n128) 302. See Christie & Bradfiel (n82) 12. This remedy was not the same as the *exceptio doli specialis*, which required the defendant to plead actual fraud.

[118] Where it was given by the praetor as a defence to strict application of the *ius civilis* to the facts of a case, when that law would produce an unjust result: Gaius *Institutes* 4 13. See, in general, *Bank of Lisbon v De Ornelas* 1988 (3) SA 580 (A) at 597 and Van der Merwe et al *Contract: general principles* 274-281.

[119] Van der Merwe et al op cit 275.

[120] Involving such matters as fictiona fulfilmen of conditions, rectificatio and estoppel. See Brand 'The role of good faith, equity and fairness in the South African law of contract: the influenc of the common law and the Constitution' (2009) 126 *SALJ* 73 and the cases he cites, together with his more recent article 'The role of good faith, equity and fairness in the South African law of contract: a further instalment' (2016) 27 *Stell LR* 238ff.

[121] See Hutchison 'Good faith in the South African law of contract' in Brownsword, Hird & Howells (eds) *Good Faith in Contract, Concept and Context* 235.

Division decided, in the landmark case of *Bank of Lisbon v De Ornelas*,[122] that it did not form part of South African law.[123] According to Joubert JA, the *exceptio* had disappeared in the Middle Ages, and, as a 'superfluou defunct anachronism', had to be laid to rest.[124] In spite of this finding the problem of doing justice between the parties persisted.[125] A solution, however, lay in Jansen JA's judgment that the *exceptio doli* was closely related to defences based on public policy and *boni mores*.[126] This *dictum* then planted the 'seed of an idea' that such concepts could be used to introduce the equitable principles of fairness and good faith into contract law,[127] although latterly they have been supplemented by reference to the Bill of Rights.[128]

(iv) *Good faith*

Good faith has always been considered one of the elements of equity, and is another legacy transmitted from Roman to Roman-Dutch law.[129] It is a general concept, broader than the fiduciar duty,[130] and more akin to a metanorm. Even so,

---

[122] 1988 (3) SA 580 (A) at 607.

[123] Cf Kerr *Principles of the Law of Contract* 641 who contends that the case was wrongly decided. See too Lewis 'The demise of the *exceptio doli*: is there another route to contractual equity' (1990) 107 *SALJ* 26ff; Van der Merwe, Lubbe & Van Huyssteen (n84) 238; Kerr 'The defence of unfair conduct on the part of the plaintiff at the time the action is brought: the *exceptio doli generalis* and the *replicatio doli* in modern law' (2008) 125 *SALJ* 246.

[124] *Bank of Lisbon* supra 607. An unsuccessful attempt was made to revive the *exceptio doli* in an appeal to the Constitutional Court in *The Crown Restaurant CC v Gold Reef City Theme Park (Pty) Ltd* 2008 (4) SA 16 (CC).

[125] As Van der Merwe et al (n118) 275 said, the problem was not use of the term *exceptio doli generalis*, but whether the South African courts were in a position to provide justice as effectively as their Roman, Dutch and pre-*Bank of Lisbon* counterparts.

[126] *Bank of Lisbon* supra 617.

[127] Brand (n120 2009) 74. See Louw 'Yet another call for a greater role for good faith in the South African law of contract: can we banish the law of the jungle, while avoiding the elephant in the room?' (2013) 16 *PELJ* 73 fn114.

[128] For a general overview see: Sutherland 'Ensuring contractual fairness in consumer contracts after *Barkhuizen v Napier* 2007 (5) SA 323 (CC) — part 1' (2008) 19 *Stell LR* 411-413; Sharrock 'Unfair enforcement of a contract: a step in the right direction? *Botha v Rich and Combined Developers v Arun Holdings*' (2015) 27 *SA Mercantile LJ* 174 for authorities cited at 181-183; Lubbe 'Taking fundamental rights seriously: the Bill of Rights and its implications for the development of contract law' (2004) 121 *SALJ* 395ff; Bhana 'The development of a basic approach for the constitutionalisation of our common law of contract' (2015) 26 *Stell LR* 3ff; Hawthorne 'Rethinking the philosophical substructure of modern South African contract law: self-actualisation and human dignity' (2016) 79 *THRHR* 286.

[129] For an overview of good faith in South African law, see Hefer 'Billikheid in die kontraktereg' (2004) 29 *JJS* 7-12 See further Lubbe '*Bona fides*, billikheid en die openbare belang in die Suid-Afrikaanse kontraktereg' (1990) 7 *Stell LR* 25.

[130] Idensohn *The Basis and Boundaries of Employee Fiduciary Duties in South African Common Law* (2015) unpublished PhD thesis, University of Cape Town 109-112 notes two significan differences. First, the duty of good faith arises from contractual relationships, whereas the fiduciar duty arises *ex lege*. Secondly: 'Duties of good faith require "loyalty" only in the sense of "having regard to" or "not acting contrary to" the interests of another. They are thus essentially concerned with mediating the parties' competing interests by avoiding certain forms of "bad faith" behaviour. Fiduciary duties, on the other hand, require "loyalty" in the absolute or "undivided" sense of acting solely and exclusively in another's interests.'

the function of good faith is restricted to the fiel of contract[131] and to assisting in the interpretation of legal documents.[132] It therefore provides a basis for the 'creative, informative and controlling functions through established rules of contract law',[133] and for applying one legal rule rather than another.[134]

On its own, however, good faith is considered too general and indeterminate to ground an action or defence in law.[135] Thus, when intervening in contractual relationships, the courts must refer, in the firs instance, to rules of positive law,[136] mainly in order to preserve legal certainty.[137] Moreover, although good faith could feasibly have performed the role previously played by the *exceptio doli,*[138] this view has not prevailed in the courts.[139] The SCA held, in *Brisley v Drotsky,*[140] that the principle cannot function as an independent basis for setting aside or refusing to enforce contractual obligations.[141]

(v) *Public policy*

Public policy is also similar to equity, in that it works as a metanorm in a legal system. But it has two points of difference. In the firs place, while public policy (like equity) has a broad scope of application, its core function is to safeguard the general interests of the citizen body, which means that the content of policy changes in accordance with society's needs from time to time.[142] The courts have

---

[131] In a case note on *Botha v Rich* 2C_4 (4) SA 124 (CC), Sharrock (n128) 174ff gives a synopsis of the role of good faith in contract, not_ng (181-182) that the SCA rejected the idea that 'good faith is an independent substantive legal prin_iple — one embodying values such as justice, reasonableness, fairness and equity — on the basis of which the courts may decline to enforce valid contractual provisions. . . . Its view is that reasonableness, fairness and good faith are no more than abstract values which perform creative, informative or controlling functions through established rules of contract law, and that the appropriate mechanism for the judicial control of contract enforcement is public policy.'

[132] Hutchison (n121) 234 Zimmermann 'Good faith and equity' in Zimmermann & Visser (n94) 242-243; Sharrock (n128) _81-183; Hawthorne (n128) 302-304; Louw (n127) 56-57.

[133] Brand (n120 2009) 81_ and see too Du Plessis 'Common law influence on the law of contract and unjustifie enrichment in some mixed legal systems' (2003-4) 78 *Tul L Rev* 239. See generally *South African Forestry Co Ltd v York Timbers* 2005 (3) SA 323 (SCA) para 27.

[134] Christie & Bradfiel (n82) 16. See also *Afrox Healthcare Bpk v Strydom* 2002 (6) SA 21 (SCA), and, as an example, *Tuckers Land & Development Corp v Hovis* 1984 (1) SA 1 (A).

[135] Described by Hutchison (n121) 213 as a 'free floatin principle'. See too *Brisley v Drotsky* 2002 (4) SA 1 (SCA) para 22; *Afrox Healthcare* supra para 32.

[136] See the authorities referred to by Du Plessis (n133) 239 fn124.

[137] Brand (n120 2009) 81_

[138] This is the contention of Zimmermann *The Law of Obligations: Roman foundations of the civilian tradition* 367-377. And, as Hawthorne (n128) 302 says, good faith was not developed into a substantive principle of our law, because its role was fulfille by the *exceptio doli.*

[139] See *Eerste Nasionale Bank van Suidelike Afrika Bpk v Saayman NO* 1997 (4) SA 302 (A) at 323, especially the minority judgment of Olivier JA. Cf Du Plessis (n133) 238.

[140] 2002 (4) SA 1 (SCA).

[141] Christie & Bradfiel (n82) 16; Du Plessis (n133) 238. Cf Kerr (n123 2008) 246. In this regard, Hawthorne (n128) 303 says that, in *Barkhuizen v Napier*, the Constitutional Court repeated the importance of public policy rather than good faith.

[142] Garner (ed) *Black's Law Dictionary* 1351. See the judgment in *Paulsen and another v Slip Knot Investments 777 (Pty) Ltd* 2015 (3) SA 479 (CC) at 86-91 for the difficulties in determining public policy, and reference of the matter in question to the legislature.

given more specifi detail to this settled point of reference, by saying that public policy reflect a common understanding of what constitutes a society's *boni mores*,[143] good morals,[144] a fundamental sense of justice[145] or, as it has sometimes been held, the basic rules of the common law.[146]

In the second place, public policy has an all-inclusive range of operation in the legal system. In this respect it differs from equity which is generally confine to private law. Policy, however, can be invoked in any branch of the law to annul rules, practices or agreements that are deemed harmful to the common weal. In practice, it is most frequently used in cases involving contracts,[147] the recognition or enforcement of foreign laws, judgments and agreements[148] and, formerly, recognition of rules of customary law in terms of the now defunct 'repugnancy proviso'.[149]

---

[143] Hawthorne (n128) 318-319, however, argues that, although public policy has been equated with *boni mores* (which generally focus on family, marriage and sexual relationships), this association is historically and dogmatically incorrect.

[144] Hutchison & Du Bois 'Contracts in general' in Du Bois (ed) *Wille's Principles of South African Law* 768, however, distinguish between public policy and good morals (768). The former applies to contracts that injure the state, aim to obstruct the administration of justice or interfere with an individual's free exercise of rights (765). Joubert *General Principles of the Law of Contract* 132ff, on the other hand, argues that the difference between public policy and good morals is difficult to establish since both are based on public interest.

[145] Van der Merwe et al (n118) 220, however, warn that the concept of 'simple justice between man and man' (cf *Jajbhay v Cassim* 1939 AD 537) in the parties' individual capacities cannot alone determine public interest. It is too crude to serve as a basis for public interest, and might lead to arbitrary decisions. See, too, *Sasfin (Pty) Ltd v Beukes* 1989 (1) SA 1 (A) at 9.

[146] Wessels (Roberts (ed)) *The Law of Contract in South Africa* vol 1 157 relied on Roman and Dutch authority for saying that contracts contravening the moral sense of the community or the common law were void. See generally Hawthorne (n128) 304ff. Christie & Bradfiel (n82) 358 also equate public policy with illegality according to the common law, and argue that it is pointless to distinguish contracts offending public policy, the common law and *boni mores*, because the three terms are interchangeable. As a result, the authors do not defin public policy; they describe it (359) as that which 'run[s] counter to social or economic expedience', is 'inimical to the interests of the community' or 'contrary to law or morality', or that which prevents 'simple justice between man and man' (*Jajbhay's* case supra 544).

[147] Many aspects of contract previously dealt with in terms of equity or public policy were identifie as ripe for legislative intervention by the South African Law Reform Commission *Report on Unreasonable Stipulation in Contracts and the Rectification of Contracts* (1998) Project 47. See further Hefer (n129) 142-154; Naude 'Unfair contract terms legislation: the implications of why we need it for its formulation and application' (2006) 17 *Stell LR* 361-385. Remedial legislation was then passed, notably the National Credit Act 34 of 2005 and the Consumer Protection Act 68 of 2008.

[148] The cases have involved: polygamous marriages (*Seedat's Executors v The Master (Natal)* 1917 AD 302); foreign contracts favouring enemy states (*Farbenfabriken Bayer v Bayer Pharma (Pty) Ltd* 1963 (1) SA 699 (FSC)) and foreign fisca laws (*Commissioner of Taxes, Rhodesia v McFarland* 1965 (1) SA 470 (W); *Cargo Motor Corp v Tofalos Transport Ltd* 1972 (1) SA 186 (W) at 195).

[149] Dating from the British colonial period, this clause barred the application of customary law if such law was 'opposed to the principles of public policy or natural justice'. The clause featured in s 11(1) of the former Black Administration Act 38 of 1927, which was then replaced by s 1(1) of the Law of Evidence Amendment Act 45 of 1988.

Since the advent of the new Constitution, the role of public policy in South African law has been overshadowed by the Bill of Rights.[150] The Constitutional Court, in *Barkhuizen v Napier*,[151] for instance, established a clear linkage between policy and the values of the Constitution: '[s]ince the advent of our constitutional democracy, public policy is now deeply rooted in our Constitution and the values that underlie it, [namely] . . . human dignity, the achievement of equality and the advancement of human rights and freedoms, and the rule of law.'[152] In fact, reference to the Bill of Rights offers a distinct advantage over public policy, because the courts can now avoid the 'unruly horse'[153] of a vaguely conceived idea of community interests by referring, instead, to a define set of fundamental rights.[154]

Nevertheless, public policy still has a role to play in the law, especially in such matters as contract, in part because not all aspects of the common weal are given legal protection by constitutional rights,[155] and in part because public policy stands for current community interests.[156] Hence, it is noticeable that, in *Barkhuizen's* case,[157] despite the Bill of Rights' status as the supreme law of the land, the Constitutional Court upheld the continued relevance of 'the general sense of justice of the community, the *boni mores*, manifested in public opinion'.[158] These terms bring to contract law the notions of fairness and justice, thereby precluding the enforcement of terms that would lead to a contrary result.[159]

Of all the elements of South African law, public policy undoubtedly has the greatest capacity to articulate a general principle of equity — and, as it happens, ubuntu. It has a broad scope of application, and it has many connections with existing concepts in the common law that are aimed at achieving the common

---

[150] See, for example, judicial intervention to determine a major question of policy, namely, the issuing of ARV drugs to counteract the HIV/AIDS epidemic, was based on the Bill of Rights: *Minister of Health and others v Treatment Action Campaign and others* (No 2) 2002 (5) SA 721 (CC).

[151] 2007 (5) SA 323 (CC) paras 28 and 29. See Kerr (n123 2008) 243ff regarding this case, and the influenc of the Constitution on the understanding of public policy.

[152] In *South African Forestry Co Ltd v York Timbers* 2005 (3) SA 323 (SCA) para 27, however, the SCA cautioned 'perceptive restraint' when considering whether to refuse to enforce contracts on the ground that the parties act in terms of the 'constitutional values such as dignity, equality and freedom'. The court referred here to *Brisley v Drotsky* 2002 (4) SA 1 (SCA) and *Afrox Healthcare Bpk v Strydom* 2002 (6) SA 21 (SCA).

[153] An image coined by Burrough J in *Richardson v Mellish* (1824) 2 Bing 229 at 259.

[154] As, for example, in *Carmichele v Minister of Safety and Security and another (Centre for Applied Legal Studies Intervening)* 2001 (4) SA 938 (CC) and *K v Minister of Safety and Security* 2005 (6) SA 419 (CC).

[155] The Bill of Rights, for instance, failed to play a decisive role in regulating contracts for gambling and sexual services. See Le Roux W 'Sex work, the right to occupational freedom and the constitutional politics of recognition' (2003) 120 *SALJ* 456-457.

[156] Louw (n127) 1ff also argues for the relevance of good faith to animate the rules and values of the Constitution in order to achieve a transformation in South African society.

[157] 2007 (5) SA 323 (CC).

[158] Paragraph 73, citing here, *inter alia*, *Schultz v Butt* 1986 (3) SA 667 (A) at 679.

[159] Sutherland (n128) 411.

good.[160] The *dicta* mentioned above in *Barkhuizen's* case make this point: when referring to community opinion as the basis for public policy, the Court included such connections as justice, fairness, *boni mores* and reasonableness.[161]

6 THE BILL OF RIGHTS

From the above discussion of the common-law devices for achieving equity, we can now consider the possibility that they — and ubuntu — have been superseded by a much more powerful instrument, ie, the Bill of Rights. The Constitution declares itself to be the supreme law of the land and that 'law or conduct inconsistent with it is invalid, and the obligations imposed by it must be fulfilled'[162] It follows that the Bill of Rights, a keystone of the Constitution, can be invoked both to resolve particular disputes and to initiate general legal change. To this end, the Bill of Rights is made applicable to all law, and is binding on 'the legislature, the executive, the judiciary and all organs of state'.[163] In addition, it binds all natural persons to the extent that it is applicable.[164] Violation of a fundamental right can therefore be used as a reason for annulling or amending any laws or juridical acts whether public or private,[165] or for founding a right held by one individual vis-à-vis another in the absence of statute or common law.[166]

If we accept the general understanding that the Bill of Rights is the most powerful mechanism for curing injustice, and that it is the repository of most (if not all) values relevant to our society, then we might be forgiven for concluding that any form of equitable doctrine — including ubuntu — may be redundant. Such thinking, however, would be wrong.

For a start, the common-law equitable principles are still playing an active role in the legal system. The functions of the *condictiones* and the fiduciar duty have certainly not been usurped by the Bill of Rights, nor have those of good faith and public policy. Unlike the Bill of Rights these principles have both a lengthy tradition of usage and particular spheres of application.

---

[160] These linkages have provided ubuntu's points of entry into the legal system. See above p 96.

[161] 2007 (5) SA 323 (CC) para 73.

[162] Section 2. Moreover, s 7(2) provides that: 'The state must respect, protect, promote and fulfi the rights in the Bill of Rights.'

[163] Section 8(1).

[164] Section 8(2) 'taking into account the nature of the right and the nature of any duty imposed by the right'.

[165] *S v Makwanyane and another* 1995 (3) SA 391 (CC) paras 301-302. In this regard see: Lubbe (n128) 395ff; Bhana (n128) 3ff; Sutherland (n128) 393 and Part 2 (2009) 20 *Stell LR* 50ff. The legislature enacted major reforms on the basis of these provisions to correct injustices inherited from the laws of the pre-democratic era. The following are examples: Labour Relations Act 66 of 1995; Prevention of Illegal Eviction from and Unlawful Occupation of Land Act 19 of 1998; Promotion of Administrative Justice Act 3 of 2000; Promotion of Access to Information Act 2 of 2000; National Credit Act 34 of 2005; Consumer Protection Act 68 of 2008. Two major examples in customary law are the Recognition of Customary Marriages Act 120 of 1998 and the Reform of Customary Law of Succession and Regulation of Related Matters Act 11 of 2009.

[166] In other words, the Bill of Rights is 'directly' horizontal in its application: *Khumalo and others v Holomisa* 2002 (5) SA 401 (CC). Cf *Du Plessis and others v De Klerk and another* 1996 (3) SA 850 (CC) paras 72-73. All other forms of horizontal application are then 'indirect'.

As for ubuntu, the previous chapter showed that it has been deployed by the courts with frequent reference to the fundamental rights. One of the reasons they did so was to modify the impact of the rights, which suggests that ubuntu is a valuable means for interpreting the new constitutional regime. This proposition becomes evident in three situations.

The firs is where the generality of a fundamental right — especially dignity or equality — has to be interpreted, and thereby refined if it is to be applied appropriately in a particular case. Ubuntu, in particular, has provided the necessary filte through which account could be taken of individual circum-stances[167] and, when necessary, the history and needs of South African society as a whole.[168] In the second situation, litigants often appeal to different rights to support their arguments, and in these cases, ubuntu has been invoked to mediate the outcome by giving additional force to one argument as opposed to the other.[169] In the third case, application of a particular right may result (paradoxically it might seem) in an unfair outcome. The intervention of ubuntu is then required to produce a better result.[170]

In all these situations, the courts have been using ubuntu to impart African values to the Bill of Rights. In this respect, ubuntu goes beyond both the Constitution and the common-law equitable remedies to bring a specificall African concept of right-doing to our legal system.[171] Indeed, in *Everfresh Market Virginia (Pty) Ltd v Shoprite Checkers (Pty) Ltd*,[172] the Constitutional Court called for the development of a new law of contract informed not only by constitutional but also traditional African values, ie, by ubuntu.[173] Similarly, in *Dikoko v Mokhatla*,[174] the Court advocated an ubuntu conception of dignity that would emphasise 'the restoration of harmonious human and social relationships where they have been ruptured by an infraction of community norms.' And, in the *Port Elizabeth Municipality v Various Occupiers*,[175] Sachs J declared that the spirit of ubuntu combines 'individual rights with a communitarian philosophy' requiring 'human interdependence, respect and concern'.

---

[167] For example, *Hoffmann v South African Airways* 2001 (1) SA 1 (CC).

[168] For example, *South African Police Service v Solidarity obo Barnard* 2014 (6) SA 123 (CC); *City of Tshwane Metropolitan Municipality v Afriforum and another* 2016 (6) SA 279 (CC); *The Citizen 1978 (Pty) Ltd and others v McBride (Johnstone and others, Amici Curiae)* 2011 (4) SA 191 (CC).

[169] For example, *Manyaishe v M&G Media Ltd and others* [2009] JOL 24238 (SCA).

[170] For example, *Savage and others v Sisters of the Holy Cross, Cape Province and others* 2015 (6) SA 1 (WCC); *Crossley and others v National Commissioner of South African Police Service and others* [2004] 3 All SA 436 (T).

[171] See above pp 97-98.

[172] 2012 (1) SA 256 (CC) paras 23-24.

[173] See Van der Sijde *The Role of Good Faith in the South African Law of Contract* (2012) unpublished LLM thesis. University of Pretoria 24-25 who links good faith and ubuntu. For the connection between these two principles, see Louw (n127) esp 74-76.

[174] 2006 (6) SA 235 (CC) para 68.

[175] 2005 (1) SA 217 (CC) para 37. Previously, with reference to the Interim Constitution, Madala J expressed similar sentiments in *S v Makwanyane and another* 1995 (3) SA 391 (CC) para 237.

7 CONCLUSION

All structured legal systems have metanorms designed to correct injustices arising from the failure of the law to address particular factual situations. The equity metanorm prevailing in continental Europe, and incorporated into Roman-Dutch law, was the species inherited by South Africa, whereas equity in England developed into a different form to become a specialised branch of the legal system. In light of the role played by equity in these legal systems, we can now return to consider the issues posed previously in this chapter: how ubuntu compares with equity, whether it is redundant to the requirements of South African law and which path it should follow for its advance into the future.

Ubuntu has one obvious similarity with all systems of equity: to soften the impact of established rules of law when their application causes an injustice. Another similarity, although of less consequence today, is the link between equity and ubuntu in the spiritual realm. In the case of equity this link is historical, coming from the belief that moral conduct derived from divine justice (which in England was taken to be via the Lord Chancellor's conscience); in the case of ubuntu, moral conduct is determined by the ancestors.[176]

Here the similarities end and the differences emerge. The use of equity in English and Roman-Dutch law is generally confine to the sphere of private law, whereas ubuntu has been invoked in all areas of the law. In English law, equity provided a cause of action, as it did in Roman-Dutch law through the *condictiones*, the *exceptio doli* and the fiduciar duty. Ubuntu, on the other hand, has not, thus far, given rise to an actionable right. Another major difference lies in a function performed by ubuntu that is absent in the case of equity. Equity is a culturally neutral concept that, notionally at least, transcends all times and societies, whereas ubuntu imports a decidedly African understanding of right-doing to the law. Thus, ubuntu has generally been invoked with the express intention of making fundamental rights or the principles of good faith and public policy more relevant to African conditions.

The latter point goes part of the way to answering the issue of redundancy, for the equitable remedies of South African law do not perform the culturally legitimating function of ubuntu. What is more, they are available in more limited circumstances than ubuntu. The *condictiones* are obviously available only when certain types of act lead to an unwarranted benefi for a particular person, and the fiduciar duty arises only when a specifi type of relationship imposes a duty of trust or the utmost good faith on a particular person. The obligations ensuing from both these institutions are therefore confine to specifi factual situations, and are generally classifie as part of private law.

Good faith and public policy have a broader scope of application, and may appear to overlap with ubuntu in that they operate as general principles to be used for justifying or interpreting rules and juridical acts. They are nevertheless distinguishable from ubuntu. Good faith has a restricted sphere of application in that it is usually invoked in private law to determine the validity of clauses in contracts or to interpret legal instruments. Public policy is applicable in both

---

[176] See above pp 43-44.

public and private law and gives effect to the common interests of society as a whole at a particular time.

This chapter explored the history of the English doctrine of equity in some depth in order to reveal its similarities to and differences from ubuntu, and thereby to suggest the future development of ubuntu. Equity in England, in the early years of its development, was invoked on a case-by-case basis without any attempt to discover a common unifying theme. The same is true of ubuntu and its present position in South African law. In the case of equity, however, ensuing complaints about uncertainty and arbitrariness led to a compilation of precedents into a fixe code of rules. As a result, equity was not only deprived of the flexibilit necessary to respond to specifi factual scenarios, but also came to be seen as a system operating in opposition to the common law.

Such an outcome is clearly not desirable for ubuntu which is currently operating not to contradict the provisions of mainstream South African law, but to complement or modify their application. In consequence, ubuntu should continue to be applied in much the same manner as equity in the civilian tradition of Roman-Dutch law, ie, as a free floatin element with no specifi area of application other than to solve individual hard cases. A problem of legal certainty might eventually begin to surface, but it is not at present a serious issue.

In any event, ubuntu has not been used, and is unlikely to develop, in a haphazard manner. In contrast with English equity, its application does not depend on a Lord Chancellor's notional 'good conscience'. The Constitution provides constant parameters for all elements of South African law, notably, 'human dignity, the achievement of equality and the advancement of human rights and freedoms'.[177]

---

[177] Section 1(a) of the Constitution.

Chapter 6

IMBIZO

1 INTRODUCTION: IMBIZO AND PUBLIC PARTICIPATION

'The structure and organisation of early African societies in this country fascinated me very much and greatly influence the evolution of my political outlook. . . . All men were free and equal and this was the foundation of government. Recognition of this general principle found expression in the constitution of the council, variously called Imbizo, or Pitso, or Kgotla, which governs the affairs of the tribe.'[1]

In this chapter we move from the normative concepts of ubuntu and equity to the factual: an ancient institution of customary law which in seTswana is termed *kgotla*,[2] in sePedi and seSotho, *pitso*[3] and in isiXhosa and isiZulu, *imbizo*.[4] (For convenience sake, the latter term and the plural *imibizo* have been used in this book.) The imbizo is a public assembly which is constituted when a traditional leader summons those under his (or sometimes her) jurisdiction to discuss any major issue affecting the common weal,[5] usually speaking for the nation as a whole,[6] the alienation of national land[7] and the appointment of a new leader.[8]

---

[1] Mandela 'Nelson Mandela's firs court statement', available at https://www.nelsonmandela.org/omalley/index.php/site/q/03lv01538/04lv01600/05lv01624/06lv01625.htm [Accessed 18 October 2015].

[2] Schapera *A Handbook of Tswana Law and Custom* 80.

[3] Derived from the verb *-bitsa* [call]. See Hamnett *Chieftainship and Legitimacy: an anthropological study of executive law in Lesotho* 78; Prinsloo *Die Inheemse Administratiefreg van 'n Noord-Sothostam* 90-93, 95 and 134-135; Prinsloo *Inheemse Publiekreg in Lebowa* 80 and 154.

[4] Derived from the verb *-biza* [call]: Mini et al *Greater Dictionary of Xhosa Volume 2* 312. The word is define in s 1 of the KwaZulu-Natal Traditional Leadership and Governance Act 5 of 2005 as 'a consultative meeting of the members of a traditional community called in accordance with custom'. The term, *indaba*, often seen in conjunction with imbizo, is considered in more detail in Chapter 7.

[5] And is translated as such in Doke & Vilakazi (eds) *The English-Zulu/Zulu-English Dictionary*: 'convocation, meeting of persons summoned (as by a chief).'

[6] *Bengwenyama-ya-Maswazi Community and others v Minister for Mineral Resources and others* 2015 (1) SA 197 (SCA) para 40.

[7] See cases to footnote 11 below.

Community members are thus provided with a forum at which to voice their opinions directly to those in power.

Imbizo and its related terms entered South African law shortly after ubuntu.[9] The arrival, however, attracted far less attention in the legal literature, which was due, in part at least, to imbizo giving no cause for concern about definition The term was already known both from references in the ethnographic literature[10] and from judgments in the colonial courts[11] — and, of course, it has a definabl physical referent, unlike ubuntu, which refers to an indeterminate abstract ideal. Moreover, use of imbizo has not had the same wide-ranging impact on the law as ubuntu. As will become apparent, it has been invoked only to discharge the state's constitutional obligation to ensure public participation in governance.

Notwithstanding these differences, ubuntu and imbizo share common ground, and their simultaneous introduction to South African law is no coincidence. First and foremost, they are both concerned with community welfare in that imbizo provides the stereotypical social setting for realizing the values of ubuntu.[12] Secondly, as in the case of ubuntu, the courts have used the vernacular word rather than an English or Afrikaans translation,[13] in order to send the message that they were referring to a specificall African institution.

Thirdly, ubuntu and imbizo have been involved with South Africa's programme of constitutional transformation,[14] and both have been closely linked to provisions in the new Constitution. In the case of imbizo, these provisions are specific s 1(d), which lists 'accountability, responsiveness and openness' amongst the founding values of the Republic,[15] and s 59(1)(a), which obliges Parliament to 'facilitate

---

[8] Holomisa 'Balancing law and tradition: the TCB and its relation to African systems of justice administration' (2011) 35 *SA Crime Quarterly* 21; Mabelebele 'Ideological objectives underpinning imbizo as a model of communication and governance' (2006) 25 *Communicare* 114ff. See, too, *Pilane and another v Pilane and another* 2013 (4) BCLR 431 (CC).

[9] For two early cases, see *Wababa and others v Premier, Eastern Cape Province and another* [1999] JOL 5801 (Ck) and *Gaika and another v Premier of the Province of the Eastern Cape and others* [2001] JOL 8286 (Ck).

[10] In addition to the sources in footnotes 2 and 3, see: Kuper 'The social structure of the Sotho-speaking peoples of Southern Africa. Part I' (1975) 45 *Africa* 72; Eckert, De Beer & Vorster 'Worldviews and decision making: natural resource management of the Laka of Mapela in an anthropological perspective' (2001) 24 *SA Tydskr Etnol* 91; Myburgh & Prinsloo *Indigenous Public Law in KwaNdebele* 41-42 and 63-64; Hunter *Reaction to Conquest: effects of contact with Europeans on the Pondo of South Africa* 394; Mönnig *The Pedi* 284-285; Krige *The Social System of the Zulus* 219; Kuper *The Swazi: a South African Kingdom* 36-38; Van Warmelo & Phophi *Venda Law* Part 4 (1949) 1758-1805, Part 5 (1967) 2658-2665; Ramsay *Tsonga Law in the Transvaal* 16.

[11] For example, *Hermannsberg Mission Society v Commissioner for Native Affairs and another* 1906 TS 135; *Mogale v Engelbrecht and others* 1907 TS 836; *Bafokeng Private Land Buyers Association and others v Royal Bafokeng Nation and others* (999/08) [2016] ZANWHC 27.

[12] Mbaya 'Social capital and the imperatives of the concept and life of ubuntu in the South African context' (2010) 104 *Scriptura* 370. Imbizo is also associated with consensual decision-making (which is dealt with in the next chapter): Murithi 'African approaches to building peace and social solidarity' (2006) 6 *African J on Conflict Resolution* 16ff.

[13] Indeed the word is now included in South African English: Silva *A Dictionary of South African English on Historical Principles* 307. Afrikaans has the term *bosberaad*, which is often seen in conjunction with imbizo and its equivalents. See fn 78 below.

[14] See below p 162-164

[15] Section 1(d) of the Constitution of the Republic of South Africa, 1996.

public involvement in the legislative and other processes of the Assembly and its committees'.

Read together these sections introduced the framework for participatory democracy to South Africa.[16] Because imbizo is open to most — if not all — members of a community, and because it involves a free exchange of views between traditional leaders and their subjects, it provides an ideal forum for achieving this purpose. Hence, although participatory democracy was an innovation for South Africa's new constitutional order, it soon became evident to judges and law-makers alike that this principle had always been present in customary law.[17]

The courts accordingly recognised imibizo as an acceptable method for fulfillin the requirements of s 59(1)(a). They thereby endorsed an existing practice established by state authorities of terming ad hoc public meetings summoned to deal with such contentious issues as labour disputes[18] or recurrent service delivery protests[19] imibizo. What is more, when the new ANC led government took office, it launched certain long-term initiatives designed to integrate public participation into administrative processes.[20] The most notable example was *Presidential Imbizo Programme*.[21]

Cultural-linguistic appropriation of this nature, however, raises serious questions. In the firs place, does an imbizo summoned by a state official bear any relation, in its composition and by its conduct, to the traditional form? In the second place, even if these meetings are called by traditional leaders, and may thereby comply with a traditional stereotype, do they meet the demands of a truly participative or direct form of democracy? As an unelected official, does the leader concerned have popular or dynastic legitimacy? And, even more important, are all those present at an imbizo given an equal opportunity to speak?

From research done on the government's various initiatives falling under the label imibizo, it appears that the term has been too loosely applied. While the imbizo considered typical of the traditional form of African government could well meet the constitutional requirements of public involvement in decision-

---

[16] See below p 128 and 134ff.

[17] A point picked up by the Constitutional Court: *Doctors for Life International v The Speaker of the National Assembly and others* 2006 (6) SA 416 (CC) para 101; *Minister of Health and another NO v New Clicks SA (Pty) Ltd and others (Treatment Action Campaign and another as Amici Curiae)* 2006 (2) SA 311 (CC) para 625.

[18] For instance, *Metrorail v SALSTAFF obo Prinsloo and others* [1998] 6 BALR 764 (IMSSA).

[19] Van der Waal 'Spatial and organisational complexity in the Dwars River Valley, Western Cape' (2005) 28 *Anthro SA* 8ff. See, too, Smith 'Dak oor kop dié begeerte by Bolanders' (30 September 2004) *Die Burger* 6 and the comments by the Constitutional Court in *Joseph v City of Johannesburg* 2010 (4) SA 55 (CC) paras 43 and 46 on the government's duty to ensure fair, respectful and responsive administration especially with regard to the delivery of public services at the municipal level.

[20] These processes included a Community Development Workers programme, Integrated Development Planning and a ward committees system: Booysen 'Public participation in democratic South Africa: from popular mobilisation to structured co-optation and protest' (2009) 28 *Politeia* 1ff.

[21] See further below pp 138ff.

making, the contemporary meetings all too often did not.[22] In fact, the labelling of meetings as imbizo seems to have functioned as a self-serving strategy to win political support, especially the support of a previously disenfranchised electorate.[23]

2 MODELS OF DEMOCRACY

The introduction of public participation in decision-making is aimed at achieving a better standard of democracy in South Africa, which implies that the representative form of democracy, that had been in operation in Southern Africa since the mid-nineteenth century, was deficient To understand why and how public participation is an improvement, a brief outline of the different models of democracy is necessary.

Any form of democracy is designed to co-opt the consent of a political community to decision-making processes in order to enhance the effectiveness and legitimacy of state decisions. In this regard, the ancient idea of direct democracy is usually held up as an ideal. It is associated with the assembly of a citizen body, when everyone was entitled to debate an issue concerned with the wellbeing of the group. While this model is derived from the government of certain ancient Greek city states,[24] it is also found in many pre-modern cultures.[25]

---

[22] Bilchitz 'Are socio-economic rights a form of political rights?' (2015) 31 *SAJHR* 92-93, who, with regard to *Merafong Demarcation Forum and others v President of the Republic of South Africa and others* 2008 (5) SA 171 (CC), notes that: 'Whilst public participation may allow the interests of the poor to be voiced, it is ultimately their representatives who must translate what they hear into legislation policies and effective programmes.' All too often this is not done: Holness 'Equality of the graveyard: participatory democracy in the context of housing delivery: Grootboom' (2011) 26 *SAPL* 9. See, too, Matshedisho 'Between imbizo and battle grounds: the deterioration of the public sphere in South Africa' Paper presented at CODESRIA 07-11 December 2008 at Yaoundé, Cameroun, available at https://www.codesria.org/IMG/pdf/Knowledge_Rajohane_Matshedisho.pdf [Accessed 23 May 2017] esp 19, who argues that the current meetings termed imibizo (which he compares with Habermas's political public space, fn 32 below) bear little relationship to their traditional form.

[23] See Piper & Nadvi 'Popular mobilisation, party dominance and participatory governance in South Africa' in Thompson & Tapscott *Citizenship, Mobilisation and Social Movements in the South: Perspectives from the Global South* 233ff with regard to the Msunduzi and eThekwini municipalities in KZN.

[24] The very word *democratia* (rule of the people), for instance, was coined in the fift century BCE to denote the political systems of certain city states in Greece, where citizen assemblies were the principal expression of popular rule. See Hornblower 'Creation and development of democratic institutions in ancient Greece' in Dunn (ed) *Democracy: the unfinished journey 508 BC — AD 1993* 8.

[25] Sen *The Idea of Justice* 328-341. In *Doctors for Life International v The Speaker of the National Assembly and others* 2006 (5) SA 416 (CC) para 101, Ngcobo J observed that institutions similar to imbizo were found in medieval Europe (most famously in the Magna Carta).

Direct democracy, however, is unworkable in large heterogeneous states,[26] and now serves mainly as a utopian ideal.[27] Not surprisingly, then, the more usual form of democracy in the modern world is representative. This model implies the citizens' right to elect representatives, who thereby have the authority to speak on their constituents' behalf.[28] Government decision-making is therefore based on a system of majority voting by the representatives in a collective assembly.

In various guises, representative democracy has been the basis of government in South Africa since the colonial era, whether in the Cape and Natal colonies, the Trekker Republics, the 1910 Union of South Africa or the apartheid Republic of 1961. It remains a keystone of the 1996 Constitution.[29] Even so, this model of democracy is far from involving citizens in the day-to-day matters of governance, because their rights are limited to exercising a periodic vote at election time.

A third form of democracy may therefore be instituted to supplement government by elected representatives.[30] Participatory democracy allows citizens to participate in the everyday decisions that affect the general public interest. This model is concerned primarily with the modalities of when and how citizens should participate,[31] and it is the basis for ss 1(d) and 59(1)(a) of the Constitution.

Finally, mention must be made of deliberative democracy.[32] This model advocates a form of citizen participation based on reasoned discussion amongst all interested parties as the basis for justifying political decision-making.[33] Public reasoning on equal terms lies at the heart of this process,[34] namely, a dialogical method for exploring the means for producing optimally effective and socially accepted decisions. This being the case, deliberative democracy seems to be implicit in the imbizo framework (and in the indaba process which is discussed in the next chapter).[35]

---

[26] Versions of direct democracy, however, have survived through to the modern era, in the form of occasional national referenda and such institutions as the Althing in Iceland and Switzerland's cantonment voting system. See Sokolon & Malone 'Democracy's march through history' in Malone (ed) *Achieving Democracy: democratization in theory and practice* 13-14.

[27] Roux 'Democracy' in Woolman & Bishop (eds) *Constitutional Law of South Africa* 10-4 to 10-10.

[28] Held *Models of Democracy* 27.

[29] Section 1(d).

[30] But not to replace it, as the courts have emphasised: *Matatiele Municipality and others v President of the Republic of South Africa and others (No 2)* 2007 (6) SA 477 (CC) para 60.

[31] Roux (n27) 10-14.

[32] Which is based on Habermas (trans Rehg) *Between Facts and Norms: contributions to a discourse theory of law and democracy*.

[33] See Fishkin *When the People Speak: deliberative democracy and public consultation* 160ff for an overview of the principles. See further Harvey 'Governing after the rights revolution' (2000) 27 *J Law & Soc* 63-68, who outlines the different strands of thinking about deliberative democracy.

[34] Cohen 'Procedure and substance in deliberative democracy' in Benhabib (ed) *Democracy and Difference: contesting the boundaries of the political* 100.

[35] Liebenberg 'Engaging the paradoxes of the universal and particular in human rights adjudication: the possibilities and pitfalls of "meaningful engagement" ' (2012) 12 *AHRLJ* 1ff argues that, in a pluralist society such as South Africa, a deliberative form of democracy, implemented in various forums, is well adapted to reconciling universalist human rights with particular situations, and thereby solving local conflicts

From what has been said above, it would appear that an imbizo can combine elements of the direct, participatory and deliberative models, and the phrase 'facilitate public involvement' in s 59(1)(a) is sufficiently broad to accommodate many different means of involvement. Even so, when talking of imbizo, the courts normally refer to it as a participatory form of democracy, thereby emphasising the citizens' simple right to take part in processes of governance.[36]

3 THE IMBIZO, ITS COMPOSITION AND STRUCTURE

The imbizo, as understood by the courts and government, is a traditional method for engaging members of a political community in decisions affecting their welfare. In order to determine whether it can properly fulfi the new constitutional mandate of facilitating public participation, we need to know more about the functioning of imibzo, and how they may have been influence by the forces of social and political change.

The use of a citizen assembly as an institution of governance is usually associated with a certain type of society: one that has weak structures of centralised power.[37] As a result, leaders cannot rely on a permanently established enforcement apparatus to back up their rule. With the exception of such famous examples as the Zulu kingdom,[38] variations of this type of polical order were common in the pre-colonial societies of Southern Africa.

In these societies, plenary authority was invested in chiefs (to use the colonial parlance),[39] or kings and paramount chiefs,[40] who represented their people in dealings with outsiders.[41] According to a common saying, however, 'a chief is a chief through his people'.[42] Thus, a ruler's authority was never continuing and unquestioned. It had to be continually recreated for specifi issues and in specifi

---

[36] For an overview, see Pateman *Participation and Democratic Theory* (1970) esp ch 2; Held (n28) 209–216; Cunningham *Theories of Democracy: a critical introduction* 123ff; Wolfe 'A defense of participatory democracy' (1985) 47 *Review of Politics* 371-376.

[37] As opposed to centralised state societies. This dichotomy is based on Fortes & Evans-Pritchard 'Introduction' in Fortes & Evans-Pritchard (eds) *African Political Systems* esp 5ff, which, despite much criticism, is still a useful model for describing precolonial African polities.

[38] A historically controversial topic see Hamilton *Terrific Majesty: the power of Shaka Zulu and the limits of historical invention*.

[39] Whatever the nuances of political structures in Southern Africa, the colonial authorities imposed the same system of classificatio on all indigenous polities and their rulers. The latter were usually termed 'chiefs' and the former 'chiefdoms' or 'chieftaincies'. See Van Rouveroy van Nieuwaal 'Chiefs and African states: some introductory notes and an extensive bibliography on African chieftaincy' (1987) 25/26 *J Legal Pluralism & Unofficial L* 5ff.

[40] Now termed 'kings', 'queens', 'senior traditional leaders' or simply 'traditional leaders' in terms of s 1(b) of the Traditional Leadership and Governance Framework Act 41 of 2003.

[41] Schapera (n2) 69; Sansom in Hammond-Tooke (ed) *The Bantu-speaking Peoples of Southern Africa* 266.

[42] In seTswana, *kgosi ke kgosi ka batho*. See Gulbrandsen 'The king is king by the grace of the people: the exercise and control of power in subject-ruler relations' (1995) 37 *Comp Stud Soc Hist* 415ff; Prinsloo (n2 *Publiekreg in Lebowa*) 161; Schapera (n2) 84.

contexts.[43] In other words, a traditional leader had to govern with the consent, or at least acquiescence, of his subjects.[44]

As the leader of his people, a chief presided over a national council of elders (which was also the highest court of the realm), and he was entitled to summon and chair imibizo.[45] The assembly took place at a place located at a conveniently central point of the political unit concerned.[46] Space permitting, this area was normally situated between the chief's cattle byre and the houses constituting his homestead.[47] In seSotho and seTswana, this area was referred to as the *kgotla*, a term that also signifie   an assembly, a court or an advisory council.[48] In isiXhosa, the area was termed the *inkundla*, a word that also had a social referent: the leader and his headmen in council (the *ibandla*), who together could constitute a tribunal to settle disputes (again referred to as *inkundla*).[49]

Factors of gender, age and birth determined not only a person's right to leadership of the nation, but also the procedures in an imbizo and the entitlement to participate. The latter right depended, for a start, on affiliation to the relevant political community, which was established mainly by birth or permission to settle there.[50] Thereafter, age and gender were critical factors. The only people with an unquestioned right to full participation were adult male subjects of the chief.[51]

---

[43] Hammond-Tooke *Command or Consensus: the development of Transkeian local government* 65. Comaroff 'Chieftainship in a South African homeland: a case study of the Tshidi chiefdom of Bophuthatswana' (1974) 1 *JSAS* 41 says that traditional authority 'suggests that the rights and duties of an incumbent are not immutably fixed   the chief and his subjects are thought to be involved in perpetual transactional process in which the former discharges obligations and, in return, receives the accepted right to influenc   policy and command people.... The degree to which his performance is evaluated as being satisfactory is held to determine the extent of his legitimacy, as expressed in the willingness of the Tshidi to execute his decisions.'

[44] Hammond-Tooke op cit 30ff. See too Hall *The Changing Past: farmers, kings and traders in Southern Africa, 2OO-186O* (1987) 65.

[45] For a general overview of official customary law, see Olivier et al 'Indigenous Law' in Joubert (ed) *Laws of South Africa* vol 32 para 81.

[46] Note that a particular subject matter might require a particular venue. *In re Kranspoort Community* 2000 (2) SA 124 (LCC) para 15, for instance, governance at a mission station was divided into religious and secular matters: the former were the preserve of a church council and the latter the preserve of a *kgotla* (which met under a large tree alongside the church).

[47] McAllister 'Ritual and social practice in the Transkei' (1997) 56 *African Studies* 283.

[48] Schapera (n2) 80; Schapera *Government and Politics in Tribal Societies* 43-46. With the Bafokeng, the *kgotla* is described as 'the core of Tswana life — so much so that one may well speak of the Tswana as "living their lives in courts" ': Gulbrandsen 'Town-state formations on the edge of the Kalahari' (2007) 51 *Social Analysis* 63. See further references in *Mathibe v Tsoke* 1925 AD 105; *S v Matlapeng* 1970 (1) SA 333 (T); *In re Kranspoort Community* 2000 (2) SA 124 (LCC) para 15. While an imbizo or pitso generally refers to an assembly of the whole nation, a *kgotla* may also refer to a much smaller unit, such as a family. A contemporary account of a family *kgotla* is given by Coertze & De Beer 'Succession to *bogosi* among the Batlhako ba Matutu in a changing dispensation' (2007) 30 *Anthro SA* 47. See, too, Myburgh & Prinsloo (n10) 57-59.

[49] McAllister (n47) 283; Masina 'Xhosa practices of *ubuntu* for South Africa' in Zartman (ed) *Traditional Cures for Modern Conflicts: African conflict 'medicine'* 171; Hammond-Tooke (n43) 141.

[50] For the terms of affiliation to a political community, see generally: Myburgh *Die Inheemse Staat in Suider-Afrika* 11-15, Prinsloo (n2 *Noord-Sothostam*) 66-69; Myburgh & Prinsloo (n48) 2-4.

[51] Gulbrandsen (n48) 63.

The panel of officials presiding over the eventual assembly was organised according to each individual's status in the community. A Tswana *kgotla*, for instance, has been described as 'intrinsically hierarchical, being chaired by the genealogically most senior man surrounded by a group of elders called *bagakolodi*, or "remembrancers" (indicating their experience and their capacity as conveyors of customs), who serve as the senior man's counselors'.[52] The marks of hierarchy could be gauged by the placement of officials in relation to one another and members of the public. The presiding officer sat facing the assembly of the people, and with the Bafokeng — as with most other groups in South Africa — the highest ranking elder sat to the right of him, and the next ranking elder sat to the left.[53] In accordance with seniority of age or status, the remaining elders were then placed in corresponding order to the presiding officer's right and left.

The order of speaking was yet another reflectio of hierarchy. A senior elder or the presiding officer usually introduced the topic under discussion. The matter was then thrown open for general debate, after which each of the elders could express his view in an inverse order of ranking, ie, a junior speaking firs and the most senior speaking last.[54] Once all interested parties had had their say, the presiding officer announced a fina decision, which should, ideally, have reflecte a common consensus.[55]

Silence was usually taken as a marker of female identity. Because of a man's supposedly superior wisdom, women were subject to male guidance, and they were obliged to accept a man's word both as a token of respect and to demonstrate their femininity.[56] Women were therefore expected to defer to older men. Even if women happened to constitute the majority of the gathering, their presence might not be felt. '[T]hey would be apologetic before they speak and ask whether they have the right to speak.'[57] Normally, however, women (and junior men and outsiders) were only allowed to listen or give evidence.[58]

This description held true of the past, and is no doubt still true in many rural areas today. To the extent that this is the case, then the composition and hierarchies implicit in imibizo will infringe the constitutional requirement of equality. First, certain members of the community may be excluded from the assembly on grounds of age, gender or birth. Secondly, the patriarchal principle determining the entitlement to speak may silence certain participants. Women are generally the

---

[52] Gulbrandsen ibid; Kuper (Social Structure Part I) 72 and 77.

[53] Gulbrandsen ibid.

[54] Gulbrandsen ibid.

[55] See generally Bennett *Customary Law in South Africa* 104-105.

[56] Cited in Brown & Duku 'Negotiated identities: dynamics in parents' participation in school governance in rural Eastern Cape schools and implications for school leadership' (2008) 28 *SA J of Education* 445.

[57] Brown & Duku op cit 424-425. See, for example, the study conducted by the Transvaal Rural Action Committee in 1990: Kompe & Small 'Demanding a place under the *kgotla* tree: rural women's access to land and power' (1991) *Third World Legal Stud* 137ff.

[58] Kompe & Small op cit 144.

most seriously prejudiced group, but also affected are men considered juniors[59] or of low status.[60]

Gender discrimination is not, however, the norm in all communities. The Lovedu, for instance, famously allowed women to occupy special positions of power.[61] Furthermore, in most communities, when female status had been enhanced by age, child-bearing or by virtue of the woman's position in the kinship structure, senior mothers and the patrilineal aunts in an agnatic family could be allowed both to attend and speak.[62] And, in all cases, patriarchal traditions may have changed to bring community meetings into closer alignment with constitutional requirements.[63]

Thus, when determining the legitimacy of an imbizo, the fair and equal right of audience is a critical factor to consider. Another, quite different factor concerning legitimacy is the right to summon an imbizo. According to customary law, this right vests in traditional leaders, but not all the current leaders acquired their positions in accordance with the rules of succession in customary law, due in large part to the interventions of colonial and apartheid governments.

When Britain began its colonisation of Southern Africa, the indigenous polities were either forced or induced to submit to its rule. In Natal, however, and later in the South African Republic, the British introduced a policy of indirect rule, whereby the existing traditional leaders were co-opted to the service of colonial rule as salaried officials,[64] but their positions came at the cost of continuing state recognition.[65] Those who were perceived to be opposed to government policies would be deposed or disregarded in matters of succession, regardless of their popular support or dynastic rights.[66] In consequence, the traditional practice of governance through dialogue and negotiation between rulers and subjects was seriously undermined.[67]

---

[59] For instance, those who have not been circumcised. See generally on the transition to adulthood: Bennett (n55) 298-300.

[60] For example, not a family head.

[61] Kuper 'The social structure of the Sotho-speaking peoples of Southern Africa. Part II' (1975) 45 *Africa* 140.

[62] Even though they may have been married into other lineages. See Coertze & De Beer (n48) 47 regarding the baTlhako.

[63] Jiyane & Ngulube 'Prevalence of use of indigenous social networks among women and girl children in a rural community in KwaZulu-Natal' (2014) 13 *Indilinga* 130.

[64] See generally Bennett (n55) 106-108.

[65] As required under s 2(7) of the Black Administration Act.

[66] Hence, if need arose, the Department could depart from the established order of succession by choosing uncles or younger brothers. See Beinart & Bundy *Hidden Struggles in Rural South Africa* 7 and Van Kessel & Oomen ' "One chief, one vote": the revival of traditional authorities in post-apartheid South Africa' (1997) 96 *African Affairs* 563-564. The Black Authorities Act 68 of 1951 thus laid the foundation for the creation of quasi-autonomous and independent homelands, and, needless to say, the major beneficiarie of this scheme were the traditional leaders who had supported the apartheid regime: Tapscott 'Government in post-apartheid South Africa' in Hofmeister & Scholz (eds) *Traditional and Contemporary Forms of Local Participation and Self-government in Africa* 294.

[67] The colonial system of indirect rule is therefore described by Mamdani *Citizen and Subject: contemporary Africa and the legacy of late colonialism* 25 as 'decentralised despotism'. This

After the Union of South Africa, indirect rule was uniformly imposed on all African polities in the country,[68] and the policy became even more deeply entrenched under apartheid.[69] In 1994, when the country entered its new constitutional era, the same traditional leaders were kept in office,[70] because the government had neither the resources nor the political infrastructure to govern the former homelands.[71] Not surprisingly, the legitimacy of many of these leaders was contested.[72]

In *Pilane and another v Pilane and another,*[73] the Constitutional Court had to decide whether the appellants — leaders of a village in the Bakgatla ba Kgafela Traditional Community — although not officially recognised by the state, were entitled to convene a *kgotha kgothe* (popular assembly). The respondents, the officially recognised leaders of Bakgatla ba Kgafela, sought to interdict them. The majority judgment of the Court found in favour of the appellants. It assumed that the right to convene a *kgotha kgothe* was to be sourced in customary law,[74] but it held the rules in question were not a matter of law, but facts, which had not been sufficiently proved on the evidence led. The Court then continued, in an *obiter dictum*, to speak of the constitutional right to public participation as well as the freedoms of expression and association.[75] These rights would have been suppressed if the respondents had been granted their interdict.

The right to summon an imbizo therefore seems to be governed by customary

---

situation was hardly surprising, because traditional rulers had long been expected to balance the difficult, and often quite contradictory, demands of traditional patriarchs and state bureaucrats: Miller 'The political survival of traditional leadership' (1968) 6 *J Modern African Studies* 183ff for a general analysis of role conflicts

[68] In terms of the Black Administration Act 38 of 1927.

[69] Under the Black Authorities Act 68 of 1951. The state could, although with due regard to customary law (*Minister of Native Affairs and another v Buthelezi* 1961 (1) SA 766 (D) at 769-770), establish three tiers of traditional authority: tribal, regional and territorial.

[70] Section 211(1) and (2) of the 1996 Constitution.

[71] It was estimated that, in the 1990s, approximately 40 per cent of the South African population were subject to traditional rule: Maloka & Gordon 'Chieftainship, civil society, and the political transition in South Africa' (1996) 22 *Crit Sociol* 37ff; Bank & Southall 'Traditional leaders in South Africa's new democracy' (1996) 37-38 *J Legal Pluralism & Unofficial Law* 407ff. Hence the position of traditional leadership was assured by ss 211 and 212 of the Constitution, 1996. See Williams 'Leading from behind: democratic consolidation and the chieftaincy in South Africa' (2004) 42 *J Modern African Studies* 113ff; Williams 'Legislating "tradition" in South Africa' (2009) 35 *JSAS* 191ff.

[72] Most were associated with the apartheid regime, and therefore suffered the taint of a corrupt and inauthentic authority. See, for example, Tapscott in Hofmeister & Scholz op cit 294-296; Hammond-Tooke (n43) 211.

[73] 2013 (4) BCLR 431 (CC). For discussion of the case, see O'Regan 'Tradition and modernity: adjudicating a constitutional paradox' (2014) 6 *CCR* 116-117.

[74] The minority judgment, on the other hand, was quite clear on this point: only those with a customary-law right were entitled to convene the *kgotha kgothe*: para 59.

[75] Paragraph 69. See the commentary on the case by Monye 'Freedom of expression and traditional communities: who can speak and when?' (2014) 29 *SAPL* 323ff, who argues that the court could have developed customary law to comply with the Bill of Rights instead of deciding the matter in terms of freedom of expression and association.

law.[76] Nontheless, for purposes of satisfying the constitutional requirements of public engagement in decision-making and freedom of associaton, *Pilane's* case would also support an argument that any ad hoc meeting called by a member of a community could qualify as an imbizo.

4 THE USE OF IMIBIZO BY THE COURTS AND LEGISLATURE

'. . .it would be a travesty of our Constitution to treat democracy as going to a deep sleep after elections, only to be kissed back to short spells of life every fiv years.'[77]

As with ubuntu, one of the primary reasons for invoking the concept of imbizo and its equivalents *pitso* and *kgotla*, was to co-opt a traditional cultural institution to the new constitutional order, and so give an ostensibly Western form of democracy an indigenous basis.[78] Prior to the new Constitution, South Africa was governed by a system of representative, parliamentary democracy that had been inherited from Britain.[79] Because Parliament was supreme, this system presented no obstacle to white minority rule: black voters were simply excluded from the voters' roll.[80]

The post-apartheid Constitution therefore instituted a decisive break with the past. Although the representative form of democracy was retained,[81] the Constitution — not Parliament — is now deemed to be the supreme source of law.[82] For present purposes, however, the most significan change was heralded by a clause in the firs section of the Constitution, which declares that the representative system is to ensure the 'accountability, responsiveness and openness' of future governments.[83] These three terms laid the foundation for a principle of public participation.

The government is accordingly obliged not only to hold elections at regular intervals, but, in addition, to be always transparent, accountable and responsive to

---

[76] A conclusion supported by *Bafokeng Private Land Buyers Association and others v Royal Bafokeng Nation and others* (999/08) [2016] ZANWHC 27 para 98.

[77] Sachs J in *Doctors for Life International v The Speaker of the National Assembly and others* 2006 (6) SA 416 (CC) para 230.

[78] *Bosberaad* was used for the same reason: *Doctors for Life* supra paras 101 and 227. The term, however, has a meaning quite different to that of imbizo. Nicol 'In the shadow of the clock' in Bell (ed) *The Making of the Constitution: the story of South Africa's Constitutional Assembly, May 1994 to December 1996* 44 says: 'The word *bosberaad* firs entered South Africa's political lexicon early in the nineties through the medium of the negotiating process. Literally translated it means "bush conference" but conveys the broader sense of a retreat — by a group of leaders, strategists or negotiators — to uninterrupted privacy in which effort is concentrated on developing strategy or findin solutions to problems.'

[79] In terms of the [Union of] South Africa Act 1909 esp ss 32 and 35. See Leacock 'The Union of South Africa' (1910) 4 *Am Polit Sci Rev* 498ff.

[80] Marriott *The Mechanism of the Modern State: a treatise on the science and art of government* 284. In fact, ss 35 and 37 of the South Africa Act 1909 simply re-enacted the voter qualification of the four provinces constituting the Union.

[81] Now based, *inter alia*, on a universal adult suffrage and a common voters roll: s 1(d) of the Constitution.

[82] Section 1(c) of the Constitution.

[83] Ibid. See, too, s 195(1) regarding the 'Basic values and principles governing public administration'.

all members of the population in all spheres of government.[84] As Sachs J observed, in the leading case *Doctors for Life International v The Speaker of the National Assembly and others,*[85] these duties are the 'constants of our democracy, to be ceaselessly asserted in relation to ongoing legislative and other activities of government'.[86] Expanding on this idea, Ngcobo J said that it allowed people to have a say in every aspect of their lives, whether 'in workplaces, communities, streets and schools',[87] and that it was relevant to decision-making in all branches of government, whether the legislature, the judiciary or the executive.[88]

Participation in governance brings an added sense of legitimacy to rule-making processes, which was a critical issue in post-apartheid South Africa.[89] In *Merafong Demarcation Forum and others v President of the Republic of South Africa and others,*[90] for example, the Constitutional Court said that the time had come 'to salvage the dignity of black people which had been ravaged by apartheid'.[91] They, like other citizens, were now entitled to speak and be listened to.[92] What is more, the Court in *Minister of Health and another v New Clicks SA (Pty) Ltd and others*[93] noted that the principle of public participation now gave all interested parties, as well as the individuals whose rights might be particularly affected, the opportunity to fin out what government was doing.

While intimated in the firs section of the Constitution, the principle of public participation is later prescribed as a mandatory rule. Section 59(1)(a) obliges Parliament to 'facilitate public involvement in the legislative and other processes of the Assembly and its committees'. (Similar provisions appear with regard to provincial government.)[94] The phrase 'facilitate public involvement' is obviously

---

[84] See *Oriani-Ambrosini v Sisulu, Speaker of the National Assembly* 2012 (6) SA 588 (CC) paras 47-51.

[85] 2006 (6) SA 416 (CC).

[86] Supra para 230.

[87] Supra para 108, citing the National Council of Provinces *Proceedings of the NCOP 4 November 2005* 102-103.

[88] With regard to the latter the Constitutional Court held in *Minister of Health and another NO v New Clicks SA (Pty) Ltd and others (Treatment Action Campaign and another as Amici Curiae)* 2006 (2) SA 311 (CC) para 628 that the operation of the public service was an area crying out 'for express legislative guidance'.

[89] See *Oriani-Ambrosini v Sisulu, Speaker of the National Assembly* 2012 (6) SA 588 (CC) para 49; Hilliard & Kemp 'Citizen participation indispensable to sustainable democratic governance and administration in South Africa' (1999) 65 *Int Rev of Administrative Sciences* 353ff.

[90] 2008 (5) SA 171 (CC) para 44.

[91] Supra para 208.

[92] Participation is a right that the Court said was 'constitutive of dignity': *Minister of Health and another NO v New Clicks SA (Pty) Ltd and others (Treatment Action Campaign and another as Amici Curiae)* 2006 (2) SA 311 (CC) para 627.

[93] Supra para 627.

[94] Sections 70(1)(b) and 118(1)(a), respectively, deal with the National Council of Provinces and provincial legislatures. As the Court held, in *Matatiele Municipality and others v President of the Republic of South Africa and others* 2006 (5) SA 47 (CC) para 72, these provisions lie at the heart of participatory democracy. Corder 'Judicial oversight of the legislative process: a South African case study' in Chirwa & Nijzink (eds) *Accountable Government in Africa* 94-96 notes that no equivalent provision was made for local government 'perhaps because it may have been seen as too onerous, or perhaps because that level of government should, by definition be close to the people it serves'.

open-ended, inviting interpretation. Accordingly, in the leading case on this provision, *Doctors for Life International v The Speaker of the National Assembly and others*,[95] the Constitutional Court observed that: 'The right to political participation is a ' "programmatic" right, which is open to experimental reformulation and which will necessarily change in the light of ongoing national experiences'.[96]

Parliament implemented s 59(1)(a) in two ways: by instituting its own opinion gathering processes prior to the enactment of new legislation,[97] and by including express provisions in new statutes to require officials and statutory bodies to facilitate similar such processes before taking administrative action.[98] The Promotion of Access to Information Act,[99] for instance, gives citizens the right to 'scrutinise, and participate in, decision-making by public bodies that affects their rights'.[100]

In *Doctors for Life*, the Constitutional Court laid down certain basic criteria for determining the nature and degree of participation.[101] In essence, the public have to be given *reasonable* opportunities to participate *effectively* in the legislative process.[102] Whether such measures can be considered 'reasonable' depends on a

---

Instead, s 152(1)(e) provides only that one of the objects of local government is 'to encourage the involvement of communities and community organisations in the matters of local government'.

[95] 2006 (6) SA 416 (CC) paras 96-97. Cited with approval in, *inter alia*, *Matatiele Municipality and others v President of the Republic of South Africa and others (No 2)* 2007 (6) SA 477 (CC) para 50; *Poverty Alleviation Network and others v President of the Republic of South Africa and others* 2010 (6) BCLR 520 (CC) paras 33-36; *Head of Department, Department of Education, Free State Province v Welkom High School and others* 2014 (2) SA 228 (CC) para 138. For a discussion of the *Poverty Alleviation* case, see Courtis 'Rationality, reasonableness, proportionality: testing the use of standards of scrutiny in the constitutional review of legislation' (2013) 5 *CCR* 36-39.

[96] As Sachs J remarked (para 239), '[n]ew jurisprudential ground is being tilled'. In *Mary Patricia King and others v Attorneys Fidelity Fund Board of Control and another* 2006 (1) SA 474 (SCA) para 22, the SCA held that: 'Public involvement might include public participation through the submission of commentary and representations: but that is neither definitiv nor exhaustive of its content. The public may become "involved" in the business of the National Assembly as much by understanding and being informed of what it is doing as by participating directly in those processes.'

[97] See, for example, the Integrated Resource Plan discussed by Calland & Nakhooda 'Participatory democracy meets the hard rock of energy policy: South Africa's National Integrated Resource Plan' (2012) 19 *Democratization* 916-917. In this respect, Parliament is assisted by the South African Law Reform Commission (established by the South African Law Reform Commission Act 19 of 1973), which is administered by the Department of Justice and Constitutional Development.

[98] With respect to housing and eviction decisions, Holness (n22) 5-6 would include more radical and less formal forms of participation, such as citizens' grass-roots organisations, social justice movements and civil society bodies.

[99] 2 of 2000. See too the Promotion of Administrative Justice Act 3 of 2000.

[100] Section 9(e)(iii). Section 2(4) of the Interim Protection of Informal Land Rights Act 31 of 1996 also makes participation in decision-making a prerequisite for securing tenure on communal land.

[101] *Doctors for Life International v The Speaker of the National Assembly and others* 2006 (6) SA 416 (CC) paras 128 and 129.

[102] Cf the analogous concept of 'meaningful engagement' which was examined by the Constitutional Court in *Occupiers of 51 Olivia Road, Berea Township, and 197 Main Street, Johannesburg v City of Johannesburg* 2008 (3) SA 208 (CC) concerning s 26(3) of the Constitution and eviction orders. See commentary by Muller 'Conceptualising "meaningful engagement" as a deliberative democratic partnership' (2011) 22 *Stell LR* 742ff.

number of factors, notably: 'the nature and importance of the legislation and the intensity of its impact on the public'; the urgency of the enactment; the time and expense involved (although savings in this regard do not justify inadequate opportunities to participate) and Parliament's own estimation of what is appropriate in view of the content, importance and urgency of the enactment in question. Hence, the general duty to facilitate public involvement entails both providing 'meaningful opportunities' and ensuring that the public is able to take advantage of them.[103]

Those responsible for framing the Constitution were fully aware of the fact that the great majority of South Africans 'had, for many years, been denied the right to influenc those who ruled over them'.[104] It followed that, because of gross inequalities in education, income and access to knowledge, mere permission to participate in a legislative process was not enough. More would be required by way of public education, access to information and the facilitation of learning and understanding.[105] Given these many requirements, the Court held that legislative bodies had 'considerable discretion' as to how they are to discharge their duties,[106] and that the courts' oversight role was confine to deciding whether the measures adopted were reasonable.[107]

In the circumstances, resort to imibizo as a valid method for ensuring public participation seemed eminently reasonable, since it provides fir grounding for a new principle of constitutional law on an indigenous African set of values and practices.[108] Indeed, in the Constitutional Court judgment on *Minister of Health and another v New Clicks SA (Pty) Ltd and others*,[109] Sachs J could justifiabl say that our 'culture of *imbizo, lekgotla, bosberaad* and *indaba* ... has become a distinctive part of our national ethos'. And a *dictum* in *Doctors for Life*[110] provided judicial authority for its use as 'both a practical and symbolic' form of participatory democracy. Thus the summoning of an imbizo even appears as a mandatory procedural rule even in certain pieces of legislation, typically, but not invariably,[111] those concerned with traditional affairs.[112]

---

[103] Public involvement is therefore 'a continuum that ranges from providing information and building awareness, to partnering in decision-making': *Doctors for Life* supra para 129.

[104] *Doctors for Life* para 130.

[105] *Doctors for Life* paras 130-131.

[106] *Doctors for Life* paras 122, 123-124 and 145. See, too, *Matatiele Municipality and others v President of the Republic of South Africa and others (No 2)* 2007 (6) SA 477 (CC).

[107] *Doctors for Life* paras 125-129.

[108] In this regard, see Froneman J's minority judgment in *Albutt v Centre for the Study of Violence and Reconciliation and others* 2010 (3) SA 293 (CC), where he held (para 91) that the principle of legality (in administrative law) could be sourced in ubuntu and the African traditions of public participation, although 'not as direct authority for its particular application to the facts of this case, but as further legitimisation that it accords with a tradition that runs deep in the lives of many people in this country'.

[109] 2006 (2) SA 311 (CC) para 625.

[110] Paragraph 101.

[111] As, for example, in reg 6 of the Disaster Management Act 57 of 2002.

[112] Such as the nomination to or election of members to Houses of Traditional Rulers. See s 4 of the Mpumalanga Traditional Leadership and Governance Act 3 of 2005; s 24(8)(c) of the Eastern Cape Traditional Leadership and Governance Act 4 of 2005. See further *Wababa and others v Premier,*

5 THE ANC'S *IMBIZO PROGRAMME*: THE POLITICS OF CULTURAL APPROPRIATION

Notwithstanding the courts' endorsement of the institution of imibizo, use of this term, on its own, clearly cannot guarantee fulfilmen of the state's duty to ensure citizen participation in decision-making. Much depends on how the meetings are actually constituted and conducted. In this respect, the government's management of imibizo programmes, especially a nation-wide and comprehensive *Presidential Participation Programme,* launched under the presidency of Thabo Mbeki,[113] shows that careful scrutiny of the facts is necessary.

From the early stages of its history, the ANC had committed itself to a participatory form of democracy.[114] When in power as the government of a now fully democratic South Africa, the Party unveiled what it called the *Presidential Participation Programme* (or simply *Imbizo Programme*).[115] This initiative was announced as a means whereby,

'the ordinary masses of our people [can] interact directly with the Governments they elected, giving further effect to our perspective of a participatory system of governance. . . . The imbizo programme helps us to address the concern that our movement has raised, of the development of what has been called social distance between our elected representatives and the masses that elected them.'[116]

Accordingly, from 1999 onwards, the ANC started to summon meetings at which it claimed to be giving the people — especially the poor — a culturally familiar forum, where authorities could listen to community concerns and complaints in order to devise solutions for deficien service delivery. The *Programme* was to run through three phases at national, provincial and local spheres of government over a period of ten years.[117] By engaging with the citizen

---

Eastern Cape Province and another [1999] JOL 5801 (Ck) 2 and *Gaika and another v Premier of the Province of the Eastern Cape and others* [2001] JOL 8286 (Ck) para 4, referring to Rules laid down in terms of the House of Traditional Leaders Act 1 of 1995 (Eastern Cape) for nominating members of the House. See, too, s 6(3)(b) of the Kwazulu-Natal Traditional Leadership and Governance Act 5 of 2005 and s 22 of the Kwazulu-Natal Traditional Leadership Regulations 2006.

[113] National Heritage Council Preserving our Heritage *Ubuntu Imbizo/Pitso Report* (2006), available at https://web.archive.org/web/20070112105507/http://www.nhc.org.za:80/contents/ubuntu_awards_2006/Ubuntu%20report%202006.pdf [Accessed 8 November 2017].

[114] Hartslief 'The South African participation programme (*imbizo*): a mechanism towards participatory democracy' (2009) 44 *J Public Admin* 329-330.

[115] See how Hartslief op cit generally regarding this initiative. Labelling meetings 'imibizo' has extended far beyond the Presidential Programme to include any large-scale gathering presided over by a state official. See, for example, Nicolson 'Zuma to hold imbizo to fin a solution to the student protests impasse' 3 October 2016 *Daily Maverick,* available at https://www.dailymaverick.co.za/article/2016-10-03-zuma-to-hold-imbizo-to-find-a-solution-to-the-student-protests-impasse/#WgLaQYhx1PY [Accessed 8 November 2017].

[116] ANC '51st National Conference: discussion documents — media in a democratic South Africa' paras 5 and 42, available at http://www.anc.org.za/show.php?id=2504 [Accessed 18 October 2015]. See further Mabelebele (n8) 103ff; Pretorius 'Government by or over the people? The African National Congress's conception of democracy' (2006) 12 *Soc Identities* 753ff; Jordan 'The African National Congress: from illegality to the corridors of power' (2004) 31 *Rev Afr Polit Econ* 209ff.

[117] See Kondlo 'Making participatory governance work — re-inventing *izimibizo* forums in South Africa' (2010) 45 *J Public Admin* 387ff.

body in this manner, state officials could undoubtedly help to fles out a more direct form of democracy, because they could communicate not only through the established media of television, radio and newspapers,[118] but could also speak face-to-face with specifi communities. Describing these meetings as imibizo was intended to invoke a network of culturally suggestive connotations,[119] and thereby forge a closer bond between the state and the electorate.[120]

Although the ANC declared that the *Imbizo Programme* was a model of communication,[121] a considerable body of fiel research into this and other imibizo suggests that such gatherings can fall far short of achieving their stated goal of public engagement in decision-making.[122] If government is to connect meaningfully with its subjects, it must ensure that a meeting meets three requirements: proper participation; equal opportunity for all members of the gathering to have their views heard; and rational discussion followed by deliberation, so that all points of view can be evaluated in light of the available opinions and evidence.[123] When working in combination, these requirements can produce a better, more consensual form of decision-making in accordance with the principles of ubuntu.[124] And, of course, citizens will have the satisfaction of contributing directly to the solution of their problems.

Criticism of the imbizo held under the *Presidential Participation Programme* and other such initiatives, however, indicated that the three requirements were not being met. Several problems were listed. One of the main ones related to the convening of imibizo at the behest of government officials and leading party activists, who were usually strangers to the targeted community. Traditionally, such assemblies would have been called by a traditional leader,[125] in which case the issues to be discussed would probably be known in advance and already informally discussed in the community.[126] The appearance of an outsider, however, created an immediate social distance requiring more time to explain

---

[118] Cf *Primedia (Pty) Ltd and others v Speaker of the National Assembly and others* 2017 (1) SA 572 (SCA) paras 28-29 regarding the duty to permit media coverage of parliamentary proceedings.

[119] Mabelebele (n8) 105. Hamilton 'Social inequality, cultural diversity and a compromised commitment to complexity in contemporary public deliberation' Paper presented at the Harold Wolpe Memorial Trust's Tenth Anniversary Colloquium 'Engaging silences and unresolved issues in the political economy of South Africa' 21-23 September 2006 at 3.

[120] Contributing not only to the solution of local problems but also to fostering social cohesion: Mabelebele (n8) 107.

[121] Jordan (n116) 209.

[122] See the detailed report in this regard by Mathagu *An Analysis and Appraisal of the Imbizo as an Instrument of Democracy in South Africa* (2010) unpublished masters thesis, UNISA, who conducted empirical research.

[123] Fishkin (n33) 46.

[124] Murithi 'African approaches to building peace and social solidarity' (2006) 6 *Afri J on Conflict Resolution* 20-21. See also the discussion of indaba in Chapter 7.

[125] Hamilton 'Uncertain citizenship and public deliberation in post-apartheid South Africa' (2009) 35 *Social Dynamics* 369.

[126] Kondlo (n117) 389-390. Wallman 'Lesotho's *pitso*: traditional meetings in a modern setting' (1968) 2 *Can J Afr Stud* 72 reports a similar problem in rural Lesotho regarding an agricultural technician appearing at a *pitso*.

points of view, and precluded the open style of debate intrinsic to a traditional imbizo.[127]

Another telling criticism, especially pertinent to imibizo held in rural communities, related to the information to be conveyed.[128] All too often, the policies, laws and facts were too compendious and too technical to be fully understood and debated by the audience. Moreover, the nature of the meetings convened by the state did not allow participants to address officials in their traditional manner. In an imbizo true to the traditional stereotype, people are used to speaking in a highly rhetorical style, which is vital to their being properly heard and understood. The new format, however, particularly the time deadlines set for the state meetings, made no allowance for such eloquence.[129]

In addition, the imibizo called by state officials did not necessarily permit the active participation of all interested parties.[130] For a start, the number of people in attendance varied enormously. With regard to the *Imbizo Programme*, the ANC claimed that 'our people ... turned up in their thousands' at some gatherings,[131] and that, at the 'people's forums' held during election campaigns, President Thabo Mbeki met 'hundreds of thousands of people' at a variety of localities.[132] If this claim were true,[133] how could everyone participate in any meaningful sense?

Indeed, over inclusiveness undermines the principles of deliberation and equality. First, the more participants there are, the more time is needed to canvass all views, and the less the likelihood is of a proper discussion presenting clear and objective evidence. Secondly, the more people who are involved, the less likely it is that all individuals can speak effectively, thereby compromising the goal of rational discussion amongst equals.[134] Thirdly, the active participants tend to be those with high status and a strong interest in the issue being debated. Those individuals do not necessarily represent a whole community.

Conversely, certain 'imbizo' gatherings were underinclusive; they were no more than 'breakfast meetings with business notables [or] popular gatherings in

---

[127] Wallman's study in Lesotho highlights this problem op cit 170.

[128] Wallman op cit 172-173. Although this point comes from a study of *pitso* in Lesotho, it is equally applicable to imibizo in South Africa.

[129] In this regard, it is interesting to speculate on the effect of digital communication on the future convening and conduct of imbizos. The study by Skuse & Cousins 'Spaces of resistance: informal settlement, communication and community organisation in a Cape Town township' (2007) 44 *Urban Studies* 991-992 revealed 'a bricolage of discursive practices' arising from new 'communication technologies allow[ing] different ways of relating to extended social networks and mobilising both the physical community and key modes of support'.

[130] See, in this connection, Fraser 'Rethinking the public sphere: a contribution to the critique of actually existing democracy' (1990) 25/26 *Social Text* 56ff, who deals with the theory of Habermas's notion of public spheres and the weakness and inequality of some members participating in public gatherings.

[131] Mbeki 'Letter from the President: izimbizo contribute to building democracy' (2004) 4 *ANC Today*, available at https://web-beta.archive.org/web/20040407170548/http://www.anc.org.za:80/ancdocs/anctoday/2004/at05.htm [Accessed 16 May 2017].

[132] ANC 'Media in a democratic South Africa' (2002) 16 *Umrabulo* para 12, available at http://www.anc.org.za/show.php?id=2932 [Accessed 18 October 2015].

[133] Pretorius (n116) 754.

[134] Fishkin (n33) 47ff.

rural villages'.[135] In such situations, could the general public interest be properly represented? And should such meetings be considered genuine imibizo?[136]

Perhaps the most significan criticism was a general one: that the ANC's *Imbizo Programme* had exploited a traditional institution to propagate an ideology that served its own political strategy.[137] By appropriating the imbizo, the Party could, at one and the same time, satisfy the public that the government was discharging its duty to implement a participatory democracy, and, at the same time, achieve partisan political purposes. Thus it has been said that the imbizo served to create an impression that the ANC and the people had a common perspective, while driving a wedge between the people and other political parties.[138]

6 CONCLUSION

As a culturally familiar institution giving citizens the right to engage directly with political authorities, the imbizo is of obvious value to both citizens and government. From the authorities' point of view, it facilitates direct communication, promotes rational deliberation, leads to better decision-making, and, in so far as a decision gains popular support, it is more likely to be fully implemented. From the citizens' point of view, an imbizo gives the satisfaction of being heard and contributing to the decision.[139]

The courts' recognition of imibizo as a typically African means for discharging the government's constitutional duty to facilitate public involvement in decision-making was therefore a sensible — and politic — method for ensuring accountability, responsiveness and openness. Nonetheless, the surface labelling of a public meeting as an 'imbizo' can be both misleading and disingenuous.

As the product of a pre-colonial society, imibizo no doubt worked effectively to achieve the objectives of a participatory and deliberative type of democracy. The institution is now being used, however, in a completely different social and political milieu, which raises questions concerning its capacity to realise its traditional functions, as well as the equality requirements specifie in the Constitution.

In answering these questions, the fact that the location for an imbizo was in a rural or urban area should not lead to any fixe assumptions about its legitimacy. It is true that imibizo run according to traditional procedures and held in rural areas might deny certain people freedom to express their opinions. but it should not be assumed that the participants are unaware of their constitutional rights.[140] Nor should it be assumed that the traditional ruler in charge has the requisite authority to convene the meeting, since he or she might lack dynastic legitimacy.

---

[135] Pretorius (n116) 754.

[136] Pretorius (n116) 753-754.

[137] Mabelebele (n8) 103.

[138] Mabelebele (n8) 111.

[139] See Chapter 7 regarding the advantages of the indaba process.

[140] A conclusion also reached by fiel work in a rural community: Claassens ' "It is not easy to challenge a chief": lessons from Rakgwadi' (2001) 9 *PLAAS Research Report* vii, available at http://www.plaas.org.za/sites/default/files/publications-pdf/PLAAS_RR9_Claassens.pd [Accessed 17 May 2017].

On the other hand, there is no reason to believe that simply because imibizo are convened in urban areas they will lack legitimacy in the eyes of the more heterogeneous group of participants. From the limited evidence available it would appear that urban communities are quite capable of keeping tradition and modernity in balance. Based on research in an urban Cape Town community, for instance, it was found that street committees were operating successfully according to both traditional and modern forms of governance.[141]

More to the point is the manner in which an imbizo is organised and conducted. Bearing in mind the criticisms levelled against the ANC's *Imbizo Programme*, the courts should take care to scrutinise an ostensible imbizo to ensure that it did, in fact, meet the requirements specifie for sufficient 'public involvement' under the Constitution. In this regard, the gathering must meet the basic criteria of 'reasonableness' and 'effectiveness' stipulated by the Constitutional Court.[142] Thus, sufficient time must be allocated for a meeting, especially when complex issues are tabled for discussion, to ensure that a full exchange of views is possible. Several days of discussion might be necessary before proposals can be properly considered and understood.[143]

In addition, the place and the medium of communication must be appropriate to the requirements of participants. In other words, all members of the designated community must be able to reach the venue selected for an imbizo within a reasonable time. They must also be able to understand the language used for the meeting and the form of address (written or oral). Given disparities in levels of education and differences in the prevailing languages of remote rural and heterogeneous urban areas, these can be critical issues.[144]

Perhaps the most important issue is whether participants are given an equal and genuine opportunity to speak. Here the answer will depend on a variety of factors: whether size of the gathering allows for each to express an opinion; whether those present constitute a fair representation of views in the community; whether the

---

[141] Note, however, that street committees are a feature of formal, established townships, not informal settlements: Skuse & Cousins (n129) 991.

[142] *Doctors for Life International v The Speaker of the National Assembly and others* 2006 (6) SA 416 (CC). Further empirical research is clearly needed to determine the actual efficacy of community participation in decision-making. See, for example, the study by Howard 'The rules of engagement: a socio-legal framework for improving community engagement in natural resource governance' (2015) 5 *Oñati Socio-legal Series* 1209ff, who conducted a detailed study of the literature with regard to natural resource governance. See further Raboshakga 'Towards participatory democracy or not? The reasonableness approach in public involvement cases' (2015) 31 *SAJHR* 4ff for a commentary on the South African case law.

[143] Regarding the reasonableness of the time allocated, see *Land Access Movement of South Africa and others v Chairperson, National Council of Provinces and others* 2016 (5) SA 635 (CC) paras 70 and 71, where the Court held that a timetable determined by the NCOP had to be subordinated to the rights guaranteed in the Constitution, not *vice versa*, and that the public had to be given sufficient opportunity to express views that were capable of influencin the decision to be taken.

[144] Phooko 'What should be the form of public participation in the lawmaking process? An analysis of South African cases' (2014) 35 *Obiter* 55.

officials presiding do in fact listen and respond to the views aired; and whether everyone is given a fair chance to speak.[145] In this regard, the community might be represented only by adult males of a certain social status; women, junior males and those not fully integrated into the community might be silenced.

Since the *Doctors' for Life* decision, the courts' approach to answering these questions seems to have become increasingly perfunctory. A study of recent Constitutional Court judgments shows that the tendency has been towards a more technical approach, in that the mere summoning of a meeting has been deemed sufficient.[146] It can, of course, be accepted that the public's engagement in decision-making should be treated as a procedural, not a substantive, requirement, meaning that the government is not obliged to accede to — or act on — the views expressed at an imbizo.[147] Even so, participatory democracy requires citizens to be at least consulted, their opinions properly considered and to be advised of any changes in policy.[148]

The state's use of imibizo is unquestionably an apposite method for discharging its constitutional duties, but the mere use of the word 'imbizo' may amount to little more than giving meetings the guise of legitimacy when they do not, in fact, meet their prescribed objectives. Hence, as watchdogs of legislative and administrative processes, the courts should be on their guard against the practice of cultural labelling.

---

[145] In *Shilubana and others v Nwamitwa* 2009 (2) SA 66 (CC) para 39, for instance, CONTRALESA argued that the Valoyi Traditional Community was never fully represented. 'Instead, as the attendance numbers revealed discussions were limited to a privileged few.'

[146] Phooko (n144) 47-49. The cases in question were *Merafong Demarcation Forum and others v President of the Republic of South Africa and others* 2008 (5) SA 171 (CC); *Poverty Alleviation Network and others v President of the Republic of South Africa and others* 2010 (6) BCLR 520 (CC); *Moutse Demarcation Forum and others v President of the Republic of South Africa and others* 2011 (11) BCLR 1158 (CC).

[147] *S v Makwanyane and another* 1995 (3) SA 391 (CC) paras 87-89, esp 88 where Chaskalson J talks of protecting the interests of minorities. See, too, *Merafong* supra para 50.

[148] Phooko (n144) 57.

Chapter 7

INDABA

1 INTRODUCTION

The previous chapter examined the imbizo, a public assembly where those present are given a forum in which to air their mutual concerns about matters of law- and policy-making. We can now go on to consider the procedures and processes typical of such meetings as an imbizo.[1]

This topic will be dealt with under the title of 'indaba', a term that is frequently used by the courts in conjunction with imbizo,[2] with the implication that the two words are synonymous.[3] Indeed, for most purposes they are. Like imbizo, indaba is a term taken from the Nguni group of languages, more specificall , isiZulu[4] and siNdebele.[5] In isiXhosa, a word with an equivalent meaning is *udaba*,[6] in siSwazi *indzaba*,[7] in seSotho[8] and seTswana *taba*.[9] In all these languages, indaba and its

---

[1] Procedure and process should be distinguished: the former implies the established or prescribed method for performing an activity, whereas the latter implies the actual interactions or activities aimed at achieving a goal.

[2] As in *Minister of Health and another NO v New Clicks SA (Pty) Ltd and others (Treatment Action Campaign and another as Amici Curiae)* 2006 (2) SA 311 (CC) para 625.

[3] Broodryk 'The philosophy of ubuntu: to improve business success' (2006) 22 *Management Today* 21 distinguishes the meanings by noting that an indaba is an 'open discussion by a group of people who share the same interest', whereas an imbizo 'is broader and on a national level and takes the form of a mass congregation or public meeting'. A *lekgotla*, on the other hand, is 'a meeting lasting hours which takes place at a secluded venue'. See above p 130.

[4] Doke et al *English-isiZulu, IsiZulu-English Dictionary: Indaba*: matter for discussion (*ukukhuluma*), topic of conversation (*inkulumo*), affair, report, information, account, law case.

[5] Elliott *Notes for a Sindebele Dictionary and Grammar and Illustrative Sentences*: '*Indaba*: affair, matter, business, case, news, report, tale.'

[6] IO Publishing *South African Multilingual Dictionary*: '*Indaba/udaba*: story, affair, case'; Pahl, Pienaar & Ndungane (eds) *The Greater Dictionary of Xhosa Vol 1*: '*Udaba*: tidings, information, intelligence, story, report, message, news of something important, affair, news, tidings.'

[7] Rycroft *Concise siSwati Dictionary: SiSwati-English, English-Siswati*: '*Indzaba*: affair, matter, subject, topic, account, report, story, news, serious matter.'

[8] Kriel *The New English-Sesotho Dictionary*: '*Taba*: affair, matter, business.'

[9] Brown *Setswana Dictionary: Setswana-English and English-Setswana*; Hartshorne, Swart & Posselt *Dictionary of Basic English/Tswana*: '*Taba*: affair, concern, meeting/public gathering.'

variants have a number of meanings, *inter alia,* news, report, topic of conversation, troublesome matter, subject of discussion or the actual gathering to undertake the discussion (when it becomes the synonym for imbizo).[10] Indaba, however, has an additional meaning that has been adopted in many forums,[11] namely, the *process* of deliberation, and it was for this reason that indaba was adopted as the heading for this chapter.

One noteworthy feature that distinguishes indaba from imbizo — and, for that matter, ubuntu — is its long accepted usage in languages having no relation to an African group. Thus, indaba, in its isiZulu form, is an established word in everyday English[12] and Afrikaans,[13] and it has spread even further afiel into an international discourse to denote conferences that have been conducted in a peculiarly South African manner.[14] Indaba was therefore chosen to describe, for example, a meeting of scouting leaders, held in Norway in 1949 (the World Scout Indaba),[15] and it is now regularly used as a brand name for major international conferences within South Africa, such as the Tourism and Design Indabas held in Durban and Cape Town,[16] and for similar events abroad.[17] In all these contexts, the word is taken to mean either the topic for discussion at the conference or the process of discussion.

The diffusion of indaba into foreign languages has been underway for over a hundred years. In 1913, for instance, it was one of the terms featured in a book on South African colloquialisms.[18] The further spread of the word outside South Africa was due in most part to its incorporation into Fanagalo, a pidgin language created on the plantations of the Eastern Cape and Natal, and subsequently in the mining industry, as a medium of communication between employers and workers from different linguistic backgrounds.[19]

---

[10] See above p 124.

[11] Notably the World Climate Change Conference in Durban and the Lambeth Bishops Conference in London, for which see below pp 157-158.

[12] Silva (ed) *A Dictionary of South African English on Historical Principles* 310: 'Indaba: First meaning: (Xhosa/Zulu) subject, topic, matter, affair, business, affairs, communication, news. Second meaning: meeting or discussion.'

[13] Buro van die Woordeboek van die Afrikaanse Taal *Woordeboek van die Afrikaanse Taal* (2015) electronically available at www.woordeboek.co.za [Accessed 18 November 2015]: '*Inda'ba: groot gebeurtenis, gedoente; ook, moles'* or '*onderlinge beraadslaging, raadpleging; konferensie, vergadering, bespreking; kajuitraad, koukus.*'

[14] See below p 157.

[15] After his tour in Africa, Lord Rowallan proposed this title. See https://en.wikipedia.org/wiki/World_Scout_Indaba [Accessed 20 November 2015].

[16] See http://www.indaba-southafrica.co.za/ [Accessed 2 December 2015].

[17] See further below p 157-158.

[18] Where three different meanings were given: news, trouble, a meeting or a discussion: Pettman *Africanderisms; a glossary of South African colloquial words and phrases and of place and other names* 225.

[19] See Mesthrie 'The origins of Fanagalo' (1989) 4 *JPCL* 211ff. Although derived primarily from isiXhosa and isiZulu, Fanagalo contained many English and Afrikaans additions: Mesthrie 'Fanagalo' in Brown & Ogilvie (eds) *Concise Encyclopedia of Languages of the World* 411-412. From South Africa, variants of Fanagalo extended beyond the South African borders: to Zimbabwe (where the version is known as Chilapalapa) and Zambia (where the version is known as Cikabanga): Mesthrie *The Origins of Fanagalo* 213. While these were useful lingua francas, they all too often

Together with imbizo and ubuntu, indaba entered South African legal discourse with the introduction of the new constitution, primarily in order to evoke the concept of a traditional African method of decision-making, rather than a more formal, typically Western process.[20] As with imbizo, indaba received no particular comment or discussion in the cases, and its meaning (or translation) has attracted no debate, doubtless because indaba was already a familiar word in all South African languages.

The functions of both imbizo and indaba complement the overarching normative goal of ubuntu, which is to achieve the common good of a community.[21] Thus imbizo is a gathering of all members of the community to participate in a decision-making indaba, a process that is open and relatively informal. From this process, the person presiding is expected to discern an overall consensus of opinion on the ultimate decision.

2 MODELS OF DECISION-MAKING

Like any other mode of discussion or deliberation, indaba is simply the manner of deciding how best to solve a problem.[22] The solution can, of course, be reached quickly, without much thought, depending on the complexity of the problem, the number of people affected and a particular institutional and cultural context. The following inquiry into indaba will concentrate on meetings of a sizeable number of people that have been called to solve complex problems in rule- or policy-making institutions.

Decision-making processes have long been the subject of study in a range of different disciplines, notably, law, psychology, economics, sociology and business management. Given these different disciplinary boundaries, agreement on essential features of these processes and the factors influencin them is bound to be elusive. Nevertheless, most types of decision-making go through six phases: recognition of a problem; the search for information relevant to the solution; processing that information; considering the objectives and options;[23] the formulation of a fina choice and the implementation of that choice.[24]

Treated as a temporal sequence, these phases are deemed rational or, more broadly, cognitive,[25] implying a particular model of decision-making. This model has always been favoured in Western systems of law, where logic and reason have

---

connoted the recipients' servile status, and so bore a mark of social inferiority: Adendorff 'Ethnographic evidence of the social meaning of Fanakalo in South Africa' (1993) 8 *JPCL* 1ff.

[20] With regard to these processes, see also below p 167 on rule-oriented and relational discourses.

[21] See above p 32.

[22] See March 'Understanding how decisions happen in organizations' in Shapira (ed) *Organizational Decision-making* 20.

[23] Clemen *Making Hard Decisions* 7.

[24] Lyles *Practical Management Problem Solving and Decision-making* vi.

[25] Because decisions result from the exercise of the human will and because humans are rational beings. Scholars of the rational model of decision theory have been strongly influence by Weber *The Theory of Social and Economic Organization* 32, 38-39, 341-343, 370-371 and 396-398.

provided a powerful basis for validating arguments.[26] Thus rationality works not only as a justification but also as authority in itself for those in dominant positions of power.[27]

A considerable body of evidence has been put forward, however, to show that, in reality, decisions seldom conform to the rational model.[28] Behaviourism, in particular, posed a significan challenge to the rational model by pointing to the fact that it failed to take sufficient account of the many variables that may override conscious reasoning.[29] An individual's personal views and circumstances, for instance, often result in decisions being taken spontaneously, impulsively or habitually.[30] When studied in these terms, decision-making theory concentrates on individual psychology[31] together with a person's likely preferences, especially in so far as they are dictated by such biases as race and culture.

For these reasons, an individual's decision is unlikely to be trusted, especially if it concerns a complex matter affecting a large number of people. In such circumstances, the authority for taking decisions with general and long-term effect is usually vested in specialised institutions, which leads to another variable that has a high probability of influencin rational decision-making: the institutional context.[32]

When individuals are bound together socially and spatially, their constant interaction requires the setting of common goals and standards of behaviour.[33] In these circumstances, decision-making is affected by such factors as the likelihood of disagreements arising amongst individuals, the need to settle disputes and for the group to act as a single entity.[34] Group decision-making therefore is 'a process of interaction in which different personalities and divergent views must blend to

---

[26] See, for example, *S v Makwanyane and another* 1995 (3) SA 391 (CC) para 156; *New National Party v Government of the Republic of South Africa* 1999 (3) SA 191 (CC) paras 19 and 24; *Pharmaceutical Manufacturers Association of South Africa: In re Ex parte President of the Republic of South Africa* 2000 (2) SA 674 (CC) paras 85 and 90; *United Democratic Movement v President of the Republic of South Africa (No 2)* 2003 (1) SA 495 (CC) para 55; *Affordable Medicines Trust v Minister of Health* 2006 (3) SA 247 (CC) paras 74-79.

[27] Miller, Hickson & Wilson 'Decision-making in organization' in Clegg, Hardy & Nord (eds) *Managing Organizations* 43; Weber (n25) 66.

[28] See, for instance, Schauer 'Legal Realism untamed' (2013) 91 *Texas L Rev* 749; Boulle 'Predictable irrationality in mediation: insights from behavioural economics' (2013) 24 *ADRJ* 8ff.

[29] See, for example, Skinner 'Cognitive science and behaviourism' (1985) 76 *British J of Psychology* 295-296. Cf Alexander 'Rationality revisited: planning paradigms in a post-postmodernist perspective' (2000) 19 *J of Planning Education & Research* 242ff who sets out to rescue rationality from its stereotypical conception by revealing its various different forms and applications.

[30] Kroeber-Riel & Haurschildt 'Decision-making' in Kuper & Kuper (eds) *The Social Science Encyclopedia* 183; Skinner op cit 296.

[31] Individual psychology is influence by many variables, such as a propensity for taking risks: Harrison *The Managerial Decision-Making Process* 141ff.

[32] Unfortunately, most of the work of legal philosophy (and that concerning the rational model) concentrates on individuals making decisions as judges or administrators at the expense of groups acting in law- and policy-making institutions.

[33] Harrison (n31) 178.

[34] Kroeber-Riel & Haurschildt (n30) 184.

produce a ... collective judgement'.[35] In this case, a consensual decision has the advantage of maintaining harmonious relationships and preserving group integrity.[36]

The reference to consensus leads to yet another significan variable affecting decision-making: culture. While cultural norms seldom feature overtly or consciously when individuals are considering their options,[37] studies of business management, especially, have revealed that different cultural environments produce marked divergences in how decisions are reached.[38] The following two sections will therefore examine decision-making in terms of what can be broadly conceived as African and Western cultural models. In the former, consensual decisions are considered the ideal, whereas in the latter, the preferred form is majoritarian voting.

3 TRADITIONAL AFRICAN PROCESSES OF DECISION-MAKING

In African systems of law and governance, a single, multi-purposed institution, the traditional leader-in-council[39] controls the making of decisions, whether they are aimed at resolving disputes, creating new laws or implementing the law.[40] If everyone in a community is affected, which happens when a far-reaching administrative decision is to be taken or a new law or policy is to be debated, the

---

[35] Harrison (n31) 177.

[36] Which are also strong forces conducing to the negative state of 'groupthink'. See below p 154.

[37] These factors are usually taken for granted (March in Shapira (n22) 20), although they may influenc the outcome to such an extent that rational preferences are subordinated to what is culturally expected: March in Shapira (n22) 17.

[38] See, for example, Alper, Tjosvold & Law 'Interdependence and controversy in group decision making: antecedents to effective self-managing teams' (1998) 74 *Organizational Behavior & Human Decision Processes* 33ff; Schweiger, Sandberg & Ragan 'Group approaches for improving strategic decision making: a comparative analysis of dialectical inquiry, devil's advocacy, and consensus' (1986) 29 *Acad Manag J* 51ff.

[39] Variants of this institution operate at different levels of the political unit — the family, ward or nation — and are presided over, respectively, by a family head, ward head or 'chief'/king.

[40] Generally speaking, because law rested on custom and tradition, the African form of governance seldom requires acts of deliberate law-making, although traditional leaders clearly have the power to take executive or legislative decisions as the needs dictate. See Schapera *Tribal Legislation Among the Tswana of the Bechuanaland Protectorate: a study in the mechanism of cultural change* and *Tribal Innovators: Tswana chiefs and social change, 1795-1940* ch 2; Hinz *Customary Law in Namibia* 95-96; D'Engelbronner-Kolff 'The people as law-makers: the juridical foundation of the legislative power of Namibian Traditional Communities' in D'Engelbronner-Kolff et al *Traditional Authority and Democracy in Southern Africa* 71ff. Nevertheless, empirical research on legislation, and by implication imibizo, is somewhat limited, because the study of decision-making has focused on dispute resolution. Cf the important works dealing with what can be considered the administrative and legislative aspects of customary law: Prinsloo *Inheemse Publiekreg in Lebowa*; Prinsloo *Die Inheemse Administratiefreg van 'n Noord-Sothostam*; Myburgh & Prinsloo *Indigenous Public Law in KwaNdebele*; Myburgh *Die Inheemse Staat in Suider-Afrika*. See, too, the early works of Schapera *Government and Politics in Tribal Societies* and Hammond-Tooke *Command or Consensus: the development of Transkeian local government*.

traditional leader must seek the views of the community by summoning a public gathering to constitute an imbizo.[41]

Once the imbizo is convened, a senior member of council of the traditional leader must put forward a proposal supported by good reasons, the merits of which can then be fully discussed and debated.[42] Notable features of this debate are the freedom given to the council and members of the public to express their opinions, and the potentially protracted nature of the process. This is to be expected, because opinions and options must be fully canvassed in order to extract a general consensus.

To this end, strict application of procedural and substantive rules is less important than finding the right answer for a problem.[43] As a result, circumstantial details, which would be excluded as irrelevant at Western-style meetings, are admitted.[44] Background information of this nature may in the long run prove useful in the search for a generally accepted solution.[45] In fact, the very measure of successful decision-makers may well be the length of time they are prepared to spend delving into details.[46]

After due discussion, a summary of the issues and the public opinion is normally presented by one of the senior elders of the council. His authority to voice an independent opinion is determined not only by his status in the community, but also by his ability to reflec a prevailing view, which a shrewd judge will appropriate to support his decision.[47] (The traditional leader who ignores the views of his subjects and councillors risks the loss of political support.)[48] The presiding officer of the gathering then pronounces the final decision: he does so with all the authority of a patriarch of a family, a position that

---

[41] See above pp 129ff, and further: Myburgh & Prinsloo op cit 41-42 and 63-64; Prinsloo op cit (*Inheemse Administratiefreg*) 134-135 and op cit (*Publiekreg in Lebowa*) 154; Hunter *Reaction to Conquest: effects of contact with Europeans on the Pondo of South Africa* 394; Mönnig *The Pedi* 284-285; Krige *The Social System of the Zulus* 219; Kuper *The Swazi: a South African kingdom* 36-38.

[42] See, for example, *Kekane v Mokgoko* 1953 NAC 93 (NE).

[43] For instance, in cases of dispute settlement, traditional courts did not apply a strict doctrine of precedent: Hamnett *Chieftainship and Legitimacy: an anthropological study of executive law in Lesotho* 94.

[44] In the case of judicial proceedings, see Dlamini 'Wither lay justice in South Africa?' (1985) 14 *Speculum Juris* 3; Van der Merwe 'Accusatorial and inquisitorial procedures and restricted and free systems of evidence' in Sanders (ed) *Southern Africa in Need of Law Reform* 147.

[45] See Van Velsen 'Procedural informality, reconciliation, and false comparisons' in Gluckman (ed) *Ideas and Procedures in African Customary Law* 138.

[46] Mqeke *Basic Approaches to Problem Solving in Customary Law: a study of conciliation and consensus among the Cape Nguni* 32. The latitude allowed by the tribunal nevertheless depends upon its overall purpose, hence, when the goal is to reconcile the parties, the approach is more flexible See Von Benda-Beckmann 'The use of folk law in West-Sumatran state courts' in Allott & Woodman (eds) *People's Law and State Law* 91.

[47] Hence, the principal source of coercion in this type of society is public opinion: Peters 'Aspects of the control of moral ambiguities a comparative analysis of two culturally disparate models of social control' in Gluckman (ed) *Allocation of Responsibility* 157.

[48] Myburgh & Prinsloo (n40) 53 go so far as to say that a traditional ruler may not act contrary to the advice of the national council.

presumes his ability to judge disputes fairly, govern wisely and ensure the good of his people.[49]

The term indaba captures the process described here, and it applies in all the decision-making bodies of the units making up a traditional community,[50] whether chiefdoms, wards or families — although procedures become more complex and rigid in the higher echelons of authority. What is more, the indaba style of discussion governs all matters, whether those aimed at the making of new rules, the implementation of laws or the resolution of disputes. In every case, the prime objective of the process is to arrive at a decision that has the support of the people involved and will secure the goal of social harmony.[51]

The political and social structures of pre-colonial African societies are largely responsible for this type of process.[52] Where a ruling body lacks the institutional backing of a centralised state, its powers of enforcement are weak, and thus dependent on the community's preparedness to accept its decisions.[53] In such a situation, those dissenting have to be convinced of the need to yield to the greater will.[54] Accordingly, prudent decision-making is seen to depend on persuasion, with an emphasis on the spirit of give and take, not on a rational and impartial application of abstract rules.[55]

In this depiction of traditional African decision-making, the extent to which the standards are still upheld will obviously vary depending on the degree of power and authority enjoyed by particular traditional leaders. Where they enjoy the backing of central government, they have less need to look to the support of their subjects.[56] This proposition is corroborated by fiel research which has shown that the democratic standards implicit in a traditional indaba process suffer whenever leaders are free to act independently of the popular will.[57]

---

[49] Hunter (n41) 392; Schapera *A Handbook of Tswana Law and Custom* 68; Hammond-Tooke (n40) 30; Mönnig (n41) 254.

[50] The term prescribed in s 2 of the Traditional Leadership and Governance Framework Act 41 of 2003.

[51] Jeppe *Ontwikkeling van Bestuursinstellings in die Westelike Bantoegebiede* 128; Hughes *Land Tenure, Land Rights and Land Communities on Swazi National Land in Swaziland* 105.

[52] In this regard, a classic work is Gluckman's study of Barotse courts in Zambia, *Judicial Process among the Barotse of Northern Rhodesia*. See further Koch et al 'Political and psychological correlates of conflic management: a cross-cultural study' (1976) 10 *Law & Soc Rev* 443.

[53] See above pp 129-130.

[54] See, for example, Gulliver 'Dispute settlement without courts: the Ndendeuli of Southern Tanzania' in Nader (ed) *Law in Culture and Society* 24ff and, generally, Gulliver *Social Control in an African Society*.

[55] See Griffiths 'The social working of legal rules' (2003) 35 *J Legal Pluralism & Unofficial L* 15; Holleman *Issues in African Law* 18. Oomen *Chiefs in South Africa: law, power and culture in the post-apartheid era* 211 shows how misleading a narrow focus on rules can be, even when customary law is taken as the primary point of reference. As Sjaastad & Cousins 'Formalisation of land rights in the South: an overview' (2008) 26 *Land Use Policy* 7, point out, 'people often draw on a diverse range of resources to argue their claims, ranging from custom to statutory law, constitutional principles, development as a desired goal, and even the Bible'.

[56] See above pp 132-134.

[57] Claassens ' "It is not easy to challenge a chief": lessons from Rakgwadi' (2001) 9 *PLAAS Research Report* 15; Claassens 'The resurgence of tribal taxes in the context of recent traditional leadership laws in South Africa' (2011) 27 *SAJHR* 522ff; Matlala 'Challenging traditional authority

4 THE WESTERN MODEL OF LEGAL DECISION-MAKING: A COMPARISON

As stated earlier, the rational model of decision-making is considered to be a distinctive mark of the Western legal tradition, but, at the outset, it must be noted that much scholarship has been devoted to showing that rationality in the law is better thought of as the expression of an ideology than an accurate reflectio of reality. With regard to dispute processing, for example, Legal Realism posed a major challenge to claims that the rational model — and the associated positivist theory — represented what actually happens in court.[58] The Realist movement set out to show that law and the legal process were fundamentally indeterminate, with the result that the formal application of rules to facts (the positivist syllogism) was only a partial explanation for judges' decisions. Several divergent schools of thought subsequently developed from Realism all sharing a basic understanding: that legal decision-making is, in fact, neither completely impartial nor determined by reference to the law alone.[59]

The Realist critique notwithstanding, decision-makers in the Western cultural mould still tend to place prime value on rationality,[60] to which they would add other factors, such as impartiality,[61] speed and efficiency,[62] individual accountability,[63] and top-down control.[64] These factors all contribute to a formal style of

---

in the platinum belt' (2014) 49 *SA Crime Quarterly* 31ff. See too *Wildlife Society of Southern Africa and others v Minister of Environmental Affairs and Tourism of the Republic of South Africa and others* 1996 (3) SA 1095 (Tks) at 1108.

[58] See Horwitz *The Transformation of American Law 1870-1960: the crisis of legal orthodoxy* 169ff, who argued that legal reasoning could not be disaggregated from morals and politics. The basic agenda of Legal Realism is described in Leiter *Naturalizing Jurisprudence: essays on American Legal Realism and naturalism in legal philosophy* 15ff American Legal Realism must be distinguished from Scandinavian Realism, for which see Pihlajamäki 'Against metaphysics in law: the historical background of American and Scandinavian legal realism compared' (2004) 52 *Am J Comp L* 469ff.

[59] For example, see Hoctor 'Legal Realism' in Roederer & Moellendorf (eds) *Jurisprudence* 158-184 for a broad overview, and Martin *Legal Realism: American and Scandinavian* 13. As Schauer (n28) 750 fn 2 says: '[T]he main lines of Legal Realism maintain that legal doctrine, whether because of the indeterminacy of individual rules or the availability of multiple ones, is more malleable, less determinate, and less causal of judicial outcomes than the traditional view of law's constraints supposes.' This understanding of Legal Realism is evident in the works of Kennedy 'Freedom and constraint in adjudication: a critical phenomenology' (1986) 36 *J Legal Educ* 518 fn 1 and Tushnet *The New Constitutional Order* 120.

[60] With insufficient sensitivity to culture and organisational behaviour: Odendaal 'Perception and individual decision-making' in Robbins et al (eds) *Organisational Behaviour* 132.

[61] Miller, Hickson & Wilson 'Decision-making in organizations' in Clegg, Hardy & Nord (n27) 59.

[62] Mangaliso 'Building competitive advantage from ubuntu: management lessons from South Africa' (2001) 15 *Acad Management Exec* 26.

[63] Schiele 'Organizational theory from an Afrocentric perspective' (1990) 21 *J Black Stud* 145.

[64] Mangaliso (n62) 23ff. All too often, this general approach to decision-making becomes instrumental, in the sense that people are regarded as a resource and a means to an end: Jackson 'Managing change in South Africa: developing people and organizations' (1999) 10 *Int J Hum Resour Man* 307. The style of business management in Japan presents a well-known contrast, since it recognises the inherent value of people in an organisation's need to serve the collective: Yoshino

deliberation,[65] which is encoded in rules laid down by statute, regulations and the common law. Under the common law,[66] for instance, a meeting must be convened by a person with the authority to do so;[67] adequate notice must be given;[68] the meeting must be properly constituted by a quorum,[69] with an authorised chairperson,[70] and proposals must be put forward by means of duly tabled motions.[71]

Perhaps the most distinctive feature of the Western procedure is the preferred method for reaching fina decisions: a vote in which the majority determines the outcome. The voting process is of course flexible and can be adapted to meet particular social requirements by imposing such modalities as the size of a necessary majority, the manner of casting a vote, the weighting of votes or restrictions on a right to vote. As a decision-making method voting has the merit of resolving disagreements amongst members of a group quickly, efficiently and relatively peacefully.[72]

An African indaba type of process can be distinguished on several grounds,[73] but the following three are especially important. First, less emphasis is placed on the need to work within a strictly rational framework. By implication, this means that there is no pressing need to preserve the values of consistency and uniformity in decision-making, which would be required if rules and precedents were to be strictly applied.[74] Instead, the African process seeks, as its principal objective, the maintenance of stability and harmony in the social group.[75] The goal is therefore to fin solutions to problems that are generally acceptable, and, to do so, the consensus of all present is required. A majority opinion obtained through formal

---

'Emerging Japanese multi-national enterprises' in Vogel (ed) *Modern Japanese Organization and Decision-making* 158.

[65] And transferring information: Karsten & Illa 'Ubuntu as a key African management concept: contextual background and practical insights for knowledge application' (2005) 20 *J Management Psychol* 608. See also rule-oriented and relational discourses below p 167.

[66] For the following requirements, see Van Blerk 'Meetings' (Revised by Du Plessis & Pugsley) in Joubert *Law of South Africa* para 184.

[67] Van Blerk op cit para 189.

[68] Van Blerk op cit paras 187-189.

[69] Van Blerk op cit paras 190-191.

[70] Van Blerk op cit para 192.

[71] Van Blerk op cit para 203.

[72] Tjosvold & Field 'Effects of social context on consensus and majority vote decision making' (1983) 26 *Acad Manag J* 500-506.

[73] For what follows below see Prozesky *Tensions between Western Business Values and African Traditional Values — a Pilot Study*. He notes that African traditional values favour, *inter alia*: the community above the individual; external (especially spiritual) control, not individual autonomy; supportiveness, not competition; time as a qualitative, not a quantitative factor; leadership as determined by care and integrity, not power and status. See too Boon *The African Way: the power of interactive leadership* 25-30.

[74] Gluckman *Order and Rebellion in Tribal Africa* 205; Hammond-Tooke *The Roots of Black South Africa* 90-94; Taylor ' "The truth the whole truth nothing but the truth": truth, community and narrative in African procedural law' (2007) 40 *CILSA* 219.

[75] Suggesting the link to ubuntu. See above pp 79ff on restorative justice.

voting would be considered ill-advised,[76] because it would probably result in a discontented minority with obvious consequences for future relationships in the community.

Second, speed and efficiency are not prime concerns at an indaba, which means that discussion about the topic in issue requires no strict rule of relevance. The process tends, rather, to be open-ended, inquisitive and co-operative, whereby all participants are allowed to contribute their views.[77] Accordingly, an indaba will sacrific brevity to allow all people present a chance to air their views and to consider alternatives.

Third, compared with the top-down control of the Western model, those presiding over an indaba style process are expected to play a listening, rather than a speaking role. Elders, not presiding leaders, generally make proposals and lead the discussion.[78] Only when the leader discerns the emergence of a workable consensus, does he or she re-enter the debate to declare the solution. Those involved can then leave with the satisfaction of having been actively listened to, and properly understood. As a result, they are more likely to be committed to the fina decision.[79]

In South African law, the Western model of decision-making is taken to be the ideal norm, but it should be appreciated that an indaba process is also available for use in almost any type of meeting, whether called by a street committee, a church council, a voluntary association or a board of trustees.[80] The ensuing benefit are numerous.

For a start, because all parties, presiding officials aside, are treated as equals, an indaba gives effect to the constitutional mandate of participatory democracy.[81] The practical advantages include: the possibility of arriving at the best solution for a problem by allowing a broader range of views to be expressed and incurring fewer difficulties in securing implementation of the solution. What is more, the consensus goal of an indaba has desirable side effects of a purely social nature: actively participating in a debate fosters more cohesive relationships within a group, as well as better communication and an improvement in trust and group

---

[76] Cf voting in traditional communities to choose a traditional leader: *Shilubana and others v Nwamitwa* 2009 (2) SA 66 (CC); *Premier of the Eastern Cape and others v Ntamo and others* 2015 (6) SA 400 (ECB). See further on voting procedures in terms of legislation: *Bakgatla-Ba-Kgafela Communal Property Association v Bakgatla-Ba-Kgafela Tribal Authority and others* 2015 (6) SA 32 (CC) paras 31-33 which sought to interpret s 5(4) of the Communal Property Association Act 28 of 1996 (regarding governance decisions of CPAs) so as to remove the gender inequalities implicit in customary law.

[77] Bennett *Customary Law in South Africa* 171-172.

[78] The elders take this role in order to save the leader loss of face if members of the public disagree with the proposals.

[79] Bennett (n77) 166-168.

[80] In the absence of any rules laid down by the organisation in question to govern procedures. See Pienaar (updated by Dendy) 'Associations' in Joubert *Law of South Africa* para 181; Bamford *The Law of Partnership and Voluntary Association in South Africa* 151-156; Van Blerk (n66) para 184.

[81] See above pp 134-136.

morale.[82] Finally, and for all these reasons, an indaba provides an optimal setting for cultivating a sense of ubuntu.

Notwithstanding these benefits an indaba is not suited to solving all problems in all situations. It works most effectively when it involves a small, homogeneous group of people, with on-going relationships and shared interests. In the converse situation of a heterogeneous group, with short-term relationships, conflictin interests and a deadline to meet, it may be impossible to reach consensus[83] without resorting to social coercion,[84] failing which, of course, a deadlock may ensue. Furthermore, a decision based on a consensus of opinion may, in the long term, prove faulty. In order to cater for a wide range of views, the ultimate decision might well be too ambiguous or general to be of much use; it may have to be revised; and, more seriously, it may prove to be biased in favour of the status quo and those in positions of power.[85]

Even in a situation ideal for instituting an indaba process and reaching a consensus decision, the wrong decision might be taken because of a phenomenon termed 'groupthink'.[86] This dynamic occurs when individual members of a group try to minimise conflic in order to reach an agreement and maintain harmonious relations. The tendency, then, is not to evaluate all options fully, and for the group to isolate itself from outside influences The result is a loss of independent thinking, which may lead to making the wrong decision. While the prospect of groupthink is a chastening caveat to an over-enthusiastic adoption of an indaba, it is not an inevitable occurrence in all groups.[87] Certain factors contribute to the phenomenon: a very high degree of group cohesiveness, a faulty internal structure, notably, a lack of impartial leadership and rules prescribing the decision-making

---

[82] Hartnett *Consensus-oriented Decision Making: the CODM model for facilitating groups to widespread agreement* 11. Schweiger, Sandberg & Ragan 'Group approaches for improving strategic decision making: a comparative analysis of dialectical inquiry, devil's advocacy, and consensus' (1986) 29 *Academy of Management J* 51ff showed, through a laboratory study, that of three very different approaches to group decision-making, those using the consensus approach did not necessarily arrive at the best result, but they nonetheless felt greater satisfaction with their decisions and wanted to continue working with their groups.

[83] Some legislation dealing with consensus seeking by administrative bodies stipulates that, in the absence of consensus, voting mechanisms should be used. See, for example: s 21 of the Commission for the Promotion and Protection of the Rights of Cultural, Religious and Linguistic Communities Act 19 of 2002; s 17 of the Mine Health and Safety Act 29 of 1996; s 23 of the National Health Act 61 of 2003; s 63 of the National Gambling Act 7 of 2004; s 11 of the Road Accident Fund Act 56 of 1996.

[84] Mansbridge *Beyond Adversary Democracy* 166-171 and 252-255.

[85] Mansbridge op cit 294-295.

[86] This idea was introduced by Irving Janis, an American psychologist, in 'Groupthink' (1971) 5 *Psychology Today* 43–46 and 84–89. He chose the term 'groupthink' to connote an invidious condition, because it implies 'a deterioration in mental efficiency, reality testing and moral judgments as a result of group pressures'. He elaborated his work in *Victims of Groupthink: a psychological study of foreign-policy decisions and fiascoes* (1972) and revised in (1983).

[87] In fact, although the benefit of consensus decision-making are seemingly threatened by groupthink, it must be appreciated that the concept was devised to explain curiously incorrect decisions reached by the United States' military. Janis therefore claimed that dysfunctional dynamics within an 'ingroup' would produce an inflate idea of its abilities *vis-à-vis* an opposing 'outgroup'. Janis (n86 1972) 4.

procedure, together with strong external pressures, such as recent failures, moral dilemmas or a situation of panic.[88]

To conclude this section, it should be borne in mind that a comparison of cultural models, such as the one above, tends to emphasise the differences at the expense of similarities. A word is therefore necessary to point out areas of similarity. For instance, there is no reason to think that the Western style of decision-making has not influence African institutions,[89] although empirical studies exploring this possibility are scarce.[90] (The few that have been undertaken concentrated on the effect of principles of equality and democracy.)[91] Western processes, on the other hand, have clearly adopted certain features typical of the African counterpart, notably, a search for consensus and all that it entails.[92] Indeed, over the last 25 years adjustments have been made in South African law with this aim in view.[93] The workplace forums established under the Labour Relations Act[94] are an example. This innovation in employer-employee relationships requires the formation of consultative bodies designed to reach consensus agreements that will promote the interests of all employees, and at the same time enhance efficiency in the workplace.[95] Other examples can be found in the now popular processes of mediation and conciliation in many different branches of the law.[96]

5 ENFORCEABILITY OF INDABA DECISIONS

The purpose for comparing African and Western modes of decision-making is to recommend the adoption of an indaba approach and with it the guiding norm of ubuntu. Although the benefit of doing so are numerous, a factor that could weigh

---

[88] Janis (n86 1972) 3.

[89] In most cases imposed by statute, notably the Traditional Leadership and Governance Framework Act 41 of 2003 regarding election of traditional council members, and the Promotion of Administrative Justice Act 3 of 2000. Moreover, *Pilane and another v Pilane and another* 2013 (4) BCLR 431 (CC) held that traditional authorities, as organs of state, must comply with the Traditional Leadership and Governance Act.

[90] See, however, Oomen (n55) for an illuminating case study of chieftainship in Sekukhuneland.

[91] See, for instance, Beal, Mkhize & Vawda 'Emergent democracy and "resurgent" tradition: institutions, chieftaincy and transition in KwaZulu-Natal' (2005) 31 *JSAS* 755ff; Tshehla 'Traditional justice in practice — a Limpopo case study' (2005) 115 *Institute for Security Studies Monographs* 1ff. See, too, Claassens & Mnisi 'Rural women redefinin land rights in the context of living customary law' (2009) 25 *SAJHR* 509 regarding women's ability to speak out about their claims to land in family forums as opposed to meetings of higher traditional authorities.

[92] V P Barabba, retired general manager of General Motors Corporate Strategy and Knowledge Development programme, for instance, was part of an extensive, long-term effort to initiate a new approach to the perception and solution of problems in the company. In his influentia book, *Meeting of the Minds* 177-211, he advocated a process of decision-making that bears close resemblance to an indaba process.

[93] See Malan *Conflict Resolution: wisdom from Africa* 74ff.

[94] Chapter 5 of Act 66 of 1995.

[95] Section 79. Unfortunately, these forums have seldom been implemented.

[96] Boniface 'African-style mediation and Western-style divorce and family mediation: reflection for the South African context' (2012) 15 *PELJ* 378ff. See, for example, the following Acts and those cited in footnote 99 below: s 6(4) of the Children's Act 38 of 2005; s 23(3) of the National Health Act 61 of 2003; s 10(1)(e)(i) of the Financial Services Ombud Schemes Act 37 of 2004.

against an indaba is the enforceability of the fina decisions: will they receive the same degree of legal recognition as those taken at meetings conducted according to common or statutory law?

The answer must depend upon the institutional context and subject matter of a meeting. If a meeting is convened to serve the purposes of a particular institution, its conduct may be governed by statute, such as the Companies Act.[97] Certain statutes, however, may require (or permit) any disputes arising within terms of the statute concerned to be settled by a consensual agreement.[98] In this situation, a decision resulting from an indaba process will qualify for legal recognition. Other statutes may require (or permit) agreements to be reached by mediation, conciliation or negotiation.[99] In these cases, the interposition of a third party mediator/conciliator does not necessarily disqualify indaba.

Voluntary associations and partnerships fall into a different category.[100] They are created and run on the basis of contracts between the members. Appropriate decision-making processes may then be provided for in the contracts constituting the associations or partnerships in question.[101] If no provision is made, members are free to choose an indaba process.

This leaves institutions falling outside the ambit of statutory or contractual regulation. Presumably, they may be governed either by the common law[102] or by customary law, which, of course, enjoys recognition on a par with the common law.[103] It follows that, if a meeting was run according to the procedures of an indaba, the decision should be afforded the same recognition as one taken in

---

[97] Section 63 of Act 71 of 2008. See, too, the collective agreements reached under s 80(7) of the Labour Relations Act 66 of 1995. Regarding meetings convened for purposes of traditional leadership and governance see, for example, s 13 of the KwaZulu-Natal Traditional Leadership and Governance Act 5 of 2005 and s 8 of the Limpopo Traditional Leadership and Institutions Act 6 of 2005.

[98] Section 21(a) of the Commission for the Promotion and Protection of the Rights of Cultural, Religious and Linguistic Communities Act 19 of 2002: 'The Commission must take decisions in a consensus-seeking manner that gives effect to the principle of unity in diversity as reflecte in the Constitution'; s 26(1) Mine Health and Safety Act 29 of 1996; s 10(6) Rental Housing Act 50 of 1999; s 63(4) National Gambling Act 7 of 2004; s 11(6) of the Road Accident Fund Act 56 of 1996; s 6 of the Sectional Titles Schemes Management Act 8 of 2011.

[99] Section 47 of the Community Schemes Ombud Service Act 9 of 2011; s 10(1)(e)(i) of the Financial Services Ombud Schemes Act 37 of 2004; s 11(1)(e) of the Commission on Gender Equality Act 39 of 1996; s 11(5)(a) of the Pan South African Language Board Act 59 of 1995; s 8 of the Human Rights Commission Act 54 of 1994; s 6(4)(b)–(d) of the Public Protector Act 23 of 1994.

[100] A voluntary association can be created by an agreement, in any form, between three or more people to form an organisation aimed at mutual co-operation to achieve a common non-profi objective: Bamford (n80) 117-119; Pienaar (n80) para 155.

[101] *Garment Workers' Union v De Vries* 1949 (1) SA 1110 (W) at 1129. According to *Govender v Textile Workers' Industrial Union (SA) Durban Branch* 1961 (3) SA 88 (D) at 91, these rules will be interpreted benevolently, depending on the circumstances and where appropriate to do so, because, if 'a narrow and close attention to the rules of the constitution are demanded, a very large number of administrative acts done by lay bodies could be upset by the Courts . . . [and] every disappointed member would be encouraged to drag his society into Court for every triflin failure to observe the exact letter of every regulation'.

[102] Van Blerk (n66) para 184.

[103] Section 211(3) of the Constitution.

accordance with a common-law procedure. A caution should nonetheless be noted. Decisions taken as the result of indabas might not qualify for recognition if certain participants were not given an equal opportunity to voice their opinions, in violation of the constitutional rule of equal treatment.[104]

6 CONCLUSION

A meeting marked by an informal discussion, whereby everyone present is given a chance to air their views, and the general focus is towards finding unanimous support for the ultimate decision, is not the exclusive preserve of an African cultural tradition. The assumed norm in Western culture, however, favours greater formality and a system of majoritarian voting. Hence, to adopt an indaba process at a meeting is to give it a distinctive African character, with the greater likelihood of encouraging ubuntu and the participatory form of democracy required by the Constitution.

Aside from these normative benefits the indaba type of process has material advantages for good decision-making. A significant attraction is the satisfaction participants will receive for fully expressing themselves and being heard by those in authority. Another is the strengthening of relationships within the group and the participants' sense of ownership in the final decision, together, of course, with the consequence of a greater likelihood of successful implementation.

There are also, of course, certain disadvantages to an indaba. In this respect, time is a critical factor, because, in emergencies, an immediate decision is needed which precludes a potentially lengthy indaba style discussion. Moreover, where a gathering is composed of a large, disparate group of people, open-ended discussion poses the prospect of a deadlock of opinion, a poorly thought out decision and even the possibility of groupthink leading to the wrong decision.[105]

The advisability of proceeding according to an indaba principle therefore needs careful consideration. It obviously functions most effectively in smaller, more cohesive groups where time is not a particular constraint. Nevertheless, even under the inauspicious circumstances of large international conferences, an indaba may prove to be a rewarding process. Two such examples are provided by the 2008 Anglican Bishops' Conference at Lambeth Palace in London and the 2011 Climate Change Conference held in Durban.

---

[104] The grounds of discrimination include, *inter alia,* race, gender, sex, ethnic or social origin, sexual orientation, age, disability and religion: s 9(3) and (5).

[105] It is unlikely, therefore, that an indaba could have solved an emergency such as that resulting from the 2009 xenophobic attack by local farm workers against 3000 Zimbabwean forced migrants, who were living in a shack settlement at De Doorns in the Western Cape. After a prolonged negotiation between the Municipality, Provincial Government and PASSOP (on behalf of the camp residents) the settlement was closed. The urgency of the situation, the conflicting interests and the absence of a neutral arbiter are some of the factors contributing to the failure of the parties involved to prevent or resolve the labour-related tensions which led to violence. See People against Suffering Suppression Oppression and Poverty (PASSOP) *The De Doorns Monitoring Report* (2010); Forced Migration Studies Programme *Violence, Labour and the Displacement of Zimbabweans in De Doorns, Western Cape* (2009) Migration Policy Brief 2 University of the Witwatersrand http://http://www.migration.org za/ [Accessed on 06 November 2017].

At the Lambeth Conference, although the parties arrived with decidedly different views — and needed to meet a deadline — the participants generally welcomed the proposal to institute an indaba.[106] It was felt that this process would provide a better method for communication (whereby conflict could be fully aired) than the potentially divisive patterns of resolution and voting (typical of a parliamentary debate).[107] As one delegate put it, indaba 'challenged the Western linear way of proceeding' and 'opened up creativity'.[108] Others felt that the indaba served to increase the amount of 'talk' and reduce the emphasis on 'resolution' or 'action', thereby encouraging discovery, analysis, goal setting and self-fulfil ment.[109] Once everyone had had an opportunity to speak, problems were clarified 'We realise that we can't just use a new wineskin to patch the old, but that we need to see a new wine fermenting.'[110]

Similarly, the lengthy talks at the World Climate Change Conference in Durban involved a heterogeneous collection of states, again with conflictin views and policies. The focus of concern, however, was a matter critical to the survival of the planet, and the original time limit had to be relaxed to allow the conference proceedings to extend three days beyond the scheduled deadline. Reaching consensus at this gathering of 195 states on a highly contentious topic was clearly going to be far from easy. The executive secretary for the UN Framework Convention on Climate Change, however, praised the indaba process as a unique, African contribution to negotiations.[111] And, according to the South African Minister of Water and Environmental Affairs, the indaba process rescued the conference from a potential impasse, and, indeed, an agreement to co-operate on a new treaty was finall reached by both developed and developing states.[112]

---

[106] This proposal was made by the Archbishop of Cape Town, who said that the indaba concept was not confine to Africa: it had been used by the Benedictine order and the Quakers.

[107] Lambeth Conference 2008 News, 23 April 2008. See http://www.anglicancommunion.org/resources/document-library/lambeth-conference/2008/section-a-introduction?author=Lambeth+Conference&year=2008. [Accessed 18 November 2015].

[108] De Santis 'Lambeth participants reshape 'indaba' process' (27 July 2008) *Anglican News*, available at http://archive.episcopalchurch.org/79901_99407_ENG_HTM.htm [Accessed 18 November 2015].

[109] http://www.indabaglobal.com/ [Accessed 18 November 2015]. The change required a shift 'from the large assembly to the face to face encounter of deeper dialogue, where we are equal partners speaking with respect but sincerity'. Anglican News Service 'Indaba means no voice is too big or small' (23 July 2008) *Anglican News*, available at http://www.anglicannews.org/news/2008/07/indaba-means-no-voice-is-too-big-or-small.aspx [Accessed 18 November 2015].

[110] Op cit.

[111] The 17th Conference of Parties to the UN Framework Convention on Climate Change. For a brief overview see http://www.environ.ie/en/Environment/Atmosphere/ClimateChange/UnitedNationsFrameworkClimateChangeConvention/ [Accessed 18 November 2015].

[112] Fabricius 'COP17 threatened by long delays' 11 December 2011 *The Sunday Independent* 7. The indaba process was again proposed by the South African delegate to the World Climate Change Conference 2015 (COP21) in Paris 8 December 2015.

Chapter 8

CONCLUSION

'[T]he presence of "uBuntu" as a guiding norm in the interpretation of our basic law is essential, in the minds of ordinary people, for the legitimation of our legal system.'[1]

Law is simply words, but, when used by institutions with the necessary authority, these are words with a social power that reaches far beyond their utterance or appearance on a page.[2] Ubuntu, imbizo and indaba are such words, and they are now being employed by courts, law-makers and scholars to advance a specificall African idea of justice, one that has made a significan contribution to South Africa's programme of transformative constitutionalism.[3]

With the fall of the apartheid regime in the late 1980s, the country might well have been torn apart by violence and revolution, but a peaceful transition to democracy was negotiated.[4] A new constitution resulted,[5] giving all citizens the right to vote, promising the abolition of all racist laws[6] and introducing a fully justiciable Bill of Rights,[7] one containing a spectrum of civil, political and socio-economic rights, including freedom from discrimination, fair labour practices, housing, education and a clean environment. The whole legal system, based on its Anglo-Roman-Dutch foundation, was therefore ripe for reform.

The South African judiciary, however, had a traditionally positivist mind set — *ius dicere non facere* — irrespective of whether the laws in question served the greater purposes of equity or the social good. The trio of words — ubuntu, imbizo and indaba — that were presented to this system augured a completely different way of thinking, one concerned with context, non-legal sources of obligation and the welfare of the community.

Derived from the Nguni group of languages, these terms appeared as words 'on loan' to English or Afrikaans, ie, not in translation. Use of the language of origin therefore signalled that these words were strangers to their new environment, implying that the adoptive language and law had an unmet need. In the case of South African law, the primary and most urgent need was for means to assist in the transformation of a society that had systematically oppressed all persons of colour

---

[1] Lenta 'Just gaming: the case for postmodernism in South African legal theory' (2001) 17 *SAJHR* 189.

[2] Austin's famous proposition regarding language philosophy: *How to Do Things with Words* 9.

[3] See below p 162.

[4] Hence, South Africa's 'revolution' did not require the overthrow of the old legal order, but rather retention of all existing laws to the extent that they were consistent with the values of a new regime. See Cornell 'Introduction: transitional justice versus substantive revolution' in Cornell (ed) *Law and Revolution in South Africa: ubuntu, dignity, and the struggle for constitutional transformation* 10-11.

[5] The Constitution of the Republic of South Africa 108 of 1996.

[6] Section 9(4) as read with s 23(1) of Schedule 6 to the 1996 Constitution.

[7] Chapter 2 of the 1996 Constitution.

and had denigrated the beliefs, values and institutions associated with their cultures. Another long-term need was for a means to help interpret the rights and freedoms enshrined in the new Constitution so as to make them more amenable to application in the special circumstances of South Africa.

The task was immense, requiring the contribution of all organs of state and all members of society.[8] How exactly were the loan words, ubuntu, imbizo and indaba, to help? In the search for answers to this question, the analytical frameworks of linguistics and comparative law were chosen, since both disciplines are concerned with the ways in which systems of language and law adapt to the importation of foreign words and concepts.

Linguistics gives valuable clues as to how loan words behave in their new environment. Although they carry with them the meanings of their languages of origin, these meanings are then added to and subtracted from according to the demands they are then put. A comparative-law study of legal transplants helps to predict how a system of law will respond to the introduction of foreign rules and institutions. Depending on whether they overlap or conflic with the system's existing rules, they may be fully integrated into the system to perform new and useful functions, or they may become dysfunctional — or simply redundant.[9]

Early predictions about the fate of ubuntu were not promising. Some academics considered it no more than an academic construct, of no real validity or worth, for its spirit was no longer alive in the country.[10] Others said that it was superfluou to the requirements of the legal system, which was already amply equipped with the equitable principles and fundamental rights capable of effecting a constitutional transformation. Still others claimed that ubuntu was too vague to function as a term of law,[11] and it is true that attempts at definin it have failed, leaving only descriptions of its characteristics,[12] or admissions that 'you can only know it when you see it'.[13]

Nevertheless, and notwithstanding the doubts and gainsaying, ubuntu, together with imbizo and indaba, were enthusiastically received by the great majority of scholars, not only in law but also in other disciplines, such as philosophy, theology and business management. What is more important for purposes of this book, however, was the fact that law-makers and judges (principally at the instigation of South Africa's new Constitutional Court) readily invoked these concepts, with the result that all three are now well established in South African law.

Their successful accommodation in the legal system can be attributed, mainly,

---

[8] According to s 8(1) and (2) of the 1996 Constitution the Bill of Rights is binding on the executive, legislature and judiciary, and all persons, natural or juristic (to the extent that it is applicable).

[9] See Chapter 2 above.

[10] Van Binsbergen 'Ubuntu and the globalisation of Southern African thought and society' (2001) 15 *Quest* 62.

[11] See, for example, English 'Ubuntu: the quest for an indigenous jurisprudence' (1996) 12 *SAJHR* 641.

[12] Mnyongani 'De-linking *ubuntu*: towards a unique South African jurisprudence' (2010) 31 *Obiter* 135.

[13] Mokgoro 'Ubuntu and the law in South Africa' (1998) 2 *PELJ* 2.

to the political role they played in bringing to the law distinctively African ideas of right-doing and decision-making. The significanc of this event deserves special mention. In the firs place, the transplanting of norms and institutions from an oral system of customary law to a highly literate and structured legal system of common law might have required a difficult period of adjustment. In the second place, the systems of customary law in South Africa have long been misunderstood, undervalued and neglected. In the event, neither of these concerns proved to be an obstacle to the reception of the transplants.

At a purely legal, technical level, the relative ease with which ubuntu was assimilated into mainstream law can be ascribed to its being a single concept, lacking any clear definition It therefore caused minimal disruption to its adoptive system, because it could be deployed as a general principle of law, a type of metanorm equivalent to such common-law principles as good faith and equity, which set standards of desirable conduct without determining the precise results.[14] With one exception,[15] the courts refrained from construing ubuntu as a rule (which would normally prescribe the performance of specifi rights and duties).[16] In consequence, ubuntu did not conflic with existing rules. Rather, it acted as a free and independent element in the law, available for use whenever the need arose to give an African interpretation of statutory and common-law rights and principles, and to provide solutons for hard cases.

The assimilation of imbizo and indaba proved even easier. As typically African institutions, aimed at creating dialogues between citizens and political authorities, they presented themselves as convenient methods for furthering South Africa's new participative form of democracy (as well as providing appropriate social settings for realising an ubuntu ethos). Government authorities and organs of civil society therefore made full use of these institutions to convey information and to discuss problems with a view to co-opting community support for new rule-making and policy initiatives.

At a political level, the assimilation of ubuntu, imbizo and indaba was assured by the timing of their entry into the legal system. In the early 1990s, when the new constitutional dispensation was being negotiated, an opportunity was presented for a complete change of policy on customary law. In 1993, it was formally recognised on a par with the common law.[17] At the same time, ubuntu appeared, albeit as an obscure term in a curious epilogue to the Interim Constitution.[18]

When read in its immediate context, ubuntu could have been taken to mean no more than an aspiration to adopt a spirit of compassion and forgiveness, one sorely

---

[14] Unlike rules which dictate a specifi result. Principles may therefore conflic with one another without affecting the legitimacy or validity of the one or the other: Dworkin *Taking Rights Seriously* 22ff.

[15] *City of Tshwane Metropolitan Municipality v Afriforum and another* 2016 (6) SA 279 (CC).

[16] Twining & Miers *How to Do Things with Rules* 132 and 139.

[17] Principle XIII of Schedule 4 to the 1993 Interim Constitution Act 200 of 1993. Full recognition of customary law is now ensured by s 211(3) of the 1996 Constitution.

[18] See above pp 27, 46 and 79 fn134.

needed if the wounds left by colonialism and apartheid were to be healed.[19] In this sense, it played a leading role in the work of the Truth and Reconciliation Commission, which presided over South Africa's programme of restorative justice.[20] Ubuntu was taken further, however. It was immediately appropriated by courts and scholars as a banner for the introduction of African values to the transforming legal system, and this has continued to be its principal function.

Although the constitutional change entailed a decisive break with the apartheid regime, it did not entail an abrupt end to all past laws and the creation of a radically new order. Rather, the change in South Africa was of a transformative nature, which, in the frequently quoted words of Karl Klare, meant

> 'a long-term project of constitutional enactment, interpretation and enforcement committed (not in isolation, of course, but in a historical context of conducive political developments) to transforming a country's political and social institutions and power relationships in a democratic, participatory and egalitarian direction.'[21]

Transformation was to be both prospective, in that all future laws and juridical acts had to conform to the Constitution, and retrospective, since the entire corpus of laws inherited from the colonial and apartheid regimes had to be overhauled.[22]

The legislature was obviously required to spearhead this process, but Parliament and the executive could not immediately attend to all requirements,[23] and, even when new laws were promulgated, inevitable ambiguities and loopholes remained.[24] The courts were therefore expected to be fully involved in the transformative mission,[25] and s 8(3) of the Constitution expressly stated that they had to 'apply, or if necessary develop' common and customary law when existing statutory rules do not give effect to the Bill of Rights.[26]

---

[19] See the Preamble to the 1996 Constitution where it was provided that the Constitution was intended to: 'Heal the divisions of the past and establish a society based on democratic values, social justice and fundamental human rights.'

[20] A function it performed in the hearings of the Truth and Reconciliation Commission. See above p 79.

[21] Klare 'Legal culture and transformative constitutionalism' (1998) 14 *SAJHR* 150. See too Langa 'Transformative constitutionalism' (2006) 3 *Stell LR* 352.

[22] Sections 2 and 3 of Schedule 6 of the 1996 Constitution.

[23] As happened in *Bhe and others v Magistrate, Khayelitsha, and others (Commission for Gender Equality as Amicus Curiae); Shibi v Sithole and others; South African Human Rights Commission and another v President of the Republic of South Africa and another* 2005 (1) SA 580 (CC), where the Constitutional Court had to call on Parliament to take action to change the customary-law rule of agnatic succession.

[24] As, for example, in the case of the Promotion of Administrative Justice Act 3 of 2000, regarding matters falling outside the definitio of 'administrative action'. See *Fedsure Life Assurance v Greater Johannesburg Metropolitan Council and others* 1999 (1) SA 374 (CC).

[25] In *Port Elizabeth Municipality v Various Occupiers* 2005 (1) SA 217 (CC) para 36, for instance, Sachs J called upon the courts to extend themselves beyond their normal functions to 'engage in active judicial management' of change.

[26] In addition, s 39(2) required the courts to 'promote the spirit, purport and objects of the Bill of Rights' when they are 'interpreting any legislation, and when developing the common law or customary law'.

The authority of the judiciary is obviously limited by the doctrine of separation of powers, but, even so, South African courts, with their positivist background, were cautious and casuistic in their approach,[27] and they drew back from a full-scale programme of law reform.[28] As a result, they were often accused of being slow on the uptake.[29] As Sachs J said, however, they could 'at least soften and minimise the degree of injustice and inequity [suffered by] . . . weaker parties in conditions of inequality or necessity'.[30]

In fact, in addition to the Bill of Rights, the judiciary had the necessary tools at hand to carry out this injunction. These were a repertoire of equitable principles drawn from the common law, notably good faith and public policy, but also reasonableness and *boni mores*.[31] While the primary function of these principles was to attend to particular cases of injustice, they could, at the same time, be put to the task of stimulating incremental constitutional reform.[32] Ubuntu presented itself as another such instrument.

The prime objection to its use could then be raised: that ubuntu was superfluou

---

[27] Bhana 'The role of judicial method in the relinquishing of constitutional rights through contract' (2008) 24 *SAJHR* 300 317 He noted (323) that, with the significan exception of *Fourie v Minister of Home Affairs* 2005 (3) SA 429 (SCA) para 139, the courts' reluctance to further the cause of transformation or to incorporate a new concept, such as ubuntu, into the interpretation of private-law principles (323-324) was due primarily to their unwillingness to sacrific legal certainty and private autonomy to the communitarian power of constitutional values of freedom, equality and dignity (328-329).

[28] Davis 'Developing the common law of contract in the light of poverty and illiteracy: the challenge of the Constitution' (2011) 22 *Stell LR* 845ff; Du Bois 'Contractual obligation and the journey from natural law to constitutional law' 2015 *Acta Juridica* 284ff. Notwithstanding these comments, judgments in the sphere of private law have repeatedly mentioned the courts' duty to develop the law. See, for example, *Brisley v Drotsky* 2002 (4) SA 1 (SCA) para 95; *Khumalo and others v Holomisa* 2002 (5) SA 401 (CC) para 30; *Fourie v Minister of Home Affairs* 2005 (3) SA 429 (SCA) para 25; *Masiya v Director of Public Prosecutions, Pretoria and another (Centre for Applied Legal Studies and another, Amici Curiae)* 2007 (5) SA 30 (CC) para 31; *Barkhuizen v Napier* 2007 (5) SA 323 (CC) para 30; *Everfresh Market Virginia (Pty) Ltd v Shoprite Checkers (Pty) Ltd* 2012 (1) SA 256 (CC) para 31; *Loureiro and others v Imvula Quality Protection (Pty) Ltd* 2014 (3) SA 394 (CC) para 34; *Paulsen and another v Slip Knot Investments 777 (Pty) Ltd* 2015 (3) SA 479 (CC) paras 54-56; *DE v RH* 2015 (5) SA 83 (CC) para 16.

[29] Davis & Klare 'Transformative constitutionalism and the common and customary law' (2010) 26 *SAJHR* 403ff.

[30] *Port Elizabeth Municipality v Various Occupiers* 2005 (1) SA 217 (CC) para 38.

[31] Because good faith gives effect to what society thinks is just and reasonable, it is arguably but an aspect of public policy, which is itself informed by the same social values: *Barkhuizen v Napier* 2007 (5) SA 323 (CC) paras 51 and 52. See Hutchison 'Non-variation clauses in contract: any escape from the *Shifren* straightjacket?' (2001) 118 *SALJ* 742.

[32] As, for example, in: *Advtech Resourcing (Pty) Ltd t/a The Communication Personnel Group v Kuhn and another* 2008 (2) SA 375 (C) para 15; *Savage and others v Sisters of the Holy Cross, Cape Province and others* 2015 (6) SA 1 (WCC); *Mayelane v Ngwenyama and another* 2013 (4) SA 415 (CC); *JT v Road Accident Fund* 2015 (1) SA 609 (GJ); *Bhe and others v Magistrate, Khayelitsha, and others (Commission for Gender Equality as Amicus Curiae); Shibi v Sithole and others; South African Human Rights Commission and another v President of the Republic of South Africa and another* 2005 (1) SA 580 (CC). Davis 'Private law after 1994: progressive development or schizoid confusion?' (2008) 24 *SAJHR* 318-319, however, contends that these equitable principles were not exploited to their full potential.

to the needs of a legal system already supplied with principles to serve the general goals of justice and transformation. This, however, is not the case. For a start, ubuntu performs, as already indicated, a political function which the other equitable principles do not: giving a sense of cultural legitimation to constitutional rights. Furthermore, these principles have a more limited sphere of operation than ubuntu, in that public policy, reasonableness and *boni mores*, for example, refer to commonly conceived ideas of justice and right behaviour of a particular society at a particular time. Ubuntu, on the other hand, is a notionally timeless, transcendent norm.[33]

In this regard, ubuntu bears a closer resemblance to the ancient European principle of equity. When used on its own, equity operates as a generalised metanorm. It has no one, clearly defined function other than to provide a broad justificatio for the courts' reluctance to apply the rules of common or statute law in certain factual situations where an inappropriate result would ensue. Ubuntu and equity thus have a similar function.[34] What is more, the two norms originated in a general spiritual conception of right-doing, and both began their development by appearing in a range of disparate cases linked by no common theme other than the need to remedy particular cases of injustice.

The subsequent development of equity in England, however, took a path that diverged from equity as conceived in civil law jurisdictions. It became a codifie set of rules separate from the common law and administered by a separate branch of the courts. In consequence, equity eventually began to create the same problems as the common law: strict application of rules which could result in unfair results. If there is a lesson to be learnt from the history of the English doctrine, it is that the South African courts should not follow the same path of development.

Like any other fundamental principle of law, the meaning and scope of ubuntu must remain broad and flexible especially since it has to perform the diverse tasks required by South Africa's constitutional transformation. Indeed, it is impossible to stipulate in advance the application of any principle with similar functions (such as reasonableness, public policy and good faith) or, for that matter, the exercise of discretionary powers (such as sentencing and parole). These devices are essential for all legal systems if they are to be responsive to unforeseen factual problems.

---

[33] A transcendence which Cornell '*uBuntu*, pluralism and the responsibility of legal academics to the New South Africa' (2009) 20 *Law & Critique* 47 construes differently to mean 'an individual is pulled out of himself or herself back towards the ancestors, forward towards the community, and towards the potential each one of us has'.

[34] Ubuntu differs from equity in three respects. First, it has been invoked in all areas of the law, whereas equity in English (and Roman-Dutch common law) is generally confine to the sphere of private law. Second, in English law, equity provided a cause of action, while ubuntu has not (so far) given rise to an actionable right. Third, equity is a culturally neutral concept which, notionally at least, transcends all times and societies, whereas ubuntu denotes a decidedly African understanding of right-doing.

The final and most serious, contender for rendering ubuntu superfluou is the Bill of Rights. As a cornerstone of the Constitution,[35] which is the supreme law of the land,[36] it transcends all other laws. It can be applied directly, both horizontally and vertically, to found causes of action;[37] it governs all laws and policies, and is regularly called upon to provide a basis for law reform.[38] Clearly, ubuntu and the other common-law equitable principles have no such all-encompassing power. Their main functions are to modify, correct or supplement the effects of the plain letter of the law. Accordingly, when discharging these functions, ubuntu can be invoked to add weight to the Bill of Rights, to interpret the rights and, on occasion, to mediate conflict between them.[39]

Hence, although ubuntu and the common-law equitable principles may play similar roles, ubuntu has a function which neither they nor the Bill of Rights can perform: that of imbuing the legal system with an African set of values, and thereby giving expression to South Africa's unique cultural and historical circumstances.[40] A classic case in point was *City of Tshwane Metropolitan Municipality v Afriforum and another*,[41] where Mogoeng CJ inveighed against the retention of colonial and apartheid era street names in Pretoria without regard for the sensitivities, history, language or culture of Africans and formerly disadvantaged groups in society.

This being the case, how far can ubuntu go to meet the need for transformation? In the last three years, this question has been given an acute urgency by radical student movements demanding a thorough decolonisation of the law and the way in which it is taught.[42] They have claimed that, for far too long, traditional African learning and knowledge have been ignored, because of the racist and eurocentric bias of South Africa's legal and educational systems. The students therefore demanded a more inclusive legal culture.[43]

---

[35] Section 7(1) of the Constitution 1996.

[36] Section 2 of the Constitution 1996.

[37] Section 8(2) of the Constitution provides that the Bill of Rights binds natural persons 'if, and to the extent that, it is applicable, taking into account the nature of the right and the nature of any duty imposed by the right'.

[38] Notably in *S v Makwanyane and another* 1995 (3) SA 391 (CC) para 307 and *Bhe and others v Magistrate, Khayelitsha, and others (Commission for Gender Equality as Amicus Curiae); Shibi v Sithole and others; South African Human Rights Commission and another v President of the Republic of South Africa and another* 2005 (1) SA 580 (CC).

[39] As, for example, in *Port Elizabeth Municipality v Various Occupiers* 2005 (1) SA 217 (CC) para 37.

[40] Cornell & Muvangua 'Introduction: the re-cognition of *uBuntu*' in Cornell & Muvangua (eds) *Ubuntu and the Law: African ideals and postapartheid jurisprudence* 8.

[41] 2016 (6) SA 279 (CC).

[42] See generally on legal education: Modiri 'The crises in legal education' (2014) 46 *Acta Academica* 1ff. The meaning and implications of decolonisation, however, are still vague: Himonga 'Decolonisation and teaching law in Africa with special reference to living customary law' paper presented at the *Workshop on Oral History and Law: writing South African legal history*' (2016) Joint Workshop of Universities of Edinburgh and North-West. See further De Sousa Santos *Decolonising the University: the challenge of deep cognitive justice*.

[43] Regarding which see: Rycroft & Le Roux 'Decolonising labour law' (2017) 38 *ILJ* 1473ff; Hutchison 'A customary insurance law?' (2017) 29 *SA Mercantile LJ* 17ff; Hutchison 'Decolonising

As it happens, the judiciary has expressed similar sentiments, although (not surprisingly) in a more moderate form. For instance, in the Constitutional Court's firs judgment, *S v Makwanyane and another*,[44] Sachs J talked of the need to source the values for South African law in African traditions. He said that the time had come to 'restore dignity to ideas and values that have long been suppressed or marginalized', especially since these were the ideas and values of the vast majority of the population.

Subsequent judgments of the Constitutional Court picked up on this point, and used it to enforce a more authentic conception of customary law than what has been termed the 'official' version, namely, the version found in textbooks, statutes and precedents.[45] In its place, the Court called for a 'living' law, which is the law created by the people themselves, not an outside authority.[46] The courts were therefore enjoined to acknowledge the values of customary law,[47] and to treat the system on its own terms, not as perceived through the prism of common law.[48]

While the Constitutional Court called for greater respect for customary law, it did not suggest a general 'africanisation' of the entire legal system, and the programme of constitutional transformation has stopped far short of this goal, or even a greater degree of integration or harmonisation of customary and common law.[49] The two regimes still largely operate independently of one another. Ubuntu, however, has succeeded in introducing to the mainstream of South African law a discreet change of discourse.[50]

South African contract law: an argument for synthesis' in Siliquini-Cinelli & Hutchison (eds) *The Constitutional Dimension of Contract Law: a comparative perspective* 151-152.

[44] 1995 (3) SA 391 (CC) paras 361ff.

[45] *Alexkor Ltd and another v the Richtersveld Community and others* 2004 (5) SA 460 (CC) para 53; *Bhe and others v Magistrate, Khayelitsha, and others (Commission for Gender Equality as Amicus Curiae); Shibi v Sithole and others; South African Human Rights Commission and another v President of the Republic of South Africa and another* 2005 (1) SA 580 (CC) paras 86-87; *Mayelane v Ngwenyama and another* 2013 (4) SA 415 (CC) paras 24-25, 32, 42-44 and 46, for which see Himonga & Pope 'Mayelane v Nwenyama and Minister for Home Affairs: a reflectio on wider implications' 2013 *Acta Juridica* 318ff. See further Costa 'The myth of customary law' (1998) 14 *SAJHR* 534 and Claassens & Budlender 'Transformative constitutionalism and customary law' (2016) 6 *CCR* 75ff. The latter authors show, however, that despite the Constitutional Court's pronouncement, the legislature has proposed a series of laws sourced in the official version of customary law thereby reinforcing the rule of traditional leaders.

[46] The validity of this law is therefore based on a people's right to culture: Himonga & Bosch 'The application of African customary law under the Constitution of South Africa: problems solved or just beginning' (2000) 117 *SALJ* 330-331.

[47] In *Bhe and others v Magistrate, Khayelitsha, and others (Commission for Gender Equality as Amicus Curiae); Shibi v Sithole and others; South African Human Rights Commission and another v President of the Republic of South Africa and another* 2005 (1) SA 580 (CC) para 44, the Constitutional Court listed some of these values: seeking consensus; encouraging family and clan meetings to prevent and resolve disputes; contributing to family unity; fostering co-operation, a sense of belonging and responsibility and the 'healthy communitarian traditions such as *ubuntu*'.

[48] *Alexkor Ltd and another v the Richtersveld Community and others* 2004 (5) SA 460 (CC) paras 51 and 56; *Gumede v President of the Republic of South Africa* 2009 (3) SA 152 (CC) para 43.

[49] See above pp 4-5.

[50] See, in this regard, Davis 'Toward a relational constitutionalism' 2008 *Acta Juridica* 239ff.

The traditional way of talking and writing about law in South Africa — which, significantl , is primarily in English or Afrikaans — reflect a positivist and rule-oriented mind set. In other words, the social complexities of rights, claims and disputes have to be simplifie into sets of relevant facts that can then be presented as causes of action to be solved by the strictly rational application of fixe rules. This syllogistic approach can be contrasted with the relational discourse of customary law. Claims and disputes are not solved solely on the basis of predetermined rules, but rather on an individual's standing in a web of social relationships.[51] Argument is therefore driven less by rules and abstract logic and more by virtues, circumstances and personal details.[52]

A relational approach to law is not, of course, unknown in South Africa — it is evident, for instance, wherever people seek to solve disputes by negotiation or mediation[53] — but ubuntu has initiated a more pervasive relational discourse,[54] one that reaches into all parts of the legal system. This form of discourse is triggered whenever the courts invoke ubuntu as a solvent for hard cases, namely, situations when application of the accepted rules of law caused an injustice.[55]

In summary, the role so far played by ubuntu in South African law has been a modest one.[56] It has not provided a radical new *Grundnorm*,[57] nor has it provided the driving force for major law reform.[58] Rather, ubuntu has provided a new criterion for interpreting rules and principles so as to inject into them the African virtues of respect, grace and compassion, together with the individual's responsibility to pay due regard to the interests of others.[59] In this way, the powerful

---

[51] Conley & O'Barr *Just Words, Law Language and Power* 67-68.

[52] As was revealed in fieldwor by Bohannan *Justice and Judgment Among the Tiv* and Gluckman *The Ideas in Barotse Jurisprudence*: Conley & O'Barr op cit 102-103.

[53] See, for instance, *Ferreira v Levin NO and others; Vryenhoek and others v Powell NO and others* 1996 (1) SA 984 (CC) para 251 esp fn 11.

[54] See Davis (n50) 252 and Cornell (n33) 48-49 citing S K Bavikatte's fieldwor amongst the San: 'A relational understanding of the self emphasises less on rights in its engagement with the world and more on virtue — virtue being define here as the sense that foregrounds one's connectedness rather than separateness. The practice of virtue on a number of occasions also resolves conflictin rights through the practice of connectedness by the manifesting of what we term here as "relational sentiments" such as graciousness, kindness, love, compassion, patience and generosity.'

[55] These are, of course, sporadic occurrences, which have led to a fear that ubuntu is undermining the predictability and certainty necessary for the rule of law. See, for instance, Pieterse ' "Traditional" African jurisprudence' in Roederer & Moellendorf (eds) *Jurisprudence* 448, who argues that, although ubuntu may serve the political purpose of cultural legitimacy, 'if it is to continue to do so it should be invoked consistently and in the correct context, and not in the current piecemeal fashion'.

[56] There is a striking analogy here with Van der Walt's idea, in 'The modest systemic status of property rights' (2014) 1 *JL Prop & Soc'y* 15ff, that property law does not play a leading role in securing such goals as dignity and equality. These are performed by the rights to dignity and equality themselves, leaving property with the more 'modest' function of simply excluding non-owners. The concept of property is then not overburdened with the complex task of promoting the human good. The same might be said of the role of ubuntu in its association with the Bill of Rights.

[57] Cornell (n4) 12.

[58] In other words, for revising substantive rules of law. Cf the Child Justice Act 75 of 2008 and *Dikoko v Mokhatla* 2006 (6) SA 235 (CC).

[59] Two of the main targets of the courts' use of ubuntu in this connection were privileged members of society — see, for example, *City of Tshwane Metropolitan Municipality v Afriforum and another*

community associations of ubuntu, expressed in the saying *umuntu ngumuntu ngabantu*, have been mobilised to protect the position of vulnerable and marginalised groups in society.[60]

Aside from the above, the courts have sought to identify ubuntu with certain rights and values of the new constitutional order (notably dignity, equality) and with equitable principles of the common-law order (notably good faith and public policy). More specificall , it has been involved with changing certain processes, most obviously the resolution of conflict (via restorative justice), the conduct of debates and discussions (via indaba) and the making of rules and policies (via imbizo).

As a flexible free floatin element in the legal system, ubuntu is now an established feature of South African law. It stands for the country's African legal heritage, a 'gift that African philosophy can bequeath on other philosophies of the world'.[61] It is an active ethic, one either practised by people in their everyday lives or calling on them to account for failing to do so. It has none of the emotional neutrality of a concept like justice. It comes rich with connotations of caring for others and a synergistic process of being an integral member of a community.[62] In this sense, ubuntu has the capacity to offer more than a principle or a value. It is also an ideal, and, as such, cannot be reduced to rational expression, but can always demand more of current behaviours and desires for an imagined future.[63]

2016 (6) SA 279 (CC) paras 2 and 11 — and officials in public service, as, for example, in: *Bertie Van Zyl (Pty) Ltd and another v Minister for Safety and Security and others* 2010 (2) SA 181 (CC) (police); *Law Society, Northern Provinces v Mogami and others* 2010 (1) SA 186 (SCA) (attorneys); *Koyabe and others v Minister for Home Affairs and others (Lawyers for Human Rights as Amicus Curiae)* 2010 (4) SA 327 (CC) (Home Affairs); *City of Johannesburg Metropolitan Municipality v Blue Moonlight Properties 39 (Pty) Ltd and another (Lawyers for Human Rights as Amicus Curiae)* 2012 (2) SA 104 (CC) (local authorities).

[60] See, for example, *Union of Refugee Women and others v Director: Private Security Industry Regulatory Authority and others* 2007 (4) SA 395 (CC) (refugees); *Port Elizabeth Municipality v Various Occupiers* 2005 (1) SA 217 (CC) (evictees); *Hoffmann v South African Airways* 2001 (1) SA 1 (CC) (HIV/AIDS victims).

[61] Teffo *The Concept of Ubuntu as a Cohesive Moral Value* 5.

[62] Cornell & Van Marle 'Exploring ubuntu: tentative reflections (2005) 5 *AHRLJ* 206-207.

[63] Cornell & Van Marle op cit 205.

BIBLIOGRAPHY

Ackermann L W H 'Equality in the South African Constitution: the role of dignity' (2000) 60 *Heidelberg J Int L* 537

Ackermann L W H 'The legal nature of the South African constitutional revolution' (2004) 4 *New Zealand LR* 633

Ackermann L W H *Human Dignity: lodestar for equality in South Africa* (2012) Juta

Adendorff R D 'Ethnographic evidence of the social meaning of Fanakalo in South Africa' (1993) 8 *JPCL* 1

Akehurst M 'Equity and general principles of law' (1976) 25 *ICLQ* 801

Albertyn C & Goldblatt B 'Equality' in S Woolman & M Bishop (eds) *Constitutional Law of South Africa* 2ed (2013) Juta 35-1

Albertyn C & Kentridge J 'Introducing the right to equality in the Interim Constitution' (1994) 10 *SALJ* 149

Albertyn C 'Women and the transition to democracy in South Africa' 1994 *Acta Juridica* 39

Alexander E R 'Rationality revisited: planning paradigms in a post-postmodernist perspective' (2000) 19 *J of Planning Education & Research* 242

Alexy R 'Reasonableness of law' in B Bongiovanni, G Sartor & C Valentini (eds) *Reasonableness and Law* (2009) Springer 5

Allen C K *Law in the Making* 7ed (1964) Clarendon Press

Almgren G 'Community' in E F Borgatta & M L Borgatta (eds) *Encyclopedia of Sociology* vol 1 (1992) MacMillan 244

Alper S, Tjosvold D & Law K S 'Interdependence and controversy in group decision making: antecedents to effective self-managing teams' (1998) 74 *Organizational Behavior & Human Decision Processes* 33

American Anthropological Association 'Statement on human rights' (1947) 49 *Am Anthropol* 539

Aristotle (trans by H Rackham) *Nicomachean Ethics* (1967) Loeb Classical Library, Harvard University Press

Ashton E H *The Basuto* (1952) Oxford University Press

Austin J L *How to Do Things with Words* 2ed (1975) Harvard University Press

Baird C J *In Defense of the Land Ethic: essays in environmental philosophy* (1989) University of New York Press

Ball C 'The vocabulary of English' in W F Bolton & D Crystal (eds) *The English Language* (1993) Penguin 165

Bamford B R *The Law of Partnership and Voluntary Association in South Africa* 3ed (1982) Juta

Bank L & Southall R 'Traditional leaders in South Africa's new democracy' (1996) 37-38 *J Legal Pluralism & Unofficial L* 407

Barabba V P *Meeting of the Minds* (1995) Harvard Business School

Barthes R (trans A Lavers & C Smith) *Elements of Semiology* (1967) Jonathan Cape

Bathia K L *Textbook on Legal Language and Legal Writing* (2010) Universal Law Publishing

Bavikatte K S & Bennett T W 'Community stewardship: the foundation of biocultural rights' (2015) 6 *JHRE* 7

Beall J, Mkhize S & Vawda S 'Emergent democracy and "resurgent" tradition: institutions, chieftaincy and transition in KwaZulu-Natal' (2005) 31 *JSAS* 755

Beinart B 'The English legal contribution in South Africa: the interaction of civil and common law' 1981 *Acta Juridica* 7

Beinart W & Bundy C *Hidden Struggles in Rural South Africa* (1987) Ravan Press

Bekker J C & Van der Merwe A 'Indigenous legal systems and sentencing: *S v Maluleke*' 2008 (1) SACR 49 (T)' (2009) 42 *De Jure* 239

Bekker J C 'Interaction between constitutional reform and family law' 1991 *Acta Juridica* 1

Bell D A & Metz T 'Confucianism and ubuntu: reflection on a dialogue between Chinese and African traditions' (2011) 38 *J of Chinese Philosophy* 78

Benda-Beckmann F von 'Who's afraid of legal pluralism?' (2002) 34 *J Legal Pluralism & Unofficial L* 37

Benda-Beckmann K von 'The use of folk law in West-Sumatran state courts' in A Allott & G R Woodman (eds) *People's Law and State Law* (1985) Foris Publications 78

Bennett T W & Munro R 'Ubuntu, indaba and. Baptist congregationalism' (2012) 21 *SABJT* 24

Bennett T W & Patrick J 'Ubuntu: the ethics of traditional religion' in T W Bennett (ed) *Traditional African Religions in South African Law* (2011) UCT Press 223

Bennett T W *A Sourcebook of African Customary Law for Southern Africa* (1991) Juta

Bennett T W *Application of Customary Law in Southern Africa* (1985) Juta

Bennett T W *Customary Law in South Africa* (2004) Juta

Benson R 'The end of legalese: the game is over' (1984-1985) 13 *New York Rev of Law & Social Change* 519

Bewaji J A I & Ramose M B 'The Bewaji, van Binsbergen and Ramose debate on ubuntu' (2003) 22 *SA J Philosophy* 378

Bhana D 'The development of a basic approach for the constitutionalisation of our common law of contract' (2015) 26 *Stell LR* 3

Bhana D 'The role of judicial method in the relinquishing of constitutional rights through contract' (2008) 24 *SAJHR* 300

Bhatia V K *Analyzing Genre: language in professional settings* (1993) Longman

Bhengu M J *Ubuntu: the essence of democracy* (1996) Novalis Press

Bhengu M J *Ubuntu: the global philosophy for humankind* (2006) Lotsha Publications

Bilchitz D l 'Are socio-economic rights a form of political rights?' (2015) 31 *SAJHR* 86

Bohannan P *Justice and Judgment Among the Tiv* (1957) Oxford University Press

Bohler-Muller N 'The story of an African value: focus: ten years after' (2005) 20 *SAPL* 266

Bolinger D 'The atomization of meaning' (1965) 41 *Language* 555

Boniface A E 'African-style mediation and Western-style divorce and family mediation: reflection for the South African context' (2012) 15 *PELJ* 377

Boon M *The African Way: the power of interactive leadership* 3ed (2007) Zebra

Boonzaier E & Sharp J 'Introduction: constructing social reality' in E Boonzaier & J Sharp (eds) *South African Keywords* (1988) David Phillip 1

Booysen S 'Public participation in democratic South Africa: from popular mobilisation to structured co-optation and protest' (2009) 28 *Politeia* 1

Botha H 'Human dignity in comparative perspective' (2009) 20 *Stell LR* 171

Boulle L 'Predictable irrationality in mediation: insights from behavioural economics' (2013) 24 *ADRJ* 8

Boyd White J *Heracles Bow — essays on the rhetoric and poetics of law* (1985) University of Wisconsin Press

Brand F D J 'The role of good faith, equity and fairness in the South African law of contract: the influenc of the common law and the Constitution' (2009) 126 *SALJ* 71

Brand F D J 'The role of good faith, equity and fairness in the South African law of contract: a further instalment' (2016) 27 *Stell LR* 238

Broodryk J 'Is ubuntuism unique?' in J G Malherbe (ed) *Decolonizing the Mind: proceedings of the second colloquium on African philosophy* (1996) UNISA Research Unit for African Philosophy 31

Broodryk J 'The philosophy of ubuntu: to improve business success' (2006) 22 *Management Today* 20

Broodryk J *Ubuntu: life lessons from Africa* (2002) Ubuntu School of Philosophy

Brown B & Duku N 'Negotiated identities: dynamics in parents' participation in school governance in rural Eastern Cape schools and implications for school leadership' (2008) 28 *SAJ of Education* 413

Brown J T *Setswana Dictionary: Setswana-English and English-Setswana* 3ed (1980) Pula Press

Bruner J S 'The narrative construction of reality' (1991) *Crit Inquiry* 1

Bruner J S *Acts of Meaning* (1990) Harvard University Press

Buckland W W & Stein P *A Text-Book of Roman Law: from Augustus to Justinian* 3ed (1963) Cambridge University Press

Bujo B (trans B McNeil) *Foundations of an African Ethic: beyond the universal claims of Western morality* (2001) Paulines Publications

Bujo B 'Springboards for modern African constitutions and development in African cultural traditions' in F M Murove (ed) *African Ethics: an anthology of comparative and applied ethics* (2009) University of KwaZulu-Natal Press 391

Burchell J M *Principles of Criminal Law* 5ed (2016) Juta

Burdick W L *The Principles of Roman Law and Their Relation to Modern Law* (1938) Lawyers Co-operative Pub Co

Buro van die Woordeboek van die Afrikaanse Taal *Woordeboek van die Afrikaanse Taal* (2015), available at www.woordeboek.co.za

Calland R & Nakhooda S 'Participatory democracy meets the hard rock of energy policy: South Africa's National Integrated Resource Plan' (2012) 19 *Democratization* 912

Callaway G *Fellowship of Veld: Sketches of Native Life in South Africa* (1926) SPCK

Cameron E, De Waal M J & Wunsh B *Honore's South African Law of Trusts* 5ed (2002) Juta

Capra F *The Web of Life: a new scientific understanding of living systems* (1996) Anchor Books

Chanock M ' "Culture" and human rights: orientalising, occidentalising and authenticity' in M Mamdani (ed) *Beyond Rights Talk and Culture Talk: comparative essays on the politics of rights and culture* (2000) David Philip 15

Chanock M 'Law, state and culture: thinking about customary law after apartheid' 1991 *Acta Juridica* 52

Chaskalson A 'Third Bram Fischer lecture — human dignity as a foundational value of our constitutional order' (2000) 16 *SAJHR* 193

Christie R H & Bradfiel G B *Christie's The Law of Contract in South Africa* 6ed (2011) LexisNexis

Cicero (trans by Rackham) *De Partitione Oratoria* (2004) Harvard University Press

Claassens A & Budlender G 'Transformative constitutionalism and customary law' (2016) 6 *CCR* 75

Claassens A & Mnisi S M 'Rural women redefinin land rights in the context of living customary law' (2009) 25 *SAJHR* 491

Claassens A ' "It is not easy to challenge a chief" ': lessons from Rakgwadi' (2001) 9 *PLAAS Research Report* 1, available at http://www.plaas.org.za/sites/default/files publications-pdf/PLAAS_RR9_Claassens.pdf

Claassens A 'The resurgence of tribal taxes in the context of recent traditional leadership laws in South Africa' (2011) 27 *SAJHR* 522

Clemen R T *Making Hard Decisions* (1991) PWS-Kent

Cockrell A ' "Can You Paradigm?" — another perspective on the public law/private law divide 1993 *Acta Juridica* 227

Coertze L I *Die Trust in die Romeins-Hollandse Reg* (1948) unpublished doctoral thesis, University of Stellenbosch

Coetzee L & Van Tonder J L 'The fiduciar relationship between a company and its directors' (2014) 35 *Obiter* 285

Coetzee P H 'Morality in African thought' in P H Coetzee & A P J Roux (eds) *Philosophy from Africa: a text with readings* 2ed (2003) Routledge 321

Cohen J 'Procedure and substance in deliberative democracy' in S Benhabib (ed) *Democracy and Difference: contesting the boundaries of the political* (1996) Princeton University Press 95

Comaroff J L 'Chieftainship in a South African homeland: a case study of the Tshidi Chiefdom of Bophuthatswana' (1974) 1 *JSAS* 36

Conaglen M 'Fiduciaries' in J McGhee *Snell's Principles of Equity* 33ed (2015) Sweet & Maxwell 137

Conley J M & O'Barr W M *Just Words, Law Language and Power* 2ed (1998) University of Chicago Press

Cook S E 'Chiefs, kings, corporatization, and democracy: a South African case study' (2005) 12 *Brown J of World Affairs* 125

Corder H 'Crowbars and cobwebs: executive autocracy and the law in South Africa' (1989) 5 *SAJHR* 1

Corder H 'Establishing legitimacy for the administration of justice in South Africa' (1995) 6 *Stell LR* 202

Corder H 'Judicial oversight of the legislative process: a South African case study' in D M Chirwa & L Nijzink (eds) *Accountable Government in Africa* (2010) UCT Press 85

Cornell D & Muvangua N 'Introduction: the re-cognition of *uBuntu*' in D Cornell & N Muvangua (eds) *Ubuntu and the Law: African ideals and postapartheid jurisprudence* (2012) Fordham University Press 1

Cornell D & Panfili K M *Symbolic Forms for a New Humanity: cultural and racial reconfigurations of critical theory* (2010) Fordham University Press

Cornell D & Van Marle K 'Exploring ubuntu: tentative reflections (2005) 5 *AHRLJ* 195

Cornell D & Van Marle K 'Ubuntu feminism: tentative reflections (2015) 36 *Verbum et Ecclesia* 1

Cornell D 'Introduction: transitional justice versus substantive revolution' in D Cornell (ed) *Law and Revolution in South Africa: uBuntu, dignity, and the struggle for constitutional transformation* (2014) Fordham University Press 1

Cornell D 'A call for a nuanced constitutional jurisprudence: ubuntu, dignity, and reconciliation' (2004) 19 *SAPL* 666

Cornell D 'Dignity violated: rethinking AZAPO through ubuntu' in D Cornell (ed) *Law and Revolution in South Africa: uBuntu, dignity, and the struggle for constitutional transformation* (2014) Fordham University Press 47

Cornell D 'Is there a difference that makes a difference between uBuntu and dignity?' (2010) 25 *SAPL* 397

Cornell D 'Socialism or radical democratic politics?: on Laclau and Mouffe' in D Cornell (ed) *Law and Revolution in South Africa: ubuntu, dignity, and the struggle for constitutional transformation* (2014) Fordham University Press 34

Cornell D 'The significanc of the living customary law for an understanding of law: does custom allow for a woman to be Hosi?' (2009) 2 *CCR* 395

Cornell D 'Ubuntu and subaltern legality' in L Praeg & S Magadla (eds) *Ubuntu: curating the archive* (2014) University of KwaZulu-Natal Press 167

Cornell D 'Ubuntu, pluralism and the responsibility of legal academics in the New South Africa' (2009) 20 *Law & Critique* 43

Cornell D 'Where dignity ends and uBuntu begins' in D Cornell (ed) *Law and Revolution in South Africa: uBuntu, dignity, and the struggle for constitutional transformation* (2014) Fordham University Press 169

Costa A 'The myth of customary law' (1998) 14 *SAJHR* 525

Cotterrell R 'Is there a logic of legal transplants?' in D Nelken & J Fest (eds) *Adapting Legal Cultures* (2001) Hart Publishing 70

Courtis C 'Rationality reasonableness, proportionality: testing the use of standards of scrutiny in the constitutional review of legislation' (2013) 5 *CCR* 33

Credo-Mutwa V *Indaba, My Children* (1998) Payback Press

Cunningham F *Theories of Democracy: a critical introduction* (2002) Routledge

Currie I & De Waal J *The Bill of Rights Handbook* 6ed (2013) Juta

D'Engelbronner-Kolff F M 'The people as law-makers: the juridical foundation of the legislative power of Namibian Traditional Communities' in F M D'Engelbronner-Kolff, M O Hinz & J L Sindano *Traditional Authority and Democracy in Southern Africa* (1998) New Namibia Books 62

Dagan H 'The Realist conception of law' (2007) 57 *UTLJ* 607

Danet B & Bogoch B 'From oral ceremony to written document: the transitional language of Anglo-Saxon wills' (1992) 12 *Lang & Communication* 95

Danet B 'Language in the legal process' (1979/1980) 14 *Law & Soc Rev* 445

David A 'The sound of the Magic Flute in legal and religious registers of the Ramesside period: some common features of two "ritualistic languages"' in A C Hagedorn & R G Kratz (eds) *Law and Religion in the Eastern Mediterranean: from antiquity to early Islam* (2013) Oxford University Press 13

Davis D M & Klare K E 'Transformative constitutionalism and the common and customary law' (2010) 26 *SAJHR* 403

Davis D M 'Constitutional borrowing: the influenc of legal culture and local history in the reconstitution of comparative influence the South African experience' (2003) 1 *Int'l J Const L* 181

Davis D M 'Developing the common law of contract in the light of poverty and illiteracy: the challenge of the Constitution' (2011) 22 *Stell LR* 845

Davis D M 'Human dignity: lodestar for equality in South Africa, Laurie Ackermann' (2013) 130 *SALJ* 878

Davis D M 'Private law after 1994: progressive development or schizoid confusion?' (2008) 24 *SAJHR* 318

Davis P C 'Toward a relational constitutionalism' 2008 *Acta Juridica* 239

De Groot G R 'Het vertalen van uidische teksten' in J P Balkema & G R De Groot (eds) *Recht en Vertalen* (1987) Kluwer 13

De Saussure F *Cours de linguistique générale* (1916) Payot

De Tejada F E 'The future of Bantu law' (1979) 11 *ARSP* 304

De Waal M J & Paisley R R N 'Trusts' in R Zimmermann, D P Visser & K C J Reid (eds) *Mixed Legal Systems in Comparative Perspective: property and obligations in Scotland and South Africa* (2004) Juta 819

De Waal M J 'Core elements of the trust: aspects of the English, Scottish and South African trusts compared' (2000) 117 *SALJ* 548

De Waal M J 'In search of a model for the introduction of the trust into a civilian context' (2001) 12 *Stell LR* 63

Deroy L *L'Emprunt linguistique* (1956) Société d'Edition Les Belles Lettres

Descheemaeker E 'Old and new learning in the law of amende honorable' (2015) 132 *SALJ* 909

Dlamini C R M 'Wither lay justice in South Africa?' (1985) 14 *Speculum Juris* 1

Doke C M & Vilakazi B W (eds) *The English-Zulu/Zulu-English Dictionary* (2006) Wits University Press

Doke C M et al *English-isiZulu, IsiZulu-English Dictionary* (1990) Wits University Press

Donne J *From Devotions upon Emergent Occasions* (1624) Augustine Mathews for Thomas Iones

Donnelly J 'Human rights and human dignity: an analytical critique of non-western conceptions of human rights' (1982) 76 *Am Polit Sci Rev* 303

Drengson A R & Inoue Y (eds) *The Deep Ecology Movement: an introductory anthology* (1995) North Atlantic Books

Du Bois F 'Contractual obligation and the journey from natural law to constitutional law' 2015 *Acta Juridica* 281

Du Plessis J E 'Common law influence on the law of contract and unjustifie enrichment in some mixed legal systems' (2003-4) 78 *Tul L Rev* 219

Du Plessis J E 'Comparative law and the study of mixed legal systems' in M Reimann & R Zimmermann (eds) *The Oxford Handbook of Comparative Law* (2006) Oxford University Press 477

Du Plessis J E *The South African Law of Unjustified Enrichment* (2012) Juta

Du Plessis L M 'Learned Staatsrecht from the heartland of the Rechtsstaat' (2005) 1 *PELJ* 1

Du Toit F 'Reflection on the bewind trust in light of the Dutch testamentary bewind' (2011) 3 *TSAR* 540

Du Toit F 'The fiduciar office of trustee and the protection of contingent trust beneficiaries (2007) 18 *Stell LR* 461

Dugmore H H et al *Itestamente Entsha Yenkosi Yetu Kayesu Kristu, Gokwamaxosa* (1842-1846) Wesleyan & Berlin Missionary Societies

Dworkin R *Taking Rights Seriously* (1977) Harvard University Press

Dzobo N K 'Values in a changing society: man, ancestors and god' in K Wiredu & K Gyekye (eds) *Person and Community: Ghanaian philosophical studies* (1992) Council for Research on Values and Philosophy 223

Ebo C 'Indigenous law and justice: some major concepts and practices' in G R Woodman & A O Obilade (eds) *African Law and Legal Theory* (1995) Dartmouth Publishing 33

Eckert B, De Beer F C & Vorster L P 'Worldviews and decision making: natural resource management of the Laka of Mapela in an anthropological perspective' (2001) 24 *SA Tydskr Etnol* 88

Eggins S *An Introduction to Systemic Functional Linguistics* (1994) Continuum

Elias T O *The Nature of African Customary Law* (1956) Manchester University Press

Eliastam J L B 'Exploring ubuntu discourse in South Africa: loss, liminality and hope' (2015) 36 *Verbum et Ecclesia* 1

Elliott W A *Notes for a Sindebele Dictionary and Grammar and Illustrative Sentences* (1913) Sindebele Publishing

English R 'Ubuntu: the quest for an indigenous jurisprudence' (1996) 12 *SAJHR* 641

Englund H 'Human rights and village headmen in Malawi: translation beyond vernacularisation' in J Eckert et al (eds) *Law against the State: ethnographic forays into law's transformation* (2012) Cambridge University Press 70

Eriksen T H *Ethnicity and Nationalism: anthropological perspectives* 3ed (2010) Pluto Press

Ewald W 'Comparative jurisprudence II: the logic of legal transplants' (1995) 43 *Am J Comp L* 489

Fagan E 'Roman-Dutch Law in its South African historical context' in R Zimmerman & D P Visser *Southern Cross: civil law and common law in South Africa* (1996) Clarendon Press 33

Fairclough N *Analysing Discourse — textual research for social research* (2003) Routledge

Falk R 'Cultural foundations for the international protection of human rights' in A A An-Na'im (ed) *Human Rights in a Cross Cultural Perspective: a quest for consensus* (1992) University of Pennsylvania Press 44

Fishkin J S *When the People Speak: deliberative democracy and public consultation* (2011) Oxford University Press

Fiske J & Hartley J *Reading Television* 2ed 2003) Routledge

Fletcher G P 'Human dignity as a constitutional value' (1984) 22 *UW Ontario L Rev* 171

Fletcher J F *Moral Responsibility* (1967) Westminster Press

Fletcher J F *Situation Ethics* (1965) SCM Press

Forster D A 'Identity in relationship: the ethics of ubuntu as an answer to the impasse of individual consciousness' in C W Du Toit (ed) *The Impact of Knowledge Systems on Human Development in Africa* (2007) UNISA Press 245

Forster D A *Self validating consciousness in strong artificial intelligence: an African theological contribution* (2006) unpublished doctoral dissertation UNISA

Fortes M & Evans-Pritchard E E 'Introduction' in M Fortes & E E Evans-Pritchard (eds) *African Political Systems* (1940) Oxford University Press

Fox D 'The nature, history and courts of equity' in J McGhee *Snell's Principles of Equity* 33ed (2015) Sweet & Maxwell 3

Francis T B *Maxims of Equity* (1824) Richmond

Fraser N 'Rethinking the public sphere: a contribution to the critique of actually existing democracy' (1990) 25/26 *Social Text* 56

Friedman L M *A History of American Law* 2ed (Revised Edition 1985) Simon & Schuster

Friedman L M *Law and Society: an introduction* (1977) Prentice-Hall

Fuller L L *The Morality of Law* 2ed (1969) Yale University Press

Gade C B N 'Restorative justice and the South African Truth and Reconciliation process' (2013) 32 *SA J Philosophy* 10

Gade C B N 'The historical development of the written discourses on *Ubuntu*' (2011) 30 *SA J Philosophy* 303

Gade C B N 'What is *Ubuntu*? Different interpretations among South Africans of African descent' (2012) 31 *SA J Philosophy* 484

Galdia M *Legal Linguistics* (2009) Peter Lang

Garner B A (ed) *Black's Law Dictionary* 10ed (2014) Thompson Reuters

Gee J P 'Critical issues: reading and the new literacy studies: reframing the national academy of sciences report on reading' (1999) 31 *J Lit Res* 355

Gee J P *Social Linguistics and Literacies: ideology in discourses* 5ed (2015) Routledge

Geertz C 'Ritual and social change: a Javanese example' (1957) 59 *Am Anthropol* 32

Ghose A *The Ideal of Human Unity* 3ed (1998) Sri Aurobindo Ashram

Glover G 'Reflection on the *sine causa* requirement and the *condictiones* in South African law' (2009) 20 *Stell LR* 468

Gluckman M *Judicial Process among the Barotse of Northern Rhodesia* 2ed (1967) Manchester University Press

Gluckman M *Order and Rebellion in Tribal Africa* (1963) Free Press

Gluckman M *The Ideas in Barotse Jurisprudence* (Reprint 1972) Manchester University Press

Golan D 'Inkatha and its use of the Zulu past' (1991) 18 *History in Africa* 113

Goodrich P 'Law and language: an historical and cultural introduction' (1984) 11 *J Law & Soc* 173

Goodrich P *Reading the law: a critical introduction to legal method and techniques* (1986) Blackwell

Goody J *Interface between the Written and the Oral* (1987) Cambridge University Press

Gosepath S 'Equality' in E N Zalta (ed) *Stanford Encyclopedia of Philosophy* (2011), available at URL = <http://plato.stanford.edu/archives/spr2011/entries/equality/

Graziadei M 'Comparative law as the study of transplants and receptions' in M Reimann & R Zimmermann (eds) *The Oxford Handbook of Comparative Law* (2006) Oxford University Press 441

Griffiths J 'The social working of legal rules' (2003) 35 *J Legal Pluralism & Unofficial L* 1

Gulbrandsen Ø 'The king is king by the grace of the people: the exercise and control of power in subject-ruler relations' (1995) 37 *Comp Stud Soc Hist* 415

Gulbrandsen Ø 'Town-state formations on the edge of the Kalahari' (2007) 51 *Social Analysis* 55

Gulliver P H 'Dispute settlement without courts: the Ndendeuli of Southern Tanzania' in L Nader (ed) *Law in Culture and Society* (1969) Aldine 24

Gulliver P H *Social Control in an African Society* (1963) Boston University Press

Gyekye K 'African ethics' in E N Zalta (ed) *Stanford Encyclopaedia of Philosophy* (2010) Center for the Study of Language and Information, Stanford University, available at http://plato.stanford.edu/entries/african-ethics/

Gyekye K 'Person and community in African thought' in H Kimmerle (ed) *I, We, and Body* (1989) John Benjamins Publishing 47, and in K Wiredu & K Gyekye (eds) *Person and Community: Ghanaian philosophical studies* (1992) Council for Research in Values and Philosophy 101

Gyekye K 'Person and community: Ghanaian philosophical studies' (1992) Council for Research in Values; reprinted as 'Person and community in African thought' in P H Coetzee & A P J Roux (eds) *The African Philosophy Reader: a text with readings* 2ed (2003) Routledge 348

Gyekye K *An Essay on African Philosophical Thought: the Akan conceptual scheme* (1987) Cambridge University Press

Habermas J (trans W Rehg) *Between Facts and Norms: contributions to a discourse theory of law and democracy* (1996) MIT Press

Hahlo H R & Kahn E *The South African Legal System and its Background* (1968) Juta

Hahlo H R 'The trust in South African law' (1961) 78 *SALJ* 195

Hall M *The Changing Past: farmers, kings and traders in southern Africa 200-1860* (1987) David Philip

Halliday M A K & Hasan R *Language, context, and text: aspects of language in a social-semiotic perspective* (1989) Oxford University Press

Halliday M A K *Language as Social Semiotic: the social interpretation of language and meaning* (1978) Edward Arnold

Hamburger M *Morals and Law: the growth of Aristotle's legal theory* (1965) Biblo & Tannen

Hamilton C 'Uncertain citizenship and public deliberation in post-apartheid South Africa' (2009) 35 *Social Dynamics* 355

Hamilton C *Terrific Majesty: the power of Shaka Zulu and the limits of historical invention* (1998) Harvard University Press

Hammond-Tooke W D *Command or Consensus: the development of Transkeian local government* (1975) David Philip

Hammond-Tooke W D *The Roots of Black South Africa* (1993) Jonathan Ball

Hamnett I *Chieftainship and Legitimacy: an anthropological study of executive law in Lesotho* (1975) Routledge & Kegan Paul

Hannum H 'The Butare colloquium on human rights and economic development in Francophone Africa: a summary and analysis' (1979) 1 *Universal Hum Rights* 63

Hapanyengwi-Chemhuru O 'Reconciliation, conciliation, integration and national healing: possibilities and challenges in Zimbabwe' (2013) 13 *AJCR* 79

Harms L T C 'Law and language in a multilingual society' (2012) 15 *PELJ* 1

Harries P 'Imagery, symbolism and tradition in a South African Bantustan: Mangosuthu Buthelezi, Inkatha, and Zulu history' (1993) 32 *History & Theory* 105

Harris R 'How does writing restructure thought?' (1989) 9 *Lang & Communication* 99

Harris R *Language, Saussure and Wittgenstein* (1988) Routledge

Harrison F *The Managerial Decision-Making Process* (1975) Houghton Mifflin

Hart H L A *The Concept of Law* (1961) Clarendon Press

Hartland E *Primitive Law* (1924) Kennikat Press

Hartnett T *Consensus-Oriented Decision Making: the CODM model for facilitating groups to widespread agreement* (2011) New Society Publishers

Hartshorne K B, Swart H A & Posselt E *Dictionary of Basic English/Tswana* (1984) Educum

Hartslief O 'The South African participation programme (*imbizo*): a mechanism towards participatory democracy' (2009) 44 *J Public Admin* 327

Harvey C 'Governing after the rights revolution' (2000) 27 *J Law & Soc* 61

Hasan R 'The disempowerment game: Bourdieu and language in literacy' (1998) 10 *Ling & Edu* 25

Hassim S 'Family, motherhood and Zulu nationalism: the politics of the Inkatha Women's Brigade' (1993) 43 *Feminist Review* 1

Hawthorne L 'Public policy: the origin of a general clause in the South African law of contract' (2013) 19 *Fundamina* 300

Hawthorne L 'Rethinking the philosophical substructure of modern South African contract law: self-actualisation and human dignity' (2016) 79 *THRHR* 286

Hefer J J F 'Billikheid in die kontraktereg volgens die Suid-Afrikaanse Regskommissie' (2000) 1 *TSAR* 142

Hefer J J F 'Billikheid in die kontraktereg' (2004) 29 *JJS* 1

Heikki E S *Comparative Legal Linguistics* (2006) Ashgate

Held D *Models of Democracy* 3ed (2006) Stanford University Press

Helfman T 'Land ownership and the origins of fiduciary duty' (2006) 41 *Real Prop Prob & Tr J* 651

Hilliard V G & Kemp N D 'Citizen participation indispensable to sustainable democratic governance and administration in South Africa' (1999) 65 *Int Rev of Administrative Sciences* 353

Himonga C & Pope A '*Mayelane v Ngwenyama and Minister for Home Affairs*: a reflection on wider implications' 2013 *Acta Juridica* 318

Himonga C & Bosch C 'The application of African customary law under the Constitution of South Africa: problems solved or just beginning' (2000) 117 *SALJ* 306

Himonga C, Taylor M & Pope A 'Reflection on judicial views of ubuntu' (2013) 16 *PELJ* 369

Hinz M O & Jonas S *Customary Law in Namibia: development and perspective* (2002) Centre for Applied Social Sciences

Hitchings H *The Secret Life of Words* (2008) John Murray

Hoad T F (ed) *Concise Oxford Dictionary of English Etymology* (1986) Oxford University Press

Hobsbawm E 'Introduction: inventing traditions' in E Hobswam & T Ranger (eds) *The Invention of Tradition* (2012) Cambridge University Press 1

Hoctor S 'Legal Realism' in C Roederer & D Moellendorf (eds) *Jurisprudence* (2004) Juta 158

Holdsworth W S *A History of English Law* (1924) Little Brown

Holleman J F *Issues in African Law* (1974) Mouton

Holmes O W 'The path of law' (1897) 1 *Harv L Rev* 457 (republished in (1997-1998) 110 *Harv L Rev* 991

Holness W A 'Equality of the graveyard: participatory democracy in the context of housing delivery: *Grootboom*' (2011) 26 *SAPL* 1

Holomisa P 'Balancing law and tradition: the TCB and its relation to African systems of justice administration' (2011) 35 *SA Crime Quarterly* 17

Hornblower S 'Creation and development of democratic institutions in ancient Greece' in J Dunn (ed) *Democracy: the unfinished journey 508 BC — AD 1993* (1992) Oxford University Press 1

Horwitz M J *The Transformation of American Law 1870-1960: the crisis of legal orthodoxy* (1992) Oxford University Press

Hosten W J et al (eds) *Introduction to South African Law and Legal Theory* 2ed (1995) Butterworths

Howard T M 'The rules of engagement: a socio-legal framework for improving community engagement in natural resource governance' (2015) 5 *Oñati Socio-legal Series* 1209

Hudson A *Equity and Trusts* 8ed (2014) Cavendish

Hughes A J B *Land Tenure, Land Rights and Land Communities on Swazi National Land in Swaziland* (1972) unpublished doctoral thesis, University of Natal

Hunter M *Reaction to Conquest: effects of contact with Europeans on the Pondo of South Africa* 2ed (1961) Oxford University Press

Hutchison A 'A customary insurance law?' (2017) 29 *SA Mercantile LJ* 17

Hutchison A 'Decolonising South African contract law: an argument for synthesis' in L Siliquini-Cinelli & A Hutchison (eds) *The Constitutional Dimension of Contract Law: a comparative perspective* (2017) Springer 151

Hutchison D & Du Bois F 'Contracts in general' in F du Bois (ed) *Wille's Principles of South African Law* 9ed (2007) Juta 733

Hutchison D 'Good faith in the South African law of contract' in R Brownsward, N J Hird & G Howells (eds) *Good Faith in Contract, Concept and Context* (1999) Ashgate 213

Hutchison D 'Non-variation clauses in contract: any escape from the *Shifren* straightjacket?' (2001) 118 *SALJ* 720

Imbo S O 'Okot p'Bitek's critique of Western scholarship on African religion' in K Wiredu (ed) *A Companion to African Philosophy* (2004) Blackwell 364

Institute of Directors in Southern Africa *King Report on Corporate Governance in South Africa* III (2009), available at http://c.ymcdn.com/sites/www.iodsa.co.za/resource/resmgr/king_iii/King_Report_on_Governance_fo.pdf

IO Publishing *South African Multilingual Dictionary* (2014) IO Publishing

Irele F A 'Francophone African philosophy' in P H Coetzee & A P J Roux (eds) *The African Philosophy Reader: a text with readings* 2ed (2003) Routledge 132

Isidore of Seville (trans S A Barney et al) *Etymologies* (2006) Cambridge University Press

Isodore Saint (trans by A Thompson) *The Treatise on Laws (Decretum DD. 1-20) with the Ordinary Gloss (Studies in Medieval and Early Modern Canon Law, Volume 2)* (1582) (1993) CUA Press

Jackson T 'Managing change in South Africa: developing people and organizations' (1999) 10 *Int J Hum Resour Man* 306

Janis I L 'Groupthink' (1971) 5 *Psychology Today* 43

Janis I L *Victims of groupthink: a psychological study of foreign-policy decisions and fiascoes* (1972) and revised in (1983) Houghton Mifflin

Jeppe W J O *Die Ontwikkeling van Bestuursinstellings in die Westelike Bantoegebiede (Tswana-Tuisland)* (1970) University of Stellenbosch

Jiyane V & Ngulube P 'Prevalence of use of indigenous social networks among women and girl children in a rural community in KwaZulu-Natal' (2014) 13 *Indilinga* 126

Jordaan D W 'Autonomy as an element of human dignity in South African case law' (2009) 9 *J Philosophy, Science & Law*, available at http://jpsl.org/archives/autonomy-element-human-dignity-south-african-case-law/

Jordan P 'The African National Congress: from illegality to the corridors of power' (2004) 31 *Rev Afr Polit Econ* 203

Joubert C P ''n Kritiese opvatting van Honoré se beskouings oor die trustreg' (1969) 31 *THRHR* 124

Joubert D J *General Principles of the Law of Contract* (1987) Juta

Kahn-Freund O 'On uses and misuses of comparative law' (1974) 37 *MLR* 1

Kalu O U 'Ancestral spirituality and society in Africa' in J K Olupona (ed) *African Spirituality: forms, meanings and expressions* (2000) Crossroad Publishing 55

Kamwangamalu M N 'Ubuntu in South Africa: a sociolinguistic perspective to a pan African concept' (1999) 13 *Crit Arts* 24

Kant I (trans & ed by A Wood & G Di Giovanni) *Religion within the Boundaries of Mere Reason* (1998) Cambridge University Press

Kant I (trans by T K Abbott) *Fundamental Principles of the Metaphysics of Morals* 2ed (1900) Longmans

Kant I (trans T K Abbot, ed & rev L Denis) *Groundwork for the Metaphysics of Morals* (2005) Broadview Press

Karsten L & Illa H 'Ubuntu as a key African management concept: contextual background and practical insights for knowledge application' (2005) 20 *J Manage Psychol* 607

Keep H & Midgley R 'The emerging role of ubuntu-botho in developing a consensual South African legal culture' in F Bruinsma & D Nelken (eds) *Recht der Werkelijkheid* (2007) Reed Business 29

Keeton G W *Law of Trusts* 8ed (1963) Pitman

Keevy I 'The Constitutional Court and ubuntu's "inseparable trinity"' (2009) 34 *JJS* 61

Keevy I 'Ubuntu versus the core values of the South African Constitution' (2009) 34 *JJS* 19

Kellogg F R 'What precisely is a "hard" case? Waldron, Dworkin, Critical Legal studies, and judicial recourse to principle' (2013) Discussion Paper for University of Edinburgh Legal Theory Research Group http://ssrn.com/abstract=2220839 or http://dx.doi.org/10.2139/ssrn.2220839

Kende M S *Constitutional Rights in Two Worlds: South Africa and the United States* (2009) Cambridge University Press

Kennedy D 'Freedom and constraint in adjudication: a critical phenomenology' (1986) 36 *J Legal Educ* 518

Kennedy D *A Critique of Adjudication [fin de Siècle]* (1998) Harvard University Press

Kenyatta J *Facing Mount Kenya: the tribal life of the Gikuyu* (1968) Secker & Warburg

Kerr A J 'The defence of unfair conduct on the part of the plaintiff at the time the action is brought: the *exceptio doli generalis* and the *replicatio doli* in modern law' (2008) 125 *SALJ* 241

Kerr A J *Principles of the Law of Contract* (revised) 6ed (2002) Butterworths

Kgosimore D L 'Restorative justice as an alternative way of dealing with crime' (2002) 15 *Acta Criminologica* 69

Khoza R J *Let Africa Lead: African transformational leadership for 21st century business* (2005) Vezubuntu

Kiralfy A K R *Potter's Historical Introduction to English Law and its Institutions* 4ed (1958) Sweet & Maxwell

Kiwanuka R N 'The meaning of "people" in the African Charter on Human and Peoples' Rights' (1988) 82 *AJIL* 80

Klare K E 'Legal culture and transformative constitutionalism' (1998) 14 *SAJHR* 146

Klinck D R *Conscience, Equity and the Court of Chancery in Early Modern England* (2010) Ashgate Publishing

Klug H *Constituting Democracy: law, globalism and South Africa's political reconstruction* (2000) Cambridge University Press

Koch K, Sodergren J A & Campbell S 'Political and psychological correlates of conflic management: a cross-cultural study' (1976) 10 *Law & Soc Rev* 443

Kock H 'Legal aspects of language policy for European communities: language risks, equal opportunities and legislating a language' in F Coulmas (ed) *A Language Policy for the European Community: prospects and quandaries* (1991) Mouton de Gruyter 147

Kohn L 'Our curious administrative law love triangle: the complex interplay between the PAJA, the Constitution and the common law' (2013) 28 *SAPL* 22

Koka K *Sage Philosophy: the significance of Ubuntu philosophy in post-colonial Africa* (1996) (unpublished paper) Ubuntu School of Philosophy, Pretoria

Kompe L & Small J 'Demanding a place under the *kgotla* tree: rural women's access to land and power' 1991 *Third World Legal Stud* 137

Kondlo K 'Making participatory governance work — re-inventing *izimibizo* forums in South Africa' (2010) 45 *J Public Admin* 384

Kriel T J *The New English-Sesotho Dictionary* (1958) APB Publishing

Krige E J *The Social System of the Zulus* 3rd imp (1965) Shuter & Shooter

Kroeber-Riel W & Haurschildt J 'Decision-making' in A Kuper & J Kuper (eds) *The Social Science Encyclopedia* (2003) Taylor & Francis 183

Kroeze I J 'Doing things with values II: the case of ubuntu' (2002) 13 *Stell LR* 252

Kroeze I J 'Doing things with values: the role of constitutional values in constitutional interpretation' (2001) 12 *Stell LR* 265

Kuper A 'The social structure of the Sotho-speaking peoples of Southern Africa. Part I' (1975) 45 *Africa* 67

Kuper A 'The social structure of the Sotho-speaking peoples of Southern Africa. Part II' (1975) 45 *Africa* 139

Kuper A *Invention of Primitive Society: transformations of an illusion* (1988) Routledge

Kuper H *The Swazi: a South African Kingdom* 2ed (1986) Holt, Rinehart & Winston

Laclau E & Mouffe C *Hegemony and Socialist Strategy* (1985) Verso

Laclau E *New Reflections on the Revolution of our Time* (1990) Routledge

Langa P 'Transformative constitutionalism' (2006) 17 *Stell LR* 351

Le Grange L 'Ubuntu/Botho as ecophilosophy and ecosophy' (2015) 49 *J Hum Ecol* 301

Le Roux W 'Sex work, the right to occupational freedom and the constitutional politics of recognition' (2003) 120 *SALJ* 452

Le Vaillant F *Voyages de M. le Vaillant dans l'Intérieur de l'Afrique par le Cap de Bonne-Espérance dans les années 1780-85* (1790) Chez Leroy

Leacock S 'The Union of South Africa' (1910) 4 *Am Polit Sci Rev* 498

Lee R W *Introduction to Roman-Dutch Law* 5ed (1953) Clarendon

Legrand P 'The impossibility of "legal transplants"' (1997) 4 *MJECL* 111

Legrand P 'What are "legal transplants"?' in D Nelken & J Feest (eds) *Adapting Legal Cultures* (2001) Hart Publishing 55

Lehnert W 'The role of the courts in the conflic between African customary law and human rights' (2005) 21 *SAJHR* 241

Leiter B *Naturalizing Jurisprudence: essays on American legal realism and naturalism in legal philosophy* (2007) Oxford University Press

Lenta P 'Just gaming: the case for postmodernism in South African legal theory' (2001) 17 *SAJHR* 173

Lewis C 'The demise of the *exceptio doli*: is there another route to contractual equity' (1990) 107 *SALJ* 26

Liebenberg S 'Engaging the paradoxes of the universal and particular in human rights adjudication: the possibilities and pitfalls of "meaningful engagement"' (2012) 12 *AHRLJ* 1

Liebenberg S 'South Africa's evolving jurisprudence on socio-economic rights: an effective tool in challenging poverty' (2002) 6 *LDD* 159

Liebenberg S 'The value of human dignity in interpreting socio-economic rights' (2005) 21 *SAJHR* 1

Liebenberg S *Socio-economic Rights: adjudication under a transformative constitution* (2010) Juta

Lotz J G 'Enrichment' in W A Joubert (ed) *Laws of South Africa* vol 9 (2005) LexisNexis Butterworths

Louw A M 'Yet another call for a greater role for good faith in the South African law of contract: can we banish the law of the jungle, while avoiding the elephant in the room?' (2013) 16 *PELJ* 1

Louw D J 'Ubuntu and the challenges of multi-culturalism in South Africa' (2001) 15 *Quest* 15

Lubbe G F '*Bona fides*, billikheid en die openbare belang in die Suid-Afrikaanse kontraktereg' (1990) 1 *Stell LR* 7

Lubbe G F 'Taking fundamental rights seriously: the Bill of Rights and its implications for the development of contract law' (2004) 121 *SALJ* 395

Luhmann N 'Autopoiesis of social systems' in F Geyer & J Van der Zouwen (eds) *Sociocybernetic Paradoxes: observation, control and evolution of self-steering systems* (1986) SAGE 172

Lyles R I *Practical Management Problem Solving and Decision-making* (1982) Van Nostrand Reinhold Company

M'Baye K 'Human rights in Africa' in K Vasak (ed) *The International Dimensions of Human Rights* (1982) Greenwood Press 583

Mabelebele J 'Ideological objectives underpinning *imbizo* as a model of communication and governance' (2006) 25 *Communicare* 103

Mabovula N N 'The erosion of African communal values: a reappraisal of the African ubuntu philosophy' (2011) 3 *Inkanyiso* 38

MacIntyre A C *After Virtue: a study in moral theory* 3ed (2007) Duckworth

Macquarrie J *In Search of Humanity: a theological and philosophical approach* (1982) SCM London

Magadla S & Chitandoin E 'The self become god: ubuntu and the "scandal of manhood"' in L Praeg & S Magadla.(eds) *Ubuntu: curating the archive* (2014) University of KwaZulu-Natal Press 176

Mahoney M R *The Other Zulus: the spread of Zulu ethnicity in colonial South Africa* (2012) Duke University Press

Malan J *Conflict Resolution: wisdom from Africa* (1997) Accord

Malan K 'The suitability and unsuitability of ubuntu in constitutional law-inter-communal relations versus public office-bearing' (2014) 47 *De Jure* 231

Maloka T & Gordon D 'Chieftainship, civil society, and the political transition in South Africa' (1996) 22 *Crit Sociol* 37

Mamdani M *Citizen and Subject: contemporary Africa and the legacy of late colonialism* (1996) Princeton University Press

Mangaliso M 'Building competitive advantage from ubuntu: management lessons from South Africa' (2001) 15 *Acad Manage Exec* 23

Mangena F 'Towards a *hunhu/ubuntu* dialogical moral theory' (2012) 13 *Phronimon* 1

Mansbridge J J *Beyond Adversary Democracy* (1980) Basic Books

Mapadimeng M S 'Ubuntu/botho, the workplace and "two economies": part two: policy and political choices' (2007) 37 *Africanus* 257

March J G 'Understanding how decisions happen in organizations' in Z Shapira (ed) *Organizational Decision-making* (2002) Cambridge University Press 9

Maré G & Hamilton G *An Appetite for Power: Buthelezi's Inkatha and South Africa* (1987) Ravan Press

Marriott J A R *The Mechanism of the Modern State: a treatise on the science and art of govern*ment vol I (1927) Oxford University Press

Martin M *Legal Realism: American and Scandinavian* (1997) P Lang

Marx C 'Ubu and ubuntu: on the dialectics of apartheid and nation building' (2002) 29 *Politikon* 49

Marx K 'On James Mill (1843)' in D McLellan (ed) *Karl Marx: selected writi*ngs (revised ed) (2000) Oxford University Press 124

Masina N 'Xhosa practices of *Ubuntu* for South Africa' in I W Zartman (ed) *Traditional Cures for Modern Conflicts: African conflict 'medicine'* (2000) Lynne Rienner 169

Masondo S 'The practice of African traditional religion in contemporary South Africa' in T W Bennett (ed) *Traditional African Religions in South African Law* (2011) UCT Press 19

Mathagu S F *An Analysis and Appraisal of the Imbizo as an Instrument of Democracy in South Africa* (2010) unpublished masters thesis, UNISA

Matlala B. 'Challenging traditional authority in the Platinum Belt' (2014) 49 *SA Crime Quarterly* 31

Matolino B & Kwindingwi W 'The end of *ubuntu*' (2013) 32 *SA J Philosophy* 197

Matolino B 'A response to Metz's reply on the end of ubuntu' (2014) 34 *SA J Philosophy* 214

Mattilla H 'European integration and legal communication' in H Petersen et al (eds) *Paradoxes of European Legal Integration* (2008) Ashgate 253

Mazrui A A *Africanity Redefined: collected essays of AA Mazrui Volume1* (2002) Africa World Press

Mbaya H 'Social capital and the imperatives of the concept and life of ubuntu in the South African context' (2010) 104 *Scriptura* 367

Mbigi L & Maree J 'Introduction' in L Mbigi & J Maree (eds) *Ubuntu: the spirit of African transformation management* (2005) Knowres Publishing 1

Mbigi L & Maree J *Ubuntu: the spirit of African transformation management* (1995) Knowledge Resources

Mbigi L 'Ubuntu' (1995) November *Enterprise* 57

Mbiti J S *Introduction to African Religion* (1975) Heinemann

Mbon F M 'African traditional socio-religious ethics and national development: the Nigerian case' in J K Olupona *African Traditional Religions in Contemporary Society* (1991) Paragon House 101

Mboti N 'May the real ubuntu please stand up?' (2015) 30 *J of Media Ethics* 125

McAllister P 'Ritual and social practice in the Transkei' (1997) 56 *African Studies* 279

McDougal M S, Lasswell H D & Chen L *Human Rights and World Public Order: the basic policies of an international law of human dignity* (1980) Yale University Press

McFarlane B 'The maxims of equity' in J McGhee *Snell's Principles of Equity* 33ed (2015) Sweet & Maxwell 87

Mdluli P 'Ubuntu-botho. Inkatha's peoples' education'(1987) 5 *Transformation* 60

Mekonnen D 'Indigenous legal tradition as a supplement to African transitional justice initiatives' (2010) 10 *AJCR* 101

Menski W *Hindu Law: beyond tradition and modernity* 2nd imprint (2009) Oxford University Press

Merry S E *Human Rights and Gender Violence: translating international law into local justice* (2006) University of Chicago Press

Merton R K *Social Theory and Social Structure* (1968) Simon and Schuster

Mesthrie R 'Fanagalo' in K Brown & S Ogilvie (eds) *Concise Encyclopedia of Languages of the World* (2009) Elsevier 411

Mesthrie R 'The origins of Fanagalo' (1989) 4 *JPCL* 211

Metz T & Gaie J B 'The African ethic of *ubuntu/botho*: implications for research on morality' (2010) 39 *J Moral Educ* 273

Metz T 'African conceptions of human dignity: vitality and community as the ground of human rights' (2012) 13 *Hum Rights Rev* 19

Metz T 'African moral theory and public governance: nepotism, preferential hiring and other partiality' in M N Murove (ed) *African Ethics: an anthology for comparative and applied ethics* (2009) University of KwaZulu-Natal Press 233

Metz T 'African values and human rights as two sides of the same coin: a reply to Oyowe' (2014) 14 *AHRLJ* 307

Metz T 'An African theory of dignity and a relational conception of poverty' in J W De Gruchy (ed) *The Humanist Imperative in South Africa* (2011) African Sun Media 233

Metz T 'Developing African political philosophy: moral theoretic strategies' (2012) 14 *Philos Afr* 61

Metz T 'Ethics in Africa and in Aristotle: some points of contrast' (2012) 13 *Phronimon* 99

Metz T 'Human dignity, capital punishment, and an African moral theory: towards a new philosophy of human rights' (2010) 9 *J Human Rights* 81

Metz T 'Just the beginning for ubuntu: reply to Matolino and Kwindingwi' (2014) 33 *SA J Philosophy* 65

Metz T 'Recent work in African ethics' (2010) 39 *J Moral Educ* 381

Metz T 'Toward an African moral theory' (2007) 15 *J Polit Philos* 321

Metz T '*Ubuntu* as a moral theory and human rights in South Africa' (2011) 11 *AHRLJ* 532

Metz T 'Ubuntu as a moral theory: reply to four critics' (2007) 26 *SA J Philosophy* 369

Metz T 'Ubuntu: curating the archive' (2014) 43 *Philosophical Papers* 447

Michaels R 'The functional method of comparative law' in M Reimann & R Zimmermann (eds) *The Oxford Handbook of Comparative Law* (2006) Oxford University Press 339

Miller N N 'The political survival of traditional leadership' (1968) *J Modern African Studies* 183

Miller S J, Hickson D J & Wilson D C 'Decision-making in organization' in S Clegg, C Hardy & W R Nord (eds) *Managing Organizations* (1999) Sage Publishing 43

Milsom S F C *Historical Foundations of the Common Law* 2ed (1981) Oxford University Press

Mini B M et al *Greater Dictionary of Xhosa Volume 2* (1989-2006) University of Fort Hare

Mkhize N 'African traditions and the social, economic and moral dimensions of fatherhood' L M Richter & R Morrell (eds) *Baba: men and fatherhood in South Africa* (2006) HSRC Press 183

Mnisi Weeks S M 'Customary succession and the development of customary law: the Bhe legacy: part III: reflection on themes in Justice Langa's judgments' 2015 *Acta Juridica* 215

Mnyaka M & Motlhabi M 'The African concept of *ubuntu/botho* and its socio-moral significance (2005) 3 *Black Theology* 215

Mnyongani F 'De-linking *ubuntu*: towards a unique South African jurisprudence' (2010) 31 *Obiter* 134

Modiri J M 'The crises in legal education' (2014) 46 *Acta Academica* 1

Mofokeng L L *Legal pluralism in South Africa: aspects of African customary, Muslim and Hindu family law* (2009) Van Schaik

Mojekwu C C 'International human rights: the African perspective' in J L Nelson & V M Green *International Human Rights: contemporary issues* (1980) Human Rights Publishing Group 85

Mokgoro J Y & Woolman S 'Where dignity ends and uBuntu begins: an amplificatio of, as well as an identificatio of a tension in, Drucilla Cornell's thoughts' (2010) 25 *SAPL* 400

Mokgoro J Y 'Ubuntu and the law in South Africa' (1998) 4 *Buff Hum Rts L Rev* 15

Mokgoro J Y 'Ubuntu and the law in South Africa' (1998) 2 *PELJ* 1

Mokgoro J Y 'Ubuntu, the Constitution and the rights of non-citizens' (2010) 21 *Stell LR* 221

Mönnig H O *The Pedi* (1967) Van Schaik

Monye S M 'Freedom of expression and traditional communities: who can speak and when?' (2014) 29 *SAPL* 323

Moore S F *Law as Process* (1978) Routledge & Kegan Paul

More M P 'South Africa under and after apartheid' in K Wiredu (ed) *A Companion to African Philosophy* (2006) Blackwell 149

Morsink J *The Universal Declaration of Human Rights: origins, drafting, and intent* (1999) University of Pennsylvania Press

Motha S 'Rationality, the rule of law, and the sovereign return' (2011) 4 *CCR* 113

Motsaathebe G 'Language, Afrikology and the tremor of the political moment: English as a main language of discourse in Africa' (2010) 9 *Indilinga* 96

Mqeke R B *Basic Approaches to Problem Solving in Customary Law: a study of conciliation and consensus among the Cape Nguni* (1997) Grocott & Sherry

Msila V 'African leadership models in education: leading institutions through ubuntu' (2014) 18 *Anthropologist* 1105

Mukheibir A 'Ubuntu and the amende honorable — a marriage between African values and medieval canon law' (2007) 28 *Obiter* 583

Mulago V 'Traditional African religion and Christianity in Africa' in J K Olupona (ed) *African Traditional Religions in Contemporary Society* (1990) Paragon House 119

Mulemfo M M *Thabo Mbeki and the African renaissance: the emergence of a new African leadership* (2000) Actua Press

Muller G 'Conceptualising "meaningful engagement" as a deliberative democratic partnership' (2011) 22 *Stell LR* 742

Mureinik E 'A bridge to where? Introducing the interim Bill of Rights' (1994) 10 *SAJHR* 31

Murithi T 'African approaches to building peace and social solidarity' (2006) 6 *African J on Conflict Resolution* 9

Mutua M W 'The Banjul Charter and the African cultural fingerprint an evaluation of the language of duties' (1995) 35 *Virginia J Int L* 339

Myburgh A C & Prinsloo M W *Indigenous Public Law in KwaNdebele* (1985) Van Schaik

Myburgh A C *Die Inheemse Staat in Suider-Afrika* (1986) Sentrum vir Inheemse Reg, UNISA

Nader L & Starr J 'Is equity universal?' in R A Newman (ed) *Equity in the World's Legal Systems: a comparative study* (1973) Établissements Émile Bruylant 125

Naude T 'Unfair contract terms legislation: the implications of why we need it for its formulation and application' (2006) 17 *Stell LR* 361

Ncube C B 'Calibrating copyright for creators and consumers: promoting distributive justice and ubuntu' in R Giblin & K Weatherall (eds) *What if We Could Reimagine Copyright?* (2017) ANU Press 253

Neels J L 'Die aanvullende en beperkende werking van redelikheid en billikheid in die kontraktereg' (1999) 4 *TSAR* 684

Neels J L 'Regsekerheid en die korrigerende werking van redelikheid en billikheid (deel 1)' (1998) 4 *TSAR* 702

Ngcobo S B 'The Bantu peoples' in G H Calpin (ed) *South African Way of Life: values and ideals of a multi-racial society* (1953) Heinemann

Nhlapo T 'Cultural diversity, human rights and the family in contemporary Africa: lessons from the South African Constitutional debate' (1995) 9 *Int J of Law, Policy & the Family* 208; and in N V Lowe & G Douglas (eds) *Families Across Frontiers* (1996) Martinus Nijhoff 237

Nicol M 'In the shadow of the clock' in P Bell (ed) *The Making of the Constitution: the story of South Africa's Constitutional Assembly, May 1994 to December 1996* (1997) Churchill Murray 40

Nkondo G M 'Ubuntu as a public policy in South Africa' (2007) 2 *Int J of African Renaissance Studies* 90

Nkrumah K *Consciencism* (1964) Heinemann

O'Regan K 'Tradition and modernity: adjudicating a constitutional paradox' (2014) 6 *CCR* 105

O'Sullivan T et al (eds) *Key Concepts in Communication and Cultural Studies* 2ed (2000) Routledge

Odendaal A 'Perception and individual decision-making' in S P Robbins et al (eds) *Organisational Behaviour* 2ed (2009) Pearson 117

Odendaal F F & Gouws R H (eds) *HAT Verklarende Woordeboek van die Afrikaanse Taal* 6ed (2015) Pearson

Ohlendorf J D 'Against coherence in statutory interpretation' (2014) 90 *Notre Dame L Rev* 735

Oladipo O 'Religion in African culture: some conceptual issues' in K Wiredu (ed) *A Companion to African Philosophy* (2004) Blackwell 355

Olivier N J J et al 'Indigenous Law' in W A Joubert (ed) *Laws of South Africa* vol 32 2ed (2009) LexisNexis Butterworths

Olivier P A *Trust Law in Practice* (1990) HUAM

Ong W J *Orality and Literacy: the technologizing of the word* 2ed (2002) Routledge

Onions C T, Friedrichsen G W S & Burchfiel R W *The Oxford Dictionary of English Etymology* (1966) Oxford Univeristy Press

Onwuanibe R C 'The human person and immortality in Ibo (African) metaphysics' in R A Wright (ed) *African Philosophy: an introduction* (1984) University Press of America 183

Oomen B 'Group rights in post-apartheid South Africa: the case of the traditional leaders' (1999) 31 *J Legal Pluralism & Unofficial L* 73

Oomen B *Chiefs in South Africa: law, power and culture in the post-apartheid era* (2005) James Currey

Oosthuizen G C 'The place of traditional religion in contemporary South Africa' in J K Olupona (ed) *African Spirituality: forms, meanings and expressions* (2000) Crossroad Publishing 35

Opoku K A *West African Religion* (1978) FEP International

Oyowe A O 'Strange bedfellows: rethinking ubuntu and human rights in South Africa' (2013) 13 *AHRLJ* 103

Pahl H W, Pienaar A M & T A Ndungane (eds) *The Greater Dictionary of Xhosa Volume 1* (1989-2006) University of Fort Hare

Pateman C *Participation and Democratic Theory* (1970) Cambridge University Press

Peart N S 'Section 11(1) of the Black Administration Act No 38 of 1927: the application of the repugnancy clause' 1982 *Acta Juridica* 99

People against Suffering Suppression Oppression and Poverty (PASSOP) *The De Doorns Monitoring Report* (2010) Forced Migration Studies Programme *Violence, Labour and the Displacement of Zimbabweans in De Doorns, Western Cape* (2009) Migration Policy Brief 2 University of the Witwatersrand http:// http://www.migration.org.za/

Peters E L 'Aspects of the control of moral ambiguities: a comparative analysis of two culturally disparate models of social control' in M Gluckman (ed) *Allocation of Responsibility* (1972) Manchester University Press 109

Pettit P H *Equity and the Law of Trusts* (2012) Oxford University Press

Pettman C *Africanderisms: a glossary of South African colloquial words and phrases and of place and other names* (1913) Longmans, Green & Co

Phooko R M 'What should be the form of public participation in the lawmaking process? An analysis of South African cases' (2014) 35 *Obiter* 39

Pienaar G J (updated by M Dendy) 'Associations' in W A Joubert (ed) *Laws of South Africa* vol 2 3ed (2015) Lexis Nexis Butterworths

Pienaar J M *Land Reform* (2014) Juta

Piers M 'Good faith in English Law — could a rule become a principle' (2011) 26 *Tul European & Civil L Forum* 123

Pieterse M ' "Traditional" African jurisprudence' in C Roederer & D Moellendorf (eds) *Jurisprudence* (2004) Juta 438

Pihlajamäki H 'Against metaphysics in law: the historical background of American and Scandinavian legal realism compared' (2004) 52 *Am J Comp L* 469

Piper L & Nadvi L 'Popular mobilisation, party dominance and participatory governance in South Africa' in L Thompson & C Tapscott *Citizenship, Mobilisation and Social Movements in the South: perspectives from the Global South* (2010) Zed Books 212

Plato (edit and trans by I A Richards) *Republic* (1966)   Cambridge University Press

Plato (trans R G Bury) *Laws* (1926) Harvard University Press

Pollock F Sir & Maitland F W *The History of English Law before the Time of Edward I* 2ed vol I (1968) Cambridge University Press

Praeg L 'An answer to the question: what is [ubuntu]?' (2008) 27 *SA J Philosophy* 367

Praeg L *African Philosophy and the Quest for Autonomy: a philosophical investigation* (2000) Rodopi

Pretorius L 'Government by or over the people? The African National Congress's conception of democracy' (2006) 12 *Soc Identities* 745

Prinsloo E 'The ubuntu style of participatory management' in J G Malherbe (ed) *Decolonizing the Mind: proceedings of the second colloquium on African philosophy* (1996) UNISA Research Unit for African Philosophy 112

Prinsloo M W 'Pluralism or unificatio in family law in South Africa' (1990) 23 *CILSA* 324

Prinsloo M W 'Unifikasi van inheemse regstelsels' 1990 (4) *TSAR* 605

Prinsloo M W *Die Inheemse Administratiefreg van 'n Noord-Sothostam* (1981) UNISA Press

Prinsloo M W *Inheemse Publiekreg in Lebowa* (1983) Van Schaik

Proculus '*Bellum juridicum*: two approaches to South African law' (1951) 68 *SALJ* 306

Proculus Redivivus 'South African law at the crossroads — or — what is our common law' (1965) 82 *SALJ* 17

Prozesky M *Tensions between Western Business Values and African Traditional Values — a Pilot Study* (2005) Unilever Ethics Centre University of KwaZulu-Natal

Raboshakga N 'Towards participatory democracy or not? The reasonableness approach in public involvement cases' (2015) 31 *SAJHR* 4

Ramose M B 'An African perspective on justice and race' (2001) 13 *Polylog: Forum for Intercultural Philosophy*, available at https://them.polylog.org/3/frm-en.htm#f4

Ramose M B 'But Hans Kelsen was not born in Africa: a reply to Thaddeus Metz' (2007) 26 *SA J Philosophy* 347

Ramose M B 'Ecology through ubuntu' in M N Murove (ed) *African Ethics: an anthology for comparative and applied ethics* (2009) University of KwaZulu-Natal Press 308

Ramose M B 'The death of democracy and the resurrection of timocracy' (2010) 39 *J Moral Educ* 291

Ramose M B 'The ethics of ubuntu' in P H Coetzee & A P J Roux (eds) *The African Philosophy Reader: a text with readings* 2ed (2003) Routledge 379

Ramose M B 'The ontology of invisible beings' (1989) 2 *Boleswa Occasional Papers* 1

Ramose M B 'The philosophy of ubuntu and ubuntu as a philosophy' in P H Coetzee & A P J Roux (eds) *The African Philosophy Reader: a text with readings* 2ed (2003) Routledge 270

Ramose M B 'Ubuntu: affirming a right and seeking remedies' in L Praeg & S Magadla (eds) *Ubuntu: curating the archive* (2014) University of KwaZulu-Natal Press 121

Ramose M B *African Philosophy through Ubuntu* revised ed (2002) Mond Books

Ramsay T D *Tsonga Law in the Transvaal* (1941) Department of Native Affairs

Ramsfiel J J *Culture to Culture: a guide to US legal writing* (2005) Carolina Academic Press

Ranganathan M A & Kaunda K D *The Political Philosophy of President Kenneth D Kaunda of Zambia* (1986) Kenneth Kaunda Foundation

Rautenbach C 'Legal reform of traditional courts in South Africa: exploring the links between ubuntu, restorative justice and therapeutic jurisprudence' (2015) 2 *JICL* 275

Reid K C J 'The idea of mixed legal systems' (2003) 78 *Tul L Rev* 5

Richardson R N 'Reflection on reconciliation and ubuntu' in R Nicolson (ed) *Persons in Community: African ethics in a global culture* (2008) University of KwaZulu-Natal Press 65

Roberts A 'South Africa: a patchwork quilt of patriarchy' (2010) 3 *Skills at Work: Theory & Practice J* 59

Roosens E E *Creating Ethnicity: the process of ethnogenesis* (1989) Sage Publications

Roux T 'Democracy' in S Woolman & M Bishop (eds) *Constitutional Law of South Africa* 2ed (2013) Juta

Ruch E A & Anyanwu K C African *Philosophy: an introduction to the main philosophical trends in contemporary Africa* (1984) Catholic Book Agency

Ryan K W *The Reception of the Trust in the Civil Law* (1959) unpublished doctoral thesis, University of Cambridge

Rycroft A & Le Roux R 'Decolonising labour law' (2017) 38 *ILJ* 1473

Rycroft D K *Concise SiSwati Dictionary: SiSwati-English, English-Siswati* (1995) Van Schaik

Sachs A 'Changing the law, changing the mind' in R Lessem & B Nussbaum (eds) *Sawubona Africa: embracing four worlds in South African management* (1996) Zebra Press 148

Samkange S & Samkange T M *Hunhuism or Ubuntuism: a Zimbabwe indigenous political philosophy* (1980) Graham Publishing

Sansom B 'Traditional rulers and their realms' in W D Hammond-Tooke (ed) *The Bantu-speaking Peoples of Southern Africa* 2ed (1974) Routledge & Kegan Paul 246

Schapera I *A Handbook of Tswana Law and Custom* (1938) (1994 reprint) Lit Verlag

Schapera I *Government and Politics in Tribal Societies* (1956) C A Watts

Schapera I *Tribal Innovators: Tswana chiefs and social change, 1795-1940* (1970) Athlone Press

Schapera I *Tribal Legislation among the Tswana of the Bechuanaland Protectorate: a study in the mechanism of cultural change* (1943) London School of Economics & Political Science

Schauer F 'Legal Realism untamed' (2013) 91 *Tex L Rev* 749

Schiele J H 'Organizational theory from an Afrocentric perspective' (1990) 21 *J Black Stud* 145

Schoeman N F 'The co-operative as an appropriate enterprise for black economic empowerment' (2006) 1 *J for Estate Planning Law* 23

Schweiger D M, Sandberg W R & Ragan J W 'Group approaches for improving strategic decision making: a comparative analysis of dialectical inquiry, devil's advocacy, and consensus' (1986) 29 *Acad Manag J* 51

Scott A W 'The nature of the rights of the "cestui que trust" ' (1917) *Colum L Rev* 269

Scott A W *The Law of Trusts* vol 1 2ed (1956) Little Brown

Scott H *Unjust Enrichment in South African Law: rethinking enrichment by transfer* (2013) Hart Publishing

Sebidi L J 'Toward a definitio of ubuntu as African Humanism' in M G Khabela & Z C Mzoneli (eds) *Perspectives on Ubuntu* (1998) Lovedale Press 62

Selden J *Table talk: being the discourses of John Selden, esq* reissued (1819) Fair- bairn & Anderson

Sen A *The Idea of Justice* (2011) Harvard University Press

Senghor L S *On African Socialism* (1964) Pall Mall Press

Setiloane G M *African Theology: an introduction* (1986) Skotaville Publishers

Shapiro F R *The Yale Book of Quotations* (2006) Yale University Press

Sharrock R 'Unfair enforcement of a contract: a step in the right direction? *Botha v Rich and Combined Developers v Arun Holdings*' (2015) 27 *SA Mercantile LJ* 174

Shiner R A 'Aristotle's theory of equity' (1993) 27 *Loyola LAL Rev* 1245

Shutte A *Philosophy for Africa* (1995) Marquette University Press

Shutte A *Ubuntu: an ethic for a new South Africa* (2001) Cluster Publications

Silva P *A Dictionary of South African English on Historical Principles* (1996) Oxford University Press

Silverman K *The Subject of Semiotics* (1983) Oxford University Press

Simons H J 'The status of customary unions' 1961 *Acta Juridica* 17

Simpson D P *Cassell's New Latin-Engish, English-Latin Dictionary* 5ed (1969) Cassel

Sjaastad E & Cousins B 'Formalisation of land rights in the South: an overview' (2008) 26 *Land Use Policy* 1

Skelton A & Frank C 'Conferencing in South Africa: returning to our future' in A Morris & G Maxwell (eds) *Restorative Justice of Juveniles: conferencing, mediation and circles* (2001) Hart Publishing 103

Skelton A 'International trends in the re-emergence of traditional systems' in C Petty & M Brown (eds) *Justice for Children: challenges for policy and practice in Sub-Saharan Africa* (1998) Save the Children Fund 99

Skelton A 'Restorative justice as a framework for juvenile justice reform: a South African perspective' (2002) 42 *British J of Criminology* 496

Skelton A 'Tapping indigenous knowledge: traditional conflic resolution, restorative justice and the denunciation of crime in South Africa' 2007 *Acta Juridica* 228

Skinner B F 'Cognitive science and behaviourism' (1985) 76 *British J of Psychology* 291

Skuse A & Cousins T 'Spaces of resistance: informal settlement, communication and community organisation in a Cape Town township' (2007) 44 *Urban Studies* 979

Smit J, Deacon M & Shutte A *Ubuntu in a Christian Perspective* (1999) Potchefstroomse Universiteit vir Christelike Hoe_r Onderwys

Smith B 'Legal relief against the inadequacies of equity' (1933) 12 *Tex L Rev* 109

Snyder R N 'Natural law and equity' in R A Newman (ed) *Equity in the World's Legal Systems: a comparative study* (1973) Établissements Émile Bruylant 33

Sokolon M K & Malone M F T 'Democracy's march through history' in M F T Malone (ed) *Achieving Democracy: democratization in theory and practice* (2011) Continuum Books 3

Sonnekus J C (trans J E Rhoodie) *Unjustified Enrichment in South African law* (2008) LexisNexis

South African Law Commission *Marriages and Customary Unions of Black Persons* (1986) Project 51 Government Printer

South African Law Reform Commission *Alternative Dispute Resolution* (1996) Project 94, Issue Paper 8, Government Printer

South African Law Reform Commission *Harmonisation of the Common Law and Indigenous Law — Report on Customary Marriages* (1999) Project 90, Government Printer

South African Law Reform Commission *Report on Unreasonable Stipulation in Contracts and the Rectification of Contracts* (1998) Project 47, Government Printer

Steiner G *After Babel: aspects of language and translation* 3ed (1998) Oxford University Press

Stråth B 'Ujamaa: the evasive translation of an elusive concept' in A Fleisch & R Stephens (eds) *Doing Conceptual History in Africa* (2016) Berghahn Books 185

Sutherland P J 'Ensuring contractual fairness in consumer contracts after *Barkhuizen v Napier* 2007 (5) SA 323 (CC) — part 1' (2008) 19 *Stell LR* 390

Sutherland P J 'Ensuring contractual fairness in consumer contracts after *Barkhuizen v Napier* 2007 (5) SA 323 (CC) — part 2' (2009) 20 *Stell LR* 50

Taljaard P C, Khumalo J N & Bosch S E *Handbook of Siswati* (1991) Van Schaik

Tapscott C 'Government in post-apartheid South Africa' in W Hofmeister & I Scholz (eds) *Traditional and Contemporary Forms of Local Participation and Self-government in Africa* (1997) Konrad-Adenauer-Stiftung

Taylor D '"The truth the whole truth nothing but the truth": truth, community and narrative in African procedural law' (2007) 40 *CILSA* 215

Teffo J *The Concept of Ubuntu as a Cohesive Moral Value* (1994) Ubuntu School of Philosophy Pretoria

Teubner G 'Legal irritants: good faith in British law or how unifying law ends up in new divergences' (1998) 61 *MLR* 11

Teubner G *Autopoietic Law: a new approach to law and society* (1988) Walter de Gruyter

Tjosvold D & Field R H 'Effects of social context on consensus and majority vote decision making' (1983) 26 *Acad Manag J* 500

Tönnies F (trans C P Loomis) *Community and Society* (1957) Courier Dover Publications

Trask R L (ed by P Stockwell) *Language and Linguistics: the key concepts* 2ed (2007) Routledge

Truth and Reconciliation Commission of South Africa *Report* (1998) Government Printer

Tshehla B 'The restorative justice bug bites the South African criminal justice system' (2004) 17 *SA Criminal LJ* 1

Tshehla B 'Traditional justice in practice — a Limpopo case study' (2005) 115 *Institute for Security Studies Monographs* 1

Tshoose C I 'The emerging role of the constitutional value of ubuntu for informal social security in South Africa' (2009) 3 *Afr J Legal Stud* 12

Turaki Y *Tribal Gods of Africa: ethnicity, racism, tribalism, and the Gospel of Christ* (1997) Crossroads Media Services

Tushnet M 'Defending the indeterminacy thesis' (1996-1997) 16 *Quinnipiac L Rev* 339

Tushnet M *The New Constitutional Order* (2009) Princeton University Press

Tutu D *No Future without Forgiveness* (1999) Rider

Twining W & Miers D *How To Do Things with Rules* 3ed (1991) Weidenfeld & Nicolson

Van Antwerpen J 'Reconciliation as heterodoxy' in J J Llewellyn & D Philpott (eds) *Restorative Justice, Reconciliation, and Peacebuilding* (2014) Oxford University Press 77

Van Binsbergen W 'Ubuntu and the globalisation of Southern African thought and society' (2001) 15 *Quest* 53

Van Blerk A E 'Meetings' (revised by E Du Plessis & E S Pugsley) in W A Joubert (ed) 2ed *Laws of South Africa* vol 17(2) (2008) LexisNexis Butterworths

Van Blerk A E 'The genesis of the modernist-purist debate: a historical bird's-eye view' (1984) 47 *THRHR* 255

Van der Merwe A 'A new role for crime victims? An evaluation of restorative justice procedures in the Child Justice Act 2008' (2013) 46 *De Jure* 1022

Van der Merwe D 'Land tenure in South Africa: a brief history and some reform proposals' (1989) 4 *TSAR* 663

Van der Merwe S E 'Accusatorial and inquisitorial procedures and restricted and free systems of evidence' in A G J M Sanders (ed) *Southern Africa in Need of Law Reform* (1981) Butterworths 141

Van der Merwe S W J et al *Contract: general principles* 4ed (2012) Juta

Van der Merwe S W J, Lubbe G F & Van Huyssteen L F 'The *exceptio doli generalis*: *requiescat in pace — vivat aequitas*' (1989) 106 *SALJ* 235

Van der Sijde E *The Role of Good Faith in the South African Law of Contract* (2012) unpublished masters thesis, University of Pretoria, available at https://repository.up.ac-.za/bitstream/handle/2263/27443/dissertation.pdf;sequence=1

Van der Waal C S 'Spatial and organisational complexity in the Dwars River Valley, Western Cape' (2005) 28) *Anthro SA* 8

Van der Walt A J & Dhliwayo P 'The notion of absolute and exclusive ownership: a doctrinal analysis' (2017) 134 *SALJ* 34

Van der Walt A J 'Dancing with codes — protecting, developing and deconstructing property rights in a constitutional state' (2001) 118 *SALJ* 258

Van der Walt A J 'The modest systemic status of property rights' (2014) 1 *JL Prop & Soc'y* 1

Van der Walt J W G 'Horizontal application of fundamental rights and the threshold of the law in view of the *Carmichele* saga' (2003) 19 *SAJHR* 517

Van der Walt J W G *Law and Sacrifice: towards a post-apartheid theory of law* (2005) Routledge

Van Kessel I & Oomen B ' "One Chief, one vote": the revival of traditional authorities in post-apartheid South Africa' (1997) 96 *African Affairs* 561

Van Niekerk G J 'A common law for Southern Africa: Roman law or indigenous African law?' (1998) 31 *CILSA* 158

Van Niekerk G J '*Amende honorable* and *ubuntu*: an intersection of *ars boni et aequi* in African and Roman-Dutch jurisprudence?' (2013) 19 *Fundamina* 397

Van Niekerk G J 'Reflection on the interplay of African customary law and state law in South Africa' (2012) 5 *SUBB Jurisprudentia* 5

Van Rouveroy van Nieuwaal E A B 'Chiefs and African states: some introductory notes and an extensive bibliography on African chieftaincy' (1987) 25/26 *J Legal Pluralism & Unofficial L* 1

Van Velsen I 'Procedural informality, reconciliation, and false comparisons' in M Gluckman (ed) *Ideas and Procedures in African Customary Law* (1969) Oxford University Press 138

Van Warmelo N J & Phophi W M D *Venda Law* Parts 1-3 (1948), Part 4 (1949), Part 5 (1967) Government Printer

Van Wyk B 'Higher education transformation in the Western Cape: on the transformative potential of ubuntu and communalism' in Y Waghid et al (eds) *African(a) Philosophy of Education: reconstructions and deconstructions* (2005) Department of Education Policy Studies, Stellenbosch University 100

Van Wyk B 'Performativity in higher education transformation in South Africa' (2005) 19 *SA J of Higher Education* 5

Van Zyl D H 'Cicero and Roman Law' (1991) 108 *SALJ* 496

Van Zyl D H 'The significance of the concepts justice and equity in law and legal thought' (1988) 105 *SALJ* 272

Van Zyl D H *Justice and Equity in Cicero: a critical evaluation in contextual perspective* (1991) Academia

Van Zyl D H *Justice and Equity in Greek and Roman Legal Thought* (1991) Academia

Vervliet C *The Human Person: African ubuntu and the dialogue of civilisations* (2009) Adonis & Abbey

Visser D P 'Unjustifie enrichment' in R Zimmermann & D P Visser (eds) *Southern Cross: civil law and common law in South Africa* (1996) Clarendon 521

Visser D P *Unjustified Enrichment* (2008) Juta

Waldron J 'Did Dworkin ever answer the Crits?' in S Hershovitz (ed) *Exploring Law's Empire: the jurisprudence of Ronald Dworkin* (2012) Oxford University Press 155

Wallman S 'Lesotho's pitso: traditional meetings in a modern setting' (1968) 2 *Can J Afr Stud* 167

Walton F P 'The civil law and the common law in Canada' (1899) 11 *Juridical Rev* 282

Watson A 'Legal transplants and law reform' (1976) 92 *LQR* 79

Watson A *Legal Transplants and European Private Law* (2000) 4 *EJCL*, available at http://www.ejcl.org/44/art44-2.html?iframe=true&width=100%&height=100%

Watson A *Legal Transplants: an approach to comparative law* (1974) Scottish Academic Press

Watson R S *Society and Legal Change* (1977) Scottish Academic Press

Weber M *The Theory of Social and Economic Organization* (1947) (1968 paper back edition) Free Press

Wessels J W (ed A A Roberts) *The Law of Contract in South Africa* vol 1 (1937) Hortors Ltd

Westen P 'The empty idea of equality' (1982) 95 *Harv L Rev* 537

Williams C *The Figure of Beatrice: a study of Dante* (1943) Boydell & Brewer

Williams J M 'Leading from behind: democratic consolidation and the chieftaincy in South Africa' (2004) 42 *J Modern African Studies* 113

Williams J M 'Legislating "tradition" in South Africa' (2009) 35 *JSAS* 191

Wilson R A *The Politics of Truth and Reconciliation in South Africa: legitimizing the post-apartheid state* (2001) Cambridge University Press

Wiredu K 'The Akan perspective on human rights' in A A An-Na'im & F M Deng (eds) *Human Rights in Africa: cross-cultural perspectives* (1990) The Brookings Institution 243

Wiredu K *Cultural Universals and Particulars: an African perspective* (1996) Indiana University Press

Wolfe J D 'A defense of participatory democracy' (1985) 47 *Review of Politics* 370

Woolman S & Swanepoel J 'Constitutional history' in S Woolman & M Bishop (eds) *Constitutional Laws of South Africa* vol 1 2ed (2013) Juta

Woolman S 'Dignity' in S Woolman & M Bishop (eds) *Constitutional Law of South Africa* vol 3 2ed (2013) Juta

Woolman S 'Humility, Michelman's method and the Constitutional Court: rereading the First Certificatio Judgment and reaffirming a distinction between law and politics' (2013) 24 *Stell LR* 281

Worthington S *Equity* 2ed (2006) Clarendon

Wydick R C *Plain English for Lawyers: teacher's manual* 5ed (2005) Carolina Academic Press

Yoshino M Y 'Emerging Japanese multi-national enterprises' in E F Vogel (ed) *Modern Japanese Organization and Decision-Making* (1975) University of California Press 146

Zahan D 'Some reflection on African spirituality' in J K Olupona (ed) *African Spirituality: forms, meanings and expressions* (2000) Crossroad Publishing 3

Zahnd E G 'The application of universal laws to particular cases: a defense of equity in aristotelianism and Anglo-American law' (1996) 59 *Law Contemp Probl* 263

Zandberg J *The Philosophy of Ubuntu and the Origins of Democracy* (2010) Lulu Enterprises Inc

Zimmermann R ' "Double cross": comparing Scots and South African law' in R Zimmermann, D P Visser & K C J Reid (eds) *Mixed Legal Systems in Comparative Perspective: property and obligations in Scotland and South Africa* (2004) Juta 1

Zimmermann R 'Good faith and equity' in R Zimmerman & D P Visser (eds) *Southern Cross: civil law and common law in South Africa* (1996) Juta 217

Zimmermann R *The Law of Obligations: Roman foundations of the civilian tradition* (1990) Juta

Zweigert K & Kötz H (trans by T Weir) *Introduction to Comparative Law* 2ed (1987) Clarendon Press

INDEX

www.ingramcontent.com/pod-product-compliance
Lightning Source LLC
Chambersburg PA
CBHW061127210326
41518CB00034B/2530